THE ULTIMATE GUIDE TO BEING A GREAT POLICE OFFICER

THE ULTIMATE GUIDE TO BEING A GREAT POLICE OFFICER

A GUIDE TO PROFESSIONAL POLICING

Dr. Jeffrey C. Fox

To order additional copies of this book, contact:
Xlibris
1-888-795-4274
www.Xlibris.com
Orders@Xlibris.com
759743

Contents

Illustrations

Preface

All that is necessary for the triumph of evil is that good men do nothing.
—Edmund Burke

This book is for anyone who is interested in becoming a police officer or who is already a police officer. For those seeking careers in law enforcement, just starting out, or wanting new tips and to brush up, my hope is you will find value in this book. This book is also great for those who supervise, train, or teach officers. The book offers a blended academic and practitioner-based approach to learning and understanding the skills needed to be a great officer.

The book goes into detail about how to prepare for a law enforcement career, how to master the skills needed to be successful during training and throughout one's career, how to act ethically, how to think critically and use excellent decision-making skills, and how to effectively communicate verbally, in writing, and through body language. The book also goes into detail regarding patrol issues, such as policing strategies, patrol techniques, enforcement issues, officer survival, and the use of force. The book provides an in-depth discussion of investigative techniques, how to deal with juveniles, understanding the use of intelligence, and report writing. Finally, the book discusses liability issues and how to deal with complaints or avoid them in the first place. The book wraps up with tips on managing your career and ending your tour of duty and moving on after having served your community, state, and country.

This book offers a deep blend of the most useful and impactful information one will learn when melding police academy training with the core academic courses offered in a criminal justice degree. To my knowledge, there are no books on the market that blends core academic topics with foundational police academy training material.

This book is designed and meant for anyone who carries a badge and gun and has powers of arrest or who wishes to pursue a career in this field of work. Typically, we think of a police officer, a sheriff's deputy, or a state trooper; but there are many others who enforce the law and/or investigate crimes at all levels of the government, from local to federal. There are also those who work in the private sector whom this book will apply to. Most colleges have police forces, as well as most large hospitals, railroad companies, etc. In the military, each branch of service has their own police force and investigative agency. There are many regulatory agencies found within state governments that have enforcement branches, such as game wardens, park police, transportation related, regulatory, etc. Likewise, each state has some sort of corrections agency that also enforce laws and provide security. This book will use the term *police officer* or *officer* as a generic term that covers all those who carry badges and guns, as well as those who are not even armed but still have investigative or other security-related duties. Those with non-badge-and-gun jobs but still have investigative duties will find this book useful.

I would be remiss if I did not offer an official caveat. The readers of this book must apply the laws of their state and locality. They must follow their department's policies and procedures. They must follow current case law.

> *Your word is a lamp to my feet and a light to my path.*
> —Psalm 119:105

Acknowledgments

The completion of this book would not have been possible without the support, patience, and love of my wife, Pam. Without her, I could not have accomplished this work. Most importantly, I owe any success I have had in my life to God. In Him, all things are possible. I thank God for allowing me to have and understand my calling in life.

I am grateful to all those who put themselves in harm's way every day to protect our communities. Our law enforcement community is made up of men and women who answer the call of service. All gave some, and some gave all. A saying I once heard has stuck with me. "Some people are meant to call the police, and others are meant to be the police. Some people will run away from the sound of gunfire, and others run toward the sound." I thank God for those who answer the call. I am personally grateful to my shift partners throughout the years who are there to answer the call, share a laugh and war stories at mealtime, and allow me to call them my brothers and sisters. I am thankful for those leaders who have hired me, trusted me, and supported my work and growth. For those of you who serve or will serve, I salute you.

Chapter One
Getting Started

The only stable state is the one in which all men are equal before the law.
—Aristotle

What is your calling?

I believe God gives us all gifts. I also believe we are put here to make a positive difference. You might say we have callings in life. In high school, I began to feel a calling to do police work. I worked for a little while after high school, but eight months after graduating, I took the plunge and joined the army. I wanted to be a military policeman (MP). I went to Fort McClellan, Alabama, and the rest was history, so to speak. After basic training, I attended advance individual training for my military occupational skill, that being a 95B or an MP. As soon as I started military police school, I knew I had made a great decision. I loved it. I felt like a duck in water. I ended up going to West Germany and guarding missiles for my first assignment. I was not crazy about that, but it was needed. When I went to Baumholder, Germany, as part of the Eighth Infantry Division, Eighth MP Company, Second Platoon, I knew I had made a great decision. We worked the road and went to the field, so it was a great mix. We had eighty some bars in town, and it was a very busy base. I learned so much there. This was my springboard into three decades of police work. I then went to Fort Myer/Davidson U.S. Army Airfield to finish out my MP career. I got out of the army on a Friday and started with my hometown police on a Monday. After almost three years there, I went to the Virginia State Police for over twenty-one years. I was so happy I was able to do police work for so many years. I made great friends, whom I would cherish forever. The memories flooded my mind. On the flip side, I saw the worst in people. Death in the most gruesome forms and violence and abuse were common to see and deal with. I saw careers crash and burn because of poor decisions. Worse of all, I have carried too many caskets of my fellow officers and attended too many line of death funerals. To say all of this did not take a toll on me would be a lie. I dealt with it in the manner one should, and I would not have changed one minute of my time for the world. I would like to think I made a difference in someone's life. Maybe that drunk driver I arrested did not kill someone that night. Maybe that child I took the time to smile at ended up becoming a police officer or did other things that helped other people. I was blessed to have another calling in life, and that was teaching. I have been training and teaching criminal justice and homeland security for over thirty years. We probably do not know each other, but I still care about you. I want you to succeed and make the right decisions in life. That is why I wrote this book. My hope and prayer is that you will come to know, or already know, what gift(s) God has given you, and if policing is your calling, this book helps you along your journey. Carpe diem!

Getting Hired

Before we go any further, you must ask yourself why you want to be a police officer. Do you know what the job really entails? Do you know if you are ready for this unique responsibility? Do you want to help people? Do you want to make a difference? Do you enjoy challenges? Do you want to make your community a safer and better place to live in? Do you enjoy being bored at times and, in a split second, being in the middle of a very high-risk situation? Do you believe in the rule of law? Do you believe all people should be treated equally before the law? Do you believe you can meet the many challenges you will face daily? If you have answered yes to these, then you might well like police work. If you have answered no, well then, you know the answer.

Okay. Now that we have addressed your readiness and desire to undertake this daunting task, let us begin our journey. How long have you thought about doing this? Have you prepared yourself for this task? If you have been preparing, then great. If you have not been readying yourself, then you need to start right now.

You might ask, "What comes next? or "How do I get started? Do I look for the job, or do I prepare?" You do both. But you must be prepared first. You must prepare mentally, physically, emotionally, and, yes, spiritually.

A great place to start is to see what the different types of jobs entail. Look at job descriptions. Spend a good amount of time researching this major decision. Try to speak with officers or police recruiters.

Possibly ask your criminal justice professors. It is good to get many different opinions and then form your own. Here are some gut check questions for you. Are you willing to use force if needed to protect your life or the life of someone else? This force might be striking a person or using your firearm. If the answer is no, then being an officer is not for you. Also, ask this: do you want to use force? If the answer is yes, then being an officer is not for you. Are you willing to put your life on the line for strangers and even people who might not like you? If the answer is no, then the job is not for you. Are you willing to arrest people or charge them with crimes or traffic offenses? If the answer is no, then the job is not for you. Finally, are you willing to see the worse part of life such as death, violence, abuse, and pure hatred? If the answer is no, then the job is not for you. This is grim stuff, is it not? I heard a saying when I was associate dean at a community college and had the police academy under my charge. "Some people are meant to call the police, and others are meant to be the police. Also, some people run to the sound of gunfire, and others run away." Which are you? By the way, it is perfectly okay if it is not for you. There are many ways you can make a positive difference in this world. There are plenty of non-badge-and-gun jobs in criminal justice as well. If you have already decided police work is not for you, there is still plenty of valuable and useful material in the book, so read on anyway.

Okay, so we have established if you are mentally and spiritually ready for this line of work. But we have more to examine. How is your heart and mind? If you have a felony record, then being an officer is out the door. If you have committed felonies, it is likely you will be out. Background investigations and polygraphs uncover a great deal of information. Then we move to misdemeanors, traffic offenses, civil matters, etc. Hopefully you have a very good and clean record. Most agencies will allow for a few small mistakes but very few. Even your credit rating and other personal matters will come into play for many agencies. Let me clearly and unequivocally say that if you should take a polygraph for employment, tell the truth and the complete truth no matter what.

How is your health? Agencies will all have different standards. A complete check will likely be done with certain thresholds applying to all sorts of things such as weight in proportion to height, eyesight, hearing, blood pressure, physical dexterity, etc. Reasonable accommodations will be made, but these are often limited for policing. Again, there are non-badge-and-gun jobs one can serve in as well. Your mental capacity will likely be tested in various ways, such as through written testing or interviews. As you can tell, many people will be eliminated from hiring through these rigorous standards. Some of these might be fixable, and others are not. The process will vary some, but it is likely it might flow something like this: review of application (automatic disqualifiers), written test, physical agility tests, initial criminal history check, interview process, background investigations, polygraph, and physical exam. If you pass all of this and make the hiring cut, then it is on to training. Please note that every agency and every state are different. The standards will vary somewhat from state to state and agency to agency.

You can prepare yourself for many of these tests and demands you will face. Work out and increase your cardio and muscles. Stay fit mentally and physically. Read and study on topics you know you will need to learn. Look at various police job advertisements and underline key words. Make sure you fit these words. Build your résumé. Volunteer, intern, etc. Get your foot in the door. Join the military. Become a dispatcher. Make sure you keep your body and mind clean. Choose your friends and the company you keep carefully. Practice shooting. I will say that you will be taught how to shoot, but if you think or know that is a problem area for you, get professional training. Do not pretend to be an officer when you are not one in any way. Practice interviewing. Set up obstacle courses to run. Work on your handgrip strength. You can talk to recruiters or officers, and they will tell you what you need to do to prepare. Later, we will cover many of the basic knowledge areas you will need to know.

Know the hiring standards and be sure you can meet them. Most agencies will have a written exam, a preliminary drug screening, a physical agility test, an interview of some sort, a preliminary background check a.k.a. a criminal history check, a thorough background investigation, a psychological evaluation or testing, and a thorough physical examination.

Some of these are easier to address than others. Keep in mind each state and agency will be different. The written exam is usually not something you can study for too much. There are exam manuals out there, and they are fine. However, reading comprehension is what it is, but you can work on this by reading and expanding your vocabulary. It is a great idea to work on memory techniques. Some exams will test your short-term-memory ability. Get plenty of rest before the exam.

Hopefully drug tests will be administered. Do not take or consume any illegal drugs. Most agencies will hire you if you have used a very small amount of marijuana in the past. Do not do drugs. Do not drink before you go to the test. Do not cheat on the test. Refrain from smoking.

Be physically fit. Find out what kind of agility test they use and practice. You want to be in great shape.

You cannot change your history, but you can determine your history before it occurs. Do not do stupid things. Having said that, most people do some stupid things when they are young to some degree. Above all else, be honest during all phases of the process. Tell the truth during the polygraph. I had a student once tell me another professor told him to lie on the polygraph. I told the student that was the stupidest thing I had ever heard. Tell the truth during all phases of the process. There are a good number of things that will keep you from being hired, and that is just a fact. Any felony conviction, and that is it. If you have committed what will be a felony but are not caught, that may well come back to haunt you. Misdemeanors are not much better.

The background investigation should go back to your communities where you lived and where you attended school down to high school. Your credit and financial situation will or should matter as well. Be mindful of the company you keep. You cannot help who your relatives are, but you can choose who you associate with. Former employers will be spoken to.

Psychological tests can come in several forms. Some will be written testing, such as personality tests. Just be honest. Some will be interviews with a psychologist. Again, just be honest.

The interview process can make a huge difference. This goes for promotions as well. Look at the position. Be ready for general questions. Be ready to show your knowledge, skills, and abilities. For entry-level jobs, they will likely not ask knowledge questions. What will be asked are questions that show your maturity, judgment, and decision-making ability. Dress for success. Wear a suit or dress. Be clean. Have a fresh haircut. Have clean shoes. Shake hands firmly and make eye contact. Make sure your voice is calm, clear, and high enough to be heard. Show confidence, but never be arrogant or cocky. Listen carefully to what is being asked. Be sure to address the question completely and thoroughly. Here is a great tip. When you see that the committee has stopped writing and laid their pencils or pens down, they have often heard enough on that answer. Make eye contact and scan between the committee members versus just fixating on one person. Smile but do it appropriately. Do not have a crazy grin or smile! If you know officers, pick their brains before you do the interview.

Hopefully you have planned for this career and have visualized what and how you will react. Sit up straight and keep your feet on the floor. Do not bring your cell phone into the interview. When done, thank them for their time and shake hands and leave. If you know the panelists, do not assume you have it in the bag or that they know all about you. Sell yourself. Be positive. Turn negative questions into positive answers. They may ask what your strongest attribute is. Tell them. They may ask what your weakest attribute is. Tell them. You should already know what it is and be working on it. Never bad-mouth another agency or people. When I had decided I wanted to be a trooper, I borrowed a trooper's state police manual and read it from cover to cover before going to the academy.

Do not be disappointed if you do not get the job. Keep trying. Try to analyze what has gone right and wrong. It might not be about you at all. They may have had others who have just ended up being higher on the list. Do not put all your eggs in one basket. Also, do not job-hop too quickly. I have sat on both sides on the interview desk a great many times. You should know not all interviews will be fair. If many people are being hired for a larger agency, you have a better chance. Smaller agencies hire fewer people. Sometimes knowing people on the panel will hurt, and sometimes it will not.

I have sat on very professional panels and some that seemed fair but were not. I was fair regardless of what others said or wanted to have as a result. I have seen a candidate make a statement, and one person loved it, and another thought it was terrible. I sat on a promotion panel once where all five of us were to make our written comments and scores without consulting with one another. We had a good number of candidates come in, and the process flowed. One candidate came in and spoke about how he prayed about his decisions. He said he and his supervisor would also pray about decisions. When he left the interview, the chairperson immediately spoke up and was literally furious and said how unprofessional that was. The others chimed in, agreeing. I saw it exactly opposite. He did not say he required anyone else to pray with him. He just said he prayed about his decisions. Frankly, I wish everyone did that. I defended this person passionately to the committee. I knew they would not like it. I also knew it would likely hurt my future, and I believe it did, but that was okay. I was sure the committee slammed this candidate for his answers. I did not.

I have seen agency heads sit in the back of a room, and after a candidate left in promotion panels, the agency head would either bad-mouth them or praise them to the committee. This was very unprofessional. I ignored the praise and condemnation. I was there to draw my own conclusions. I have been before panels for promotions where I was treated like dirt and where I was treated great. I have been before panels where the panelists should not have been there based on their bad histories or past behaviors. Life is not and will not be fair, so get used to it. I have seen panels where, no matter what the panel said, the decision had already been made. This sort of behavior is wrong and insulting to the invited panelists. I was on one panel where a candidate for a job with our agency praised another local agency. One panel member was highly offended by this and did not want to hire him. The interviewee was right; the local agency was a great agency. It probably was not the smartest thing to do, but I did not hold that against him. He was hired.

I have had candidates come before a promotion or hiring panel who on paper looked great, but the interviews were horrible. Sometimes people just have a bad day. The worse I ever saw was a candidate who answered his cell phone during the interview. Never ever do that! One candidate told us he would be great for the job since he had been an informant before. I said, "How were you an informant?" He said because he had gotten busted for selling marijuana and had to work it off. He was never convicted, though. He was not hired. I had a candidate for a secretary position cry during an interview when she spoke of her old boss who had died. After we hired her, she told me she was sure she did not get the job because she cried. We should consider the circumstances. Normally, crying in an interview would be a very bad thing to do. It was okay in this scenario.

Physical examinations usually look at blood pressure, height in proportion to weight, eyesight, hearing, physical dexterity, and so forth. You should know what the hiring standards are before you start the process. Some things you can fix, and others you cannot. I have known people who have gotten corrective eye surgery to improve their vision.

Academy and Post Academy Training

Academies will vary greatly. Most academies will be commuter academies, that is, you will not stay there at night. In some academies, such as state police academies, you will stay there 24/7 or at least five days a week. Some academies are more stressful than others. Some stress is good. Be prepared for this. Follow the rules all the time. For some, this is their first time away from home. You might be leaving loved ones behind. Prepare them and yourself for this time. Remember, it is not forever, but you cannot be an officer if you do not complete the academy. Academies run from possibly eight weeks but more likely fourteen to sixteen weeks up to thirty to forty weeks. When you are done, you will look back on this time fondly. You will make lifelong friends. You will form bonds that you do not get anywhere else other than the military. It will be a great, life-changing experience that you can be proud of forever. Do not give up. Do not quit. See it through. Remember, if you get there and you have done your best and for whatever reason it does not work, it does not mean you are a lesser person or a failure. It means that job, at this point in your life, is not for you. Things happen for reasons. Hold your head high and find what God put you here for. Hopefully you will do great and graduate. That is the reason for this book.

Before, during, or after the academy or a combination thereof, you will most likely go through a field training program. You will ride with a seasoned officer, a field training officer (FTO), who will train and evaluate you. This is a great opportunity to see if you like the work and if the work fits you. Do your best. Listen and always have a great attitude. I hope you get a great FTO, but you might not. Make the best of it either way.

Once you complete the academy and had your field training, you will be released on your own. You will likely be on probation for six months up to a year. Be careful. Learn your area. Learn the agency. Do your best. Work your way into the job. Do not go out and try to conquer the world or solve all problems in your first year. Do take your calls. Do enforce the law. Just use great judgment and think about what you are doing. You will make mistakes. Keep these mistakes small and infrequent. If you make a mistake, always tell the truth. If you make a mistake and see you are square in the middle of a bad one, do not keep drudging ahead. Take a step back. Try to resolve the mistake. Learn from it. Sometimes you are better off to punt if you can. You must know the laws. However, if you find yourself on a self-initiated activity and you are not sure about the law, then let it go until next time. In certain calls, you go on, you cannot punt, and you must know the law. We will get into this later.

Training and Education

Education is so important for so many reasons. Maybe you already have a degree, or maybe you are going to start working on a degree. Either way, that is great. If you do not have a college degree, I highly encourage you to earn one as soon as possible. I want you to be as competitive and as marketable as possible. Having a degree in hand helps you reach this goal. If you do not have a degree, you can still get hired by a vast number of departments. If you do not have a degree and are already an officer, I encourage you to earn a degree. This will make you more competitive for promotion and life after your police career. Also, a degree will help you with your job. It will help you read and write better. It will help you manage your time better and to think better. This is not to take away from someone who does not have a degree. I have known plenty of people who have degrees and make poor officers and many who do not have degrees who are great officers. Common sense, honesty, bravery, and hard work might be innate but can be learned in many ways. These traits are best learned through emulation and self-discipline.

College does not teach these core competencies. Finally, a degree will provide some level of insurance in case you decide you no longer want to do police work, or heaven forbid, you get hurt to the point you can no longer carry a badge and gun. The suggestions and advice to follow might apply to your college educational endeavors or police training or both in many cases. Of course, you must be guided by the rules and regulations of the academy or college.

I taught police classes for over twenty years to basic students and in-service and specialized classes. Likewise, I was the assistant training director for the Virginia State Police. Further, I have been teaching and administering college courses and programs for going on twenty years. I was a field training officer for many years. My goal was and is for each student or trainee to be as good as they could be. I wanted everyone to pass, graduate, and learn a great deal. Sadly, this was not always the case. I have seen many police trainees (cadets) fail out of training for a variety of reasons. These reasons always ended up being tied back to our domains of learning. Cognitively, some students just could not pass written tests. Psychomotor-wise, some students have difficulty with performance-based skills, such as driving, shooting, physical contact, etc. Finally, some students administered self-inflicted blows by way of the affective or attitudinal domain. In other words, they were unethical. Usually, it was cheating, lying, or failing to follow rules.

It always saddens me to see someone fail out for whatever reason. Let me say here and now that if that has happened to you, it is not the end of the world. Reevaluate yourself and what happened. Decide on the next step in your life based on a reasoned and logical assessment and move on. I have seen students fail cognitively who have tried again later and succeeded. The main reason I have written this book is evident in this paragraph right here. I want you to succeed, to make a positive difference in the world, and to go on to help others do the same. I have seen students who are not number one in their class become great officers and some who are top academically turn out not to be so great. What is in the heart matters as much as what is in the mind.

Commitment Issues

You must be mentally, emotionally, and physically mature and have a serious purpose. You need to know the why and how of things. You must understand the subject matter. You must be truly committed to earning a degree or completing the academy. Do you really want to do what you are doing? Are you self-motivated? If you are going into an academy half-heartedly, then do not go.

Self-esteem also comes into play. This goes both ways, being too little or too much. Fear of the unknown or change can be daunting for some learners. Anxiety is often high with students. It is normal to have some anxiety and, yes, even fear. Do not let fear and anxiety control you. You control it. The job you are embarking on is hard. It is not for the faint of heart or meek and mild. You should and will be challenged in academy training because, in real life, it might be a matter of life or death. On more than one occasion, I have seen people complete the training; and the first time they must fight or see a dead body, they realize the job is not for them. Do a serious gut check before you start. It is okay if it is not for you.

Why do students fail?

- ✓ Lack of a positive self-image—the main barrier to success
- ✓ Unfair treatment (This does occur, but I do not think it is high on the list.)
- ✓ Physical discomfort, illness, or fatigue (short or long term)
- ✓ Failure to understand what is being taught (possibly cognitive issues)
  - ○ Reading comprehension
  - ○ Cognitive impairments
- ✓ Personality conflict with instructor or other students
- ✓ Fear, anxiety, or worry
- ✓ Immaturity
- ✓ Lack of motivation

Almost all of these reasons are the responsibility of the student—you. It is for you to deal with. You must have a positive self-image but not be cocky or arrogant. You will experience discomfort that comes with the job. You must learn to deal with conflict in a positive manner. Immaturity has no place in police work. Finally, being lazy or lacking motivation is not acceptable. You are in control of your destiny. If you have any of these issues, recognize them, fix them, and charge onward.

If you are struggling or are doing well but want to do better, consider these strategies. Remedial strategies may include but are not limited to the following:

- ✓ Flash cards (create them)
- ✓ Spelling quizzes
- ✓ Commentary driving
- ✓ Group study
- ✓ Simulation
- ✓ Role-playing
- ✓ Reverse role-playing
- ✓ Reading assignments
- ✓ Self-critique
- ✓ Reading aloud
- ✓ Taping notes and playing them back
- ✓ Tutoring

These remedial strategies can be used for students in a pure academic environment. Consider preparing for the training before you start. Read as much as you can on what will be taught.

Learning Tips and Ideas

Planning and preparation, along with excellent time management, are essential keys to success. Every day, I practice the art of *Kaizen*, that is, trying to better whatever it is I am doing in some way. I do this through introspection, as well as feedback from others. Always display and have grace, dignity, high expectations, respect, knowledge, and excellent customer service in every endeavor or transaction you have with anyone. Attitude goes a long way. There is nothing that will hurt you more than a bad attitude.

Practice makes perfect only if perfect practice. Of course, no one is perfect, but we should strive to be as good as possible at whatever task we set out to accomplish. Also, we need to correct poor or underperforming behavior—or work, if you will—early on and often. Do not create repetitions that are incorrect action. To do so will build incorrect muscle memory, which now must be unlearned.

Understand the difference between the letter of the law and the spirit of the law. One should interpret the law strictly—or legalistically, if you will. Words mean things. Then they should apply the law through the spirit of the law. Consistency in life is important and expected for many people. Of course, life is not always consistent, so we must be able to deal with such inconsistencies.

Helping You Achieve

The following are hints or advice to help you achieve success.

Attend all classes. If you want to get good grades, you must attend every class, not most classes. When you miss classes, you miss lectures, notes, class discussions, homework explanations, and assignments.

Be organized. Use an assignment planner, notebook, or electronic device. Take the assignment notebook to every class, and record each assignment under the date due. Use a three-ring binder or notebook for notes. Use a laptop, if allowed, for note-taking purposes only. Keep important information in the front of the notebook. Save all computer files on disk, thumb drives, etc. I highly recommend an external computer backup. Keep all returned papers, quizzes, and tests. Record instructors' phone numbers. This will also help you develop good work habits.

Manage time well. Do not overextend yourself. If you feel that you are doing more than you can handle, look for ways to make your life more manageable, and make the needed changes. Plan ahead. Look at what you need to do and then think about how you can get it done most efficiently. Create a plan. A calendar is a great tool to use. Create a time budget. Consciously make choices about how you use your time. Also, look for ways to streamline and combine tasks. Learn how to multitask or improve at multitasking.

Be successful in the classroom. Learn how to adapt to different instructors. Part of your education is learning how to adapt to different personalities, teaching styles, and expectations. Be ready for each class. Have all assignments completed before class. Lectures will then be easier to follow, and you will get more out of class. Sit in front of the class whenever possible. Communicate with your instructors. Do not hesitate to contact an instructor whenever you have a question, concern, or problem. Be on time for all classes. Participate in class. Be a good team member.

Take good notes. Be an active listener. Take notes to help you focus. Learn to recognize important information. Take notes that are easy to read. Go over your notes often. Get notes if you are absent.

Know how to read a textbook or course material. Scan by reading subtitles, words in **bold** and *italic* print, summaries, charts, and review questions. Read with a purpose. Review by scanning the material to check your comprehension. Reading out loud involves more senses and thus raises the retention level. Consider reading aloud and taping your reading. Listen to your taped reading of the text and notes whenever possible. This is also good when studying for promotion exams.

Study smart. Find a good place to study free from distractions. Get started. Know your learning style. Organize your study time. Know how to study for tests. Learn how to memorize and remember information. Know how to use technology. Know how to write a paper. Use tricks when making a presentation or speech. Tricks may be looking toward objects behind the audience or having a friend helping you with timing.

Use test-taking strategies. Get off to a good start. Develop a plan. Mark questions that you want to return to later. Increase your odds on multiple-choice questions. Look for key words in true/false questions. Watch for *never* and *always* and double negatives. Be prepared for open-book tests. Go over all returned tests. If you have a question about a wrong answer, ask for clarification, but look it up yourself first.

Reduce test anxiety. Start studying early. Mentally practice going through the testing experience. Avoid late nights and alcohol consumption.

Try common relaxation techniques. Take a deep breath and hold it and then slowly release your breath. Start at the tip of your head, flexing and then relaxing each part of your body. Close your eyes and let your arms hang down at your sides. Visualize the tension from your head, neck, and shoulders flowing down your arms and out your fingertips. Think of a place where you feel very relaxed and calm; close your eyes and visualize being in that place.

Know about and use available services. Most of your questions can be answered and your problems solved if you go to the appropriate person or office. You must take the initiative and ask for the help you need. Whenever you have an academic question or problem, see your adviser, mentor, counselor, etc. Check your college, course, or program catalog to find which services are offered and make a point to use them.

Takeaways

- ✓ Begin to plan and prepare early for what lies ahead in the job hunt, testing, and training.
- ✓ Never lie.
- ✓ Be careful with whom you associate.
- ✓ Do not put all your eggs in one basket.
- ✓ If you are married, your spouse must be on board with this grueling career choice.
- ✓ The more senses you involve, the higher the level of retention.
- ✓ Prepare yourself mentally and physically for the testing and training process.
- ✓ Practice interviewing.
- ✓ Make yourself as marketable and as competitive as possible.
- ✓ Go to college. Get your foot in the door. Join the military. Volunteer or intern when possible.
- ✓ The training and academy will be hard. Do not quit.
- ✓ Practice or perform a task until it is done successfully each time and to a high level.
- ✓ Keep positive.
- ✓ Check your communication techniques.
- ✓ Never be disruptive.
- ✓ Be sure you manage all aspects of your study time.

- ✓ Stay engaged.
- ✓ Learn to think critically, instinctively, and intuitively.
- ✓ Think remedial strategies and employ them as needed.
- ✓ Planning and preparation are important, along with excellent time management, and are keys to successful learning.
- ✓ Practice makes perfect only if perfect practice (or as near perfect as possible).
- ✓ Do not create improper repetitions of any performance, thereby creating improper muscle memory.
- ✓ Understand, recognize, and achieve your full potential.
- ✓ Use good discretion and common sense with everything.
- ✓ It is up to you to learn and succeed.
- ✓ Is police work your calling?
- ✓ Be sure you understand what the career entails.
- ✓ Seek advice and guidance from trustworthy sources.
- ✓ Different types of police jobs have different missions. Be sure you want to and can do the mission.
- ✓ Pray about your decisions.

Above all else, guard your heart, for it is the wellspring of life. Put away perversity from your mouth; keep corrupt talk far from your lips. Let your eyes look straight ahead, fix your gaze directly before you. Make level paths for your feet and take only ways that are firm. Do not swerve to the right or the left; keep your foot from evil.
—Proverbs 4:23–27

Chapter Two
Mastering the Needed Skill Sets

Good people do not need laws to tell them to act responsibly,
while bad people will find a way around the laws.

—Plato

Know your strengths and weaknesses.

Everyone has their kryptonite! Prior to joining the army, I had shot a gun one time in my life. I was not scared of guns and felt comfortable with them. It came time in training to shoot and qualify. I was okay with the rifle. I was fine with the M60 machine gun. I was good with hand grenades. But then came my kryptonite—the good old .45-caliber semiautomatic pistol. To be an MP, you had to qualify with this weapon. So off we went to the range. At close distances, I was okay. The further away, the worse it got. I think we shot from fifty yards out at the furthest with the .45. I did not qualify at first. I could feel a sense of dread coming over me. I felt the pressure build. I thought, *What will happen now? Will I have to switch my military occupational skill (MOS)? Will I end up with crossed spoons in the mess hall versus crossed pistols as an MP?* The drill sergeants, who were extremely hard normally, and the range instructors were fine with me. I was doing very well in my training overall and had no problems academically. So I went back to the range and practiced more. After several attempts, I qualified. Thank God! I was so relieved and jumped right back in where I left off with my other training. It was a gut check for me. I felt like a complete failure during that brief time and felt very alone.

I realized over the years that I was not alone. Many others needed extra practice. In all of my years involving training, we never had someone fail out for not being able to shoot. We got everyone qualified. For twenty-seven more years, I shot and qualified each time the first time. We switched handguns many times, but each time, it was fine. I was never one you would put on a pistol competition, but I knew I would do just fine if I ever had to use my gun to stop a threat. Because of this, I have always had a special place in my heart for those who struggled in firearms, test taking, or whatever skill set was required. Having said that, I knew that if I did not qualify, I would not be an MP. I would have been devastated, but I knew life would be okay. I knew I would have taken another path to being an officer. I knew I would practice much more in order to become an officer. I mentioned that everyone qualified. We did not lower standards. We did have one fellow whom we let go, but it was because of his attitude, not his ability to shoot. We had noticed he had an attitude and were monitoring him. While shooting, when he did not do well, he would kind of jerk the gun downrange as if to throw bullets. His temper was coming through. He was cracking under pressure. He was let go. His attitude did him in. You see, when we get squeezed or feel pressure, we are like a tube of toothpaste. What is inside comes out for all to see.

While you are in college or in the academy, you will use all three domains of learning. In the academy, you will use the psychomotor domain. Many students will struggle with one or more of these domains of learning, so it is prudent and useful to discuss each one. Each of these domains offers their own challenges and benefits.

The cognitive domain deals with thinking—or knowledge, if you will. The psychomotor domain deals with applying knowledge in some way through physical activity or, put another way, using one's muscular and skeletal system to manipulate something in some way with the use of skills. Finally, the attitudinal or affective domain deals with appreciation or, put another way, values, ethics, morals, and empathy and relates to the understanding of knowledge about a given topic and possibly involving the use of a skill in dealing with an activity, event, or situation. Techniques involve the use of all domains.

Cognitive Skills

Cognitive Domain Examined - Mental Attributes (Mind)

When discussing and considering the cognitive domain, it is important and appropriate to examine several key terms. One such term is the word *paradigm*. Paradigms are taken-for-granted commonsense perspectives and unwritten rules. Paradigms are the way we and our organization(s) do things. Paradigms typically can result in damaging perceptions. Examples of harmful paradigms are phrases we are probably all familiar with and maybe have even said. "It is our way or the highway." "We have always done it that way, so it must be right."

One way to overcome paradigms is through personal mastery. Personal mastery requires one to

- ✓ understand who he or she is,
- ✓ recognize one's level(s) of competence and commitment,
- ✓ understand one's level of self-esteem,
- ✓ recognize how fit one is to hold his or her position.

Personal mastery can be achieved through the practice of introspection. This is the process of self-analysis and reflection. It can lead to a deeper understanding of ourselves and the beliefs, values, attitudes, and organizational culture that frame our motives.

Your paradigm is the source from which your attitude and behavior flows. A paradigm is like a pair of glasses. It affects the way you see everything in your life. If you look at things through the paradigm of correct principles, what you see in life is dramatically different from what you see through any other centered paradigm.

Another important and related term is *satisficing*. The influence of illogical factors on our decision-making process causes individuals to engage in a process known as satisficing. This process occurs when an individual selects a solution that is just good enough instead of selecting the best course of action. Individuals often engage in satisficing to handle a problem with the least uncertainty and risk to themselves. The easiest way out is also caused by the need to appear decisive. This method only addresses the short term and fails to consider the long-term outcomes and impacts.

Introspection requires one to assess one's strengths and weaknesses, to understand what and who one is, and to evaluate personal and organization expectations. Further, introspection requires one to be realistic, not expect perfection from oneself or others, and assess one's capacity to recognize and deal with problems. Finally, introspection requires one to understand one's personal biases and to change those values and behaviors that need to be changed.

The last term we will look at is called *Kaizen*. One way to respond to the results of one's self-evaluation is to practice the art of *Kaizen*. Every day, find some small way to improve yourself and the way you perform your function(s).

Each student will come with different levels of confidence and cognitive ability. I have dealt with students who did not know they had learning disabilities at first. Something as simple as eyesight can make a difference in student success. Students come with different life and educational experiences. While having the ability to learn, process, and remember is critical, what is in the heart is equally important. I have seen so many students graduate at the top of the class academically but are outperformed by others in the field based on common sense and a great work ethic.

Emotional Skills

Emotional - Affective/Attitudinal Attributes (Heart)

A quick recap might be in order here. The affective or attitudinal domain deals with our ethics, values, motivation/drive, view of excellence, and how we treat others. As we have seen, the cognitive domain drives everything, including the psychomotor domain, and the same is true of the affective domain. Without cognition, we will be unable to be aware of anything and thus not able to function. Students do not show up ready to learn as a blank slate. They bring all their experiences they have had in life, be they good, bad, or indifferent. A person will have a predetermined outlook or view on life and specific parts of it when he or she begins a venture of any sort. He or she might have no idea and have never considered the issue before. We have discussed this earlier when we have looked at paradigms. Paradigms fit very well into the scope of the affective or attitudinal domain. Many people have misconceptions based on a number of factors, but what they see in movies or television shows is probably one of the biggest false factors. I see this all the time with students in forensic science classes. It is so bad that we have a name for it—"the CSI effect." This false sense of reality brings havoc in courtrooms. This topic can get kind of sensitive, so buckle up.

Contrary to what some in modern society think, there still is right and wrong. Ethics are standards or rules of conduct by which we live. Ethics relate to what is right and wrong. Ethics are not about preferences or likes or dislikes. When an employee disagrees with his or her assignment or work, that in and of itself is not an ethical issue. It is a matter of preference in most cases.

Integrity is derived from the word *wholeness*. Integrity means having character that develops hope, honesty, courage, empathy, etc. It means "the state of being complete." Words and deeds match up. Loyalties are not divided, not pretentious in nature. A person of integrity means one who has established a system of values against which all life is judged. Integrity is more than what we do; it is who we are. Who we are determines what we do, how we act. We are all faced with conflicting desire. Integrity is the factor that determines which desire will prevail. Coupled with values, it should enable each of us to set the example. Image is what people think we are. Integrity is what we really are. I have seen so many people fooled by image. It sounds trite, but you really cannot judge a book by its cover.

Attitude is an important part of anyone's makeup. Life is 10 percent what happens to us and 90 percent how we react to it. I have seen so many people worry about rumors they have heard that have never come to fruition. I have been guilty of this but, over the years, have worked hard to not fall prey to rumors and worry. This does not mean we should walk around in a state of perpetual ignorance either. Being aware of one's surroundings and circumstances is important for everyone.

Attitudes determine what we see and how we handle our feelings. These two factors greatly determine our success. Ralph Waldo Emerson said, "What lies behind us and what lies before us are tiny matters compared to what lies within us." Our attitudes cannot stop our feelings, but they can keep our feelings from stopping us.

Remember, as an officer, you are a leader. Leadership, in its true form, has to do less with position as it does with disposition. A leader's attitude is caught by his or her followers more quickly than his or her actions. Paul Meier said, "Attitudes are nothing more than habits of thought, and habits can be acquired. An action repeated becomes an attitude realized." Reframe your attitudes by keeping paramount that, while you may not be able to change the world you see around you, you can change the way you see the world within you.

Self-discipline is derived from the Greek word meaning "to grip" or "to take hold of." Aristotle says, "The ability to test desire by reason." He further explains that people who are not controlled have strong desires that seduce them from the way of reason, but to succeed, they must keep those desires under control.

Sadly, we live in an emotion-driven world. Children are inundated with emotionally charged stimuli from a very early age. Such constant conditioning must be purposely changed. Maybe this severely emotionally driven mind-set is offset or stymied by parents and other caregivers who set character-driven examples. Maybe by luck or chance, a series of events helps the young child grow into young adulthood; and by some miracle, he or she develops strong character-driven behaviors. If the latter is not the case, we need to develop character-driven qualities in ourselves. I will argue that, hopefully, the hiring process picks up on character-driven behavior already. Regardless, such behavior will need to be instilled and reinforced. How do we do this? You've guessed it—through excellent and consistent training and modeling. Let us see what these two mind-sets look like in the table below. I hope you find you are character driven.

Character- or Emotion-Driven Behaviors

Character Driven	Emotion Driven
Do right, feel good	Feel good, do right
Commitment driven	Convenience driven
Principle-based decisions	Popularity-based decisions
Action controls attitude.	Attitude controls action.
Believe it and then see it.	See it and then believe it.
Create momentum	Wait for momentum
Ask: "What are my responsibilities?"	Ask: "What are my rights?"

(Massey, 1980)

A student can score 100 percent on a test, but that does not tell me if he or she knows when to act or when not to act or how to treat people. All too often, we leave this critical domain to chance. We tend to focus on the cognitive and psychomotor and assume this domain is okay or we overlook it completely.

The pessimist complains about the wind.
The optimist expects it to change.
The leader adjusts the sails.

—William A. Ward

Physical Skills

Attributes – Psychomotor Skills (Body)

It must be understood that with few exceptions, if any, the psychomotor domain cannot function without using the cognitive domain first. Of course, there are times where we act first and think second. This usually does not end well. However, we do want to train to a level where we can reduce the time needed to think and then act. Also, physical dexterity and muscle memory will be very important in this domain. You need to be able to think critically yet intuitively and instinctively given a scenario or situation. Of course, there are occasions where we have plenty of time to consider options and think through what to do and even seek guidance from others. When possible, this is the best option. However, in policing, this is a luxury that is not often available.

In the academy, you will do a great deal of performance-based training (PBT). This is a method of training individuals to master tasks required for a successful job performance. Contextual-based training takes PBT one step further, that is, it involves the added element of coaching and training in context. By telling, showing, and having the student do or perform the task and then coaching or providing feedback, the retention level can rise to 90 percent.

No artifacts should be used in training. You might not be able to control this, but at least be aware of it. Artifacts are very important to discuss. Artifacts involve anything that is added to training that will not be in a real situation. Often, artifacts are added for convenience or to save money. Sometimes artifacts are added for safety. The only time artifacts should be added is for safety. Years ago, some police agencies would have their officers take the time to dump spent cartridges into their hands and then into their pockets to save time during range cleanup. They were putting spent cartridges in their pockets! Remember, training and reaction is all about proper muscle memory. A shootout occurred in California, called the Newhall incident, in the early 1970s. California Highway Patrol officers became involved in a shootout with some criminals. Officers were killed, and when they found their bodies at the scene of the shooting, they discovered spent cartridges in their pockets. Under stress, they reacted the way they had been trained. Valuable time was lost dumping spent ammo (casings) into their hands and then into their pockets.

Other examples of artifacts involve such things as driving vehicles on the range that one will not drive on patrol, as well as traditional firearms ranges where the only training is "Ready on the right, ready on the left. The firing line is ready. On command, pull your weapon and fire one or two rounds." Shooting from barricades can be another example. Remember, safety is first and foremost. When we begin to teach such skills as firearms training, we must take baby steps. Classroom comes first and then dry firing and so forth. We do need to shoot in the traditional range fashion for practice and qualification. However, it should not end there. I applauded the Virginia State Police when they recognized we needed more dynamic training; we did it. It cost money and added an element of risk, but it was controlled and made as safe as possible. The more dynamic the exercise, such as combat shooting and moving and shooting, the more care and oversight are needed.

Whatever it is you are learning, if it is a psychomotor skill, avoid artifacts at all costs. Something as simple as firing two shots while holding a radio in one hand and then calling in what you have is better than nothing. Hold the radio, shoot or call for help, etc. Practice cover while reloading, combat loading, or adding stress. Use decision-making drills. In shootouts, there is a phenomenon called sympathetic shooting. One person fires, so others do as well. This should never occur. We must train officers to first know this exists and can happen and then train and condition them to avoid such a reaction. Remember, we want our people to be able to say, "Been there, done that successfully." If not, then the officer may have to improvise or, in some cases, may avoid acting when action is required. These artifacts can be found in any profession or discipline. Under stress, one will revert to one's instincts (training).

Contextual training is normally performance based—pass/fail. Some scores can be attached to certain skills such as firearms, driving, etc. Contextual-based training will, if done correctly, expand a student's comfort zones. Comfort zones can be described like a V—like an air conditioner thermostat sixty-five degrees to seventy-two degrees. When outside this range, the system cuts on to get back into the comfort zone. We function best within our zone of comfort. We want to expand this comfort zone. This is what great athletes do. Anyone who competes in the Olympics would never put minimal effort into their preparation. Your life might hang in the balance, or someone else's life might depend on you. Peak performance occurs when people are at the peak or edge of their comfort zone. With good training, we can expand comfort zones. Comfort zones show visual impact on a person's physiology. When someone is out of their comfort zone, you will likely see sweating, shaking, stammering, voice cracking, blood pressure going up, etc. Grossman and Christensen (2008) do an excellent job explaining the physiological impact of stress and fear. They provide a color-coded system based on heart rate and the impact all this has on the body.

While it may not be realized, contextual-based training involves or should involve critical thinking. This brings together all three domains of learning: cognitive, psychomotor, and affective or attitudinal. Critical thinking must become intuitive so that the officers' reaction time will not be adversely affected. This process must be fine-tuned and instinctive.

With the psychomotor domain and performance-based training, you will first learn the topic or subject. Next, you will be shown how to perform the task. Then you will practice the task. Finally, you will have to demonstrate proficiency in and with the task. This covers many areas of training, such as firearms, driving, defensive tactics, patrol procedures, crime scene investigations, traffic crash investigations, fingerprinting, weapon use, handcuffing, first aid, CPR, etc. These areas are normally in the latter half of the academy for the most part. I have seen students struggle here. This is where the rubber hits the road. Here you have to walk and chew gum at the same time while under stress in some cases. You are involving all three domains of learning now.

Thinking is the active process by which we develop understanding of ourselves, others, and our world. The process of thinking enables us to solve problems, interpret information, make sense of our feelings and attitudes, discuss important issues, establish beliefs, and work toward the completion of goals. Thinking is an essential component in our life as a human being.

Critical Thinking (Decision Making and Problem-Solving)

Practice Visualizing Future Outcomes

There will likely be times in your life where you will have to make split-second decisions that might be life and death in nature. Late one night, a pursuit began in another county and worked its way into my area. There were four of us working that night. A female was driving a medium-sized car and would not stop. This occurred on the interstate. The pursuit had gone on for some time. It was not a matter of her outrunning us, and traffic was moderate at this time of the night. The interstate was under construction and would go from two to three lanes back and forth. When it went to two lanes, a concrete jersey wall would be on the shoulder. I and another trooper were in front of her, with others to her rear. I had her in the right lane, and she went to the shoulder, so I took the right lane. We were approaching a concrete jersey wall, and she did not appear to be willing to stop. She had three choices. She could hit me on the side, stop, or hit the jersey wall head-on. The choice was hers. I decided I would give her one more chance. I gave her the right lane back. The two of us stayed ahead of her for a while longer. Finally, we came to a place where we could slow to a stop, and she could not go around us. She still had a choice of hitting us or stopping. She stopped. When you do a running roadblock, you put yourself at great risk. One of the troopers behind her ran up, broke the window out, and dragged her out of the car. We then realized she had a baby in a baby carrier on the front seat beside her. The carrier was not a car seat, and it was not buckled in. The baby was okay. I think back to that decision from time to time. I know, without a doubt, if she had hit the concrete jersey wall, that baby would have died. It would have been her decision to not stop, and she could have, but I would have had to live with that the rest of my life. Making split-second decisions will be the hardest part of your job. You will be second-guessed. Be sure you can live with your decisions. It is important to note that the liability and fault would have been hers, but I had other options. Sometimes just because you can does not mean you should.

Common Sense

There is absolutely no substitute for common sense. It is, without a doubt, a key component to great policing.

What is critical thinking?

Critical thinking is the ability to think about one's thinking in such a way as to recognize its strengths and weaknesses and, as a result, to recast the thinking in improved form. Universal intellectual criteria and standards are as follows:

- ✓ Clarity
- ✓ Accuracy
- ✓ Precision
- ✓ Relevance
- ✓ Depth
- ✓ Breadth
- ✓ Logicalness

Critical thinking is the intellectually disciplined process of actively and skillfully conceptualizing, applying, analyzing, synthesizing, and/or evaluating information gathered from or generated by observation, experience, reflection, reasoning, or communication as a guide to belief and action (Paul and Elder, 2002).

What are the rules of critical thinking?

- ✓ Consistency. The critical thinker attempts to discover and eliminate contradictions in thinking.
- ✓ Coherency. The critical thinker attempts to connect all the various dimensions of thinking.
- ✓ Applicability. The critical thinker attempts to ensure that the model of understanding really fits human experiences.
- ✓ Adequacy. The critical thinker attempts to ensure that the model of understanding is flexible enough to incorporate new experiences and data.
- ✓ Communicability. The critical thinker recognizes that thinking, knowing, and learning occur in a community of human beings; and thereby the critical thinker attempts to ensure that the model of understanding is understandable to others (Paul and Elder, 2002).

Adult learning and critical thinking equal

- accumulation of information;
- change in behavior;
- improved performance or proficiencies;
- change in knowledge, attitudes, and skills;
- a new sense of meaning;
- cognitive restructuring;
- personal transformation (Paul and Elder, 2002).

Critical Thinking

A vast majority of my students are or want to be members of the first responder community. First responders must be able to think instinctively and intuitively but also critically. These responders cannot afford *analysis paralysis*. Literacy, writing, and critical thinking skills are tools everyone should possess; but each takes years of work to develop and even more years, actually a lifetime, to maintain. These three skills feed on and reinforce one another. No one is a critical thinker through and through (Paul and Elder, 2002). Critical thinking can be seen as having two components: (1) a set of skills to process and generate information and beliefs and (2) the habit, based on intellectual commitment, of using those skills to guide behavior.

Thinking is the active process by which we develop understandings of ourselves, others, and our world (Paul and Elder, 2002). The process of thinking enables us to solve problems, interpret information, make sense of our feelings and attitudes, discuss important issues, establish beliefs, and work toward the completion of goals. Thinking is an essential component in our life as a human being (Paul and Elder, 2002).

Critical thinking is active and purposeful thinking about how we arrive at our understandings of ourselves, others, and our world and selecting those modes of thinking that are most successful in clarifying and enhancing our understanding (Paul and Elder, 2002). Critical thinking, moreover, examines the assumptions of our beliefs, the connections between our beliefs, and the consequences of beliefs to discover how our beliefs impact our understanding. Further, critical thinking is the ability to think about one's thinking in such a way as to recognize its strengths and weaknesses and, as a result, to recast the thinking in improved form (Paul and Elder, 2002).

Universal intellectual criteria and standards are clarity, accuracy, precision, relevance, depth, breadth, and logicalness (Paul and Elder, 2002). Once again, we see these attributes of critical thinking apply equally to literacy, writing, and thinking. These attributes are the strategy to be employed in all things we do. Critical thinking is the intellectually disciplined process of actively and skillfully conceptualizing, applying, analyzing, synthesizing, and/or evaluating information gathered from or generated by observation, experience, reflection, reasoning, or communication as a guide to belief and action.

Decision-Making

Decision-making is the process utilized in rationally choosing between several alternatives. Sometimes your alternatives are very limited. Some decisions you must make in a split second. Some you can ponder on when time permits. Many will require action within a few minutes. You must follow codified law, as well as case law, in all decision making. You must follow policy and your training. To do all of this, you must still employ critical-thinking and problem-solving skills in your decision-making process. The following offers a road map for these endeavors. You will be presented with a plethora of situations on any given shift. Some will require immediate enforcement or investigative action. Others will involve more strategic thinking and action.

Problem-solving is a dynamic that involves

- ✓ facts,
- ✓ emotions,
- ✓ unknowns,
- ✓ distortions,
- ✓ competition,
- ✓ analysis,
- ✓ observation,
- ✓ communication.

The sheer number of these factors inhibits effective decision making and problem-solving.

The Process

Identify and define the problem:

- ✓ Is the problem real?
- ✓ Is the problem yours?
    - In other words, do you have any authority to deal with it? Be careful here. There will be times where you have no authority to act or even offer comment or advice.

Obtain all the facts:

- ✓ Find the cause of the problem.
- ✓ Analyze and evaluate the data.
- ✓ Develop alternatives.
- ✓ Make a decision.
- ✓ Evaluate the decision.

Problem-Solve

Obstacles

- ✓ Fear
- ✓ Lack of management support
- ✓ Politics
- ✓ Competition
- ✓ Too many alternatives
- ✓ Lack of facts
- ✓ Lack of trust

These obstacles can come from many places. They might be your internal issues. It might be the stakeholders who are involved or affected by the issue. It might be the larger community or even your own agency. It might be those who have nothing to do with it but interject themselves anyway.

Follow Up

- ✓ Do not expect to make the right decision at all times.
    - ○ However, in matters of law, you must make the correct (legal) decision.
- ✓ Evaluate.
- ✓ Make sure the decision is implemented.
- ✓ Make sure your desired outcome is realized.

Reevaluate

- ✓ Times change.
- ✓ Issues change.
- ✓ Conditions change.
- ✓ Needs change.

What is your problem-solving style?

- ✓ Ambassador
    - ○ Strives for mutual agreement (consensus)
    - ○ Easily influences others
    - ○ Conforms to prevailing group
    - ○ Idea person

- ✓ Thinker
    - ○ Researches history of the problem
    - ○ Analyzes similar situations
    - ○ View issues in "black and white"
    - ○ Tends to be indecisive when faced with several possible solutions

- ✓ Charger
    - ○ Is occupied with the outcome
    - ○ Likes to test theories
    - ○ Has a do-it-yourself attitude
    - ○ Values the institution
    - ○ Tends to make on-the-spot decisions

None of these are necessarily bad. In fact, a combination of them might be good and might be needed depending on the situation.

Summary

✓ Most first-line decisions involve operational issues.
✓ Problems should be prioritized.
✓ Decisions should be made at the lowest possible level.
✓ Good officers see decision making as a challenge rather than a chore.

Understand your paradigms. Do not use stopgap measures. In hostile, aggressive, or volatile situations, you may have to use stopgap steps. Do not practice satisficing unless it is a volatile matter. Do practice *Kaizen* and introspection. Set the benchmark for others.

There are a variety of problem-solving models available. One such model is called SARA or scanning, analysis, response, and assessment.

SARA Problem-Solving Model

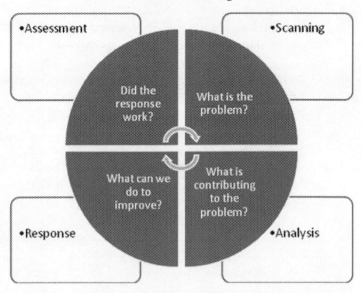

Takeaways

✓ Empathy is an important trait for an officer, but do not let it keep you from doing your job.
✓ The cognitive domain deals with thinking or knowledge.

- ✓ The psychomotor domain deals with applying knowledge in some way through physical activity or, put another way, using one's muscular and skeletal system to manipulate something in some way with the use of skills.
- ✓ The attitudinal or affective domain deals with appreciation or, put another way, values, ethics, morals, and empathy and relates to the understanding of knowledge about a given topic and possibly involving the use of a skill in dealing with an activity, event, or situation.
- ✓ Paradigms are taken-for-granted perceived commonsense perspectives and unwritten rules, which may be damaging.
- ✓ Overcome paradigms through personal mastery.
- ✓ The influence of illogical factors on our decision-making process causes one to engage in a process known as satisficing.
- ✓ Introspection requires one to assess one's strengths and weaknesses, to understand what and who one is, and to evaluate personal and organization expectations.
- ✓ Expand your comfort zones through training.
- ✓ Critical thinking must become intuitive and instinctive so as not to reduce your reaction time.
- ✓ Be sure your actions and behavior are always worthy of emulation.
- ✓ Be sure you can live with your decisions.
- ✓ Just because you can does not mean you should.
- ✓ Is the problem real, and is the problem yours?
- ✓ Obtain the facts.
- ✓ Do not suffer from analysis paralysis.
- ✓ There is no substitute for common sense. Practice it always.
- ✓ Learn to think critically, intuitively, and instinctively at all times.

Therefore, render to Caesar the things that are Caesar's, and to God the things that are God's.

—Matthew 22:21

Chapter Three
Criminal Procedures and Understanding the Law

*The Constitution is not an instrument for the government to
restrain the people, it is an instrument for the people to restrain the
government—lest it come to dominate our lives and interests.*
—Patrick Henry

Understand the law.

This is a two-part story. I was working midnight shift, and I had
a trainee with me. I was on patrol, and I heard someone on the
citizens band (CB) radio talking about selling crack cocaine at the
local truck stop. It was an ice-snow mix falling. I went to the truck
stop area and parked my patrol car a distance away from the place
where I knew passenger vehicles normally parked. My trainee and
I walked through the falling ice and snow and slushy ice on the
ground until we came to the corner of the building. I watched from
around the corner as two people made a drug transaction. One
person reached out his window with a twenty-dollar bill as the
other one began to give him a piece of aluminum foil. I came out
quickly and interceded in seizing the money and foil. The foil had
crack cocaine inside. I arrested the subjects. Fast-forward to several
months, the drug dealer, who had a terrible record, was before the
jury. I had heard about this fellow, and none of it was good. I had
been warned to watch out for him. A good lawyer should never ask a
question he or she did not already have the answer to. However, the
drug dealer's lawyer did just that. He asked me if I had ever heard
of his client before. I just looked at him and then at the prosecutor.
The lawyer asked again, and I said, "Well, yes, I had heard things
about him." The lawyer continued. He said, "What have you heard?"
I said I heard he was a drug dealer and that he carried an automatic
weapon on him. The jury looked amazed. I think even they knew
that was a bad question the lawyer asked. The jury found the drug
dealer guilty and gave him the maximum sentence.

The lawyer had made a fatal mistake, and I knew it. I would have
normally never been allowed to say such a thing based on hearsay,
but he asked. When the trial was over, the lawyer approached me
angrily in the hallway and tried to chastise me. I calmly explained

to him that he was the one who asked the question, and I had not volunteered such a statement. He walked away in a tizzy. It was critical to know all the rules of evidence and criminal procedure. My concern about answering his terrible question was that it might produce a mistrial or provide the defendant with an argument for inadequate defense.

The United States is a nation of laws. While our criminal justice system is far from perfect, it is and has always been the best system the world has ever known. Police officers are given the awesome duty to uphold and enforce the law. Never take this duty lightly.

We will delve deep into several core areas that form the foundation and basis for our legal system. We will examine constitutional law, rules of evidence, criminal procedure, and court procedure. We will not delve into the many and vast local, state, and federal sets of codified laws. Localities, states, and the federal government create law through the legislative process. This law becomes what is known as codified law. Before we jump off the deep end of the pool, it is prudent to offer a few tips. One should read the law strictly—or literally, if you will. However, one should enforce the law through the spirit of the law. When I say "read the law," literally, I mean just that. It is essential to focus on these six items when reading the law. The words "may" and "shall" offer very different meanings and instructions when reading the law. "May" allows some latitude. "Shall" means you must. The words "and" and "or" are also critical. "And" means something follows; in most cases, that is applicable. "Or" might allow an option. Finally, a comma (,) and a period (.) mean a great deal when reading the law. A comma, when used, may create two sentences that can stand alone but are joined by a comma. And when reading a code or law, one must read the entire code or law. All too often, I have seen officers focus on the part of the law that fits what they are looking for. The law must be viewed in its entirety at all times.

Now comes the question of how does an officer know what the spirit of the law means? The spirit of the law actually means what the legislative intent is. This does not help the officer much, does it? The legislative intent is rarely, if ever, written into the law or attached to the law. One can apply common sense and good judgment—or discretion, if you will—but that is not a guarantee you will know the legislative intent. This is where case law, which is derived from higher court decisions, comes into play. So now we must know the law and the applicable case law that instructs us as to how to apply the law.

One more thing before we dive in. In any given locality or state, there might be thousands of criminal and traffic laws. As I mentioned, these are codified. They are given code sections, and we have a typical phase we use to make a charge. Within this framework, you will have felonies, misdemeanors, traffic offenses, and even civil charges in some cases. You are not expected to memorize code numbers. You will learn the most used ones with experience and use. However, you must know the elements of each offense. Determining when to warn, summons, arrest, or ignore will be discussed in another chapter. So without further ado, come on in, the water's fine.

Constitutional Law

The Constitution's Purpose

The purpose of the Constitution is to establish a central government authorized to deal directly with individuals rather than states and to incorporate a system of checks and balances that will preserve the fundamental concepts contained in the Magna Carta, that is, to limit the power of the government. The first three articles of the Constitution establish the legislative, executive, and judicial branches of the government and the system of checks and balances. The balance of power is established vertically through the separation of power between the federal government and the states and laterally through the three branches of the government with the system of checks and balances. In the supremacy clause, the Constitution declares itself the supreme law of the land (Gardner and Anderson, 2010; Harr, Hess, and Orthmann, 2011; Samaha, 2012).

U.S. Legal System

The basic purpose of the U.S. legal system is to ensure fairness in balancing individual and societal rights and needs while preventing excessive government power. This balance between individual and societal rights and needs is represented by the scales of justice.

Our legal system has its roots in the common law of England, the judge-made early English law based on custom and tradition and followed throughout the country. In American law, common law is synonymous with case law. Stare decisis is a common-law doctrine requiring that precedent set in one case shall be followed in all cases having the same or similar circumstances, thus ensuring consistency in the law. The Constitution ensures individual rights by limiting government power. And although the law, in fairness, must be consistent, it is also flexible.

In addition to common law, our legal system also relies upon statutory or codified law, which is promulgated by legislatures or governing bodies. The U.S. legal system categorizes offenses into two specific areas: civil and criminal. Civil laws deal with personal matters and wrongs against individuals—called torts. Criminal laws deal with wrongs against society—called crimes. An act may be both a tort and a crime. When civil or criminal laws are broken, the courts' two main functions are to settle controversies between parties and to decide the rules of law that apply in specific cases (Gardner and Anderson, 2010; Harr et al., 2011; Samaha, 2012).

Judicial Structure

The U.S. judicial system is two tiered, consisting of state and federal court systems because both the federal and state governments need their own court systems to apply and interpret their laws. Both the federal and state constitutions attempt to do this by spelling out the jurisdiction of their respective court systems. Each tier includes specific levels of courts—a trial court, appellate courts, and a supreme court.

Federal Court System

The term "federal court" refers to one of two types of courts. The first type of court is an Article III court. These courts are so named because they derive their power from the Article III of the Constitution. These courts include (1) the U.S. district courts, (2) the U.S. circuit courts of appeal, and (3) the U.S. Supreme Court. They also include two special courts: (a) the U.S. Court of Claims and (b) the U.S. Court of International Trade. These courts are different because, unlike the other courts, they are not courts of general jurisdiction. Courts of general jurisdiction can hear almost any case. Justices and judges of Article III courts are appointed by the president of the United States with the advice and consent of the Senate and hold office for life (Gardner and Anderson, 2010; Harr et al., 2011; Samaha, 2012).

The second type of courts is also established by Congress. These courts are (1) magistrate courts, (2) bankruptcy courts, (3) the U.S. Court of Military Appeals, (4) the U.S. Tax Court, and (5) the U.S. Court of Veterans' Appeals. The judges of these courts are appointed by the president with the advice and consent of the Senate. They hold office for a set number of years, usually about fifteen. Magistrate and bankruptcy courts are attached to each U.S. district court. The U.S. Court of Military Appeals, U.S. Tax Court, and U.S. Court of Veterans' Appeals are called Article I or legislative courts (Gardner and Anderson, 2010; Harr et al., 2011; Samaha, 2012).

State Court Systems

No two state court systems are identical. However, there are enough similarities to describe a typical state court system. Most state court systems are made up of

1. two sets of trial courts
   a. trial courts of general jurisdiction or main trial-level courts
   b. courts of limited jurisdiction (probate, family, traffic, etc.);
2. intermediate appellate courts; and
3. the highest state courts—called by various names.

Unlike federal judges, most state court judges are not appointed for life but are either elected or appointed, or a combination of both, for a certain number of years (Gardner and Anderson, 2010; Harr et al., 2011; Samaha, 2012).

The United States Supreme Court

The Supreme Court consists of the chief justice of the United States and such number of associate justices as may be fixed by Congress. The number of associate justices is currently fixed at eight (28 U.S.C. § 1). The power to nominate the justices is vested in the president of the United States, and appointments are made with the advice and consent of the Senate (Gardner and Anderson, 2010; Harr et al., 2011; Samaha, 2012).

Appellate jurisdiction has been conferred upon the Supreme Court by various statutes, under the authority given Congress by the Constitution. The basic statute effective at this time in conferring and controlling jurisdiction of the Supreme Court is 28 U.S.C. § 1251 et seq. and various special statutes.

The complex role of the Supreme Court derives from its authority to invalidate legislation or executive actions that, in the court's judgment, conflict with the Constitution. This power of "judicial review" has given the court a crucial responsibility in assuring individual rights, as well as in maintaining a "living Constitution" whose broad provisions are continually applied to complicated new situations (Gardner and Anderson, 2010; Harr et al., 2011; Samaha, 2012).

While the function of judicial review was not explicitly provided in the Constitution, it had been anticipated before the adoption of that document. Prior to 1789, state courts had already overturned legislative acts that conflicted with state constitutions. Moreover, many of the founding fathers expected the Supreme Court to assume this role in regard to the Constitution; Alexander Hamilton and James Madison, for example, had stressed the importance of judicial review in the *Federalist Papers*, which urged adoption of the Constitution (Gardner and Anderson, 2010; Harr et al., 2011; Samaha, 2012).

Despite this background, however, the court's power of judicial review was not confirmed until 1803, when it was invoked by Chief Justice John Marshall in *Marbury v. Madison*. In this decision, the chief justice asserted that the Supreme Court's responsibility to overturn unconstitutional legislation was a necessary consequence of its sworn duty to uphold the Constitution. That oath could not be fulfilled any other way (Gardner and Anderson, 2010; Harr et al., 2011; Samaha, 2012).

The Constitution limits the court to dealing with "cases" and "controversies." John Jay, the first chief justice, clarified this restraint early in the court's history by declining to advise Pres. George Washington on the constitutional implications of a proposed foreign policy decision. The court does not give advisory opinions; rather, its function is limited to deciding specific cases. When the Supreme Court rules on a constitutional issue, that judgment is virtually final. Its decisions can be altered only by the rarely used procedure of constitutional amendment or by a new ruling of the court. However, when the court interprets a statute, new legislative action can be taken (Gardner and Anderson, 2010; Harr et al., 2011; Samaha, 2012). Researching the Law

Information may be written at a popular level for the layperson, at a professional level for the practitioner, or at a scholarly level for the researcher. Sources of legal information are classified as primary or secondary. Primary sources are statutes, codes, and cases—the authoritative, original legal information. Primary sources are the law and must be followed by courts unless the court is changing the law. Secondary sources are things that discuss the primary sources—periodicals, treatises/texts, legal encyclopedias, and legal dictionaries. Secondary sources are not authoritative and do not establish precedents. Courts do not need to follow them because they are considered only persuasive, not binding (Gardner and Anderson, 2010; Harr et al., 2011; Samaha, 2012).

Many legal case citations are found within the information sources. A legal citation is a standardized way of referring to a specific legal source. It has three basic parts: a volume number, an abbreviation for the title, and a page or section number. The year of the decision should also be included with the citation. The National Reporter System publishes seven regional sets of volumes of legal cases, as well as individual sets for specific states (Gardner and Anderson, 2010; Harr et al., 2011; Samaha, 2012).

A legal opinion usually contains (1) a description of the facts, (2) a statement of the legal issues presented for decision, (3) the relevant rules of law, (4) the holding, and (5) the policies and reasons that support the holding. The skills and process needed to read case law are (1) thinking in reverse, (2) untangling the interplay of the basic components, and (3) drawing inferences (Gardner and Anderson, 2010; Harr et al., 2011; Samaha, 2012). Most case briefs contain the case name and citation, a summary of key facts, the legal issues involved, the court's decision, the reasons for that decision, and any separate opinions or dissents.

Shepardizing a case involves using *Shepard's Citations*, a reference that tracks cases so legal researchers can easily determine whether the original holding has been changed through any appeals. An invaluable tool in researching the law is the Internet. However, a note of caution when using the Internet for legal research: to evaluate the reliability of information found on the Internet, consider the credibility of the source and the currency of the information (Gardner and Anderson, 2010; Harr et al., 2011; Samaha, 2012).

Equal Protection under the Law and Due Process of Law

The Constitution states only one command twice. The Fifth Amendment says to the federal government that no one shall be "deprived of life, liberty or property without due process of law." The Fourteenth Amendment, ratified in 1868, uses the same words, called the due process clause, to describe a legal obligation of all states. These words have, as their central promise, an assurance that all levels of American government must operate within the law and provide fair procedures.

While the text of the due process clause is extremely general, the fact that it appears twice makes it clear that it states a central proposition. The requirement that the government function in accordance with the law and with a commitment to legality is at the heart of all advanced legal systems, and the due process clause embodies that commitment (Gardner and Anderson, 2010; Harr et al., 2011; Samaha, 2012).

To ensure "liberty and justice for all," two additional amendments were added to the Constitution following the Civil War. The Thirteenth Amendment, ratified in 1865, abolished slavery. The Fourteenth Amendment, ratified in 1868, granted citizenship to all persons born or naturalized in the United States and forbade states to deny their citizens due process of law or equal protection of the law. Thus it made certain provisions of the Bill of Rights applicable to the states. The Supreme Court did not directly confront civil rights until the 1950s and 1960s (Gardner and Anderson, 2010; Harr et al., 2011; Samaha, 2012).

The equal protection clause of the Fourteenth Amendment prohibits states from denying any person within its jurisdiction the equal protection of the laws. In other words, the laws of a state must treat an individual in the same manner as others in similar conditions and circumstances. A violation will occur, for example, if a state prohibits an individual from entering into an employment contract because he or she is a member of a particular race. The equal protection clause is not intended to provide "equality" among individuals or classes but only "equal application" of the laws. The result, therefore, of a law is not relevant so long as there is no discrimination in its application. By denying states the ability to discriminate, the equal protection clause is crucial to the protection of civil rights. The Fourteenth Amendment is not by its terms applicable to the federal government. Actions by the federal government, however, that classify individuals in a discriminatory manner will, under similar circumstances, violate the due process of the Fifth Amendment (Gardner and Anderson, 2010; Harr et al., 2011; Samaha, 2012).

Selective Incorporation

The doctrine of selective incorporation holds that only the provisions of the Bill of Rights that are fundamental to the American legal system are applied to the states through the due process clause of the Fourteenth Amendment. However, this area continues to evolve, and today there are controversial areas currently involving constitutional issues and federal powers, such as the immigration issue and the role of unions in public safety organizations (Gardner and Anderson, 2010; Harr et al., 2011; Samaha, 2012).

The First Amendment

"Congress shall make no law respecting an establishment of religion, or prohibiting the free exercise thereof; or abridging the freedom of speech, or of the press; or the right of the people peaceably to

assemble, and to petition the government for a redress of grievances."
The First Amendment protects the right to freedom of religion and
freedom of expression from government interference. The Supreme
Court interprets the extent of the protection afforded to these rights.
The First Amendment has been interpreted by the court as applying
to the entire federal government, even though it is only expressly
applicable to Congress. Furthermore, using selective incorporation,
the court has ruled that the due process clause of the Fourteenth
Amendment protects the rights contained in the First Amendment
from interference by state governments (Gardner and Anderson,
2010; Harr et al., 2011; Samaha, 2012).

The most basic component of freedom of expression is the right
of freedom of speech. The right to freedom of speech allows
individuals to express themselves without interference or constraint
by the government. The Supreme Court requires the government
to provide substantial justification for the interference with the
right of free speech where it attempts to regulate the content of the
speech. A less stringent test is applied for content-neutral legislation.
The Supreme Court has also recognized that the government may
prohibit some speech that may cause a breach of the peace or
cause violence, such as advocating illegal action, fighting words,
commercial speech, and obscenity (Gardner and Anderson, 2010;
Harr et al., 2011; Samaha, 2012).

Free speech also includes other mediums of expression that
communicate a message. The level of protection that speech receives
also depends on the forum in which it takes place. Freedom of
expression consists of the rights to freedom of speech, the press,
and assembly and the right to petition the government for a redress
of grievances and the implied rights of association and belief. The
expression/speech does not need to be verbal to be protected and
can be a symbolic act (Gardner and Anderson, 2010; Harr et al., 2011;
Samaha, 2012).

Despite popular misunderstanding, the right to freedom of the
press guaranteed by the First Amendment is not very different
from the right to freedom of speech. It allows individuals to express
themselves through publication and dissemination. It is part of the
constitutional protection of freedom of expression. It does not afford
members of the media any special rights or privileges not afforded

to citizens in general (Gardner and Anderson, 2010; Harr et al., 2011; Samaha, 2012).

The right to assemble allows people to gather for peaceful and lawful purposes. Implicit within this right is the right to association and belief. The Supreme Court has expressly recognized that a right to freedom of association and belief is implicit in the First, Fifth, and Fourteenth Amendments. This implicit right is limited to the right to associate for First Amendment purposes (Gardner and Anderson, 2010; Harr et al., 2011; Samaha, 2012).

The government may prohibit people from knowingly associating in groups that engage and promote illegal activities. The right to associate also prohibits the government from requiring a group to register or disclose its members or from denying government benefits on the basis of an individual's current or past membership in a particular group. There are exceptions to this rule where the court finds that governmental interests in disclosure/registration outweigh interference with First Amendment rights. The government may also, generally, not compel individuals to express themselves, hold certain beliefs, or belong to particular associations or groups (Gardner and Anderson, 2010; Harr et al., 2011; Samaha, 2012).

The right to petition the government for a redress of grievances guarantees people the right to ask the government to provide relief for a wrong through the courts (litigation) or other governmental action. It works with the right of assembly by allowing people to join together and seek change from the government (Gardner and Anderson, 2010; Harr et al., 2011; Samaha, 2012).

Prisoners' diminished rights based on the First Amendment involve censorship of mail, expression within the institution, association within the institution, religion, appearance, and visitation rights (Gardner and Anderson, 2010; Harr et al., 2011; Samaha, 2012).

The Second Amendment

"A well-regulated militia, being necessary to the security of a free state, the right of the people to keep and bear arms, shall not be infringed" (Gardner and Anderson, 2010; Harr et al., 2011; Samaha, 2012).

The Fourth Amendment

"The right of the people to be secure in their persons, houses, papers, and effects, against unreasonable searches and seizures, shall not be violated, and no warrants shall issue, but upon probable cause, supported by oath or affirmation, and particularly describing the place to be searched, and the persons or things to be seized" (Gardner and Anderson, 2010; Harr et al., 2011; Samaha, 2012).

At the very core of restrictions on the government's infringing on an individual's freedom is the Fourth Amendment, which forbids unreasonable searches and seizures. These two key words—*search* and *seizure*—are fundamental to understanding the Fourth Amendment. A search is an examination of person, place, or vehicle for the contraband or evidence of a crime. A seizure is a taking by law enforcement personnel or other government agents of contraband, evidence of a crime, or a person into custody (Gardner and Anderson, 2010; Harr et al., 2011; Samaha, 2012).

The Fourth Amendment has continued to evolve constitutionally, both substantively and procedurally through both case and statutory law, and it governs much of what police officers are legally permitted to do as they "serve and protect." Until the 1960s, the Supreme Court has tended to view the two key Fourth Amendment clauses—unreasonable searches and seizures and no warrants without probable cause—as closely connected and constitutionally intertwined. Since the 1960s, the court has tended to view the clauses as separate. This means that there are instances where a search may be conducted without either a warrant or probable cause and still be considered reasonable (Gardner and Anderson, 2010; Harr et al., 2011; Samaha, 2012).

Again, the Fourth Amendment forbids only unreasonable searches and seizures and requires that any search or arrest warrant be based on probable cause. The Constitution does not provide an absolute right to be free from government intrusion, only unreasonable interference. If a person is an employee of any governmental agency or is an agent of the government in any capacity, that person is bound by the Fourth Amendment. The Fourth Amendment does not apply to private parties (Gardner and Anderson, 2010; Harr et al., 2011; Samaha, 2012).

Probable cause is the legal metric normally used to determine when officers may execute lawful searches and arrests with or, in some cases, without a warrant. Probable cause to search means officers reasonably believe that evidence, contraband, or other items sought are where police believe these items to be. Probable cause to arrest means officers reasonably believe that a crime has been committed by the person they seek to arrest. All warrants are to be based on probable cause. When executing a search or arrest warrant, the general rule is that, for an entry into a home to be constitutional, police must first knock and identify themselves and their purpose—the knock-and-announce rule (Gardner and Anderson, 2010; Harr et al., 2011; Samaha, 2012).

A stop is a brief detention of a person based on specific and articulated facts for the purpose of investigating suspicious activity. A frisk is a limited pat-down search for weapons for the protection of the government agent and others. It is not automatically permitted with a stop but only when the agent suspects the person is armed and dangerous. The law of stop and frisk deals with that time frame during which officers follow up on their suspicions but before the time that the requisite probable cause is established to justify an arrest (*Terry v. Ohio*, 1968). The *Terry* decision established that, in what is termed a *Terry* stop, an officer with articulated reasonable suspicion that a crime is occurring, has occurred, or is about to occur may conduct a brief investigatory stop, including a pat down for weapons if the officer has reason to suspect the person is armed and dangerous (Gardner and Anderson, 2010; Harr et al., 2011; Samaha, 2012).

An unlawful search or seizure can have two serious consequences: (1) the evidence may be excluded from court—the exclusionary rule—and/or (2) internal sanctions, as well as civil and criminal liability, may be incurred. The exclusionary rule is a judicially created rule promulgated by the Supreme Court to prevent police misconduct. It prohibits evidence obtained in violation of a person's constitutional rights from being admissible in court (*Weeks v. United States*, 1914) (Gardner and Anderson, 2010; Harr et al., 2011; Samaha, 2012).

The primary purpose underlying the exclusionary rule is to deter government misconduct. *Mapp v. Ohio* (1961) has made the exclusionary rule applicable at the state level. As with most judicial evidentiary doctrines, there are exceptions to the rule. Among the exceptions to the exclusionary rule are the inevitable discovery doctrine, existence of a valid independent source, harmless error, and good faith (Gardner and Anderson, 2010; Harr et al., 2011; Samaha, 2012).

Seizures

The *Terry* case established that the authority to stop and frisk is independent of the power to arrest. A stop is not an arrest, but it is a seizure within the meaning of the Fourth Amendment and, therefore, requires reasonableness. How long a stop may last depends on factors that indicate the suspect has not been detained for an unreasonably long time, including the purpose of the stop and the time and means the investigation required (Gardner and Anderson, 2010; Harr et al., 2011; Samaha, 2012).

A seizure occurs when a reasonable person believes he or she is not free to leave. An arrest is a formal restraint on one's freedom of movement. A seizure need not necessarily be an arrest, but all arrests are seizures. To arrest is to deprive a person of liberty by legal authority, taking the person into custody for the purpose of holding him or her to answer a criminal charge. The elements of an arrest are (1) intending to take a person into custody, (2) exercising authority to do so, (3) detaining or restraining the person to be arrested, and (4) the arrestee understanding what is happening. Officers can usually make a lawful arrest for any crime committed in their presence, for any felony if they have probable cause, and with an arrest warrant (Gardner and Anderson, 2010; Harr et al., 2011; Samaha, 2012).

Police may, without a warrant, arrest for any crime committed in their presence. Police may, without a warrant, arrest for an unwitnessed felony based on probable cause. Police may make a warrantless arrest based on probable cause in a public place or in a private place that a suspect has retreated to from a public place. Police may not make a nonconsensual, warrantless arrest inside a person's home or arrest a guest within that home without exigent circumstances. Exigent circumstances include hot pursuit of a fleeing felon, prevention of imminent destruction of evidence, and prevention of a suspect's escape (Gardner and Anderson, 2010; Harr et al., 2011; Samaha, 2012).

Foreign diplomats—including ambassadors, ministers, their assistants and attachés, and their families and servants—generally have complete immunity from arrest. Foreign consuls and their deputies, as well as some legislators and out-of-state witnesses, may also have limited immunity (Gardner and Anderson, 2010; Harr et al., 2011; Samaha, 2012).

Officers may stop motorists only for violations of the law, which may include equipment violations, erratic driving, or invalid vehicle registration. Because a traffic stop is brief and occurs in public, it is not considered an arrest (Gardner and Anderson, 2010; Harr et al., 2011; Samaha, 2012).

The use of roadblocks and checkpoints in which every vehicle is stopped is permissible provided they pass a balancing test established by the Supreme Court in *Brown v. Texas* (1979), which considers three factors:

1. The gravity of the public concerns served by the roadblock

2. The degree to which the roadblock is likely to succeed in serving the public interest

3. The severity with which the roadblock interferes with individual liberty (Gardner and Anderson, 2010; Harr et al., 2011; Samaha, 2012).

Checkpoints at ports of entry or near our international borders need no justification to stop all vehicles to check for illegal entrants into the United States (Gardner and Anderson, 2010; Harr et al., 2011; Samaha, 2012).

Use of Force

When making an arrest, police officers can use only as much force as is reasonably necessary to overcome resistance and gain compliance. Excessive force may result in civil and perhaps even criminal liability for the officer(s) involved. Two Supreme Court cases have framed the degree of force constitutionally permissible when police are making an arrest (Gardner and Anderson, 2010; Harr, et al, 2011; Samaha, 2012).

Garner v. Tennessee (1985)

At about 10:45 p.m. on October 3, 1974, a Memphis police officer, responding to a prowler call, began chasing a fleeing suspect, Edward Garner. Garner—fifteen years old—stopped at a six-foot-high chain-link fence at the edge of the yard. With the aid of a flashlight, the officer was able to see Garner's face and hands. He saw no sign of a weapon and, though not certain, was "reasonably sure" and "figured" that Garner was unarmed. He thought Garner was seventeen or eighteen years old and about 5'5" or 5'7" tall. While Garner was crouched at the base of the fence, the officer called out, "Police! Halt!" and took a few steps toward him. Garner then began to climb over the fence. Convinced that if Garner made it over the fence he would elude capture, the officer shot him. The bullet hit Garner in the back of the head. Garner was taken by ambulance to a hospital, where he died on the operating table. Ten dollars and a purse taken from the house were found on his body (Gardner and Anderson, 2010; Harr et al., 2011; Samaha, 2012).

In using deadly force to prevent the escape, the officer was acting under the authority of a Tennessee statute and pursuant to police department policy. The statute stated that "if, after notice of the intention to arrest the defendant, he either fled or forcibly resisted, the officer may use all the necessary means to affect the arrest." The department policy was slightly more restrictive than the statute but still allowed the use of deadly force in cases of burglary. The incident was reviewed by the Memphis Police Firearm's Review Board and presented to a grand jury. Neither took any action (Gardner and Anderson, 2010; Harr et al., 2011; Samaha, 2012).

Garner's father initiated a civil action seeking damages under 42 U.S.C. 1983 for asserted violations of Garner's constitutional rights. The federal trial court concluded that the officer's actions were authorized by the Tennessee statute, which in turn was constitutional. The trial court believed that the officer had employed the only reasonable and practicable means of preventing Garner's escape. Garner had "recklessly and heedlessly attempted to vault over the fence to escape, thereby assuming the risk of being fired upon" (Gardner and Anderson, 2010; Harr et al., 2011; Samaha, 2012).

The court of appeals reversed and remanded. It reasoned that the killing of a fleeing suspect was a "seizure" under the Fourth Amendment and was therefore constitutional only if "reasonable." The Tennessee statute failed as applied to this case because it did not adequately limit the use of deadly force by distinguishing between felonies of different magnitudes. On appeal, the Supreme Court agreed with the court of appeals and held that

> the use of deadly force to prevent the escape of all felony suspects, whatever the circumstances, is constitutionally unreasonable. It is not better that all felony suspects die than that they escape. Where the suspect poses no immediate threat to the officer and no threat to others, the harm resulting from failing to apprehend him does not justify the use of deadly force to do so. It is no doubt unfortunate when a suspect who is in sight escapes, but the fact that the police arrive a little late or are a little slower afoot does not always justify killing the suspect. A police officer may not seize an unarmed, nondangerous suspect by shooting him dead. The Tennessee statute is unconstitutional insofar as it authorizes the use of deadly force against such fleeing suspects.

The court did not rule out the use of deadly force in all instances but simply concluded it could not be used indiscriminately across the board when attempting to arrest a fleeing felon (Gardner and Anderson, 2010; Harr et al., 2011; Samaha, 2012).

Graham v. Connor (1989)

Graham, a diabetic, asked a friend, Berry, to drive him to a convenience store to purchase orange juice to counteract the onset of an insulin reaction. Upon entering the store and seeing the number of people ahead of him, Graham hurried out and asked Berry to drive him to a friend's house instead. Connor, a city police officer, became suspicious after seeing Graham hastily enter and leave the store, followed Berry's car, and made an investigative stop, ordering the pair to wait while he found out what had happened in the store. Backup police officers arrived on the scene, handcuffed Graham, and ignored or rebuffed attempts to explain and treat Graham's condition. During the encounter, Graham sustained multiple injuries. He was released when Connor learned that nothing had happened in the store. Graham filed suit in the district court under 42 U.S.C. § 1983 against the officers, alleging that they had used excessive force in making the stop, in violation of "rights secured to him under the Fourteenth Amendment to the United States Constitution" and 42 U.S.C. (Gardner and Anderson, 2010; Harr et al., 2011; Samaha, 2012).

Both the district trial court and the appeals court rejected Graham's argument on the basis of the then-existing subjective standard used to evaluate police actions in excessive force lawsuit—whether the force was applied in a good faith effort to maintain and restore discipline or maliciously and sadistically for the very purpose of causing harm. On appeal, the Supreme Court, in a 9–0 ruling, reversed the lower courts' rulings and held that "all claims that law enforcement officials have used excessive force—deadly or not—in the course of an arrest, investigatory stop, or other 'seizure' of a free citizen are properly analyzed under the Fourth Amendment's 'objective reasonableness' standard, rather than under a 'substantive due process standard.'"

The result of these cases is not that police cannot use force but that the force used must be reasonable under the circumstances. In general, the only justification for use of deadly force is self-defense or protecting the lives of others. The courts appreciate that, on the streets, a split-second decision is often required, and that too is a factor in a reasonableness analysis (Gardner and Anderson, 2010; Harr et al., 2011; Samaha, 2012).

Even the use of a Taser might be considered unreasonable excessive force if the subject is not a flight risk, a dangerous felon, or an immediate threat (*Bryan v. McPherson*, 2009).

Searches

The fundamental constitutional rules that apply to challenges under Fourth Amendment protection are (1) there must be governmental action; (2) the person making the challenge must have standing, that is, the conduct violates the challenger's reasonable expectation of privacy; and (3) general searches are unlawful and restrict government from going beyond what is necessary. All searches must be limited in scope. General searches are unconstitutional and never legal (Gardner and Anderson, 2010; Harr et al., 2011; Samaha, 2012).

Searches conducted with a warrant must be limited to the specific area and specific items described in the warrant. Although warrantless searches are presumed unreasonable, exceptions to the warrant requirement include the following: (1) with consent, (2) frisking for officer safety, (3) plain feel/view evidence, (4) incident to lawful custodial arrest, (5) automobile exceptions, (6) exigent (emergency) circumstances, and (7) open fields, abandoned property, and public places (Gardner and Anderson, 2010; Harr et al., 2011; Samaha, 2012).

In the first exception, consent searches, the consent to search must be voluntary. The search must be limited to the area specified by the person granting permission. The person may revoke the consent at any time. In the second exception, stop-and-frisk situations, if a frisk is authorized by the circumstances of an investigative stop, only a limited pat down of the detainee's outer clothing for the officer's safety is authorized. In the third exception, plain feel/view, if in the lawful course of a frisk officers feel something that training and experience causes them to believe is contraband, there is probable cause to expand the search and seize the object—plain feel/touch. In addition, unconcealed evidence that officers see while engaged in a lawful activity may be seized and is admissible in court—plain view (Gardner and Anderson, 2010; Harr et al., 2011; Samaha, 2012).

In the fourth exception, searches incidental to a lawful custodial arrest, the search must be contemporaneous and must be limited to the area within the person's reach (*Chimel v. California*, 1969). A search incident to lawful arrest allows seizure of property or containers not immediately connected with the arrestee's body but under his or her immediate control, including backpacks, briefcases, luggage, or other packages. In the fifth exception, the automobile exception, *Carroll v. United States* (1925) established that vehicles can be searched without a warrant provided (1) there is probable cause to believe the vehicle's contents violate the law, and (2) the vehicle will be gone before a search warrant can be obtained. The sixth exception, exigent circumstances, includes danger of physical harm to officers or another person, danger of destruction of evidence, driving while intoxicated, hot pursuit situations, and individuals requiring "rescuing." The seventh exception—open fields, abandoned property, and public places—involves the lack of expectation of privacy; therefore the Fourth Amendment protection does not apply (Gardner and Anderson, 2010; Harr et al., 2011; Samaha, 2012).

The Supreme Court has ruled that routine border searches and searches at international airports are reasonable under the Fourth Amendment. Prison inmates, probationers, and parolees have limited Fourth Amendment rights because, while incarcerated or under supervision, they should not expect the degree of privacy enjoyed by law-abiding citizens (Gardner and Anderson, 2010; Harr et al., 2011; Samaha, 2012).

Electronic Searches

Electronic surveillance is a form of search and seizure and, as such, is governed by the Fourth Amendment. For a search to have occurred, government agents need not physically go onto someone's property. Information obtained whenever there is a reasonable expectation of privacy constitutes a search (Gardner and Anderson, 2010; Harr et al., 2011; Samaha, 2012).

The Fourth Amendment does not limit the use of electronic equipment that merely enhances officers' senses but does not interfere with a person's reasonable expectation of privacy. Lights, photography from aircraft, and telescopes fall within this area. However, the use of thermal imaging without a search warrant to detect illegal activity inside a residence is unconstitutional. To obtain an electronic surveillance warrant, probable cause that a person is engaging in particular communications to pursue an illegal activity must be established by the court, and normal investigative procedures must have already been tried (Gardner and Anderson, 2010; Harr et al., 2011; Samaha, 2012).

The Fifth Amendment

> No person shall be held to answer for a capital, or otherwise infamous crime, unless on a presentment or indictment of a grand jury, except in cases arising in the land or naval forces, or in the militia, when in actual service in time of war or public danger; nor shall any person be subject for the same offense to be twice put in jeopardy of life or limb; nor shall be compelled in any criminal case to be a witness against himself, nor be deprived of life, liberty, or property, without due process of law; nor shall private property be taken for public use, without just compensation. (Gardner and Anderson, 2010; Harr et al., 2011; Samaha, 2012)

The Fifth Amendment outlines basic constitutional limits on police procedure. The grand jury clause and the due process clause come from the Magna Carta, dating back to 1215. The Fifth Amendment provides five distinct constitutional rights:

1. Grand juries for capital crimes

2. Prohibition on double jeopardy

3. Prohibition against required self-incrimination

4. Guarantee that all criminal defendants will have a fair trial

5. A promise that the government will not seize private property without paying market value.

While the Fifth Amendment originally only applied to federal courts, the U.S. Supreme Court has interpreted the Fifth Amendment's provisions as now applying to the states through the due process clause of the Fourteenth Amendment (Gardner and Anderson, 2010; Harr et al., 2011; Samaha, 2012).

Grand Juries

Normally, grand jurors are selected from the pool of prospective jurors who can serve on a given day in any juror capacity. While state legislatures may set the statutory number of grand jurors anywhere within the common-law requirement of twelve to twenty-three, statutes setting the number outside of this range violate the Fifth Amendment. Federal law has set the federal grand jury number as falling between sixteen and twenty-three (Gardner and Anderson, 2010; Harr et al., 2011; Samaha, 2012).

A person being charged with a crime that warrants a grand jury has the right to challenge members of the grand juror for partiality or bias. These challenges differ from peremptory challenges, which a defendant has when choosing a trial jury. When a defendant makes a peremptory challenge, the judge must remove the juror without making any proof; but in the case of a grand juror challenge, the challenger must establish the cause of the challenge. Grand juries possess broad authority to investigate suspected crimes but may not conduct "fishing expeditions" and may not hire individuals to locate testimony or documents. Ultimately, grand juries may make a presentment. In a presentment, the grand jury informs the court that they have a reasonable suspicion that the suspect committed a crime (Gardner and Anderson, 2010; Harr et al., 2011; Samaha, 2012).

Double Jeopardy

The double jeopardy clause protects an individual from harassment through successive prosecutions of the same alleged act. Courts have interpreted the double jeopardy clause as accomplishing these goals by providing the following three distinct rights: a guarantee that a defendant will not face a second prosecution after an acquittal, a guarantee that a defendant will not face a second prosecution after a conviction, and a guarantee that a defendant will not receive multiple punishments for the same offense. Jeopardy refers to the danger of conviction. Thus jeopardy does not attach unless a risk of the determination of guilt exists. If some event or circumstance prompts the trial court to declare a mistrial, jeopardy has not attached if the mistrial only results in minimal delay and if the government does not receive added opportunity to strengthen its case (Gardner and Anderson, 2010; Harr et al., 2011; Samaha, 2012).

Double jeopardy may not preclude federal prosecution for essentially the same act. For example, if a defendant was acquitted at a state trial for an offense and that offense could be framed as a federal offense, say, a civil rights violation, the defendant could be tried in federal court for that offense (Gardner and Anderson, 2010; Harr et al., 2011; Samaha, 2012).

Self-Incrimination

The Fifth Amendment protects criminal defendants from having to testify if they may incriminate themselves through the testimony. A witness may "plead the Fifth" and not answer if the witness believes answering the question may be self-incriminatory. In the landmark case *Miranda v. Arizona* (1966), the Supreme Court extended the Fifth Amendment protections to encompass any situation outside of the courtroom that involves the curtailment of personal freedom. Any time that law enforcement takes a suspect into custody, they must make the suspect aware of all rights. Known as *Miranda* rights and warnings, these rights include the right to remain silent, the right to have an attorney present during questioning, and the right to have a government-appointed attorney if the suspect cannot afford one (Gardner and Anderson, 2010; Harr et al., 2011; Samaha, 2012).

If an officer fails to *Mirandize*, courts will often suppress any statements by the suspect as a violation of the Fifth Amendment's protection against self-incrimination unless, of course, the suspect waived these rights. A waiver occurs when a suspect waives the rights knowingly, intelligently, and voluntarily. To determine if a knowing, intelligent, and voluntary waiver has occurred, courts consider the totality of the circumstances, which considers all relevant facts and circumstances surrounding the statement. If a suspect makes a spontaneous statement while in custody and prior to being made aware of the *Miranda* rights, law enforcement can use the statement against the suspect as long as police interrogation does not prompt the statement (Gardner and Anderson, 2010; Harr et al., 2011; Samaha, 2012).

After Congress passed the 1968 Crime Control and Safe Streets Act, there was concern that the statute essentially overruled the requirements of *Miranda*. Some also believed that Congress had the authority to do so because they felt that *Miranda* represented a matter of judicial policy rather than an actual declaration of Fifth Amendment protections. However, in *Dickerson v. United States* (2000), the Supreme Court rejected these arguments and ruled that the 1964 court had derived *Miranda* directly from the Fifth Amendment (Gardner and Anderson, 2010; Harr et al., 2011; Samaha, 2012).

Due Process

Due process requires the government to respect all the rights, guarantees, and protections of the U.S. Constitution and applicable statutes before the government may deprive a person of life, liberty, or property. Due process essentially guarantees that the affected party will receive a fundamentally fair, orderly, and just judicial proceeding. While the Fifth Amendment only applies to the federal government, the identical text in the Fourteenth Amendment means that this due process requirement applies to the states as well (Gardner and Anderson, 2010; Harr et al., 2011; Samaha, 2012).

Courts recognize two aspects of due process: procedural due process and substantive due process. Procedural due process ensures fundamental fairness by guaranteeing a party the right to be heard, to receive proper notification throughout the judicial proceeding, and to be before a court that has the jurisdiction to render a judgment. Thus procedural due process rights are rights that dictate how the government can lawfully go about taking away a person's freedom or property or life when the law gives it the power to do so (Gardner and Anderson, 2010; Harr et al., 2011; Samaha, 2012).

Substantive due process rights are those rights that reserve to the individual the power to possess or to do certain things, despite instances of the government's desire to the contrary. These are rights like freedom of speech and religion. This is a significant legal doctrine because it greatly expands the power of judicial review exercised by the federal courts. Advocates of the doctrine argue that it is a simple recognition that no procedure can be just if it is being used to unjustly deprive a person of his basic human liberties and that the due process clause is intentionally written in broad terms to give the court flexibility in interpreting it (Gardner and Anderson, 2010; Harr et al., 2011; Samaha, 2012).

Sixth Amendment

"In all criminal prosecutions, the accused shall enjoy the right to a speedy and public trial, by an impartial jury of the state and district wherein the crime shall have been committed, which district shall have been previously ascertained by law, and to be informed of the nature and cause of the accusation; to be confronted with the witnesses against him; to have compulsory process for obtaining witnesses in his favor, and to have the assistance of counsel for his defense" (Gardner and Anderson, 2010; Harr. et al., 2011; Samaha, 2012).

The Sixth Amendment provides criminal defendants with seven basic liberties and protections: (1) the right to a speedy trial, (2) the right to a public trial, (3) the right to an impartial jury, (4) the right to be informed of pending charges, (5) the right to confront and to cross-examine adverse witnesses, (6) the right to compel favorable witnesses to testify at trial through the subpoena power of the judiciary, and (7) the right to legal counsel (Gardner and Anderson, 2010; Harr et al., 2011; Samaha, 2012).

The Sixth Amendment originally applied only to criminal actions brought by the federal government. However, all the protections guaranteed by the Sixth Amendment have been made applicable to the states through selective incorporation via the Fourteenth Amendment. As we know, under this doctrine, the due process and equal protection clauses of the Fourteenth Amendment require each state to recognize certain fundamental liberties that are enumerated in the Bill of Rights because such liberties are deemed essential to the concepts of freedom and equality. Together with the supremacy clause of Article VI, the Fourteenth Amendment prohibits any state from providing less protection for a right conferred by the Sixth Amendment than is provided under the federal Constitution (Gardner and Anderson, 2010; Harr et al., 2011; Samaha, 2012).

Speedy Trial

The right to a speedy trial is to prevent defendants from waiting in jail—or even out of jail—for an indefinite period before trial, to minimize the time in which a defendant's life is disrupted and burdened by the anxiety and scrutiny associated with a criminal trial, and to reduce the chances that a prolonged delay before trial will impair the ability of the accused to prepare a defense. The longer a trial is postponed, the more likely it is that witnesses will disappear, that evidence will be lost or destroyed, and that memories will fade. The right to a speedy trial attaches only after the government has arrested, indicted, or otherwise formally accused someone of a crime. There is no set time that constitutes lack of a speedy trial, and courts will use a balancing test to decide the question. If a court finds in favor of an accused in such a case, the usual remedy is to dismiss the charges (Gardner and Anderson, 2010; Harr et al., 2011; Samaha, 2012).

Public Trial

The founding fathers believed that public criminal proceedings would operate as a check against malevolent prosecutions, corrupt or malleable judges, and perjury by witnesses. The public nature of criminal proceedings also aids the fact-finding mission of the judiciary by encouraging citizens to come forward with relevant information, whether inculpatory or exculpatory. The right to a public trial is personal to the defendant and may not be asserted by the media or the public in general, although both the public and media have a qualified First Amendment right to attend criminal proceedings. The First Amendment does not accommodate everyone who wants to attend a particular proceeding, and it does not require courts to televise any given legal proceeding. For example, oral arguments before the U.S. Supreme Court have never been televised (Gardner and Anderson, 2010; Harr et al., 2011; Samaha, 2012).

Trial by an Impartial Jury

> The guarantees of jury trial in the Federal and State Constitutions reflect a profound judgment about the way in which law should be enforced and justice administered. A right to jury trial is granted to criminal defendants in order to prevent oppression by the Government. Those who wrote our constitutions knew from history and experience that it was necessary to protect against unfounded criminal charges brought to eliminate enemies and against judges too responsive to the voice of higher authority. The framers of the constitutions strove to create an independent judiciary

DR. JEFFREY C. FOX

but insisted upon further protection against arbitrary action. Providing an accused with the right to be tried by a jury of his peers gave him an inestimable safeguard against the corrupt overzealous prosecutor and against the compliant, biased, or eccentric judge. . . . [T]he jury trial provisions . . . reflect a fundamental decision about the exercise of official power—a reluctance to entrust plenary powers over the life and liberty of the citizen to one judge or to a group of judges. Fear of unchecked power . . . found expression in the criminal law in this insistence upon community participation in the determination of guilt or innocence. (Gardner and Anderson, 2010; Harr et al., 2011; Samaha, 2012)

Duncan v. Louisiana (1968)

The Sixth Amendment entitles defendants to a jury pool that represents a fair cross section of the community. During the voir dire questioning process of jury selection, the presiding judge, the prosecution, and defense attorneys are allowed to ask members of the jury pool a variety of questions intended to reveal any latent biases, prejudices, or other influences that might affect their impartiality. The presence of even one biased juror is not permitted under the Sixth Amendment (Gardner and Anderson, 2010; Harr et al., 2011; Samaha, 2012).

Although a jury must be impartial, there is no Sixth Amendment right to a jury of twelve persons. The Supreme Court has ruled that a jury of at least six persons is "large enough to promote group deliberation, free from outside attempts at intimidation, and to provide a fair possibility for obtaining a cross-section of the community" (*Williams v. Florida*, 1970). However, the court has also ruled that a jury of only five members is unconstitutionally small (*Ballew v. Georgia*, 1978) (Gardner and Anderson, 2010; Harr et al., 2011; Samaha, 2012).

To Be Informed of the Nature and Cause of the Accusation

The constitutional right to be informed of the nature and cause of the accusation entitles the defendant to insist that the indictment apprise him of the crime charged with such reasonable certainty that he can make his defense and protect himself after judgment against another prosecution on the same charge (*United States v. Cruikshank*, 1876). This right has been interpreted to have two elements: (1) a defendant must receive notice of any criminal accusations that the government has lodged through an indictment, information, complaint, or other formal charge; and (2) a defendant may not be tried, convicted, or sentenced for a crime that materially varies from the crime set forth in the formal charge—no surprises (Gardner and Anderson, 2010; Harr et al., 2011; Samaha, 2012).

To Be Confronted with the Witnesses against Him

> The primary object of the constitutional provision in question was to prevent depositions of ex parte affidavits . . . being used against the prisoner in lieu of a personal examination and cross-examination of the witness in which the accused has an opportunity not only of testing the recollection and sifting the conscience of the witness, but of compelling him to stand face to face with the jury in order that they may look at him, and judge by his demeanor upon the stand and the manner in which he gives his testimony whether he is worthy of belief. (*Mattox v. United States*, 1895) (Gardner and Anderson, 2010; Harr et al., 2011; Samaha, 2012)

As with most constitutional rights, the confrontation right is not absolute; and in extraordinary situations, a defendant may be prevented from confronting their accusers face-to-face. If a judge determines that a fragile child will be traumatized by testifying in front of a defendant, the Sixth Amendment authorizes the court to videotape the child's testimony outside the presence of the defendant and later replay the tape during trial. The Sixth Amendment does permit courts to remove defendants who are disorderly, disrespectful, and abusive (*Illinois v. Allen*, 1970). Additionally, if an unruly defendant insists on remaining in the courtroom, the Sixth Amendment authorizes courts to take appropriate measures to restrain him. In some instances, courts have shackled and gagged recalcitrant defendants in the presence of the jury (Gardner and Anderson, 2010; Harr et al., 2011; Samaha, 2012).

To Have Compulsory Process for Obtaining Witnesses in His Favor

The Sixth Amendment has another witness-related guarantee, the right to use the compulsory process of the judiciary to subpoena witnesses who can provide exculpatory testimony or who have other information that is favorable to the defense. The Sixth Amendment guarantees this right even if a defendant is indigent and cannot afford to pay the expenses that accompany the use of judicial resources to subpoena a witness. Naturally, this is not a carte blanche right, and a court will make a determination of the applicability of this right in instances objected to by the prosecution (Gardner and Anderson, 2010; Harr et al., 2011; Samaha, 2012).

To Have the Assistance of Counsel for His Defense

Although today we take this right for granted in all instances, such was not the case until fairly recently. Shortly after the ratification of the Sixth Amendment, Congress enacted two statutory provisions that seemed to indicate an understanding that the guarantee was limited to assuring that a person wishing to and able to afford counsel would not be denied that right. There was no thought of what to do if someone could not afford an attorney. Up until 1930, there was little expansion of this right. However, in 1932, the Supreme Court set aside the convictions of eight black youths sentenced to death in a hastily-carried-out trial without benefit of counsel. The defendants were indigent and could not have afforded counsel, but the court concluded that, under the circumstances,

> the ignorance and illiteracy of the defendants, their youth, the circumstances of public hostility, the imprisonment and the close surveillance of the defendants by the military forces, the fact that their friends and families were all in other states and communication with them necessarily difficult, and above all that they stood in deadly peril of their lives . . . the necessity of counsel was so vital and imperative that the failure of the trial court to make an effective appointment of counsel was likewise a denial of due process within the meaning of the Fourteenth Amendment . . . In a capital case, where the defendant is unable to employ counsel, and is incapable adequately of making his own defense because of ignorance, feeble mindedness, illiteracy, or the like, it is

the duty of the court, whether requested or not, to assign counsel for him as a necessary requisite of due process of law. (*Powell v. Alabama*, 1932) (Gardner and Anderson, 2010; Harr et al., 2011; Samaha, 2012)

Finally, in *Gideon v. Wainright* (1963), the right to counsel was essentially expanded to how we have come to understand it today. In a unanimous decision, the Supreme Court ruled that "in our adversary system of criminal justice, any person hauled into court, who is too poor to hire a lawyer, cannot be assured a fair trial unless counsel is provided for him" (Gardner and Anderson, 2010; Harr et al., 2011; Samaha, 2012). More recently, the court has held that the right applied to any misdemeanor case in which imprisonment was imposed—that no person may be sentenced to jail who was convicted in the absence of counsel, unless he validly waived his right (*Scott v. Illinois*, 1979). The right to the assistance of counsel also applied in juvenile proceedings (*In re Gault*, 1967).

Unlike many of the Sixth Amendment rights, the right to counsel does not attach at the onset of a criminal prosecution but only at what are termed "critical stages" of prosecution. From a practical standpoint, there may be little difference, but a critical stage of prosecution includes every instance in which the advice of counsel is necessary to ensure a defendant's right to a fair trial or in which the absence of counsel might impair the preparation or presentation of a defense. The Supreme Court has ruled that the denial of counsel during a critical stage amounts to an unconstitutional deprivation of a fair trial, warranting the reversal of conviction (*United States v. Cronic*, 1984) (Gardner and Anderson, 2010; Harr et al., 2011; Samaha, 2012).

Critical stages of prosecution will include things such as interrogation, bail hearings, suppression of evidence hearings, trial matters, jury selection, and sentencing. Things generally not considered to be critical stages will include pretrial scientific analysis of evidence items or probable cause hearings. These types of events are considered preliminary elements of a prosecution. The Sixth Amendment right to counsel presumes counsel is effective. Unfortunately, that is not always the case, which undermines the right. Thus there is case law and standards for determining when such representation has been ineffective to the point of unfairly prejudicing a defendant (Gardner and Anderson, 2010; Harr et al., 2011; Samaha, 2012).

The Eighth Amendment

"Excessive bail shall not be required, nor excessive fines imposed, nor cruel and unusual punishments inflicted." The Eighth Amendment has three provisions: (1) the excessive bail clause, which limits judicial discretion in setting the amount of bail for the release of someone accused of a criminal activity between the time of their arrest and their trial; (2) the excessive fines clause, which limits the amount that a state or the federal government may fine someone convicted of a crime; and (3) the cruel and unusual punishment clause, which limits the severity of the punishment that a state or the federal government may impose on someone convicted of a crime (Gardner and Anderson, 2010; Harr et al., 2011; Samaha, 2012).

Excessive Bail

Trial-level court judges are given some degree of latitude under the excessive bail clause. Bail is the amount of money, property, or bond that a defendant must pledge to the court as security for his or her appearance at trial. If the defendant meets bail or is able to pay the amount set by the court, the defendant is entitled to recover the pledged amount at the conclusion of the criminal proceedings. However, if the defendant fails to appear as scheduled during the prosecution, then he or she forfeits the amount pledged and still faces further criminal penalties if convicted of the offense or offenses charged (Gardner and Anderson, 2010; Harr et al., 2011; Samaha, 2012).

When fixing the amount of bail for a defendant, a court considers a number of factors: (1) the seriousness of the offense; (2) the weight of the evidence against the accused; (3) ties that the accused has to the community where he or she will be prosecuted, such as family or employment; (4) the ability to pay a given amount; and (5) the likelihood that the defendant will flee the jurisdiction if released (Gardner and Anderson, 2010; Harr et al., 2011; Samaha, 2012).

In applying these factors, courts usually attempt to set bail for a reasonable amount. Setting bail for an unreasonable amount would unreasonably restrict the freedom of someone who, at this point in the legal process, has only been accused of wrongdoing and who is presumed innocent until proven guilty. Plus, this person is entitled to pursue a living and to support a family. At the same time, courts are aware that bail needs to be set sufficiently high to ensure that the defendant will return for trial. Defendants are less likely to flee the jurisdiction if they will forfeit large sums of money as a result. Courts are also aware that they must protect communities from the harm presented by particularly dangerous defendants. Accordingly, the Supreme Court has permitted lower courts to deny bail for a defendant who will create an abnormally dangerous risk to the community if released (Gardner and Anderson, 2010; Harr et al., 2011; Samaha, 2012).

Cruel and Unusual Punishment

Appellate courts usually defer to lower courts' decisions when a criminal penalty is challenged under the excessive fines and excessive bail clauses of the Eighth Amendment. However, appellate courts give much greater scrutiny to criminal penalties challenged under the cruel and unusual punishments clause. State and federal governments may not inflict cruel and unusual punishment on a defendant, no matter how heinous the crime committed. The prohibition against cruel and unusual punishment has been made applicable to the states through the doctrine of selective incorporation, by which selective liberties in the Bill of Rights have been applied to the states as a result of the Supreme Court's interpretation of the due process and equal protection clauses of the Fourteenth Amendment (Gardner and Anderson, 2010; Harr et al., 2011; Samaha, 2012).

The Eighth Amendment requires that every punishment imposed by the government be commensurate with the offense committed by the defendant. This concept is known as the proportionality principle and deems sentences cruel and unusual if they are "grossly disproportionate" to the "gravity of the offense. Punishments that are disproportionately harsh will be overturned on appeal." Examples of punishments that have been overturned for being unreasonable are two Georgia statutes that have prescribed the death penalty for rape and kidnapping, *Coker v. Georgia* (1977) and *Eberheart v. Georgia* (1977) (Gardner and Anderson, 2010; Harr et al., 2011; Samaha, 2012).

A minority of judges believe the Eighth Amendment requires no proportionality principle, or if so, that it is up to the legislature to decide what sentences are disproportionate. The Supreme Court has also ruled that criminal sentences that are inhuman, outrageous, or shocking to the social conscience are cruel and unusual. Although the court has never provided specific definitions for these punishments, the relevant cases speak for themselves. For instance, the Georgia Supreme Court has stated that the Eighth Amendment is intended to prohibit barbarous punishments such as castration, burning at the stake, and quartering (*Whitten v. Georgia*, 1872). Similarly, the U.S. Supreme Court has stated that the cruel and unusual punishments clause prohibits crucifixion, breaking on the wheel, and other punishments that involve a lingering death (*In re Kemmler*, 1890). The Supreme Court has also invalidated an Oklahoma law that has compelled the state government to sterilize "feeble-minded" or "habitual" criminals in an effort to prevent them from reproducing and passing on their deficient characteristics (*Skinner v. Oklahoma*, 1942). However, the Supreme Court, fifteen years earlier, has let stand a Virginia law that authorized the sterilization of mentally retarded individuals who are institutionalized at state facilities for the "feeble-minded" (*Buck v. Bell*, 1927) (Gardner and Anderson, 2010; Harr et al., 2011; Samaha, 2012).

A constitutional standard that permits judges to strike down legislation that they find shocking but to let stand other legislation they find less disturbing has an inherently subjective quality and has caused the raising of some legal eyebrows. A punishment that seems outrageous to one judge on a particular day might seem reasonable to a different judge on the same day or to the same judge on a different day. In *Hudson v. McMillian* (1992), the Supreme Court reviewed a case in which a prisoner had been handcuffed by two Louisiana corrections officers and beaten to the point where his teeth were loosened and his dental plate cracked. Seven Supreme Court justices ruled that the prisoner had suffered cruel and unusual punishment under the Eighth Amendment, but two disagreed (Gardner and Anderson, 2010; Harr et al., 2011; Samaha, 2012).

Another somewhat vague standard by which the constitutionality of criminal sentences is reviewed has resulted in the Supreme Court invalidating punishments that are contrary to "the evolving standards of decency that mark a maturing society" (*Trop v. Dulles*,

1958). Under the *Trop* standard, the court determines whether a particular punishment is offensive to society at large, not merely shocking or outrageous to a particular justice. In these instances, the court will survey state legislation to determine if the punishment is authorized by a majority of jurisdictions. If most states authorize a particular punishment, the court will not invalidate that punishment, as it is not contrary to "evolving standards of decency" (Gardner and Anderson, 2010; Harr et al., 2011; Samaha, 2012).

Applying this standard, the court ruled that the death penalty could be imposed upon a sixteen-year-old who had been convicted of murder because a national consensus, as reflected by state legislation, supported capital punishment for juveniles of that age (*Stanford v. Kentucky*, 1989). However, in 2005, in a 5–4 decision, the court ruled that state laws authorizing capital punishment for sixteen- and seventeen-year-olds who committed murder violated the Eighth Amendment and were therefore unconstitutional. The action reversed the death sentences of seventy-two convicted murderers who committed their crimes as juveniles (*Roper v. Simmons*, 2005). The court stated that a national consensus had emerged in opposition to the execution of juveniles. However, dissenting justices said the fact that twenty states authorized the death penalty for juveniles was proof that no such consensus had emerged (Gardner and Anderson, 2010; Harr et al., 2011; Samaha, 2012).

In a similar instance, the Supreme Court permitted the state of Texas to execute a mentally retarded person who had been convicted of murder, despite claims that the defendant's handicap minimized his moral culpability (*Penry v. Lynaugh*, 1989). In the years after the Supreme Court decided *Penry*, several states, including Texas, prohibited the execution of mentally retarded individuals. Also, very few of the states that did not prohibit such executions actually executed mentally retarded defendants. Then in 2002, the court concluded that, because so few states allowed execution of the mentally retarded, the practice had indeed become "unusual." The court stated further that justifications for the death penalty, such as retribution on the part of the defendant and deterrence of capital crimes by prospective offenders, did not apply to the mentally retarded. Accordingly, the court prohibited the death penalty from being imposed on the mentally retarded on the grounds that it violated the Eighth Amendment (*Atkins v. Virginia*, 2002). *Atkins* clearly demonstrated that the Eighth Amendment, like other constitutional provisions, evolves as society evolves (Gardner and Anderson, 2010; Harr et al., 2011; Samaha, 2012).

Although for many people capital punishment may appear to be cruel and unusual, the Supreme Court has not held this to be the case. However, in certain instances, the court has found states to be in violation of its citizens' due process protection in the manner in which the death penalty was imposed. *Furman v. Georgia* (1972) was the landmark case in which the Supreme Court called for a ban on the death penalty in Georgia, ruling that its law was capricious and, hence, cruel and unusual punishment. In *Gregg v. Georgia* (1976), the Supreme Court reinstated the Georgia death penalty by approving its revised death penalty law. The death penalty itself was not cruel and unusual punishment per se, but a capital case required two proceedings: one to determine guilt or innocence and a second proceeding to determine the sentence (*Gregg v. Georgia*, 1976) (Gardner and Anderson, 2010; Harr et al., 2011; Samaha, 2012).

The Supreme Court continues to consider specific instances of punishment in order to determine whether they violate the Eighth Amendment. In *Hope v. Pelzer* (2002), the court has considered a case where Alabama prison officers have handcuffed a prisoner to a hitching post on two occasions, once for more than seven hours without water or a restroom break. Use of a hitching post, according to the court, has violated the Eighth Amendment (Gardner and Anderson, 2010; Harr et al., 2011; Samaha, 2012).

The Seventh Amendment

The underlying rationale of the Seventh Amendment is also to preserve the historic line separating the province of the jury from that of the judge in civil cases. Although the line separating questions of law from questions of fact is often blurred, the basic functions of judges and juries are clear. Judges are charged with the responsibility of resolving issues concerning the admissibility of evidence and instructing jurors regarding the pertinent laws governing the case. Judges are also permitted to comment on the evidence, highlight important issues, and otherwise express their opinions in open court as long as each factual question is ultimately submitted to the jury. However, a judge may not interject his or her personal opinions or observations to such an extent that they impair a litigant's right to a fair trial (Gardner and Anderson, 2010; Harr et al., 2011; Samaha, 2012).

There are limitations to the Seventh Amendment right to a jury trial. The Seventh Amendment right to a jury trial only applies in federal court. This right is one of the few liberties enumerated in the Bill of Rights that has not been made applicable to the states through the doctrine of selective incorporation (*Minneapolis & St. Louis Railroad v. Bombolis*, 1916). The Seventh Amendment does not apply in state court even when a party is enforcing a right created by federal law. However, today most state constitutions also provide the right to trial by jury in civil cases (Gardner and Anderson, 2010; Harr. et al., 2011; Samaha, 2012).

The Seventh Amendment forbids federal judges to "reexamine" any "fact tried by a jury" except as allowed by the common law. This provision means that no court, trial or appellate, may overturn a jury verdict that is reasonably supported by the evidence (*Taylor v. Curry*, 1994). A jury must be allowed to hear a case from start to finish unless it presents a legal claim that is completely lacking an evidentiary basis (*Gregory v. Missouri Pacific Railroad*, 1994). A judge may disregard a jury's verdict only if he or she believes it overwhelmingly contradicts the evidence. Even in such a case, however, the judge may not enter his or her own verdict but may only order a new trial on the matter (Gardner and Anderson, 2010; Harr et al., 2011; Samaha, 2012).

Ninth Amendment

"The enumeration in the Constitution, of certain rights, shall not be construed to deny or disparage others retained by the people." The Ninth Amendment is somewhat of an enigma. It provides that the naming of certain rights in the Constitution does not take away from the people rights that are not named. Yet neither the language nor the history of the Ninth Amendment offers clues or hints about the nature of the rights it is designed to protect. Every year, federal courts are asked to recognize new unenumerated rights "retained by the people"; and typically, they turn to the Ninth Amendment. However, the federal judiciary does not base rulings exclusively on the Ninth Amendment. Courts normally cite the amendment as a secondary source of fundamental liberties. Most notably, however, the Ninth Amendment has played a major role in the establishment of a constitutional right to privacy (Gardner and Anderson, 2010; Harr et al., 2011; Samaha, 2012).

The Tenth Amendment

"The powers not delegated to the United States by the Constitution, nor prohibited by it to the states, are reserved to the states respectively, or to the people." As with the Ninth Amendment, the Tenth Amendment was also a compromise between the Federalists and Anti-Federalists in the effort to ratify the Constitution by seeking an acceptable balance of power between the federal government and the states and individuals. "The Tenth Amendment was intended to confirm the understanding of the people at the time the Constitution was adopted, that powers not granted to the United States were reserved to the States or to the people. It added nothing to the instrument as originally ratified" (*United States v. Sprague*, 1931). It was basically a declaration of the relationship between the national and state governments as established by the Constitution. Its purpose was to address fears that the new national government might seek to exercise powers not granted and that the states might not be able to exercise fully their reserved powers (Gardner and Anderson, 2010; Harr et al., 2011; Samaha, 2012).

Criminal Law

Fundamentals of Criminal Law

Everything about criminal law in America today (defining, classifying, prohibiting, and punishing) is in the hands of the legislature or the lawmaking body for each jurisdiction. Crimes are "owned" by the state and prosecuted by the state, and the only thing separating a civil wrong from a criminal wrong is that fine line that exists because some legislature says it exists (Gardner and Anderson, 2010; Harr et al., 2011; Samaha, 2012).

A Typical Statutory Law Scheme

According to Gardner and Anderson (2010), Harr et al. (2011), and Samaha (2012), it should be apparent by now that all crime is an injury against society. Indeed, there does not even have to be a victim (victimless crimes) or someone to complain (consensual sex acts). Society as a whole, via its legislatures, has presumably made a collective judgment that certain behaviors are harmful to certain "societal interests." This brings us to the most important characteristic of criminal law as follows:

The essence of criminal law is its common punishment. No matter what the offense, from felony to misdemeanor to infraction or violation, the reaction expresses the moral contempt of society. Even for a minor traffic violation, there is always the slightest hint that one has injured society and broken the collective, agreed-upon rules (Gardner and Anderson, 2010; Harr et al., 2011; Samaha, 2012).

To better understand the way criminal law manipulates statuses and roles in society, it is probably a good idea to understand the way the law classifies things. The oldest way of classifying crime is to make these distinctions:

1. Crimes mala in se—acts that are wrong in themselves. Anything wrong under natural law and virtually every act proscribed under common law are mala in se. The conduct is unlawful because the transaction or contact between people is unnatural or immoral. Examples include murder, rape, burglary, and so forth.

2. Crimes mala prohibita—acts that are wrong because prohibited. Anything that interferes with positive law and much of statutory law is mala prohibita. The conduct is unlawful because it infringes on other's rights or just because it is prohibited. Examples include drunk driving, gambling, and so forth (Gardner and Anderson, 2010; Harr et al., 2011; Samaha, 2012).

Another way of classifying crime is to focus on the potential penalties imposed:

1. Capital felonies—crimes that are punishable by death or, in states without the death penalty, life imprisonment without parole. An example is aggravated murder.

2. Felonies—broadly defined, crimes that are punishable by a year or more in a prison. Historically, it is a serious crime involving forfeiture of all worldly possessions, imprisonment, and/or death. Another definition is an infamous crime, one which by its nature or character indicates a depravity in perpetration or intent to pervert justice and propagate falsehood that forever destroys the accused's credibility. Examples include murder, manslaughter, rape, larceny, robbery, arson, sodomy, mayhem, and—in the case of infamous crime—anything involving falsehood, like treason, forgery, perjury, or bribery.

3. Misdemeanors—broadly defined, misdemeanors are crimes punishable by jail sentences, fines, or both. A gross misdemeanor is a very great, or high, misdemeanor typically carrying a sentence of close to a year in jail. They often involve moral turpitude, which by their commission imply a base, vile, or depraved nature regarding the private and social duties that a person owes to others or to society in general. It implies something is immoral in itself. Examples include obscenity, profanity, and solicitation. The doctrine of merger requires that if a misdemeanor is part of a felony, the less important crime ceases to have an independent existence and is merged into the felony, but this does not apply to lesser included offenses common in plea bargaining or prosecutorial overcharging common in creating the impression of multiple counts that are really multiple degrees of the same offense.

4. Infractions (or violations)—typically, these are traffic offenses or the breaking of municipal ordinances that are punishable only by suspension of privileges (administrative law) or fines (quasi-criminal law). Technically, they are not even crimes since they do not result in a record of criminal conviction in most

jurisdictions. However, it is possible to be jailed on a violation if the city in question has a municipal court. Such a court can impose a fine, but they cannot imprison for failure to pay the fine, only for failure to comply with a court order (Gardner and Anderson, 2010; Harr et al., 2011; Samaha, 2012).

The best way of classifying crime is to use a jurisprudential approach. Jurisprudence has many meanings but generally refers to the science or philosophy of law as a whole.

1. The concept of legality combines the two principles we learned earlier and says there can be no crime without law. There must be public respect for the law and for the office, if not the officeholders (which is the concept of legitimacy). Laws not based on societal norms are unlikely to gain general compliance.

2. The concept of actus reus (a phrase meaning "evil or bad deed") is derived from an old Latin phrase and, in many ways, is what separates criminology from theology because, as much as we might like to, those of us who work with criminals all the time cannot be concerned with, or inclined to punish, bad thoughts (Gardner and Anderson, 2010; Harr et al., 2011; Samaha, 2012).

   From a legal point of view, "communication" is a form of action. A whole set of laws exist for what are called inchoate crimes (incomplete crimes), such as conspiracy, attempt, possession, solicitation, terrorist threats, assault, sexual harassment, inciting to riot, aiding and abetting, and being an accomplice or accessory. Once again, mental state is largely irrelevant because the criminal statutes have usually described the behavior so well that the principle of vicarious liability applies. Anybody who participates in the planning, design, or cover-up of a crime is subject to the same penalties as a person who actually carries it out. This is a controversial area, and in all fairness, some statutes require a combination of communication (words) and conduct (deeds); but then again, once you open the door to combinations, evidence of bad thoughts may even be admissible. The closest term we have for when wicked thoughts are assumed to apply to the act (and the intent) is *malice*. Malice is among the many things that can be inferred from other evidence and imputed to a defendant (Gardner and Anderson, 2010; Harr et al., 2011; Samaha, 2012).

3. The concept of causation is one of the more advanced concepts in criminal law. An act by itself is not punishable in itself because it is assumed to be the cause of something else, the effect, or social harm that the criminal law is presumably more concerned with and because all crimes are cause-and-effect relationships. Establishing a cause-and-effect relationship is no simple matter with legal reasoning or, for that matter, in any social science (Gardner and Anderson, 2010; Harr et al., 2011; Samaha, 2012).

   The most important types of causes in criminal law are "causes in fact" (also called direct causes), proximate causes (also called legal causes), intervening causes, and superseding causes.

4. The concept of social harm is a fairly undeveloped concept in criminal Law, and it is what separates criminology from victimology. The criminal law exists for a public purpose, not a private purpose. The criminal law is not concerned with the protection or vindication of individual victims but rather society as a whole (Gardner and Anderson, 2010; Harr et al., 2011; Samaha, 2012).

5. The concept of concurrence requires that any act (actus reus) causing social harm must coincide, or be accompanied, with a criminal state of mind (mens rea). Both act and intent must concur in point of time. It is part of a basic formula in criminal law:

   The legal requirement of concurrence is usually taken care of by proving motive. Intent and motive are not the same thing. In criminal law, motive is that which leads or tempts the mind to indulge in a criminal act, such as an impulse, incentive, or reason for committing the crime. Intent is the mind being fully aware of the consequences. Many criminal statutes require intent as an element of the crime, but motive is never stated as an essential element of a crime in any criminal statute. Motive can be used to assist in establishing intent, but more likely, motive is introduced as an admitted piece of evidence, often circumstantial, along with evidence of opportunity, to impress the judge or jury. The presence of motive is evidence tending to presume guilt, and the absence of motive is evidence tending to presume innocence (Gardner and Anderson, 2010; Harr et al., 2011; Samaha, 2012).

6. The concept of mens rea (a phrase meaning "evil or bad mind") is a well-developed concept and perhaps the most complex and confusing concept in criminal law. The best way to understand mens rea (often mislabeled as intent) is to realize that it is always invisible. You cannot really prove intent like you can with motive. You also cannot really blame someone for their motive (it is understandable), only for their intent. Intent is different for every person and for every case, and it is impossible, as well as futile, to get inside the "mind" of each and every criminal offender. Confessions are the closest thing to direct evidence of mens rea, and even then, they must be corroborated. Therefore the criminal law has established certain objective tests for inferring the subjective mental state (intent) of criminal offenders. To do this requires certain assumptions about responsibility, and by adding in the rules for inferring intent, called determining culpability, we arrive at a way to attach blameworthiness (Gardner and Anderson, 2010; Harr et al., 2011; Samaha, 2012).

Traditionally, this stance has been softened somewhat by mutually agreed-upon recognitions. I have not said "exceptions." There are no exceptions to the freewill assumption. However, there are the "three Is" of insanity, infancy, and involuntary. The criminal law "recognizes," to varying degrees, that insane people, extremely young people, and those with certain involuntary "medical" conditions should not be assumed to be responsible for their actions. These are best understood as special defenses that get to the idea of voluntariness of acts or volition (the ability to exercise free will). Insanity and infancy are fairly self-explanatory, but the following is a list of involuntary "medical" conditions: reflexive behavior, unconscious behavior, behavior while asleep (sleepwalking), convulsive behavior (epilepsy), and involuntary intoxication (drugged against your will) (Gardner and Anderson, 2010; Harr et al., 2011; Samaha, 2012).

General intent is the kind of intent that a judge or jury can easily infer or presume from the act itself. The intended result does not matter. The prosecution need not establish why the crime occurred. It must be shown, however, that the defendant had an "awareness" of a criminal act being committed. Battery is a good example because the extent of injuries or why the fight started does not matter (Gardner and Anderson, 2010; Harr et al., 2011; Samaha, 2012).

Specific intent is the kind of intent that legislatures have put in the language of the criminal statute. Usually, it requires a particular result beyond the act itself, such as "with purpose to defraud an insurance company" in the crime of arson for profit. It requires the prosecution to prove additional elements and cannot be presumed by a judge or jury (Gardner and Anderson, 2010; Harr et al., 2011; Samaha, 2012).

Strict liability intent involves regulatory crimes where intent does not matter at all. Intent is not an element of the crime. It is immaterial whether the accused acted in good faith or knew they were violating the law (Gardner and Anderson, 2010; Harr et al., 2011; Samaha, 2012).

Transferred liability intent involves cases where the accused intended to harm one victim but instead harmed another. It relieves the prosecution of the need to prove the chain of events leading to harm. It is the basis of felony murder rule (Gardner and Anderson, 2010; Harr et al., 2011; Samaha, 2012).

Constructive intent involves cases where the accused should have known their behavior created a high or unreasonable risk of injury. It is also called criminal negligence and replaces any specific intent contained in statute, thereby constructing or converting an innocent act to a crime (Gardner and Anderson, 2010; Harr et al., 2011; Samaha, 2012).

Scienter is a requirement in some statutes that the accused had some additional degree of knowledge beyond knowing a possible criminal act was being committed. Examples include knowing that the victim is a law enforcement officer, knowing that the materials are stolen property, or knowing that the hitchhiker is an escaped fugitive (Gardner and Anderson, 2010; Harr et al., 2011; Samaha, 2012).

The following limits on criminal law are in alphabetical order:

Adversary System - a limitation on criminal law that controls the establishment of guilt. It guarantees the average citizen the right to have a prosecutor and a defense counsel oppose each other in a trial if they are unwilling or unable to dispose of the case prior to trial. The prosecution also has the burden of proof initially (Gardner and Anderson, 2010; Harr et al., 2011; Samaha, 2012).

Bill of Attainder - This refers to any legislative act that inflicts punishment without a criminal trial.

Bill of Rights - The first ten amendments to the Constitution limit the ability of the government to define certain acts as criminal, and they also have important things to say about the enforcement of criminal law.

Corpus Delicti -- This Latin phrase meaning "body of the crime" means that the prosecution must prove all elements of a crime. To do this, the prosecution must consult the specific statute of the state that has jurisdiction. Although there are presumptions that the prosecution will also prove the identity of the accused and be able to produce a victim, those factors are not technically part of the concept of corpus delicti. For example, the corpus delicti of burglary consists of six elements: (1) breaking (2) and entering (3) the dwelling (4) of another (5) at nighttime (6) with the intent to commit a felony therein. In the law of homicide, however, one of the elements is death; and in this case, the ability to find or account for the body is part of the corpus delicti of homicide (Gardner and Anderson, 2010; Harr et al., 2011; Samaha, 2012).

Corroboration of Confession - The general rule is that a conviction cannot rest alone upon an accused's out-of-court confession. Admission of the confession is only permitted if proof of corpus delicti will be presented later (Gardner and Anderson, 2010; Harr et al., 2011; Samaha, 2012).

Cruel and Unusual Punishment - This is an Eighth Amendment protection where the words "cruel" and "unusual" have never really been adequately defined. A piecemeal approach has been followed in which the distinction is made between "ancient" and "modern" forms of punishment with the assumption being that ancient methods are unconstitutional and that most modern methods are upheld. Recent issues have involved the question of proportionality, where habitual offenders with prior records receive stiffer sentences for the same crime as those committed without prior records (Gardner and Anderson, 2010; Harr et al., 2011; Samaha, 2012).

Double Jeopardy - The same sovereign entity cannot prosecute the same individual twice for the same act or the same crime. This gets at the matter of jurisdiction and what is theoretically possible and what is done in practice. As a practical matter, both federal and state governments do not prosecute the same person, although they theoretically can, unless there are some dissimilarities to be found in the nature of the crime, or the first jurisdiction to prosecute does so unsuccessfully (Gardner and Anderson, 2010; Harr et al., 2011; Samaha, 2012).

Due Process of Law - a phrase found in the Fifth and Fourteenth Amendments, as well as every state constitution that forbids the government from taking life, liberty, or property without due process of law. At the fundamental level, due process ensures, at a minimum, the right to fair notice and a fair hearing. On other levels, it guarantees certain inalienable rights and freedoms. On a practical level, it is usually determined by various balancing tests that pit the needs of the individual against the needs of the government. The implied right to privacy also prohibits making crimes out of behavior protected by the right of privacy (Gardner and Anderson, 2010; Harr et al., 2011; Samaha, 2012).

Equal Protection of Law - The government cannot make a law applicable to only one sex, race, or religion or treat one group of citizens differently from other groups without a rational reason. This idea is related to the notion of due process at the level of fundamental freedom, tying together fairness and inalienable right. The principle is that all persons must be treated alike, not only in law enactment but also in law enforcement. Historically, it has been used to strike down miscegenation laws, and contemporary examples include the "powder-rock" cocaine controversy for blacks and "sexual harassment" statutes for women (Gardner and Anderson, 2010; Harr et al., 2011; Samaha, 2012).

Ex Post Facto Laws - Both the federal and state governments are prohibited from altering the law in any way so as to be detrimental to an accused person retroactively. This can occur in many ways:

1. The legislature passes a new law, and someone is prosecuted for committing the act before the law was enacted (unless there is a "savings" clause in the statute).

2. The legislature increases the penalties for an existing law, and someone is punished under the new penalty when they committed the act while the old penalty was in effect.

3. The legislature decreases the burden of proof or in any way makes it easier for the prosecution to convict. Persons who committed crime under the old system must be tried under the old rules. (Note: this does not apply to evidentiary rule changes.)

4. The legislature adjusts the amount of good time credit or eligibility for parole to alleviate prison overcrowding and then restores the old formula once the overcrowding problem has been solved (Gardner and Anderson, 2010; Harr et al., 2011; Samaha, 2012).

Jurisdiction - The court system is organized by this, and there are three different types of jurisdiction: person, place, and type of crime. Different courts are limited by jurisdiction in what cases can be brought before them (Gardner and Anderson, 2010; Harr et al., 2011; Samaha, 2012).

Presumption of Innocence - All the presumptions of law independent of evidence are in favor of the accused, and every person is presumed innocent until proven guilty. This concept is closely related to the reasonable doubt standard and the notion of moral certainty. Reasonable doubt is the last presumption of innocence in criminal procedure, and actually, it is an "entitlement" to the benefit of acquittal. Moral certainty is a term for the judgment call that remains to be made after reasonable doubt has been eliminated (Gardner and Anderson, 2010; Harr et al., 2011; Samaha, 2012).

Status Offenses - The law cannot make being a certain kind of person a crime. This determination is made through analogy with a chronic medical condition: the law cannot criminalize having a "common cold." Most cases of chronic alcoholism do not qualify, but drug laws criminalizing the status of being an "addict" do. In practice, the law has many kinds of status offenses (Gardner and Anderson, 2010; Harr et al., 2011; Samaha, 2012).

Statute of Limitations - This places a time limit on the period from commission of the offense to filing of the criminal charges. The Supreme Court has decided that it only applies when the suspect is in custody. States are free to devise their own statutes of limitations, and there is widespread variation, but in general, misdemeanors usually have one year and felonies longer. There are two ways to extend the statute of limitations: (1) an arrest warrant extending it indefinitely or for a specified period; or (2) tolling the statute of limitations by not counting the period equal to the accused's absence from the jurisdiction (Gardner and Anderson, 2010; Harr et al., 2011; Samaha, 2012).

Void-for-Vagueness Doctrine - This requires that legislatures use clear and precise language so that people of common intelligence do not have to guess at the meaning of a law or its application. If the language of a statute or ordinance is vague, it is unconstitutional, and the law must be struck down. Sometimes the doctrine is applied just to the words like "ill repute" or "lewd," and at other times, whether the law entraps citizens or is difficult for police to enforce is considered. A modern example is the "racial profiling" controversy (Gardner and Anderson, 2010; Harr et al., 2011; Samaha, 2012).

Principle of Criminal Liability

Criminal liability is what unlocks the logical structure of the criminal law. Each element of a crime that the prosecutor needs to prove (beyond a reasonable doubt) is a principle of criminal liability. There are some crimes that only involve a subset of all the principles of liability, and these are called "crimes of criminal conduct." Burglary, for example, is such a crime because all you need to prove beyond a reasonable doubt is an actus reus concurring with a mens rea. On the other hand, there are crimes that involve all the principles of liability, and these are called "true crimes." Homicide, for example, is such a crime because you need to prove actus reus, mens rea, concurrence, causation, and harm. The requirement that the prosecutor must prove each element of criminal liability beyond a reasonable doubt is called the "corpus delicti rule" (Gardner and Anderson, 2010; Harr et al., 2011; Samaha, 2012).

Liability needs to be distinguished from the following concepts:

- ✓ Culpability (purposely, knowingly, recklessly, negligently) - infers intent
- ✓ Capacity (infancy, intoxication, insanity) - capacity defenses
- ✓ Responsibility (volition, free will, competency) - presumptions

There are five principles of liability in criminal law:

- ✓ Principle of actus reus
- ✓ Principle of mens rea
- ✓ Principle of concurrence

✓ Principle of causation
✓ Principle of resulting harm

The Principle of Actus Reus

Involuntariness - Sleepwalking, hypnotic behavior, etc., are seen as examples of acting upon forces beyond individual control and are therefore not normally included in the principle of actus reus. However, certain "voluntarily induced involuntary acts," such as drowsy driving, might arguably be included if the prior voluntary act has created the risk of a future involuntary act (Gardner and Anderson, 2010; Harr et al., 2011; Samaha, 2012).

Manifest criminality - caught red-handed, clear-cut case of actus reus proven beyond a reasonable doubt (Gardner and Anderson, 2010; Harr et al., 2011; Samaha, 2012).

Possession - The law recognizes various degrees of this. Actual possession means physically on your person. Constructive possession means physically under your control. Knowing possession means you know what you are possessing. Mere possession means you do not know what you are possessing. Unwitting possession is when something has been planted on you. The only punishable types of possession are the ones that are conscious and knowable (Gardner and Anderson, 2010; Harr et al., 2011; Samaha, 2012).

Procuring - obtaining things with the intent of using them for criminal purposes, e.g., precursor chemicals for making narcotics, "pimping" for a prostitute, and procuring another to commit a crime ("accessory before the fact") (Gardner and Anderson, 2010; Harr et al., 2011; Samaha, 2012).

Status or condition - Sometimes a chronic condition qualifies as action, e.g., drug addiction and alcoholism, on the assumption that the first use is voluntary. Sometimes the condition, e.g., chronic alcoholism, is treated as a disease that exculpates an individual. Most often, it is the punishment aspect of criminal law in these kinds of cases that triggers an Eighth Amendment issue. Equal protection and other constitutional issues may be triggered (Gardner and Anderson, 2010; Harr et al., 2011; Samaha, 2012).

Thoughts - Sometimes, not often, the expression of angry thoughts (e.g., "I'll kill you for that") is taken as expressing the resolution and will to commit a crime; but in general, thoughts are not part of the principle of actus reus. Daydreaming and fantasy are also not easily included in the principle of mens rea (Gardner and Anderson, 2010; Harr et al., 2011; Samaha, 2012).

Words - These are considered "verbal acts," e.g., sexual harassment, solicitation, terroristic threats, assault, inciting to riot (Gardner and Anderson, 2010; Harr et al., 2011; Samaha, 2012).

The Principle of Mens Rea

- ✓ Circumstantial - determination of mens rea through indirect evidence
- ✓ Confessions - clear-cut, direct evidence of mens rea beyond a reasonable doubt
- ✓ Constructive intent - One has the constructive intent to kill if they are driving at high speeds on an icy road with lots of pedestrians around.
- ✓ General intent - the intent to commit the actus reus of the crime one is charged with, e.g., rape and intent to penetrate
- ✓ Specific intent - the intent to do something beyond the actus reus of the crime one is charged with, e.g., breaking and entering with intent to burglarize
- ✓ Strict liability - crimes requiring no mens rea or liability without fault, e.g., corporate crime or environmental crime
- ✓ Transferred intent - the intent to harm one victim but instead harm another (Gardner and Anderson, 2010; Harr et al., 2011; Samaha, 2012)

The Principle of Concurrence

Attendant circumstances - Some crimes have additional elements that must accompany the criminal act and the criminal mind, e.g., rape (Gardner and Anderson, 2010; Harr et al., 2011; Samaha, 2012).

Enterprise liability - In corporate law, this is the idea that both the act and the agency (mens rea), for it can be imputed to the corporation, e.g., product safety (Gardner and Anderson, 2010; Harr et al., 2011; Samaha, 2012).

Year-and-a-day rule - It is a common-law rule that the final result of an act must occur no later than a year and a day after the criminal state of mind. For example, if you struck someone on the head with intent to kill but they did not die until a year and two days later, you could not be prosecuted for murder. Many states have abolished this rule or extended the time limit (Gardner and Anderson, 2010; Harr et al., 2011; Samaha, 2012).

Vicarious liability - Sometimes, under some rules, the guilty party would not be the person who committed the act but the person who intended the act, e.g., supervisors of employees (Gardner and Anderson, 2010; Harr et al., 2011; Samaha, 2012).

The Principle of Causation

Actual cause - a necessary but not sufficient condition to prove causation beyond a reasonable doubt; the prosecutor must also prove proximate cause (Gardner and Anderson, 2010; Harr et al., 2011; Samaha, 2012)

But-for or sine qua non causation - setting in motion a chain of events that sooner or later led to the harmful result, but for the actor's conduct, the result would not have occurred (Gardner and Anderson, 2010; Harr et al., 2011; Samaha, 2012)

Intervening cause - unforeseen events that still hold the defendant accountable (Gardner and Anderson, 2010; Harr et al., 2011; Samaha, 2012)

Legal causation - a prosecutor's logic of both actual and proximate cause (Gardner and Anderson, 2010; Harr et al., 2011; Samaha, 2012)

Proximate cause - the fairness of how far back the prosecutor goes in the chain of events to hold a particular defendant accountable; literally means the next or closest cause

Superseding cause - unforeseen events that exculpate a defendant (Gardner and Anderson, 2010; Harr et al., 2011; Samaha, 2012).

Responsibility for Crime: Presumptions

Presumptions are court-ordered assumptions that the jury must take as true unless rebutted by evidence. Their purpose is to simplify and expedite the trial process. The judge, for example, at some point in testimony may remind the jury that it is okay to assume that all people form some kind of intent before or during their behavior. It is wrong, however, for the judge to order the jury to assume intent or a specific kind of intent in a case. Presumptions are not a substitute for evidence. Presumptions are supposed to be friendly reminders about safe scientific assumptions about human nature or human behavior in general. The most common presumptions are:

- ✓ reminders that the accused is considered innocent until proven guilty and
- ✓ reminders that the accused is to be considered sane, normal, and competent (Gardner and Anderson, 2010; Harr et al., 2011; Samaha, 2012).

It is important to understand that presumptions are not inferences. Presumptions must be accepted as true by the jury. Inferences may be accepted as true by the jury, but the trick is to get the jury to believe they have thought of it first.

Accomplice Law

An accomplice is someone who knowingly, voluntarily, and with common interest participates in the commission of a crime and can be charged with the same crime(s) for which the accused will be tried. Complicity means association in a wrongful act. Principal means anyone involved in committing a crime. An accessory before the fact aids, incites, or abets but is not physically present. An accessory after the fact receives, comforts, relieves, or assists a felon to avoid apprehension and conviction (Gardner and Anderson, 2010; Harr et al., 2011; Samaha, 2012).

In accomplice law (complicity), the statutory law has evolved much beyond the common law, and the case law is extensive and confusing about exactly where the lines are drawn. Complicity is a concept that can be abused by prosecutors. Only a few basic restrictions exist: (1) the law does not recognize accomplices to any misdemeanor or the crime of treason; (2) an accomplice must normally be physically present during commission of the crime, but advice or words of encouragement beforehand, as well as providing material assistance afterward, will create a liability; (3) no one can be convicted on the uncorroborated testimony of an accomplice alone; and (4) persons giving postcrime aid are punished less severely than those furnishing precrime aid (Gardner and Anderson, 2010; Harr et al., 2011; Samaha, 2012).

Being an accomplice is not the same as the following:

Accessory after the fact - This remains, in some jurisdictions, a separate and less serious offense for giving aid and comfort (harboring) to a fugitive. The law sees it as a separate offense because it is really helping someone avoid arrest or escape punishment more than helping someone commit a crime. Accessories always have a claim to less punishment (Gardner and Anderson, 2010; Harr et al., 2011; Samaha, 2012).

Conspiracy - Conspiracy is a completely different crime; according to the *Pinkerton* rule, a person can be charged with both conspiracy to commit a crime and the crime itself under the law of accomplices (for example, two people agree to commit murder, and one acts as a lookout while the other kills somebody; both can be charged with conspiracy to commit murder and murder itself) (Gardner and Anderson, 2010; Harr et al., 2011; Samaha, 2012).

Facilitation or solicitation - These are separate offenses related to the ideas, respectively, of making it easier for someone to commit a crime and enticing someone to commit a crime that never occurs (for example, aiding a juvenile who is used in a crime to limit someone's exposure to prosecution and soliciting a prostitute; of the two, facilitation is closest to accomplice law) (Gardner and Anderson, 2010; Harr et al., 2011; Samaha, 2012).

There are two doctrines in this area to remember:

1. The doctrine of complicity - This establishes the notion of "accomplice liability," which for anyone aiding, abetting, or giving counsel to a known felon has that felon's actus reus and mens rea attributed to them. Their participation is what creates the liability as if they have committed the crime alone.

2. The doctrine of respondeat superior - This establishes the notion of "vicarious liability," where a master is responsible for the illegal conduct of their servant. The relationship is what creates the liability. It dispenses with the element of actus reus in the same way strict liability dispenses with the element of mens rea. It often comes up in business, where a corporation (as an entity, not a person) cannot commit a crime (cannot form criminal intent), but it can be held "criminally liable" if the only punishment sought is a fine or seizure of property. Officers of a corporation can be punished by imprisonment only if the corporation has been held "criminally liable" first; the officer has been found guilty of malfeasance, misfeasance, or nonfeasance by their corporation; and (unless stated otherwise in statute) the officer causes, requests, commands, or in any way authorizes the illegal act to be committed (Gardner and Anderson, 2010; Harr et al., 2011; Samaha, 2012).

Incomplete (Inchoate) Crimes

Anticipatory, incipient, incomplete, and preliminary crimes are all other words for inchoate crimes—acts that imply an inclination to commit a crime even though the crime is never completed. The word *inchoate* means "underdeveloped or unripened." Because of the social need to prevent crimes before they occur, the common law long ago has established three separate and distinct categories of inchoate crimes—the crimes of attempt, conspiracy, and solicitation. Over the years, there has been little addition to this category of crime, with the possible exception of possession (as in possession of burglar tools, bomb materials, gun arsenal, etc.) and another seldom-heard offense based on the notion of preparation, which has normally not been associated with inchoate crimes (Gardner and Anderson, 2010; Harr et al., 2011; Samaha, 2012).

Traditionally, inchoate crimes have always been considered misdemeanors; but over the years, they have been merged into felonies, as society has put more power in the hands of law enforcement and prosecutors to deal with recalcitrant problems, such as organized crime, white-collar crime, and drug crime. Traditional rules that exist are (1) a person should not be charged with both the inchoate and choate offense, according to the so-called doctrine of merger, with the exception of conspiracy, which can be a separate charge; (2) lesser penalties should ideally be imposed for inchoate crimes, but in many cases, the penalty should be exactly the same as for the completed offense; (3) inchoate crimes should have specific intent, spelling out clearly what the mens rea elements are; and (4) some overt action or substantial step should be required in the direction of completing the crime. This set of rules is sometimes referred to as the doctrine of inchoate crimes (Gardner and Anderson, 2010; Harr et al., 2011; Samaha, 2012).

It is best to discuss the three inchoate crimes in alphabetical order, as well as for another reason—attempt is considered to stand closest to a completed crime, conspiracy is considered to be further removed, and solicitation is considered the furthest removed.

Attempt

Criminal attempt, in many ways, is all about failure (not being a very good criminal), for example, shooting at somebody and missing. The law of attempt is also about nipping violence in the bud, so under certain circumstances, even certain words (threats, challenges) might qualify as attempts. There is no such thing as a crime called "attempt." Most states allow the prosecutor to pick what the crime is that is being attempted; that is, most states do not try to define attempted murder, attempted robbery, attempted rape, and so forth. Most states typically have a general attempt statute that specifies a punishment (usually the same as for the completed offense) and allows the word "attempted" to be placed before the target crime (Gardner and Anderson, 2010; Harr et al., 2011; Samaha, 2012).

The elements of attempt include the following:

1. Specific intent - This means that "purposely" is the only mens rea that qualifies. All inchoate crimes are

specific intent crimes, and all specific intent crimes do not allow such states of mind as reckless, negligent, or strict liability.

2. An overt act toward commission - This is intended to weed out the plotters from the perpetrators, but the standards vary widely by jurisdiction. Acts of preparation do not count. Some places use fairly loose language like "some steps," while other places use the more rigorous "all but last act" standard (Gardner and Anderson, 2010; Harr et al., 2011; Samaha, 2012).

   There are at least four tests used in various places:

   a. Physical proximity doctrine - This focuses upon space and time and establishes the "last act" standard, which requires looking at the remaining steps.

   b. Probable desistance approach - This considers whether the attempt would naturally lead to commission but, for some timely interference, not related to bad luck.

   c. Equivocality approach - This looks at whether the attempt can have no other purpose than commission of a crime.

   d. Substantial steps test - This is a Model Penal Code–recommended approach that looks for corroborating evidence in the form of conduct that tends to concur or verify a criminal purpose.

3. Failure to consummate the crime - The law looks at the reasons why the crime failed, and in some cases, the reason mitigates the punishment or removes the liability, as in the following:

   a. Legal impossibility - a defense that what was attempted is not a crime (raping a mannequin, for example, because rape requires a human victim); prosecutors have the burden of proving legal possibility, as well as apparent ability

b. Factual impossibility - a defense that some extraneous factor or outside force made it impossible to complete the crime; most jurisdictions will not accept this on the presumption that "luck" does not count (same as no defense)

c. Renunciation - This is the idea of abandonment, and to be a successful defense, the actor must have given up for moral reasons, not just because of the risk of apprehension (Gardner and Anderson, 2010; Harr et al., 2011; Samaha, 2012)

Different courts use different tests, but with the law of attempt, all courts distinguish between mere preparation to commit the crime and an actual attempt to commit it. Only the latter is prohibited. Federal courts generally use the "substantial steps" test borrowed from the Model Penal Code. The substantial steps test is as follows: "if, acting with the kind of culpability otherwise required for commission of the crime, [the offender] . . . purposely does or omits to do anything that, under the circumstances as he believes them to be, is an act or omission constituting a substantial step in a course of conduct planned to culminate in his commission of the crime" (*United States v. Hsu*, 3d Cir., 1998). In sum, the law looks at attempt as something more than just trying to do something (Gardner and Anderson, 2010; Harr et al., 2011; Samaha, 2012).

Conspiracy

The essence of conspiracy is an agreement. It does not have to be a written one; a "meeting of the minds" will do. Usually, it is inferred from the facts or circumstances. What the agreement has to be about doesn't even have to be criminal, only "unlawful." Because a conspiracy by itself is almost treated as a substantive crime in itself, this is the only inchoate offense that the law permits a person to be charged with, in addition to the target crime (that is, a person can be charged with both murder and conspiracy to commit murder, for example). This probably will not be reduced by plea bargaining (Gardner and Anderson, 2010; Harr et al., 2011; Samaha, 2012).

Solicitation

Solicitation is best thought of as a substantive crime in itself, remote from being thought of as an attempt at a substantive crime. Solicitation occurs when the solicitation is made. Another way of saying this is that the crime of solicitation is over with the asking. The crime of solicitation is inherently incomplete (inchoate) because the law does not even care if the solicitation is influential or not. The exception is murder. Solicitation of murder (a.k.a. contract killing, a.k.a. murder for hire) is a common crime of solicitation but generally results in a charge of homicide, not just solicitation. It also does not matter if it is a crowd or an individual being solicited, and it is even possible to perpetrate solicitation through an intermediary. What does matter is the thing being solicited—the crime of solicitation should be restricted to certain serious felonies. At common law, these are would-be crimes that breach the peace or obstruct justice (Gardner and Anderson, 2010; Harr et al., 2011; Samaha, 2012).

Solicitation, specifically the actus reus of it, consists of words— words that create an *inducement*, defined as advising, commanding, counseling, encouraging, enticing, entreating, importuning, inciting, inducing, instigating, ordering, procuring, requesting, soliciting, or urging another to commit a serious felony with the specific intent that the person solicited commit the crime. This list is sometimes called the list of proper utterances for the crime of solicitation (Gardner and Anderson, 2010; Harr et al., 2011; Samaha, 2012).

Justifications

Self-defense

Self-defense, or self-help, has always been a recognized justification, and it has many variations. It does not apply to preemptive strikes or paybacks, but it does cover a wide range of behaviors that make the crime seem justified, in fact, so justified that self-defense is called a perfect defense (the defendant "walks"). Other justifications and excuses may only be imperfect defenses that are treated as mitigating circumstances resulting in a lesser punishment (Gardner and Anderson, 2010; Harr et al., 2011; Samaha, 2012).

The law of self-defense revolves around the notion of reasonableness. The person claiming it must have had a reasonable belief in imminent danger and used a reasonable degree of force. Some states have specifically mentioned that self-defense can be used when the danger is a specific felony, such as rape, sodomy, kidnapping, and robbery. Reasonable force means that if someone slaps your face and you shoot them, that is unreasonable because you escalated force too far when just returning a slap in the face might have been more reasonable (Gardner and Anderson, 2010; Harr et al., 2011; Samaha, 2012).

Imminent is a word meaning "in progress or about to happen right now." You cannot use self-defense for continuing and ongoing danger, although a few states have allowed this. Most states use an objective test to determine the sense of being imminent, and their statutes either spell out the grounds for a reasonable belief or use a reasonable man standard. Other states use a subjective test or honest belief (Gardner and Anderson, 2010; Harr et al., 2011; Samaha, 2012).

Some states also adhere to the retreat doctrine. This is the rule that defenders must have taken all means to avoid or escape before attacking in self-defense, although in some jurisdictions retreat is not necessary. Some states, however, adhere to the castle doctrine, the idea that when attacked in one's home, you should hold your ground and not be required to retreat. Self-defense can include protecting family, friends, and loved ones (Gardner and Anderson, 2010; Harr et al., 2011; Samaha, 2012).

Excuses

Duress

The main type of excuse is the defense of duress. The principle is that when people are forced to do something wrong, it ought not to count against them. There is widespread disagreement, however, over how duress is defined and what kinds of crimes can be excused by duress. States differ. Some permit only having a gun pointed to your head, others permit threats of bodily harm ("I'll hurt you if you don't do that"), and still others are fairly lenient in permitting such things as "If you don't do that, I'll tell other people something nasty about you." Whatever the threat, it must be immediate, not some ongoing situation of extortion or blackmail. And whatever the threat, the crime must be minor and not serious. Murder, for example, can never be excused by duress (Gardner and Anderson, 2010; Harr et al., 2011; Samaha, 2012).

Intoxication

There are different ways to get intoxicated, and the law recognizes two ways: voluntary and involuntary. Voluntary intoxication goes to the element of mens rea (ability to form the capacity to understand purpose or intent) and is logically a justification. Involuntary intoxication, on the other hand, is an excuse because the person's body does not know it is under the influence. There is also an assumption of duress with involuntary intoxication (Gardner and Anderson, 2010; Harr et al., 2011; Samaha, 2012).

Mistake

Mistake or ignorance of fact has always excused criminal responsibility under some circumstances, and in all circumstances, it is always acceptable that anyone holding a genuine and sincere belief in something that, if true, will negate their criminal liability should believe in something that does. The principle of mistake of fact excuses when it negates a material element in the crime. For example, taking the wrong umbrella when leaving the room because it resembles your own umbrella negates the element of mens rea (forming criminal intent to steal). The principle of mistake of law, ignorance of the law, excuses criminal behavior if a person has made a reasonable effort to learn the law. Normally, ignorance of the law is not a valid excuse, though. In practice, it is difficult to distinguish between mistakes of fact and law, and the law must be careful to not open the door to allowing everybody to claim ignorance (Gardner and Anderson, 2010; Harr et al., 2011; Samaha, 2012).

Infancy

This is one of the three Is (intoxication, infancy, and insanity) that make up the capacity defenses to crime. The principle is that age always affects criminal liability. At common law, under age seven, there is an irrefutable presumption that someone is incapable of committing a crime. Under age fourteen, there is a rebuttable presumption that someone is incapable of committing a crime. Changes in juvenile law and the increasing practice of waivers to adult court have substantially changed this common law; however, society seems increasingly ready to recognize that young people can, and do, commit serious crimes (Gardner and Anderson, 2010; Harr et al., 2011; Samaha, 2012).

Entrapment

Entrapment is a perfect defense (the defendant "walks"), but it is often just a way to shift the burden of persuasion to the prosecution. It is not a constitutional right. It is a twentieth-century invention that has its origins in sympathy for the accused. The principle, if there is one, of entrapment is that there is limited sympathy because of the need to balance the needs of law-abiding citizens. It also depends on the crime. The law looks negatively at police entrapment in cases of consensual, victimless crimes. In order for entrapment to occur, police must initiate the encouragement of crime, specifically by any of the following:

- ✓ Pretending to be victims
- ✓ Enticing suspects to commit crimes
- ✓ Communicating the enticement to suspects
- ✓ Influencing the decision to commit crimes
- ✓ Making repeated requests to commit a crime
- ✓ Forming personal relationships with suspects and appealing to the personal
- ✓ Promising benefits from committing the crime
- ✓ Supplying essential materials and/or contraband to complete the crime (Gardner and Anderson, 2010; Harr et al., 2011; Samaha, 2012)

The key to entrapment is the person must be predisposed to commit the crime. If the state cannot show the person was predisposed, then entrapment has occurred.

Insanity

The insanity principle bestows upon the government the authority to incarcerate without convicting people who are abnormal and not average, everyday criminals. The defense is usually only seen when the crimes are very serious and the punishment quite severe. A successful insanity defense is not about going free ("walking") but quite the opposite. Insanity impairs mens rea, but it operates by affecting the brain (the body) via a mental illness. This is sometimes expressed as insanity being a legal concept and mental illness a medical condition. The law reserves the right to not have to conform its definitions to those of the medical community and to treat the whole issue of curability as irrelevant. Insanity is an affirmative defense—the defense has to prove it if they raise it, but in practice, whoever brings up the issue first in court has the burden of persuasion. Over the years, various tests have been used to determine insanity, including the following:

M'Naghten rule, or right-wrong test - The focus is on the intellectual capacity to know right from wrong, pure intellectual awareness, cognition, or being able to grasp the act's true significance, not just a feeling or emotional sensation that something is wrong.

Irresistible impulse test - a revised type of *M'Naghten* rule in which the focus is on volition, whether the defendants have exercised any free will in an attempt to inhibit their criminal behavior or if they have suffered from a "disease of the mind" so strong that they suddenly lost the power to avoid doing the act. If the crime is the product of a mental illness itself, this is considered satisfaction of the *Durham* rule.

Substantial capacity test - a focus on the loss of "substantial," not "total," mental capacity; it is the majority test in most jurisdictions because it conforms to the ALI (American Legal Institute) definition: "if at the time of such conduct as a result of mental disease or defect, he lacks substantial capacity either to appreciate the wrongfulness of his conduct or to conform his conduct to the requirements of law." It substitutes the word "appreciate" for "knowing" and allows for the possibility of affective or emotional understanding. The phrase "conform his conduct" is intended to replace the idea of "suddenness" in other tests, and the code's definition of "mental disease or defect" excludes antisocial personality disorders, psychopaths, and sociopaths (Gardner and Anderson, 2010; Harr et al., 2011; Samaha, 2012).

Automatism

This is the preferred defense, instead of insanity, whenever it is claimed the defendant acted unconsciously or semiconsciously because of either a physical problem (such as epilepsy, concussion, or unexplained blackout) or mental problem (such as childhood trauma, mental things other than insanity, intoxication, and brainwashing) (Gardner and Anderson, 2010; Harr et al., 2011; Samaha, 2012).

Diminished Capacity

These are syndromes that are always emerging but, in general, are perhaps best exemplified by the various stress and stress-related disorders. The principle of diminished capacity is that there are some mental diseases and defects that do not affect people sufficiently enough to make them insane, but the law recognizes them nonetheless. The law has really backed itself into a corner because it reserves the right to depart from definitions of the medical community, so all sorts of "legal diseases and defects," so to speak, are possible (Gardner and Anderson, 2010; Harr et al., 2011; Samaha, 2012).

The Law of Homicide

Homicide is a neutral term. It describes an act with no moral judgment. *Murder* is the term that is non-neutral. It describes an act with moral judgment. The law of homicide has the most complex degree (grading) system of any area in criminal law. This grading system is reproduced below. The first two fall in a category called "perfect" defenses. The last four fall in a category called "imperfect" defenses. Perfect defenses always involve justifications and excuses.

1. Justifiable Homicides - These are "no fault" homicides. They ordinarily involve the death of someone under circumstances of necessity or duty (commanded or

authorized by law). Examples are self-defense, capital punishment, and police shootings.

2. Excusable Homicides - These are misadventures, accidents, or acts of insanity. They ordinarily involve acts of civil fault, error, or omission. There is not enough fault to criminal negligence. There is a legal defense to this act.

3. First-Degree Criminal Homicide (Murder) - These are acts involving the death of someone in "cold blood" or by "lying in wait." They are distinguishable by the mental state of "purposely," which is defined in homicide law as having three elements: (a) premeditated, meaning fixed or obsessed; (b) deliberate, meaning "cool"; and (c) malicious, meaning scheming or clever. Also, the crime of felony murder (someone dies during commission of a felony) is automatically first-degree homicide.

4. Second-Degree Criminal Homicide (Murder) - These are acts involving the death of someone in the "heat of passion." It is basically a catchall category today for acts such as shooting bullets up in the air. But historically, a number of older terms were associated with this grade, such as the "year and a day" rule (for when the death had to occur) and the idea of "malice aforethought" (which meant wicked, evil, depraved, spiteful, or with depraved heart); of these terms, only the phrase "depraved heart murder" is still used. Heat-of-passion murder does not require provocation, but it still requires proof of intent.

5. Voluntary Manslaughter - Manslaughter, in general, involves acts involving the death of someone without thinking. It involves "sudden passion." There is no premeditated deliberation. The requirement is "adequate provocation," and there are three tests: (a) the person loses the ability to reflect coolly, (b) there is no sufficient time to cool off, or (c) the provocation must have caused action. Voluntary manslaughter is often what the jury will return as a verdict when they are deadlocked on the homicide charges.

6. Involuntary Manslaughter - This is the crime of criminal negligence. It is the least serious offense in the law of homicide. It typically involves acts related to public safety, such as operating a motor vehicle, railroad, or bus. Specifically, it involves the careless use of firearms, explosives, animals, medicine, trains, planes, ships, and automobiles. Many states have sorted out a separate category called vehicular manslaughter for cases involving automobiles (Gardner and Anderson, 2010; Harr et al., 2011; Samaha, 2012).

Premeditated Deliberation

This is the idea of planned-in-advance coolness. There is some inconsistency in definition, but the phrase generally refers to anything "cold-blooded." It is defined as "a careful thought and weighing of consequences, a judgment or plan, carried out cooly and steadily, according to a preconceived plan." "Planning" in the long term is not required. A few seconds will suffice at law as long as there is sufficient maturity and mental health. There is also something called the deadly weapon doctrine, which allows the inference of intent if a deadly weapon is used (Gardner and Anderson, 2010; Harr et al., 2011; Samaha, 2012).

Adequate Provocation

This is the idea of extenuating circumstances. Only certain kinds of circumstances will reduce the crime in terms of degree. The reasonable person standard is used to determine if there is a reasonable belief in being in danger of losing one's life or suffering great bodily harm. The law on this point also recognizes the frailty of human nature, such as reacting without thinking (Gardner and Anderson, 2010; Harr et al., 2011; Samaha, 2012).

Assault, Battery, and Related Crimes

The idea behind these crimes, commonly called "offenses against the person," is that every person has a personal space that should not be violated without consent. There are old common-law traditions protecting personal security and bodily integrity. It goes back to the Magna Carta and involves the practice of touching people without their permission. Many forms of violence are punished at law to preserve order in society, and the trick is to determine the punishment proportional to the crime (Gardner and Anderson, 2010; Harr et al., 2011; Samaha, 2012).

One of the things that the law looks at is the victim. It matters a great deal who the victim is. Traditionally, felonies have been reserved for victims who are police officers, paramedics, or other persons acting in the line of duty. The law has been slow in helping the victims of spousal abuse, but it is now a felony in many states. Child abuse is different because, traditionally, it has always included neglect as a form of abuse. Elderly abuse is a new area copied from the child abuse model. Hate crime is also a new area of concern (Gardner and Anderson, 2010; Harr et al., 2011; Samaha, 2012).

Assault

Assault is either (1) an attempted battery or (2) the placing of the victim in apprehension of receiving an immediate battery. Endangerment is a related offense to assault (but usually a misdemeanor) that involves recklessly endangering the safety of others. Hazing is a form of endangerment involving initiation rites that pose a threat to the health of the applicant. Aggravated assault is a generic term for the most serious kinds of assaults, and this crime exists in order to tailor the punishment more efficiently (Gardner and Anderson, 2010; Harr et al., 2011; Samaha, 2012).

Battery

Battery is the unlawful, unconsented touching of one human being by another human being. Some states have the offense of aggravated battery but not all.

Rape

Rape is the unlawful, unconsented "carnal knowledge" of a woman by a man. Sex crimes are treated as especially serious matters in criminal law, only one step below murder. Criminal sexual conduct does not have to involve physical injury to the victim. In 1970, most states have abolished the requirement that the victim's testimony of resistance has to be corroborated. In addition, most states have passed rape shield laws prohibiting any testimony about a women's past sexual history. Many states also have abolished the requirement that a rape has to be reported promptly. And many states have abolished the marital exception. All forms of sexual penetration— vaginal, anal, and oral—fall under today's criminal sexual assault statutes. And the law is now gender-neutral (Gardner & Anderson, 2010; Harr, et al, 2011; Samaha, 2012).

The elements of rape are (1) actus reus of penetration, (2) actus reus of use of force or threat of force, (3) the circumstance of nonconsent, and (4) mens rea of engaging in sexual activity by force or threat of force without consent. Penetration is defined as "however slight." Merely putting a finger between the folds of skin over a vagina is penetration, and according to the intrinsic force standard, the act of penetration subsumes, or includes by inference, the act of force. Threats of force must have created an objectively reasonable fear or a real fear of imminent bodily harm. Words do not have to be exchanged to express a threat. The law looks at the age, size, and mental condition of both perpetrator and victim. The physical location and relationship (if position of authority or domination) is also looked at. Proof of nonconsent does not require the prosecution to prove or disprove that the victim has announced any consent. The law looks at the physical actions rather than words. Statutory rape does not require force, intent, or nonconsent. Immaturity in age substitutes for all these elements (Gardner and Anderson, 2010; Harr et al., 2011; Samaha, 2012).

False Imprisonment

False imprisonment is the unlawful, unconsented confinement of a human being.

Kidnapping

Kidnapping is the unlawful, unconsented movement of a person from one place to another place or holding a person against their will at any location.

Threats

The crime of threatening, sometimes called menacing or terrorizing, is the making of unequivocal, immediate, and specific threats with the intent to create fear in the victim. Depending on the state, the intent to create great bodily harm is required, but the main focus is the victim's fear. The threat can be conveyed by a third party or in any form. It is commonly used to prosecute bomb threats that cause evacuations of public places. Coercion, also called intimidation, is a related offense involving inducing a person to do something against their will, such as participate in a crime or refrain from operating a competing business. Intimidation does not require the threat of violence, only the desire to control the behavior of somebody. Extortion, for example, does not necessarily require the element of violence but the usual payment of money or blackmail. Stalking is a related offense that requires proof of intent and repeated attempts to follow the victim or engage in other forms of harassment where there is no legal justification to do so (Gardner and Anderson, 2010; Harr et al., 2011; Samaha, 2012).

Burglary has evolved from a medieval concept of trespass (a broad offense intended to protect churches, walled towns, and places likely to attract people) to common-law burglary (limited to dwellings, at nighttime, and with intent to commit a felony therein) to modern burglary statutes (breaking and entering but also remaining with intent to commit any crime). It is necessary to understand the six common-law elements of burglary because some of these elements continue to function as core or aggravating factors today, even though the crime no longer carries the death penalty (Gardner and Anderson, 2010; Harr et al., 2011; Samaha, 2012).

Common-Law Elements of Burglary

1. Breaking - The term "breaking" refers to any forceful parting, separating, piercing, or disintegration of a solid substance. Breaking is not the same as causing damage. Breaking is closer to the concept of trespass. All that is required is that some part of the structure was moved, a doorknob was turned, a door was opened, or a window was raised. Breaking is sometimes broken down into two types: actual (involving some minimal

use of force) and constructive (involving entry by means of fraud, conspiracy using an accomplice, or false pretenses). Entering structures in an unusual manner, such as via a chimney, is also considered constructive breaking (Gardner and Anderson, 2010; Harr et al., 2011; Samaha, 2012).

2. Entering - This element involves the placing of any portion of the body or item connected to the body inside the slightest portion of the dwelling, even momentarily. It is intended to get at various items called "burglary tools" (pry bars, augers, picks, etc.), but offenses can include just placing a finger or sticking the point of a gun inside a windowsill or doorway. Entry items can be inanimate or animate, and they are connected to a person's body via the mens rea (or intent) of burglary. The point of entry is determined by "breaking the close," an imaginary geometric plane that defines the physical confines of the house. A "close" is different from a "curtilage." Here is a breakdown of different state versions:

   ✓ Strict entry requirement - This is the kind described above, e.g., tip of the finger.
   ✓ Unprivileged entry requirement - This looks at the relationship between the owner and an intruder.
   ✓ Surreptitious remaining requirement - This looks at when it is lawful to be somewhere and when it is unlawful (after closing time, for example).

Eliminated entry requirement - This is the kind that includes attempt (Gardner and Anderson, 2010; Harr et al., 2011; Samaha, 2012).

3. Dwelling - At common law, any structure intended for sleep is considered a dwelling. Modern statutes tend to define it as any structure or building adapted for the accommodation of persons or the carrying on of business, whether or not occupied. Abandoned properties do not ordinarily qualify as dwellings, but it is not the presence or absence of people that matter but rather the character or use of the building (such as if it is someone's summer

home or vacation cabin). States normally punish the burglary of an inhabited dwelling more severely than that of an uninhabited dwelling. Any adjacent building within the "curtilage" of a main structure is considered part of the dwelling, such as a garage, barn, stable, cellar, or shed. Vacant apartments are considered the same as houses, but like houses under construction, the common-law rule is that a structure becomes a dwelling when the first occupants move in and ceases to become a dwelling when the last occupants move out (because of the building being condemned, permanently vacated, or scheduled for demolition). Four walls and a roof do not constitute a dwelling. Most states have expanded the concept to include motor vehicles, boats, airplanes, tents, camping areas, and unenclosed spots in a yard (Gardner and Anderson, 2010; Harr et al., 2011; Samaha, 2012).

4. Of Another -- The structure must be used as a dwelling by someone other than the accused. Ownership does not matter, as an owner can commit burglary of their own structure if it is rented and used by another. Whether or not a dwelling belongs to another depends on the right of possession, if they take care of it, fix it up, maintain it, or have some "sweat equity" in it. In cases of husband-and-wife dissolution or separation, an important consideration is the unauthorized entry requirement. The spouse keeping the house must control access (such as by changing the locks) to the home in order for the "of another" element to be satisfied. The fact of marriage only gives an estranged husband an economic interest, not a possessory one (Gardner and Anderson, 2010; Harr et al., 2011; Samaha, 2012).

5. Nighttime -- Technically, this begins one-half hour after sunset and ends one-half hour before sunrise; but legally, it is defined as whenever it is too dark to discern a person's face or to recognize them. This element is intended to get at the characteristics of stealth, disguise, or cover-up common to burglaries. Only about half of all burglaries are committed at night, however, and all states today recognize daytime burglaries with

nighttime intrusions as an aggravating circumstance. Some states have eliminated the nighttime element completely. Burglary does not require one-night action; a person can commit a "breaking" on one night and an "entering" on another night (Gardner and Anderson, 2010; Harr et al., 2011; Samaha, 2012).

6. Intent to Commit a Felony - Felonious intent must be present at the time of entry, not at some point once inside the dwelling. The most common reason for committing a burglary is to place oneself in a position to look around and commit a theft. It is the intent to steal something of value, not the act of theft, that satisfies this element of burglary. Burglary is not the same as theft. The act of breaking and entering at nighttime with the intent to commit any felony (e.g., homicide, rape, larceny, or mischief) is burglary. The law wishes to avoid arguments over exactly what and how much the burglar intends to steal once inside. Therefore most states have modified this mens rea element to the intent to commit any crime, thus avoiding the argument of whether or not the intended crime is a felony. A mental state of purposely, knowingly, or recklessly intending to inflict injury or commit harm will usually suffice. It is immaterial whether the intended crime is committed or not; what matters is whether there is a specific intent to commit a crime (other than burglary) prior to actually gaining entrance. This leaves open the question of what to do with offenders who, say, break in to keep warm or escape from harm and who, once inside, see an item of value and decide to steal it. Such offenders cannot be charged with burglary, and most states charge them with robbery or some other attempted felony, although a burglary conviction may still hold because completion of a criminal act is presumption of a mens rea for burglary. On the other hand, the intent to steal cannot be inferred from the act of unlawful entry. Intent can only be inferred from a set of circumstances: forcible entry, point of entry (rear or side entrance), type of building (items a burglar might be interested in), time of entry, and hiding

or attempting to escape when interrupted (Gardner and Anderson, 2010; Harr et al., 2011; Samaha, 2012).

Modern Burglary Law

Burglary is sometimes graded into first degree (assaults a person present), second degree (carries a weapon), third degree (intends a felony or gross misdemeanor), and fourth degree (intends any misdemeanor); but more commonly, the distinction is made between simple burglary and aggravated. Burglaries of the first and second degree will be the same as aggravated because these grades all involve inhabited dwellings and the offender being armed with a deadly weapon (Gardner and Anderson, 2010; Harr et al., 2011; Samaha, 2012).

"Breaking and entering" is a term used by some states that have not modified their burglary statutes to define what a dwelling is. Breaking and entering (B&E) is usually reserved for structures other than residences where people sleep, e.g., offices, stores, shops, warehouses, factories, and vehicles. If the targeted location is used for conducting business, the offense is sometimes called commercial burglary (Gardner and Anderson, 2010; Harr et al., 2011; Samaha, 2012).

Criminal trespass involves entering or remaining on property without permission. The property must be marked in some way (No Trespassing signs), or the offender must have been told to leave. Anyone who remains under these conditions is usually charged with the related offense of trespass. Trespassing on vacant land is usually a misdemeanor, but a common defense is that the area is an established and well-defined pathway, trail, or public beach. An honest belief that the owner will have granted permission, if asked, also serves as a good defense. Necessity (e.g., using any old port in a storm) is also a defense, and some states exclude abandoned buildings from trespass laws, although other states include them to go after homeless squatters (Gardner and Anderson, 2010; Harr et al., 2011; Samaha, 2012).

Trespass can be tricky. As an officer, you do not have the authority to tell someone they are trespassing. Unless it is posted, you must know the property owner has told the person they are trespassing and must leave. This might be in a written form. It might be verbal. Then if the person does not leave, you can charge. When I was an officer, I worked a case where someone broke into the home of an elderly lady. He kicked the door open, walked into the kitchen, stood there, and then left. I quickly tracked the person down. He was a juvenile. He was at home in bed. He had run there quickly and lied to his parents. I was able to charge him. The charge I placed was breaking and entering. Before court, his lawyer got with me, and we had a good discussion. His lawyer was right. I did not have a breaking and entering. I know it sounded like I did. All I had was a vandalism of property and a trespass. I could not prove the juvenile was going to commit any other crime. I could not show intent to commit another crime. Of course, the kid was not going to admit to anything else. Absent some intent to commit another crime, all I had was trespass by his breaking the plane of the doorway and vandalism for kicking the door open. Now your state might have different statutes, but in my state, that was all I had. This makes a big difference. Breaking and entering is a felony. Trespass and vandalism are usually misdemeanors. This not only changes the offense but it also changes when and how you can arrest them. A felony, you can arrest whenever. To arrest for a misdemeanor, the crime has to be committed in your presence or with a warrant. There are exceptions in each state for being able to arrest on a misdemeanor not committed in an officer's presence. Years later, I was a trooper, and another trooper asked a question about this exact same scenario. I told him exactly what he had, but he preferred to believe another troop who told him he had a felony! He did not have a felony without some other intent being proven. The law can be complicated.

Arson Law

"Setting a fire that reaches a structure" and "burns" are the essential elements of arson. Explosions are also treated as burnings for the purposes of arson law. It does not matter how much burning takes place. The common-law rule is that however slight the burning, the arson is complete. A few states distinguish between "sooting" (smoke damage), "scorching" (blistering), "charring" (external surfaces destroyed), and so forth; but the main point is that a structure does not have to burn to the ground. The kind of structure and the amount of damage are circumstances to be considered.

Arson can occur inside a house if the item damaged qualifies as a permanent fixture (Gardner and Anderson, 2010; Harr et al., 2011; Samaha, 2012).

There is a difference between "setting a fire" and "burns" in that it is possible to set fire to something, but it gets extinguished before any burning occurs. For this reason, it is important that you read the precise wording of the state statute. If the statutory language contains the word "or" sandwiched in between "setting a fire" and "burns," then that particular state considers the act of setting a fire an arson even if no burning occurs (Gardner and Anderson, 2010; Harr et al., 2011; Samaha, 2012).

Arson is a crime of general, rather than specific, intent. At common law, the mens rea of arson is "willfully and maliciously"; but as a crime of general intent, malice can be inferred from the act itself. All that is necessary is proof that the person intentionally, even recklessly—although that is called reckless burning in some states— started the fire. The criminal intent with arson, therefore, is intent or purpose to start a fire, even if there is no intent to burn a structure. This is often called a fire of incendiary origin (as opposed to one of unknown origin) (Gardner and Anderson, 2010; Harr et al., 2011; Samaha, 2012).

Arson is typically graded into first degree (homes, schools, churches), second degree (unoccupied structures, vehicles), and third degree (personal property). Arson is a crime against possession, not ownership, so it is possible for a person to be charged with burning their own house or committing arson against themselves. There are clearly differences between arson for profit, revenge arson, and pyromania. Some states reserve their harshest punishments for arson with intent to defraud (arson for profit or arson for hire). Some states have the offense of aggravated arson, which is like felony murder but carries additional penalties if a firefighter gets injured while trying to put out the fire. A person who is party to the crime is typically charged with arson rather than being an accomplice to the crime. Actions preliminary to arson, like pouring accelerant on the floor of a building or possessing firebombs, may be offenses related to arson under some state statutes. Making a false bomb threat or false fire alarm is also a separate but related offense in most states (Gardner and Anderson, 2010; Harr et al., 2011; Samaha, 2012).

Vandalism – Malicious Mischief

This is the crime of damaging or destroying the property of another, and it is called criminal damage or vandalism in some states. It is not generally more than a misdemeanor, but it can be a felony in some cases where there are large financial losses or a serious inconvenience to the general public. Complete destruction of property is not required, but there must be some physical damage that impairs the utility of the property or materially diminishes its value. The property can be inanimate or animate; the family pet can be vandalized. Most, but not all, states attempt to grade the offense by the amount of financial loss involved, with felonies starting in the one-thousand-dollar range normally (Gardner and Anderson, 2010; Harr et al., 2011; Samaha, 2012).

Because this is primarily a juvenile crime, the law first considers whether there are any justifications, excuses, or mitigating factors for the behavior. The mental state required is at least recklessness in a general intent approach to "malice," but "willful or wanton disregard" for property is often spelled out in some statutes. Some states and cities have separated out graffiti vandalism and possession of graffiti materials as more serious crimes, and most jurisdictions treat cemetery vandalism and highway sign vandalism as quite serious. Interruption of public service (such as knocking out streetlights, cutting telephone lines, throwing stink bombs in school, etc.) is also mischief, but some states treat it as criminal tampering. The trend is toward state statutes that spell out specific types of mischief—institutional mischief, for example, when schools or churches are involved and environmental mischief when environmental damage is caused. Many states and cities have passed laws making parents responsible for the financial costs of their children's mischief (Gardner and Anderson, 2010; Harr et al., 2011; Samaha, 2012).

Elements of Larceny

Larceny is the wrongful taking and carrying away of personal property that is in the possession of another with the intent to convert it or permanently deprive the owner thereof.

1. Wrongful taking - The state must show that there was an element of control, however brief, over someone else's property by the defendant. Control does not mean touching. If you sell someone else's bicycle to a passerby, even if you have not touched it, you have taken it. It's the same with financial transactions; you do not need to actually handle money to take it. A common defense to this element is "borrowing." Since larceny is a specific intent crime, the law requires considering whether there is an intent to steal or a genuine intent to return something (Gardner and Anderson, 2010; Harr et al., 2011; Samaha, 2012).

   There is no such thing as "finders keepers" for lost or mislaid property under theft law. Some states have little-known statutes establishing the standards by which a reasonable effort must be made to find the true owner. However, if there is no real way of ever finding the true owner, like finding a dollar bill on the sidewalk, the taking does not constitute larceny. Many states have constructed three levels of taking:

   - ✓ Larceny (theft) by trick - con games, schemes, and swindles
   - ✓ Larceny (theft) by deception - stings, scams, price altering
   - ✓ Larceny (theft) by fraud - inside trading, telemarketing, credit card (Gardner and Anderson, 2010; Harr et al., 2011; Samaha, 2012).

2. Carrying away - In legal jargon, this is called asportation. It means that the property is completely moved (however slightly) from the place it is taken. Partial or incomplete movements, such as shuffling or rearranging an object, do not count. Carrying away can be done by an innocent third person if, say, the item has been stashed on them without their knowledge. A common defense in shoplifting occurs when the shoplifter senses they will be stopped and therefore drops or abandons the item before leaving the store. Some state laws will say this is still carrying away since the item left its

merchandise area; other states will require the shoplifter have passed beyond the final point of purchase. The element of asportation is settled on the basis of common sense (Gardner and Anderson, 2010; Harr et al., 2011; Samaha, 2012).

The above two elements are often decided on the basis of something called trespassory taking, which looks at whether the person involved has "larceny in their heart." There are four rules (exceptions) associated with this, and the following types of persons cannot take anything in legal sense:

- ✓ Employees cannot normally possess their employer's property because they have custody over it. (Thus employees are not usually charged with shoplifting but with pilfering or embezzlement.)
- ✓ People normally consent to "loan" their property to repairmen but do not relinquish possession. (Thus repairmen can only be charged with larceny by trick or false pretenses if there is a transfer of title.)
- ✓ Bank tellers (or others authorized to handle money) are involved in transfers of custody, not possession. (Thus cashiers can only be charged with larceny by trick or false pretenses.)
- ✓ Parking lot attendants (who have their customers' keys) cannot wrongfully take and carry away property because they possess it (Gardner and Anderson, 2010; Harr et al., 2011; Samaha, 2012).

3. Personal property - Under the old common law, only movable property counted as personal property, but under modern statutes, almost anything qualifies as personal property. There are generally seven categories of property:

- ✓ Real property - real estate, trees, items attached to the land

- ✓ Tangible property - movable, anything not affixed to the land
- ✓ Documents - money, tickets, paper, anything of value
- ✓ Services - labor, utilities, lodging, food, transportation
- ✓ Information - records, computer files, some services
- ✓ Intellectual - skills, talents, abilities, or products thereof
- ✓ Contraband - illegal items, unlikely to be reported stolen (Gardner and Anderson, 2010; Harr et al., 2011; Samaha, 2012).

The value of the property stolen determines whether the charge is a misdemeanor or felony. Grand larceny, a felony, involves property generally worth more than two hundred dollars on average, but the dividing line differs in each state. Petty larceny, a misdemeanor, generally involves anything worth less than two hundred dollars on average. Some states also have particular interests in certain kinds of property. Some states also use a "market value" approach to determining worth; others use "replacement cost." Evidence rules sometimes require experts or appraisers to testify as to the worth of property (Gardner and Anderson, 2010; Harr et al., 2011; Samaha, 2012).

4. In possession of another - The law requires that the owner of the property testify that the taking was without his or her consent and to identify the stolen property in open court. Sometimes, as in the case of jewelry, it is difficult for the owner to make an identification. For this reason, law enforcement investigators often have a policy of marking objects of stolen property at the time of search and seizure. It must also be proven that the owners have not abandoned the property, leaving open the honest belief that they do not care if it has been taken (Gardner and Anderson, 2010; Harr et al., 2011; Samaha, 2012).

5. With the intent to convert or permanently deprive - Larceny is a specific intent crime. The intent may be proven by direct or circumstantial evidence and, at a minimum, by a substantial risk of permanent loss but more typically if the thief is counting on, but not hoping for, some "reward" or gain by the sale or return of the property. The substantial risk of loss is a fairly new element intended to encompass cases like joyriding, where the thief plans to eventually return the property, but the risk of permanent loss is present. If it turns out the thief truly believes the property is theirs, this is called the claim of right, a common defense to larceny (Gardner and Anderson, 2010; Harr et al., 2011; Samaha, 2012).

Embezzlement

Embezzlement is the conversion of lawfully acquired property into something for unlawful purposes (personal use or profit). The property converted must have come into the suspect's possession via a position of trust, commonly called a fiduciary relationship. For example, employees, parking lot attendants, dry cleaning services, auto shops, and bankers typically occupy such positions of trust. The actus reus elements of embezzlement are the same as larceny except that the element of taking is relaxed, and the element of breach of trust is added. All that is necessary to prove breach of trust is that the property has been handled in a manner inconsistent with the trust arrangement (Gardner and Anderson, 2010; Harr et al., 2011; Samaha, 2012).

Embezzlement is a specific intent crime. The requisite mental state is an intent to defraud and convert property. This mental state is sometimes proven by considering what happened after the act of larceny. If the person claims he or she has intended to return the exact same property, it is false pretenses. If the person has intended to return similar or identical property because he or she has already spent the profit or covered up the losses in some way because of the physical impossibility of returning the original property, it is embezzlement (Gardner and Anderson, 2010; Harr et al., 2011; Samaha, 2012).

Receiving Stolen Property

Receiving, concealing, possessing, buying, and transferring stolen property are typically the behaviors associated with the crimes of fencing or trafficking in stolen goods. Receiving is generally defined as a single act, while concealing, possessing, buying, and transferring are conceived of as continuing acts. Fencing and trafficking are the continuing acts of being a middleman or distributor. The crime of receiving stolen property is a specific intent crime requiring proof that the person has gained control over an item, known that the item has been obtained in a criminal manner, and (at any level of intent) intended to permanently deprive the rightful owner of his or her interest in the property. Control of the property can be actual or constructive, and it is the material fact of the item being stolen that matters, not the belief that it is stolen. If someone hides something he or she thinks is stolen but it is not in fact stolen, then the person has not received anything stolen. The level of mens rea is lessened in this crime to include negligence because a person should know, for example, that when they get "too good" a deal on something, it is probably stolen. This lowered culpability requirement is aimed at junk dealers and pawnbrokers (Gardner and Anderson, 2010; Harr et al., 2011; Samaha, 2012).

Elements of Robbery

Robbery and extortion are hybrid crimes, both against person and property. It is also sometimes said that these are "aggravated" forms of larceny. The elements of robbery are as follows:

1. Taking - The general rule is that the victim and the offender must confront each other. There must be immediate possession and direct control, not "control" in the looser sense associated with larceny.

2. Carrying away - The offender must gain immediate possession of the property and retain it in such a way as to make it immediately impossible for the rightful owner to regain possession. Only a slight movement of the property is necessary to fulfill this requirement if the element of impossibility is present or if the threat of harm accompanies the taking. Victims must relinquish

their property because they honestly and reasonably fear the robbers' threats. The victim is compelled to acquiesce in the taking of the property.

3. Property of others - Actual ownership of the property by the victim does not matter; mere possession is sufficient.

4. From their person or in their presence - The general rule is that the property must be on the person or in the immediate vicinity.

5. By immediate or threatened force - This is the key element in robbery. There must be forceful intimidation (force or threat of force to inflict harm to the person, property, or rights of another). The threat can be to the victim, the victim's family, the victim's dwelling, or another person present. Threats to dwellings do not count in some jurisdictions. If there is no force or threat of force, the crime is larceny, not robbery. If there is a struggle, the force must be sufficient to overcome the victim's resistance; otherwise, the crime is attempted robbery. Some states do not require force at the time of taking, only at the time of escape.

6. With the intent to permanently deprive - The intent required for robbery is the same as for larceny (Gardner an Anderson, 2010; Harr et al., 2011; Samaha, 2012).

Most states have divided robbery into degrees:

✓ First-degree robbery - also called strong-arm robbery or mugging. This requires the presence of a deadly weapon (play weapon suffices), serious injury, or the intent to create serious injury. A variant called home invasion robbery occurs when the robber follows the victim home, knocks on the door to gain entry, or lies in wait after a break-in.
✓ Second-degree robbery - This requires the presence of an accomplice or accomplices, any display of weapon, any injury, or threat of injury.

✓ Third-degree robbery - also called simple robbery, unarmed robbery, or forcible stealing. This simply requires use or threat of force (Gardner and Anderson, 2010; Harr et al., 2011; Samaha, 2012).

Extortion

Extortion is the only general intent crime against property. It is synonymous with the term *blackmail*. It is the unlawful taking of property from another by threats of future harm. The element of time is what distinguishes extortion from robbery. Extortion is the threat of some future harm rather than immediate harm. There is also no need for the victim and the offender to confront each other. Extortion can be committed over the phone, by mail, or by e-mail; but this, of course, makes it a federal crime. As a general intent crime, the motives for it do not really matter. It also does not matter if the victim cooperates (i.e., there is no such thing as attempted extortion). Here are some typical extortions:

✓ Threats to drive someone out of business
✓ Threats to destroy somebody's good name
✓ Threats to expose somebody's family or personal secret
✓ Threats to kidnap or injure somebody's friends or family
✓ Threats to collect a debt by illegal means
✓ Threats to hurt somebody if they do not do something
✓ Threats to tamper with something that belongs to somebody (Gardner and Anderson, 2010; Harr et al., 2011; Samaha, 2012)

Forgery and Fraud

The world of business and/or commerce operates on the basis of documents, be they paper or electronic. It has been this way ever since the merchant class became literate, and documents took on the quality of expressing legal rights and obligations. In today's world, we prove important things by producing documents, e.g., birth certificates, drivers' licenses, titles, invoices, bills of sale. False documents represent a threat to social stability and order. They undermine confidence in the authenticity of documents (Gardner and Anderson, 2010; Harr et al., 2011; Samaha, 2012).

Forgery and fraud offenses refer to a variety of criminal behaviors designed to cheat a person, a business, or a government agency out of their money, goods, or services. This aspect of the criminal behavior—cheating or deceiving—is the resemblance between these offenses and property crime. Indeed, many states do not have separate fraud statutes; they include such crimes under theft or larceny by fraud statutes. Another aspect of fraudulent behavior is its similarity to a white-collar crime. Indeed, because it often involves the falsification of documents, it is a good example of this, but simple frauds are not often committed by persons of high or respectable social status (which fits the definition of white-collar crime). Another aspect of forgery and fraud offenses is that they corrupt the very foundation of public administration and/or government regulation (Gardner and Anderson, 2010; Harr et al., 2011; Samaha, 2012).

Although most crimes against business are distinguished by the means used to carry them out, forgery is a specific intent crime, while fraud is a general intent crime. Forgery requires a rather unusual mental state that easily distinguishes it from other crimes of theft. With fraud, it is sometimes said that it must always be intentional as distinguished from negligent, but there are so many different forms of fraud, spelling out so many different circumstances, that it is probably better to refer to fraud as requiring constructive intent (Gardner and Anderson, 2010; Harr et al., 2011; Samaha, 2012).

Element of Forgery

Forgery is the false making or material alteration of a writing where the writing has the apparent ability to defraud and is of apparent legal efficacy with the intent to defraud (Gardner and Anderson, 2010; Harr et al., 2011; Samaha, 2012).

1. False making - The person must have taken paper and ink and created a false document from scratch. Forgery is limited to documents. There can be no such thing as a forgery of art or forgery of machine because these items are not written documents. "Writing" includes anything handwritten, typewritten, computer generated, printed, or engraved (Gardner and Anderson, 2010; Harr et al., 2011; Samaha, 2012).

2. Material alteration - The person must have taken a genuine document and changed it in some significant way. It is the writing itself that must be false, not the document. This element is intended to cover situations involving false signatures or improperly filling in blanks on a form.

3. Ability to defraud - The document or writing has to at least look genuine enough to fool people. Forgeries of completely ridiculous things—like titles to swamp land in Florida, deeds to land on the moon, or a license to kill—do not qualify as having the apparent ability to fool most people (Gardner and Anderson, 2010; Harr et al., 2011; Samaha, 2012).

4. Legal efficacy - The document or writing has to have some legal significance affecting at least another person's right to something, usually some property right, broadly defined to include intellectual property like the form of a signature. Legal significance is distinguished from social significance. A writing of social significance cannot be the subject of forgery, e.g., a letter of introduction. Similarly, if you found an old book by a famous author and wrote their signature inside the front cover to make it look like an autographed edition, you would not be guilty of forgery because this has social and not legal significance. But if you were to sell the autographed book at an auction, you would be guilty of false pretenses (Gardner and Anderson, 2010; Harr et al., 2011; Samaha, 2012).

5. Intent to defraud - The specific state of mind for forgery does not require an intent to steal, only an intent to fool people. The person must have intended that other people regard something false as genuine. A forgery is complete upon having created such a document with this requisite intent. No use need ever be made of the document, nor does it ever need to be tried out or circulated by the offender. The test is whether anyone might have been defrauded (Gardner and Anderson, 2010; Harr et al., 2011; Samaha, 2012).

Elements of Uttering

Uttering a forged instrument is the passing or making use of a forged writing or document with knowledge of its forged nature. This is the more usual pattern—to charge the offender with both forgery and uttering—because forgery is used to accomplish some other crime, like false pretenses, some other property offense, or something as simple as purchasing alcohol with a fake ID. Falsification of information on employment applications has also been held to involve uttering (Gardner and Anderson, 2010; Harr. et al., 2011; Samaha, 2012).

1. Passing or making use - This is any putting into circulation of a writing or document that involves forgery. Any form of material gain may be the motive, but generally, financial gain is the motive as in the common practice of passing a bad check. Motive is not the distinguishing factor, however. There must be some legal significance to the circulation.

2. Intent to defraud - This is the same as intent to defraud under forgery law.

3. Knowledge of forgery - This is held to exist even in the case of the person passing something without saying anything, like "This isn't my real name, or there might not be enough money in the balance to pay this, but can you cash the check anyway?" In other words, silence (when knowing about something unusual) qualifies as satisfying this element. Merely attempting to offer something as genuine that is suspected to be false qualifies as offering or transferring (i.e., uttering) (Gardner and Anderson, 2010; Harr et al., 2011; Samaha, 2012).

Elements of Fraud

Fraud consists of various deceitful means to convert or permanently deprive a person, business, or government agency of property, goods, or services. The statutory elements are usually the same as under the law of theft, although some states have separate fraud statutes that spell out the actus reus (like "bait and switch") more precisely. Fraud is always intentional (fraudulent intent), intentional by appearance (constructive intent), or intentional by inference from the act (general intent) (Gardner and Anderson, 2010; Harr et al., 2011; Samaha, 2012).

The investigation of fraud, like public order offenses, often requires law enforcement to engage in certain unethical practices, like infiltration, entrapment, and sting operations. The variety of fraud offenses is sometimes amazing and constantly growing (Gardner and Anderson, 2010; Harr et al., 2011; Samaha, 2012).

Regulation of Marital Status and Sexual Behavior

Adultery and fornication involve the same act of sexual intercourse when being out of wedlock, the former offense when at least one of the partners is married. Prosecution of these crimes is so rare as to make the laws all but nonexistent (Gardner and Anderson, 2010; Harr et al., 2011; Samaha, 2012).

Bigamy law prohibits a person from having more than one spouse at the same time. Most states allow a good faith exception if it is believed a previous spouse is dead or a previous marriage dissolved. No mens rea is required for this offense (Gardner and Anderson, 2010; Harr et al., 2011; Samaha, 2012).

Buggery or bestiality is any type of sexual intercourse with an animal.

Cohabitation requires no proof of sexual intercourse. It is "living together" outside of wedlock. It is the least prosecuted public order crime.

Incest law prohibits sexual intercourse between a male and a female who are too closely related. Typically, any relationship (or consanguinity) of being first cousins or closer is included as incest. The law tends to base relationship on family ties, not genetic ties. Therefore adopted and "step" relatives are included (Gardner and Anderson, 2010; Harr et al., 2011; Samaha, 2012).

Regulation of Sex-Related Vice Behavior

Prostitution is legal in parts of Nevada but illegal throughout the rest of the United States. Prostitution laws vary as do definitions of the term "prostitute."

The typical elements of prostitution are as follows:

1. Offering to engage or soliciting in - This is any offer of agreement or, in the case of soliciting, getting another to make the offer of agreement.

2. Any sexual contact - This generally includes any kind of contact with the genitals; it is questionable from a constitutional standpoint if self-masturbation (as in peep show) constitutes prostitution.

3. For a fee - This is generally accomplished by exchange of money (Gardner and Anderson, 2010; Harr et al., 2011; Samaha, 2012).

Obscenity laws are enforced with variable success and are unofficially tolerated if kept within certain "vice zones" where some communities have approached the problem by manipulating zoning ordinances and business permits. The Supreme Court, in recent years, has been accepting numerous obscenity cases, and the Communications Decency Act of 1996 doubles the penalties if computers are used to transmit child pornography, among other things (Gardner and Anderson, 2010; Harr et al., 2011; Samaha, 2012).

The typical elements of obscenity are the following:

1. Average person - This is the reasonable person standard.

2. Applying contemporary community standards - This refers to local norms about what is patently offensive. The material or performance must, as a whole, lack serious literary, artistic, political, and scientific value.

3. Appeal to prurient interest in sex - This means that there is a one-sided, almost obsessive fascination with sex. Generally, this involves masturbation, excretory functions, sadism, masochism, lewd depictions of genitalia, genitalia in a state of arousal or turgid state, or depiction of a device designed primarily for genital stimulation (Gardner and Anderson, 2010; Harr et al., 2011; Samaha, 2012).

Controlled Substances

The federal government and all fifty states have controlled substance acts that are quite uniform in nature. Under such laws, it is a crime to do any of the following:

- ✓ Manufacture or deliver a controlled substance
- ✓ Possess a controlled substance
- ✓ Possess with intent to manufacture or deliver
- ✓ Create, deliver, or possess with intent to deliver a counterfeit
- ✓ Offer or agree to deliver and then deliver something not a substance
- ✓ Keep a dwelling or property resorted to by persons using substances
- ✓ Acquire possession of a substance by misrepresentation or deception

Some states follow a "trace amount" rule that does not require the amount to be usable; other states follow a "usable amount" rule. Possession can be either actual or constructive (if within an accessible area of control). Intent to deliver is determined by the quantity of drugs (and, among other things, if baggies and any lists of customers are present). Delivery is generally the transfer of drugs from a supplier to a dealer or distributor and from a dealer or distributor to a user. Possession of lower scheduled drugs is usually a misdemeanor, while delivery is usually a felony (Gardner and Anderson, 2010; Harr et al., 2011; Samaha, 2012).

Michigan v. Long, 463 U.S. 1032 (1983), was a decision by the United States Supreme Court that extended *Terry v. Ohio*, 392 U.S. 1 (1968), to allow searches of car compartments during a stop with reasonable suspicion. This case dealt with the driver of a vehicle making furtive movement as the officer approached. When such furtive movement was made, it allowed the officer to search the immediate area surrounding the driver for weapons for officer safety (Gardner and Anderson, 2010; Harr et al., 2011; Samaha, 2012).

Sokolow v. United States, 490 U.S. 1 (1989), dealt with drug couriers. The Supreme Court found reasonable suspicion to exist when federal drug enforcement agents detained an airline passenger who met several characteristics of a "drug courier" profile developed by the Drug Enforcement Administration (DEA). These characteristics included the fact that the passenger traveled to a major drug source city, used cash to purchase tickets, traveled under an alias, had no checked bags, was visibly nervous when observed during the trip, and remained only forty-eight hours in the source city in spite of the fact that a round-trip took twenty hours (Gardner and Anderson, 2010; Harr et al., 2011; Samaha, 2012).

Whren v. United States, 517 U.S. 806 (1996), is a unanimous United States Supreme Court decision that declares that any traffic offense committed by a driver is a legitimate legal basis for a stop. The court has held that the temporary detention of a motorist upon probable cause to believe that he has violated the traffic laws does not violate the Fourth Amendment's prohibition against unreasonable seizures, even if a reasonable officer will not have stopped the motorist absent some additional law enforcement objective. In other words, it does not matter if the traffic stop is pretextual so long as there is independent justification for the stop (Gardner and Anderson, 2010; Harr et al., 2011; Samaha, 2012). Follow your agency policy regarding pretextual stops. Many judges do not like this, but it is clearly established case law with unanimous agreement by the court. You may be stopping a vehicle to look further regarding a crime, such as drugs, but as long as there is a clear and real violation of the law, the pretextual nature of the stop is permissible. A key question will be, would you stop anyone else and everyone else for the same violation at any given time? If the answer is no, you will likely have an issue in court.

Drug Offenses

With drug offenses, possession must be proven. There are many ways to prove possession. However, in general, the law only recognizes two kinds of possession. These are actual (direct) possession or constructive possession. There are other types of possession, but these are the main two.

Definitions

Possess (Possession)

To occupy in person; to have in one's actual and physical control; to have the exclusive detention and control of; to hold as property; to have a just right to (Garner and Black, 2014)

A person who knowingly has direct physical control over a thing, at a given time, is then in actual possession of it. A person who, although not in actual possession, knowingly has both the power and the intention at a given time to exercise dominion or control over a thing, either directly or through another person or persons, is then in constructive possession of it (Garner and Black, 2014).

The law recognizes also that possession may be sole or joint. If one person alone has actual or constructive possession of a thing, possession is sole (Garner and Black, 2014).

Actual Possession

Exists where the thing is in the immediate occupancy and control of the party (Garner and Black, 2014)

Constructive Possession

A person has constructive possession of property if he has power to control and intent to control such item. It is being in a position to exercise dominion or control over a thing (Garner and Black, 2014).

The defendant must have had dominion and control over the contraband (Garner and Black, 2014).

Dominion

The generally accepted definition of *dominion* is "perfect control in right of ownership." It implies title and possession (Garner and Black, 2014).

Control

Verb – to exercise restraining or directing influence over (Garner and Black, 2014)

Noun – power or authority to manage, direct, restrict (Garner and Black, 2014)

Often, the offenders would hide the drugs or paraphernalia that contained drugs. So you must prove they knew the drugs were there and that they had control over them. I used to ask them if they knew what latent fingerprints were. They usually said no. I would then explain what a latent print was. I would then ask them how they would explain it if I sent the item in question off to the lab and their latent fingerprints came back on the item. Almost without fail, the person would admit they had touched the item. They might confess fully, but they almost always gave me enough to provide dominion and control. I could have tested the item for latent prints, but I never had to do that. It was a great interrogation tool.

Elements of Perjury

Perjury is the willful taking of a false oath in a judicial proceeding in regard to material matter at issue before the court. The essential elements are as follows:

1. Willful taking of false oath - An "oath" or some other form of oath allowed at law is an essential element. The reasons are historical. Throughout history, perjury is a minor misdemeanor because the supernatural consequences of lying under oath are considered more severe than whatever the law can do to a person.

2. Judicial proceeding - Historically, the crime of perjury could only be committed in open court, but states have expanded it to include affidavits, depositions, testimony, and statements in other proceedings.

3. Material matter at issue - The person must lie about a subject that has a significant outcome at trial. The significant outcome does not have to be guilt or innocence, but it must be more than social significance, such as lying about your age or place of birth.

4. General or constructive intent - The person need not know positively that his or her statement is false. It is sufficient if proven that one is merely uncertain about his or her statement but has gone ahead anyway and made the statement. It is a matter of determining if the person cares or does not care about telling the truth. Under common law, the requirement is that two witnesses are needed to support the intent to commit perjury, but modern law allows a single witness plus circumstantial evidence, or circumstantial evidence alone (Gardner and Anderson, 2010; Harr et al., 2011; Samaha, 2012).

Elements of Bribery

Bribery is the tender (or receipt) of anything of value to (or by) a public office holder with the intent that the public office holder will be influenced in the performance of his or her official duties. In addition to bribery, public office holders can be additionally charged with conflict of interest (personally profiting from office) and/or criminal misconduct (where applicable) (Gardner and Anderson, 2010; Harr et al., 2011; Samaha, 2012).

1. Tender (or receipt) - At law, it does not matter how something of value is transferred or even if anything is exchanged at all. Making, giving, and accepting a bribe are all the same. There is no such thing as attempted bribery.

2. Anything of value - The law does not even try to define this loose term; generally, anything will suffice.

3. Public office holder - Some states will specify the exact officeholders that can be involved in bribery. Other states identify certain legal categories such as legislators, judges, jurors, law enforcement officers). Other states include corporate officers, athletes, etc. And still other states just refer to anyone, public or private, that has influence over anything.

4. General or constructive intent - Although the definition of *bribery* spells out an intent to influence the performance of public office because some states have watered down the "public" office requirement, a general intent, inferred from the act of bribery, to influence is usually the case. Some states, however, require a "mutual" intent between two parties (Gardner and Anderson, 2010; Harr et al., 2011; Samaha, 2012).

Elements of Contempt

Contempt is the willful disregard of the authority of a court or legislative body. Anything that frustrates the dignity of these institutions can be held in contempt. All orders and judgments of a court must be complied with promptly. A person can appeal but absent a stay (of judgment); the person must still comply even if they have appealed. If a person is obstinate enough, they may be held in criminal contempt, which is a form of punishment. "Civil" contempt is used to compel people to do things until they do it (Gardner and Anderson, 2010; Harr et al., 2011; Samaha, 2012).

1. Willful disregard - There is no contempt unless there is some sort of willful disregard, some degree of intentional wrongdoing. Falling asleep in court or being late for reasons not your own, for example, cannot be subject to contempt. Failure to pay a fine, for being unable or unemployed, is not a defense to contempt.

2. General intent - direct contempt - Direct contempt occurs in full view of open court or the legislative body. It may be punished summarily, meaning there is no opportunity for a hearing about it. An example is when Larry Flynt has started shouting obscenities at his trial.

The general rule is that there must be a personal attack on a trial judge in the form of a vicious slander or angry insult. Isolated uses of street vernacular, like "chicken shit," have not been held sufficient to support contempt charges. I will never push my luck!

3. Constructive intent - indirect contempt - Indirect contempt occurs out of the presence or hearing of a court or legislative body. A person so charged is entitled to a hearing on it before submitting to punishment for it (Gardner and Anderson, 2010; Harr et al., 2011; Samaha, 2012).

Rules of Evidence

Introduction

Rules of evidence can be thought of as the gates through which information passes to the judge and jury in a courtroom. A brief understanding of the history of these rules can help explain the rules today. These rules help protect the rights of the accused, as well as the public interest in seeing that justice is done. American law, including the rules of evidence, has its primary roots in the judge-made law, called the common law, of England prior to 1776 (Gardner and Anderson, 2010; Harr et al., 2011; Samaha, 2012).

The American Declaration of Independence (1776) drew in part from the Magna Carta and recognized habeas corpus. The declaration rejected the divine right of kings to rule and declared that government power came from the people and that people had certain rights granted by natural law. Rights existed independent of government largesse. One of the criticisms of the U.S. Constitution (1789) was that it did not contain a Bill of Rights to protect people from the newly created federal government. To deal with these concerns, a Bill of Rights (First through the Tenth Amendment to the Constitution) was ratified in 1791 (Gardner and Anderson, 2010; Harr et al., 2011; Samaha, 2012).

Many of the provisions of the Bill of Rights deal with criminal proceedings. The Sixth Amendment gives defendants a right to a speedy and public trial. It also grants rights to counsel, to subpoena witnesses, to confront and cross-examine witnesses, and to be informed of the charges. The Fifth Amendment grants a privilege against self-incrimination. The Fourth Amendment prohibits unreasonable searches and seizures and establishes minimum requirements for warrants. Although originally intended to limit only the power of the federal government, most of the Bill of Rights also apply against state governments (incorporation) (Gardner and Anderson, 2010; Harr et al., 2011; Samaha, 2012).

The American Criminal Justice System

The U.S. Constitution establishes a form of government known as federalism. Government power is divided between the states and the federal government. This results in fifty-one separate sets of criminal laws, rules of evidence, courts, and law enforcement agencies. In spite of the variety of laws, the U.S. Constitution is the supreme law of the land, and any other law (including a rule of evidence) or government action that is inconsistent with the Constitution is null and void. The federal courts utilize the Federal Rules of Evidence, which were initially adopted in 1975. Many state rules of evidence are modeled on the federal rules. The exception to the state and federal systems being separate is most evident in the interstate commerce clause (Gardner and Anderson, 2010; Harr et al., 2011; Samaha, 2012).

The American system of justice, both civil and criminal, is an adversary system. The two sides do not cooperate but actively challenge each other. The trial judge is the umpire or referee and enforces the rules of evidence and procedure. Each side attempts to present evidence favorable to its position and critical of the opponent's position. Each side uses the rules of evidence to attempt to prevent the opponent from getting its evidence admitted. If evidence is admitted, the jury or judge can consider it. If it is not admitted, the judge or jury is not allowed to learn of it. The American criminal justice system is also accusatorial. The government must prove guilt but may not coerce the defendant to confess or provide incriminating evidence.

In the adversary system, each side challenges the admissibility of evidence offered by the other side. They object to their opponent's evidence primarily based on three requirements for admissibility— relevance, reliability, and competence. Nonrelevant evidence is not admissible, even though in some circumstances relevant evidence can be excluded. Reliable evidence is evidence that is reasonably thought to be valid or true (Gardner and Anderson, 2010; Harr et al., 2011; Samaha, 2012).

The *Fry v. Pliler* (2007) and *Holmes v. South Carolina* (2006) decisions established that persons have a constitutional right to present a complete defense. Even if evidence is relevant or reliable, it can still be excluded if it is deemed incompetent because some other rule makes it inadmissible (Gardner and Anderson, 2010; Harr et al., 2011; Samaha, 2012).

Although the system is an adversarial one, under certain circumstances, the law requires parties to disclose evidence to the opponent. For instance, the government must disclose evidence suggesting the defendant is innocent (*Brady* rule). If the government loses, misplaces, or destroys important evidence, this can be a violation of due process if the government has acted in bad faith and if the evidence is significant to the defense. If the government uses false or perjured testimony, this can result in civil or criminal liability for those involved. Such action will also require that the defendant get a new trial (Gardner and Anderson, 2010; Harr et al., 2011; Samaha, 2012).

Using Evidence to Determine Guilt or Innocence

Ultimately, the rules of evidence will determine what evidence can be considered by the judge or jury at trial. However, the evidence will be evaluated by others before trial, and cases will be weeded out (dropped, dismissed, etc.) if there are evidence problems. Both the defense and prosecution will evaluate the admissibility and strength of the evidence when deciding upon a strategy. In some localities, the evidence is reviewed by a team (evidence review team), in addition to the defense and prosecution. As about 40 percent of criminal homicides are not cleared, this type of review has increased efficiency and clearance rates. The team evaluates physical evidence, witnesses and corroboration, the suspect, confessions, and incriminating statements before advising whether the case should proceed (Gardner and Anderson, 2010; Harr et al., 2011; Samaha, 2012).

Direct and Circumstantial Evidence, Inferences, and Presumptions

Evidence consists of the materials, testimony, exhibits, etc., that are presented to the trier of fact (judge in a bench trial, jury in a jury trial) to prove something. Proof is the result of evidence. This proof may include oral evidence or oral confessions, which means they are verbal rather than written (Gardner and Anderson, 2010; Harr et al., 2011; Samaha, 2012).

The burden of proof in a case is what the party must ultimately prove by the end of the trial to win the case. In a criminal case, the burden of proof is on the prosecution to prove guilt beyond a reasonable doubt. The burden of production means that a party who wants an issue to be part of the case must present some evidence that the fact in issue exists. If a party does not meet their burden of production, they may lose the case on a directed verdict for the other party (Gardner and Anderson, 2010; Harr et al., 2011; Samaha, 2012).

There are many ways to classify evidence. One such scheme classifies it as direct or circumstantial. Direct evidence proves a fact without the need to draw inferences or conclusions. For instance, a witness testifies that they saw the defendant shoot the victim. Circumstantial evidence is indirect evidence; it proves the fact to be useful to drawing inferences or conclusions. An example of an inference from circumstantial evidence is that the defendant has had some form of intent because people intend the natural and probable consequences of their deliberate acts. An example will be inferring intent to kill from the fact that the defendant has stabbed the victim in the chest (Gardner and Anderson, 2010; Harr et al., 2011; Samaha, 2012).

Using either direct or circumstantial evidence is important when trying to prove the use of the Internet in child pornography. This has often been difficult for the prosecution. However, the PROTECT Act of 2003, found by the Supreme Court to be constitutional, defines as a crime the posting and, therefore, distribution of suggestive images of children in sexual poses (child pornography) (Gardner and Anderson, 2010; Harr et al., 2011; Samaha, 2012).

To challenge evidence (i.e., victim's testimony), a defendant may introduce past violent acts of the victim(s) if he or she can show he or she had an awareness of the victim's reputation (*People v. Harris*, 1998).

Defendants frequently challenge their convictions on the basis that there is not sufficient evidence to prove guilt beyond a reasonable doubt. However, circumstantial evidence alone is enough to justify a conviction. It frequently takes the form of showing that the defendant has the motive, opportunity, and means to commit the crime. Other examples are footprints or fingerprints found at the scene of the crime. If the defendant is in possession of large quantities of illegal drugs, the jury may infer that it has been possessed with intent to sell or deliver it to others (Gardner and Anderson, 2010; Harr et al., 2011; Samaha, 2012).

Some rules of law, however, do not permit the drawing of inferences. For instance, the jury may not infer guilt from the fact that the defendant has not testified or that the defendant has remained silent after his or her arrest, whether *Miranda* has been given or not (e.g., *State v. Mainaaupo*, 2008). Presumptions are jury instructions that the jury must draw certain inferences if the proper foundation is met. Jury instructions about inferences give the jury the option of whether or not to draw the inference (Gardner and Anderson, 2010; Harr et al., 2011; Samaha, 2012).

Witness Competency

To present testimony, a witness must meet three requirements. First, unless testifying as an expert, they must have personal knowledge. Second, they must swear or declare that they will testify truthfully by oath or affirmation. Third, they must be deemed competent. *Competent* means that they have adequate capacity to observe, remember, narrate their memory, and understand the duty to tell the truth (Gardner and Anderson, 2010; Harr et al., 2011; Samaha, 2012).

Adult witnesses are presumed to be competent. The party opposing their testimony must convince the judge that they are not competent.

If the witness is a child, the judge or attorneys will question the child (voir dire) to determine competence. *Washington v. Crawford* (2004) and *State v. Hughes* (2007) limits the admissibility of some child hearsay (Gardner and Anderson, 2010; Harr et al., 2011; Samaha, 2012).

Truthfulness

The law uses several methods to help ensure that witnesses tell the truth. First, witnesses must take an oath or affirmation that they will tell the truth. Second, they must testify in person at the trial. Third, witnesses are subject to being cross-examined by the opposing side. Fourth, witnesses who lie may be prosecuted for the crime of perjury. Finally, witnesses may be held in contempt of court and punished for misconduct as a witness (Gardner and Anderson, 2010; Harr et al., 2011; Samaha, 2012).

Witness Credibility

The trier of fact, judge or jury, must determine whether the witness is credible and believable and how much weight should be given to their testimony. The trier of fact may consider any bias, prior inconsistent statements, or the witness's demeanor (Gardner and Anderson, 2010; Harr et al., 2011; Samaha, 2012).

Testimony Admissibility Requirements

Even though a witness may be deemed competent to testify, the testimony, like all forms of evidence, is not admissible unless it is material, relevant, and competent. The fact that the proponent is attempting to prove is material if it will have some effect on the outcome of the trial. The testimony or evidence is relevant if it tends to make a material fact more or less probable. Finally, the evidence itself must be competent; it must not be inadmissible under some other rule of evidence (Gardner and Anderson, 2010; Harr et al., 2011; Samaha, 2012).

Eyewitness Testimony

Eyewitness testimony is powerful direct evidence testimony. However, research shows that is frequently unreliable. The U.S. Constitution and state rules of evidence control the admissibility of such evidence to prevent misidentification and wrongful convictions (Gardner and Anderson, 2010; Harr et al., 2011; Samaha, 2012).

Witnesses and a Defendant's Constitutional Rights

The defendant at a criminal trial has several constitutional rights regarding witnesses. Under the Sixth Amendment, the defendant has the right to compel the attendance (subpoena) of witnesses and a right to confront and cross-examine witnesses. Under the Sixth Amendment and due process, defendants have a right to testify if they so desire (Gardner and Anderson, 2010; Harr et al., 2011; Samaha, 2012).

Opinion Testimony

In general, ordinary (nonexpert) witnesses are not allowed to give their opinions. Though there are exceptions, they are expected to limit their testimony to facts. On the other hand, persons who are experts can offer opinions within their field of expertise. *Dawson v. State* (2009) has established that knowledge by the witness of the defendant can support an opinion (i.e., gestures, manner of speaking) (Gardner and Anderson, 2010; Harr et al., 2011; Samaha, 2012).

Questioning a Witness

Witnesses are questioned first by the party that called them. This is called direct examination. During direct examination, the opponent may challenge the questions based on a number of rules of evidence by making objections. After direct examination is completed, the opposing side has an opportunity to cross-examine the witness to show bias, lack of opportunity to observe, prior inconsistent statements, etc. These will damage the credibility of the witness.

During cross-examination, the questioner may attempt to "impeach" the witness. The believability of a witness may be challenged by making the trier of fact aware of certain types of conviction of crime or of prior inconsistent statements by the witness. Due process requires the government to disclose to the defendant information regarding witness credibility prior to the trial (*Napue v. Illinois*, 1959). The party calling the witness may also impeach the witness. This is sometimes done for "damage control" so the other side cannot make it worse.

After a witness has been cross-examined, they may be questioned again by the party that called them to clear up matters raised on cross-examination. This is called redirect examination. After redirect examination, the opponent may cross-examine the witness about new matters brought out on redirect examination (Gardner and Anderson, 2010; Harr et al., 2011; Samaha, 2012).

Testimonial Privileges of Witnesses

Self-Incrimination

The law of evidence recognizes certain privileges in which persons cannot be compelled to testify about privilege matters. The best known privilege is the Fifth Amendment privilege against self-incrimination. The privilege can be asserted in any judicial proceeding where the person is asked questions that might implicate them in crime. This rule is a mainstay of our adversarial and accusatorial approaches that requires that guilt be proven by means other than compelling the suspect to confess. This privilege only applies to evidence that is testimonial or communicative. It does not apply to physical evidence, such as hair or blood samples or appearing in a lineup. The privilege can be utilized even when the person claims he or she is innocent. When a defendant refuses to testify at trial or respond after *Miranda* warnings, this may not be used against the person (Gardner and Anderson, 2010; Harr et al., 2011; Samaha, 2012).

Attorney-Client

The attorney-client privilege was created to encourage frank and open communication between the attorney and the client so that the attorney can effectively represent the client. The attorney cannot be made to testify about any communications from the client. However, for the privilege to apply, there must be a formal attorney-client relationship. The privilege protects disclosures about past wrongdoing by the client but does not include disclosures about future wrongdoing. The privilege does not apply when the client seeks advice on how to best commit a crime or fraud. Most jurisdictions hold that the privilege does not protect physical evidence of crime given to the attorney by the client. The attorney must give the evidence to police (Gardner and Anderson, 2010; Harr et al., 2011; Samaha, 2012).

In re Grand Jury Subpoena (2006) has strengthened the crime-fraud exception. Even if the attorney didn't know the client sought advice about committing a crime but that was the client's intent, then the privilege does not apply. Losing the attorney-client privilege often involves written documents, and how these are managed may result in the waiver of the privilege (e.g., *U.S. v. Ary*, 2008). State privilege laws most often protect clients in attorney-client relationships. Client confessions to his or her attorney are inadmissible, even when another person is sentenced for the crime (Gardner and Anderson, 2010; Harr et al., 2011; Samaha, 2012).

Marital

To foster harmony in marriages and encourage confidentiality between husband and wife, the law recognizes a husband-wife (or marital) privilege. A spouse cannot be required to testify as to what he or she has been told by his or her spouse. To qualify as a privileged communication, it must be made in confidence while the couple is legally married. However, there are some exceptions to this privilege. First, it does not apply when the husband and wife are committing crimes together. Second, it does not apply when one of the spouses has committed crimes against the other or their children. Kentucky courts, in *Lynch v. Commonwealth* (Ky. 2002), have held that the violence-against-spouse exception applies to persons outside the immediate family of the accused. Third, the privilege of communication between spouses extends only to the content of the conversation, not that the communication occurred (*Humphrey v. State*, 2008) (Gardner and Anderson, 2010; Harr et al., 2011; Samaha, 2012).

Physician-Patient

To encourage full communication between patients and physicians, most jurisdictions recognize a physician-patient privilege. In many jurisdictions, there are a number of exceptions to this privilege. See *State v. Poetschke* (2008) for a decision narrowing the waiver of this privilege. Some states also recognize a similar psychotherapist-client privilege. Some jurisdictions recognize a "dangerous patient" exception to this privilege, requiring the therapist to notify or take steps to protect persons who are seriously threatened by their clients. A number of jurisdictions also recognize certain privileges between counselors and their clients (Gardner and Anderson, 2010; Harr et al., 2011; Samaha, 2012).

Clergy-Penitent

Nearly two-thirds of the states recognize a privilege for communications between clergy and a person who has consulted the clergy for religious reasons (Gardner and Anderson, 2010; Harr et al., 2011; Samaha, 2012).

Reporter–Confidential Source

Reporters and the media have not been able to convince the U.S. Supreme Court that their communications with (and the identity of) confidential sources should be privileged under the First Amendment. A number of states, however, have created reporter-source privileges. Currently at issue is the leaking of government information to the press by government employees (Gardner and Anderson, 2010; Harr et al., 2011; Samaha, 2012).

Parent-Child

Most courts have refused to recognize a parent-child privilege.

Miscellaneous Government-Related Privileges

Most, if not all, jurisdictions recognize a privilege of the government not to reveal the identity of confidential informants. Without the guarantee of confidentiality, many persons will be afraid to provide information to the police. However, when necessary to protect important constitutional rights of defendants, courts may order that the identity of the informant be revealed, or the charges will be dismissed (Gardner and Anderson, 2010; Harr et al., 2011; Samaha, 2012).

Grand jury proceedings are secret, and the defendant has no right to attend or testify. In general, members of the grand jury may not disclose information relative to their participation.

Judicial Notice

To prevent wasting time proving matters of common knowledge and other incontrovertible facts, courts and legislatures have created the device called judicial notice. All jurisdictions recognize this device, which is a shorter substitute for offering witnesses, documents, etc. A party will ask the judge to take judicial notice of some fact, and the opposing party will have an opportunity to oppose the motion. If the judge agrees that the fact is appropriate for judicial notice, the judge will instruct the jury about the existence of this fact (Gardner and Anderson, 2010; Harr et al., 2011; Samaha, 2012).

The oldest use of judicial notice is for matters generally known within the community or state. An example will be the location of well-known places. Courts may also take judicial notice of facts contained in recognized reports, dictionaries, treatises, or newspapers. An example will be data about the weather at a particular place or time. Finally, a court may take judicial notice that a scientific technique or procedure is recognized as reliable. For example, a judge can take judicial notice of the theory underlying DNA profiling. The court must be careful when taking judicial notice. In *State v. Gagnon* (2007), it has been concluded that information must be "generally known," not just that the court has the information (Gardner and Anderson, 2010; Harr et al., 2011; Samaha, 2012).

Hearsay

The testimony of witnesses is central to most trials. To help ensure that the truth comes out, witnesses must testify under oath and be present at trial and subject to cross-examination. However, these protections are defeated when a witness does not testify to what they personally saw or heard but rather testify as to what someone else told them. This someone else is frequently referred to as the "declarant" or "out-of-court declarant." Because the out-of-court declarant is not under oath and cannot be observed or cross-examined, the witness on the witness stand is ordinarily precluded from passing on statements from out-of-court declarants under the rule against hearsay (Gardner and Anderson, 2010; Harr et al., 2011; Samaha, 2012).

The definition of hearsay from the Federal Rules of Evidence is as follows: "'Hearsay' is a statement, other than one made by the declarant while testifying at the trial or hearing, offered in evidence to prove the truth of the matter asserted" (Rule 801(c)). Hearsay can involve oral or written statements. To qualify as hearsay, the out-of-court declarant's statement must be an assertive statement and be offered to prove the truth of the out-of-court declarant's statement. Nonverbal communication, such as a nod, can also be hearsay. Not all types of evidence that may appear to be hearsay are hearsay. If the evidence is offered to prove knowledge, feelings, state of mind, or effect on the hearer, it is not being offered to prove the truth of the matter asserted and is not hearsay (Gardner and Anderson, 2010; Harr et al., 2011; Samaha, 2012).

The rules against hearsay and exceptions thereto are a complex area of the law that varies somewhat from jurisdiction to jurisdiction. The issue is further complicated by the fact that the use of hearsay can also affect a defendant's Sixth Amendment right to confront and cross-examine witnesses (Gardner and Anderson, 2010; Harr et al., 2011; Samaha, 2012).

Not Hearsay

Rule 801(d) Federal Rules of Evidence

A statement is not hearsay if:

(1) Prior statement by witness. The declarant testifies at the trial or hearing and is subject to cross-examination concerning the statement, and the statement is (A) inconsistent with the declarant's testimony, and was given under oath subject to the penalty of perjury at a

trial, hearing, or other proceeding, or in a deposition, or (B) consistent with the declarant's testimony and is offered to rebut an express or implied charge against the declarant of recent fabrication or improper influence or motive, or (C) one of identification of a person made after perceiving the person; or

(2) Admission by party-opponent. The statement is offered against a party and is (A) the party's own statement, in either an individual or a representative capacity or (B) a statement of which the party has manifested an adoption or belief in its truth, or (C) a statement by a person authorized by the party to make a statement concerning the subject, or (D) a statement by the party's agent or servant concerning a matter within the scope of the agency or employment, made during the existence of the relationship, or (E) a statement by a coconspirator of a party during the course and in furtherance of the conspiracy. The contents of the statement shall be considered but are not alone sufficient to establish the declarant's authority under subdivision (C), the agency or employment relationship and scope thereof under subdivision (D), or the existence of the conspiracy and the participation therein of the declarant and the party against whom the statement is offered under subdivision (E). (Gardner and Anderson, 2010; Harr et al., 2011; Samaha, 2012)

Hearsay Exceptions

The general rule is that hearsay testimony is not admissible. However, over the years, a number of exceptions to that ban have developed in the law of evidence.

Both the rule against hearsay and the confrontation clause deal with the problem of not being able to confront and cross-examine the (out-of-court) declarant. The U.S. Supreme Court's early confrontation clause cases (e.g., *Ohio v. Roberts*) have generally allowed exceptions to confrontation if the statement has some indicia of reliability. The existence of a well-established exception to the hearsay rule is usually accepted as an indication that the statement has some indicia of reliability. Thus to a certain extent, if a statement is admissible under some well-established exception to the hearsay rule, it is admissible under the confrontation clause. That approach, at least for "testimonial" evidence, has changed with the U.S. Supreme Court's decision in *Crawford v. Washington* (2004) (Gardner and Anderson, 2010; Harr et al., 2011; Samaha, 2012).

Davis v. Washington (2006) and companion case, *Hammon v. Indiana* (2006), have established a test to distinguish between testimonial and nontestimonial out-of-court statements. The court has concluded that statements are nontestimonial when made to law enforcement during an ongoing emergency; they are testimonial if there is no such emergency and if the purpose of questioning is to establish or prove past events (Gardner and Anderson, 2010; Harr et al., 2011; Samaha, 2012).

Thus for nontestimonial statements, it appears that the traditional exceptions to the hearsay rule are still viable. Although the rules vary from jurisdiction to jurisdiction, some of the hearsay exceptions require that the declarant be unavailable (i.e., has died, cannot be located) before the exception applies. In *Giles v. California* (2008), the court has rejected the idea that forfeiture by wrongdoing depends only on a defendant making a witness unavailable. The court has adopted the rule that requires a showing of intent to do so (Gardner and Anderson, 2010; Harr et al., 2011; Samaha, 2012).

Reliability Standard

Exceptions to the hearsay rule are generally allowed when there is something about the statement (or the situation under which it was made) that indicates that it is likely to be more reliable than typical hearsay. It is also necessary to distinguish some so-called exceptions that are not really exceptions to the ban on hearsay but are not hearsay at all because they are not offered to prove the truth of the matter asserted. There are two broad categories of exceptions: (1) when the declarant's availability is immaterial and (2) when the declarant is unavailable. Some of the well-established exceptions and their rationales follow (Gardner and Anderson, 2010; Harr et al., 2011; Samaha, 2012).

Declarant's Availability Immaterial

Rule 803 Federal Rules of Evidence - Hearsay Exceptions; Availability of Declarant Immaterial

According to Gardner and Anderson (2010), Harr et al. (2011), and Samaha (2012), the following are not excluded by the hearsay rule, even though the declarant is available as a witness:

(1) Present sense impression. A statement describing or explaining an event or condition made while the declarant was perceiving the event or condition, or immediately thereafter.

(2) Excited utterance. A statement relating to a startling event or condition made while the declarant was under the stress of excitement caused by the event or condition.

(3) Then existing mental, emotional, or physical condition. A statement of the declarant's then existing state of mind, emotion, sensation, or physical condition (such as intent, plan, motive, design, mental feeling, pain, and bodily health), but not including a statement of memory or belief to prove the fact remembered or believed unless it relates to the execution, revocation, identification, or terms of declarant's will.

(4) Statements for purposes of medical diagnosis or treatment. Statements made for purposes of medical diagnosis or treatment and describing medical history, or past or present symptoms, pain, or sensations, or the inception or general character of the cause or external source thereof insofar as reasonably pertinent to diagnosis or treatment.

(5) Recorded recollection. A memorandum or record concerning a matter about which a witness once had knowledge but now has insufficient recollection to enable the witness to testify fully and accurately, shown to have been made or adopted by the witness when the

matter was fresh in the witness' memory and to reflect that knowledge correctly. If admitted, the memorandum or record may be read into evidence but may not itself be received as an exhibit unless offered by an adverse party.

(6) Records of regularly conducted activity. A memorandum, report, record, or data compilation, in any form, of acts, events, conditions, opinions, or diagnoses, made at or near the time by, or from information transmitted by, a person with knowledge, if kept in the course of a regularly conducted business activity, and if it was the regular practice of that business activity to make the memorandum, report, record or data compilation, all as shown by the testimony of the custodian or other qualified witness, or by certification that complies with Rule 902(11), Rule 902(12), or a statute permitting certification, unless the source of information or the method or circumstances of preparation indicate lack of trustworthiness. The term "business" as used in this paragraph includes business, institution, association, profession, occupation, and calling of every kind, whether or not conducted for profit.

(7) Absence of entry in records kept in accordance with the provisions of paragraph (6). Evidence that a matter is not included in the memoranda reports, records, or data compilations, in any form, kept in accordance with the provisions of paragraph (6), to prove the nonoccurrence or nonexistence of the matter, if the matter was of a kind of which a memorandum, report, record, or data compilation was regularly made and preserved, unless the sources of information or other circumstances indicate lack of trustworthiness.

(8) Public records and reports. Records, reports, statements, or data compilations, in any form, of public offices or agencies, setting forth (A) the activities of the office or agency, or (B) matters observed pursuant to duty imposed by law as to which matters there was a duty to report, excluding, however, in criminal cases matters observed by police officers and other law enforcement personnel,

or (C) in civil actions and proceedings and against the Government in criminal cases, factual findings resulting from an investigation made pursuant to authority granted by law, unless the sources of information or other circumstances indicate lack of trustworthiness.

(9) Records of vital statistics. Records or data compilations, in any form, of births, fetal deaths, deaths, or marriages, if the report thereof was made to a public office pursuant to requirements of law.

(10) Absence of public record or entry. To prove the absence of a record, report, statement, or data compilation, in any form, or the nonoccurrence or nonexistence of a matter of which a record, report, statement, or data compilation, in any form, was regularly made and preserved by a public office or agency, evidence in the form of a certification in accordance with rule 902, or testimony, that diligent search failed to disclose the record, report, statement, or data compilation, or entry.

(11) Records of religious organizations. Statements of births, marriages, divorces, deaths, legitimacy, ancestry, relationship by blood or marriage, or other similar facts of personal or family history, contained in a regularly kept record of a religious organization.

(12) Marriage, baptismal, and similar certificates. Statements of fact contained in a certificate that the maker performed a marriage or other ceremony or administered a sacrament, made by a clergyman, public official, or other person authorized by the rules or practices of a religious organization or by law to perform the act certified, and purporting to have been issued at the time of the act or within a reasonable time thereafter.

(13) Family records. Statements of fact concerning personal or family history contained in family Bibles, genealogies, charts, engravings on rings, inscriptions on family portraits, engravings on urns, crypts, or tombstones, or the like.

(14) Records of documents affecting an interest in property. The record of a document purporting to establish or affect an interest in property, as proof of the content of the original recorded document and its execution and delivery by each person by whom it purports to have been executed, if the record is a record of a public office and an applicable statute authorizes the recording of documents of that kind in that office.

(15) Statements in documents affecting an interest in property. A statement contained in a document purporting to establish or affect an interest in property if the matter stated was relevant to the purpose of the document, unless dealings with the property since the document was made have been inconsistent with the truth of the statement or the purport of the document.

(16) Statements in ancient documents. Statements in a document in existence twenty years or more the authenticity of which is established.

(17) Market reports, commercial publications. Market quotations, tabulations, lists, directories, or other published compilations, generally used and relied upon by the public or by persons in particular occupations.

(18) Learned treatises. To the extent called to the attention of an expert witness upon cross-examination or relied upon by the expert witness in direct examination, statements contained in published treatises, periodicals, or pamphlets on a subject of history, medicine, or other science or art, established as a reliable authority by the testimony or admission of the witness or by other expert testimony or by judicial notice. If admitted, the statements may be read into evidence but may not be received as exhibits.

(19) Reputation concerning personal or family history. Reputation among members of a person's family by blood, adoption, or marriage, or among a person's associates, or in the community, concerning a person's

birth, adoption, marriage, divorce, death, legitimacy, relationship by blood, adoption, or marriage, ancestry, or other similar fact of personal or family history.

(20) Reputation concerning boundaries or general history. Reputation in a community, arising before the controversy, as to boundaries of or customs affecting lands in the community, and reputation as to events of general history important to the community or State or nation in which located.

(21) Reputation as to character. Reputation of a person's character among associates or in the community.

(22) Judgment of previous conviction. Evidence of a final judgment, entered after a trial or upon a plea of guilty (but not upon a plea of nolo contendere), adjudging a person guilty of a crime punishable by death or imprisonment more than one year, to prove any fact essential to sustain the judgment, but not including, when offered by the Government in a criminal prosecution for purposes other than impeachment, judgments against persons other than the accused. The pendency of an appeal may be shown but does not affect admissibility.

(23) Judgment as to personal, family or general history, or boundaries. Judgments as proof of matters of personal, family or general history, or boundaries, essential to the judgment, if the same would be provable by evidence of reputation.

Declarant Unavailable

Rule 804 Federal Rules of Evidence - Hearsay Exceptions; Declarant Unavailable

(a) Definition of unavailability.

"Unavailability as a witness" includes situations in which the declarant—

(1) is exempted by ruling of the court on the ground of privilege from testifying concerning the subject matter of the declarant's statement; or

(2) persists in refusing to testify concerning the subject matter of the declarant's statement despite an order of the court to do so; or

(3) testifies to a lack of memory of the subject matter of the declarant's statement; or

(4) is unable to be present or to testify at the hearing because of death or then existing physical or mental illness or infirmity; or

(5) is absent from the hearing and the proponent of a statement has been unable to procure the declarant's attendance (or in the case of a hearsay exception under subdivision (b)(2), (3), or (4), the declarant's attendance or testimony) by process or other reasonable means.

A declarant is not unavailable as a witness if exemption, refusal, claim of lack of memory, inability, or absence is due to the procurement or wrongdoing of the proponent of a statement for the purpose of preventing the witness from attending or testifying.

(b) Hearsay exceptions.

The following are not excluded by the hearsay rule if the declarant is unavailable as a witness:

(1) Former testimony. Testimony given as a witness at another hearing of the same or a different proceeding, or in a deposition taken in compliance with law in the course of the same or another proceeding, if the party against whom the testimony is now offered, or, in a civil action or proceeding, a predecessor in interest, had an opportunity and similar motive to develop the testimony by direct, cross, or redirect examination.

(2) Statement under belief of impending death. In a prosecution for homicide or in a civil action or proceeding, a statement made by a declarant while believing that the declarant's death was imminent, concerning the cause or circumstances of what the declarant believed to be impending death.

(3) Statement against interest. A statement that:

(A) a reasonable person in the declarant's position would have made only if the person believed it to be true because, when made, it was so contrary to the declarant's proprietary or pecuniary interest or had so great a tendency to invalidate the declarant's claim against someone else or to expose the declarant to civil or criminal liability; and

(B) is supported by corroborating circumstances that clearly indicate its trustworthiness, if it is offered in a criminal case as one that tends to expose the declarant to criminal liability.

(4) Statement of personal or family history. A statement concerning the declarant's own birth, adoption, marriage, divorce, legitimacy, relationship by blood, adoption, or marriage, ancestry, or other similar fact of personal or family history, even though declarant had no means of acquiring personal knowledge of the matter stated; or a statement concerning the foregoing matters, and death also, of another person, if the declarant was related to the other by blood, adoption, or marriage or was so intimately associated with the other's family as to be likely to have accurate information concerning the matter declared.

(5) Forfeiture by wrongdoing. A statement offered against a party that has engaged or acquiesced in wrongdoing that was intended to, and did, procure the unavailability of the declarant as a witness.

Because it may be traumatic for a child to testify in court in front of an accused abuser, many states have created exceptions for the statements of child victims. How many of these rules survive *Crawford v. Washington* remains to be seen. Many of these rules may have to be changed, as *Crawford* seems inconsistent with the court's 1990 decision (*Idaho v. Wright*) allowing such statements in certain situations (Gardner and Anderson, 2010; Harr et al., 2011; Samaha, 2012).

Exclusionary Rule

Evidence obtained in violation of a defendant's rights under the U.S. Constitution is generally not admissible at trial to prove guilt. This rule is known as the exclusionary rule and applies in both state and federal courts. This rule is created by the U.S. Supreme Court, and the primary rationale for the exclusionary rule is to deter law enforcement misconduct. The rule applies primarily to violations of the Fourth, Fifth, and Sixth Amendments and due process and includes violations of *Miranda* rights (Gardner and Anderson, 2010; Harr et al., 2011; Samaha, 2012).

For most of U.S. history, there were no exclusionary rules. In 1914, the U.S. Supreme Court made the rule mandatory in federal courts (*Weeks v. U.S.*); and in 1961, the court made the rule mandatory in state courts (*Mapp v. Ohio*) (Gardner and Anderson, 2010; Harr et al., 2011; Samaha, 2012).

Fruit of the Poisonous Tree

The exclusionary rule applies not only to evidence obtained directly by violation of a constitutional right but also to evidence obtained indirectly from the violation of the right. This is called the "fruit of the poisonous tree" doctrine or derivative evidence rule. Thus any evidence obtained directly or indirectly from a constitutional violation must be excluded (Gardner and Anderson, 2010; Harr et al., 2011; Samaha, 2012).

Exceptions

The U.S. Supreme Court has created exceptions to the exclusionary rule and "fruit of the poisonous tree" doctrine. Below are three of the main exceptions (Gardner and Anderson, 2010; Harr et al., 2011; Samaha, 2012).

Independent Source

First, even if unconstitutional police conduct leads to discovery of the evidence, the independent source exception may apply. The police must show that they also got to the evidence by an independent source that did not include a violation of rights (Gardner and Anderson, 2010; Harr et al., 2011; Samaha, 2012).

Inevitable Discovery

Second, if the government can show that it will undoubtedly have obtained the evidence later through means independent of any constitutional violation, the evidence does not have to be excluded. This is the inevitable discovery exception (Gardner and Anderson, 2010; Harr et al., 2011; Samaha, 2012).

Attenuation of the Taint

Third is the attenuation of the taint doctrine. The government must show that events occurring between the unconstitutional police conduct and obtaining the evidence have weakened or attenuated the causal connection between the police misconduct and obtaining the evidence (Gardner and Anderson, 2010; Harr et al., 2011; Samaha, 2012).

The Supreme Court and many state courts have been reluctant to apply the "fruit of the poisonous tree" doctrine in *Miranda* violation cases. Usually, only the unlawfully obtained statement is excluded, and any evidence derived from or obtained by exploitation of this statement is not excluded. Some justices are in favor of modifying the scope of the exclusionary rule, as the level of police misconduct is often negligible. There is also currently no regard for the seriousness of the evidence (Gardner and Anderson, 2010; Harr et al., 2011; Samaha, 2012).

While rules are necessary to prevent police misconduct in the "knock and announce" approach when serving a search warrant, the Supreme Court in *Hudson v. Michigan* (2006) has ruled that serving a search warrant in this fashion does not require a certain amount of time for a person to answer. Certainly, key evidence can be destroyed if a lengthy amount of time elapsed. Therefore the exclusionary rule, the court has said, is inapplicable (Gardner and Anderson, 2010; Harr et al., 2011; Samaha, 2012).

The federal exclusionary rule has been made applicable to the states in 1961 in the U.S. Supreme Court's decision in *Mapp v. Ohio*. Many states have their own exclusionary rules. These states thus have two exclusionary rules. On the other hand, a few states have limited or deleted their state exclusionary rule (Gardner and Anderson, 2010; Harr et al., 2011; Samaha, 2012).

Exclusionary Rule Not Applicable

There are four basic cases in which the exclusionary rule will not apply. First, if there is no violation of a constitutional rule, there is no wrong to remedy. For instance, if there has been no Fourth Amendment violation, there is no need to consider the exclusionary rule. Second, there are exceptions to the exclusionary rule. Here there has been a constitutional violation, but for policy reasons, the Supreme Court has decided not to apply the exclusionary rule. An example will be the good faith exception that the police has acted in good faith and made an honest mistake. Third, the defendant may not have "standing" (a legal right) to raise the issue. And fourth, by consent or waiver, a person can give up, or waive, his or her rights and thus be left without a remedy such as the exclusionary rule (Gardner and Anderson, 2010; Harr et al., 2011; Samaha, 2012).

There are situations where rights are violated, but the courts will not apply the exclusionary rule. In these cases, the courts have concluded that the officers have acted in a reasonable fashion and that the social cost of the loss of relevant reliable evidence outweighs the deterrent effect of excluding the evidence. In *U.S. v. Leon*, the Supreme Court has refused to suppress evidence obtained pursuant to a valid search warrant because a magistrate has issued the warrant, and a reasonable police officer can believe the warrant is valid. Also, in *U.S. v. McClain* (2005), the good faith doctrine is upheld on this basis. In other cases, if police have acted reasonably but made an honest mistake, the Supreme Court has not found a Fourth Amendment violation or has created an exception to the exclusionary rule (Gardner and Anderson, 2010; Harr et al., 2011; Samaha, 2012).

Like all the first eight amendments in the Bill of Rights, the protections apply only against the government. A private citizen acting totally on his or her own (without police encouragement, payment, or cooperation) cannot violate those rights. Because there is no violation of rights, the exclusionary rule does not come into play. However, as found in *People v. Wilkinson* (2008), a private search can become a government search when the government participates in the search (Gardner and Anderson, 2010; Harr et al., 2011; Samaha, 2012).

There are numerous types of proceedings where the exclusionary rule does not apply. It does not apply in civil cases, grand jury proceedings, or probation and parole revocation hearings.

The exclusionary rule does not apply to evidence obtained in a consent search (e.g., *U.S. v. Drayton*, 2002). The two requirements for the use of evidence obtained in a consent search are (1) proof that consent has been given voluntarily and (2) proof that consent has been obtained from a person with actual or apparent authority to give consent. The person giving consent may limit the area to be searched or may revoke the consent at any time. Consent is not needed in exigent circumstances (Gardner and Anderson, 2010; Harr et al., 2011; Samaha, 2012).

In *Georgia v. Randolph* (2006), the court held that, while cohabitants might invite persons on the property (i.e., consent to police search), no one cohabitant could override the wishes of another (i.e., another cohabitant refused consent to search) (Gardner and Anderson, 2010; Harr et al., 2011; Samaha, 2012).

DR. JEFFREY C. FOX

Legal Standing to Invoke the Exclusionary Rule

To raise a legal issue, a person must have "standing." They must have legal authority to raise the issue. A criminal defendant does not have standing to raise the issue of a constitutional violation or the exclusionary rule unless his or her rights are violated. Violation of someone else's rights does not give standing. In a Fourth Amendment search case, the defendant must show that he or she had an expectation of privacy in the place searched. For instance, a mere passenger in a car may not have standing to challenge the search of the car (Gardner and Anderson, 2010; Harr et al., 2011; Samaha, 2012).

Abandoned Property

If a person abandons property, they give up their rights to challenge government searches or seizures of that property. They have given up their Fourth Amendment rights by abandoning the property. However, if the abandonment (e.g., throw down of illegal drugs) is the result of police misconduct (i.e., illegal arrest), the abandonment doctrine will not be applied. A person who denies ownership of property (including contraband) will be deemed to have abandoned the property. In some instances, property is deemed abandoned if it is left after the expiration of the rental agreement for a room, home, or locker. Evidence is also frequently found in abandoned vehicles, and such evidence is deemed to be abandoned. When a person places items in their trash or garbage and sets it on the curb to be picked up, they have abandoned the property. If the police seize and search that trash, there has been no Fourth Amendment violation (Gardner and Anderson, 2010; Harr et al., 2011; Samaha, 2012).

Open Fields

The U.S. Supreme Court has held that the Fourth Amendment does not apply to government intrusions into open fields (i.e., pastures, rangeland). A piece of land does not have to literally be a "field" to qualify. A swamp or forest, for example, can be an open field for Fourth Amendment purposes. Thus a warrantless entry by police into open fields is not a Fourth Amendment violation. However, the curtilage (the area immediately around the house, such as the lawn, swimming pool, etc.) does have Fourth Amendment protection (Gardner and Anderson, 2010; Harr et al., 2011; Samaha, 2012).

Special Needs Exceptions

The general rule is that searches and seizures without warrants violate the Fourth Amendment. However, the U.S. Supreme Court has recognized numerous exceptions to this general rule, or presumption, such as searches incident to a lawful arrest (Gardner and Anderson, 2010; Harr et al., 2011; Samaha, 2012).

The Supreme Court has recognized a special set of exceptions involving "special needs" of the government not directly related to law enforcement. In these cases, the presumption of the need for a warrant is weaker than in most other types of cases. These cases generally involve administrative functions rather than law enforcement functions. The general rationale is that the government interests outweigh the intrusion on the rights of the individual and that requiring warrants or even probable cause will make it extremely difficult for government to protect these interests. In the case of health and housing code enforcement, the Supreme Court has relaxed the usual requirements for obtaining search warrants. Searches and seizures at airports, courthouses, etc., have become commonplace. Everyone is screened, and no warrants, probable cause, or even suspicion are required (Gardner and Anderson, 2010; Harr et al., 2011; Samaha, 2012).

Inspections for the purpose of enforcing health and housing codes are seen by the Supreme Court as posing little threat to core Fourth Amendment values. If the owner does not consent, officials can get a warrant much easier than in most cases, or they can get a warrant to search an area of the community. Public school students while in school have less protection than usual. Many types of searches in this environment can be conducted by school officials (but not the police) on reasonable suspicion alone. The courts have allowed random drug testing and/or drug testing on reasonable suspicion of public employees in certain critical positions. Examples are peace officers and prison workers (Gardner and Anderson, 2010; Harr et al., 2011; Samaha, 2012).

In two cases, the U.S. Supreme Court has allowed random drug testing of public school athletes and those involved in extracurricular activities, without a showing of suspicion. No warrants are required. Certain businesses that involve dangerous activities or strong public interests (e.g., coal mines, pharmacies, taverns) have weakened Fourth Amendment protection as compared to other businesses or industries. They may be inspected without warrants, probable cause, or even suspicion as long as there is a regular administrative procedure for such inspections (Gardner and Anderson, 2010; Harr et al., 2011; Samaha, 2012).

Supervisors of public employees may search work facilities and items (e.g., desks, file cabinets, computer logs) as long as the search is work related. No warrants or suspicion of wrongdoing is required. However, personal items brought to work, such as purses and lunch bags, will have greater Fourth Amendment protection if the employee has a reasonable expectation of privacy with regard to that item (Gardner and Anderson, 2010; Harr et al., 2011; Samaha, 2012).

Checkpoints (roadblocks) are a relatively common law enforcement technique. Every vehicle is stopped, and no suspicion is required for any individual vehicle. The courts have permitted such temporary seizures for DWI enforcement, checking drivers' licenses and vehicle registrations, intercepting illegal aliens, apprehending fleeing criminals, and preventing violent terrorist activities. The U.S. Supreme Court has also approved a checkpoint run by police to gather information about a fatal accident in the affected area. However, such stops without suspicion cannot be used for general law enforcement purposes, including drug enforcement (Gardner and Anderson, 2010; Harr et al., 2011; Samaha, 2012).

Federal border agents do not need "particularized suspicion" to view files of laptop computers as decided in *U.S. v. Arnold* (2008).

Although the issue has not reached the U.S. Supreme Court, a number of courts have upheld sham roadblocks. In this type of situation, the police post a conspicuous sign along the highway that there is a drug checkpoint ahead. There is no such checkpoint, but people who throw items out of their car after seeing the sign are stopped. Their activity after seeing the sign is deemed to constitute reasonable suspicion to stop the vehicle (Gardner and Anderson, 2010; Harr et al., 2011; Samaha, 2012).

At issue currently are identification checkpoints in public housing projects. Both residents of and visitors to public housing have been subjected to these identification checks. A number of state courts have held that this violates the Fourth Amendment, e.g., *State v. Hayes* (2006) and *People v. Pope* (2002) (Gardner and Anderson, 2010; Harr et al., 2011; Samaha, 2012).

There are also special needs exceptions cases dealing with searches and seizures of the homes of probationers and parolees and jail and prison searches. The holding in *Samson v. California* (2008) has found that officers can—without suspicion—conduct a search of a parolee, as this is not prohibited by the Fourth Amendment. Further, convicted persons in certain sexual assault treatment programs may, in spite of the Fifth Amendment, be required to discuss other crimes they have committed. The government is not required to provide them with immunity from prosecution (Gardner and Anderson, 2010; Harr et al., 2011; Samaha, 2012).

Confessions

Confessions are extremely powerful pieces of evidence, and numerous rules of evidence surround their use. One of these rules, applicable in most jurisdictions, is the corpus delicti rule, which prohibits conviction of a person based solely on a confession. The confession must be corroborated, as this establishes the "trustworthiness" of the confession (Gardner and Anderson, 2010; Harr et al., 2011; Samaha, 2012).

Admissibility of Confessions - Voluntariness

There are four constitutional rules that can affect the admission of confessions. First, confessions must be voluntary. Confessions obtained by torture, threats, or certain types of promises are inadmissible under the privilege against self-incrimination. This is the first and oldest test. Courts look at the totality of circumstances in each individual case to determine whether the confession is voluntary (e.g., *Lincoln v. State*, 2004). Promises of leniency in exchange for confessions result in being involuntary (e.g., *U.S. v.*

Lopez, 2006) (Gardner and Anderson, 2010; Harr et al., 2011; Samaha, 2012).

Admissibility of Confessions - *Miranda*

Because of difficulty in administering the voluntariness test and Supreme Court concerns about the rights of suspects, the court has added another requirement in the case of *Miranda v. Arizona*. The purpose of *Miranda* warnings is to help protect the privilege against self-incrimination. The prosecution must show that three requirements are met before a confession is admissible. First, the defendant must be given the proper warnings. Defendants must be warned/notified that they have the right to remain silent, that anything they say can be used against them, that they have a right to an attorney at questioning, and that if they cannot afford an attorney, one will be provided by the government. Second, it must be shown that the suspect has understood these rights. Third, it must be shown that the suspect voluntarily waived these rights (Gardner and Anderson, 2010; Harr et al., 2011; Samaha, 2012).

Because *Miranda* is designed to counteract the effect of coercive police conduct, it applies only when two conditions are met. First, the suspect must be in custody; and second, the suspect must be interrogated by government agents. If one of these is missing, *Miranda* is not applicable. Challenges to *Miranda* include the 2006 case of *U. S. v. Gonzales-Lauren*, where evidence of a crime has been shown to the suspect before giving *Miranda* rights. The Supreme Court has concluded that this delay does not affect the Fifth Amendment rights, and the confession that ensued has been upheld (Gardner and Anderson, 2010; Harr et al., 2011; Samaha, 2012).

There are a number of situations where *Miranda* does not apply. It does not apply to ordinary traffic stops or *Terry* stops. *Miranda* does not apply to questioning by private citizens, nor does it apply to routine booking questions (i.e., name, address, etc.) (Gardner and Anderson, 2010; Harr et al., 2011; Samaha, 2012). There is also a public safety exception to *Miranda*. In emergency situations, suspects in custody may be questioned without the warnings and waiver.

No Comment Rule

On the issue of silence, *Miranda*, and impeachment, in *U.S. v. Caruto* (2008), the Supreme Court concluded that due process was violated when the prosecutor was permitted to highlight omissions in the defendant's initial statement because the defendant could not explain why an earlier statement was less detailed than the trial testimony without disclosing that she had invoked *Miranda* rights. The court found that this action would invite the jury "to draw meaning from silence," which is not permitted (Gardner and Anderson, 2010; Harr et al., 2011; Samaha, 2012).

Confessions and the Sixth Amendment Right to Counsel

The Sixth Amendment provides for the assistance of counsel. To have a constitutional right to a free or retained attorney before trial, two things must be shown. A criminal prosecution must have begun (e.g., indictment), and the occurrence must qualify as a critical stage. Interrogation by the police is a critical stage. Thus a defendant who meets these two requirements may not be interrogated unless an attorney is present or the right to an attorney is waived (Gardner and Anderson, 2010; Harr et al., 2011; Samaha, 2012).

There are two situations in which the government may not proceed unless the person has an attorney or has waived that right: during custodial interrogations if the person is not free to leave and after a person is formally charged with a crime. There are practices that have been established by state law, court decisions, or established procedure. These practices include permission to make a phone call and to immediately post bail and be released (unless on a serious charge) and advice that, if he or she is appearing in a lineup, he or she may have an attorney present. Persons testifying before a grand jury are allowed to have an attorney present, but the attorney is not allowed in the hearing itself (Gardner and Anderson, 2010; Harr et al., 2011; Samaha, 2012).

The Supreme Court has determined in *Rothgery v. Gillespie County* (2008) that criminal prosecution begins by the initiation of adversarial criminal proceedings—formal charge, indictment, preliminary hearing, or arraignment. Therefore counsel must be appointed if the person is indigent when proceedings begin, as these trigger the Sixth Amendment's right to counsel.

There is also a right to an attorney at interrogation under *Miranda*. The Sixth Amendment right, however, does not require custody. Further, unlike *Miranda*, the Sixth Amendment right is offense specific. Under *Miranda*, once a suspect asserts their rights, interrogation must stop; and in general, the suspect may be not be interrogated about any offenses. The Sixth Amendment right applies only to offenses for which a criminal prosecution has begun (Gardner and Anderson, 2010; Harr et al., 2011; Samaha, 2012).

Confessions and Codefendants

The *Bruton* rule involves a situation where A makes a confession that also implicates B. If the two are tried together and A's confession is admitted in evidence (and A does not testify), it is a violation of B's right to confront and cross-examine adverse witnesses. A cannot be called as a witness by either the prosecution or a codefendant B. One solution is to delete (redact) mention of B from A's confession. Another solution is to try the defendant separately (Gardner and Anderson, 2010; Harr et al., 2011; Samaha, 2012).

Confessions and Incarcerated Persons

Persons in prison or jail are clearly in custody and are generally entitled to *Miranda* warnings before being interrogated by the government. One exception is when the questioning is done by an undercover officer acting as another inmate or when another inmate is cooperating with police. *Miranda* does not apply because the defendant does not know the other inmate is an officer or working for the police; this is not the kind of police-dominated, coercive atmosphere *Miranda* is designed to alleviate. In Sixth Amendment cases, there is a violation only if there is questioning or deliberate inducement of incriminating remarks (Gardner and Anderson, 2010; Harr et al., 2011; Samaha, 2012).

Polygraphs

Defendants cannot be forced to take a polygraph or lie detector test, and evidence that they have refused to take such a test is not admissible. Further, the results of lie detector tests are not admissible in most jurisdictions. In most jurisdictions, voice spectrograph evidence is not admissible. For both of these types of evidence, one of the main concerns is the reliability of these techniques (Gardner and Anderson, 2010; Harr et al., 2011; Samaha, 2012).

Identification Issues

In addition to proving that a crime has been committed, the government must prove that the defendant is the perpetrator. This is usually accomplished by some form of identification evidence by victims or witnesses (Gardner and Anderson, 2010; Harr et al., 2011; Samaha, 2012).

Eyewitness identification is powerful evidence. However, research and experience show that it is frequently unreliable. The human brain often incorrectly records, or we interpret even what we see inaccurately. Interestingly, studies have found that eyewitness identifications are less reliable if the race of the witness is different than the person identified. In addition, there are two key rights that must be respected when dealing with eyewitness identification (Gardner and Anderson, 2010; Harr et al., 2011; Samaha, 2012).

First, the defendant is entitled to due process. The witness identification procedures used must meet certain minimum standards of fairness. Second, if a criminal prosecution has begun (i.e., the defendant has been indicted), the defendant has a right to an attorney at all proceedings that constitute a critical stage. Identification procedures by witnesses will usually, but not always, constitute critical stages. Violation of either of these rights will result in suppression of the identification evidence (Gardner and Anderson, 2010; Harr et al., 2011; Samaha, 2012).

Methods of Identifications

There are three primary techniques of suspect identification—show-up, lineup, and a photographic display (Gardner and Anderson, 2010; Harr et al., 2011; Samaha, 2012).

A show-up is a one-on-one confrontation between the suspect and witness. Although they can be unfair because of the suggestiveness, the courts have allowed such identifications in many cases. To pass court muster, show-ups must generally take place shortly after the crime. The U.S. Supreme Court has approved a delayed show-up when the witness is near death in the hospital (Gardner and Anderson, 2010; Harr et al., 2011; Samaha, 2012).

Lineups involve a group of suspects with similar appearances being viewed by the witness. Although it is unlikely that a show-up will be held before a criminal prosecution has begun, a defendant has a right to an attorney at both show-ups and lineups if they occur after a criminal prosecution has begun (Gardner and Anderson, 2010; Harr et al., 2011; Samaha, 2012).

The National Council of Judges has suggested rules for procedures for police lineups. These include reasonable notice of the lineup and that an attorney may be present for such. The lineup should consist of at least six people as alike in appearance as possible. Persons in lineup may be requested to speak, using same words, for voice identification. No one but the witness should indicate a suspect. The lineup should be viewed by one witness at a time and should not be subsequently discussed. It is also recommended that there be sequential lineups (one person at a time), instead of all at once. Additionally, it is suggested that there be double-blind administration of lineups in which the officer assigned has no involvement or knowledge of the suspect or the case (Gardner and Anderson, 2010; Harr et al., 2011; Samaha, 2012).

The third common procedure is for police to show witnesses a number of photographs of persons. One of the photographs is of the person the police suspect. Officers should always preserve a copy of the array shown to the witnesses and make a detailed report of the procedure. Courts have even allowed identifications in some cases when only one photograph has been shown to the witness.

In general, there is no Sixth Amendment right to an attorney at a photographic display. A number of organizations and courts have suggested guidelines for each of these three procedures (Gardner and Anderson, 2010; Harr et al., 2011; Samaha, 2012).

All three of these procedures must meet due process requirements. Due process requires that identification procedures be fair and reasonably nonsuggestive. The key focus is on the reliability (accuracy) of the identification. The basic test is whether the identification procedure is so impermissibly suggestive as to cause a very substantial likelihood of irreparable misidentification (Gardner and Anderson, 2010; Harr et al., 2011; Samaha, 2012).

Although courts consider the totality of the circumstances of the identification process, courts look primarily at five factors in making such determinations. First, at the time of the crime, did the witness have a good opportunity to view the perpetrator? Second, at the time of the crime, what was the witness's attention level? Third, how consistent was the witness's description with the characteristics of the person identified? Fourth, how confident was the witness about the identification? Finally, how soon after the crime did the identification occur? (Gardner and Anderson, 2010; Harr et al., 2011; Samaha, 2012)

Other Methods of Identification

Police also use other methods of identification. These too must meet due process requirements. Sketches rather than photographs can be used. There may be fingerprints or surveillance camera footage available. Witnesses can be asked to listen to the suspect speak the same words that have been used during the crime. However, the use of voiceprint or spectrogram evidence is prohibited in most jurisdictions. DNA evidence is also used as a method of identification. Biometric identification utilizing biological reference systems, rather than documents, aids in solving cases as well. The Amber Alert system (immediate information is relayed to the public when there is a suspected child abduction) is another way of obtaining identification (Gardner and Anderson, 2010; Harr et al., 2011; Samaha, 2012).

Before trial, the defendant can also ask that in-court identification be prohibited on the basis that it has been tainted by an illegal pretrial identification. When permitted at trial, victims and witnesses will usually be asked to make an in-court identification of the defendant. These witnesses may also be allowed to testify as to pretrial identifications if these have not been suppressed (Gardner and Anderson, 2010; Harr et al., 2011; Samaha, 2012).

Mistaken Identification

Significant information was found in the 2008 study of innocent persons mistakenly incarcerated, and this should serve to address and correct by our criminal justice system. All too often, the innocent are mistakenly identified and wrongly convicted. There are steps that can be taken to lessen these convictions based on eyewitness testimony. Prosecutors should screen the witnesses' identifications more carefully, judges and juries should demand a higher burden of proof, and more expert testimony should be allowed, as well as corroborating evidence. To control undue influence or suggestion, witnesses to a crime should be separated and interviewed separately (Gardner and Anderson, 2010; Harr et al., 2011; Samaha, 2012).

Physical Evidence

Physical evidence (e.g., weapons, drugs, documents, clothing) is crucial in many prosecutions. However, the admissibility of such evidence may be challenged on many grounds, including violations of the Fourth Amendment. It is thus important for criminal justice personnel to have a firm understanding of the basics of Fourth Amendment law. Much evidence is discovered after an arrest, during warrant executions, etc. However, if the arrest, warrant, or warrant execution is invalid, the evidence may have to be excluded (Gardner and Anderson, 2010; Harr et al., 2011; Samaha, 2012).

The U.S. Supreme Court has stated that there is a strong preference for warrants. All warrants require probable cause. However, the court has recognized numerous exceptions to the warrant requirement. One of these exceptions is stop and frisk (Gardner and Anderson, 2010; Harr et al., 2011; Samaha, 2012).

Persons - Stop and Frisk

A stop is a Fourth Amendment seizure of a person, and a frisk is a Fourth Amendment search of a person. However, not all police-citizen contacts implicate the Fourth Amendment. Voluntary encounters or conversations are not searches and are not covered by the Fourth Amendment. Any evidence discovered or handed over while the encounter is still a voluntary one is not protected by the First Amendment. A police-citizen contact is covered by the Fourth Amendment only when there is a search or seizure as defined under the Fourth Amendment. A seizure of a person occurs when a reasonable person in the suspect's situation will not feel free to leave (Gardner and Anderson, 2010; Harr et al., 2011; Samaha, 2012).

If at any time during a *Terry* stop the officer obtains a reasonable suspicion that a person is armed and dangerous, the officer may conduct a pat down of the outer clothing to detect and seize weapons. In *U.S. v. Arvizu* (2002), the Supreme Court has found that the totality of the circumstances can support an officer's decision to stop a vehicle (Gardner and Anderson, 2010; Harr et al., 2011; Samaha, 2012).

Many states require a person who is stopped to identify himself or herself in response to an officer's request (e.g., *Hibel v. Sixth Judicial District Court of Nevada*, 2004). The court in *Hibel* stated that an officer asking for identification does not constitute a Fourth Amendment seizure (Gardner and Anderson, 2010; Harr et al., 2011; Samaha, 2012).

There are two basic kinds of seizures of persons. A *Terry* stop is a temporary investigative detention that is permissible only when the officer has reasonable suspicion that criminal activity is afoot or that the person is involved in a completed crime. An arrest, however, requires probable cause. If the officer makes a valid arrest, the officer may, without a warrant or further probable cause, search the person for evidence or weapons. If the person is arrested in a vehicle, the passenger compartment may be searched for evidence and weapons (Gardner and Anderson, 2010; Harr et al., 2011; Samaha, 2012).

Inventory Search

Any time the police validly seize a property (e.g., arrestee's property before entering jail, validly seized automobile), they may search and inventory the seized property. The purpose of this is not to gain evidence of crime but to protect the police and the rights of the owner of the property (Gardner and Anderson, 2010; Harr et al., 2011; Samaha, 2012).

Private Premises

The general rule is that police must have a search warrant to enter a suspect's home. Further, that warrant (arrest or search warrant) must be properly executed. This means that, in the absence of a legally recognized exception (e.g., possible destruction of evidence), the police must knock, announce their identity and purpose, and wait a reasonable amount of time for someone to come to the door. The general rule is that a person may not be arrested in their home unless there is an arrest or search warrant, consent to enter, or some exigent or emergency circumstances. In *Brigham City v. Stuart* (2006), the Supreme Court has held that as long as an officer's actions are objectively reasonable, the Fourth Amendment is not violated. In this case, the court has determined that ongoing violence has justified entry into a residence (Gardner and Anderson, 2010; Harr et al., 2011; Samaha, 2012). A person may also be arrested in a public place without a warrant for certain offenses.

Automobiles

Stops of motor vehicles require at least reasonable suspicion except at valid checkpoints as discussed previously. During a traffic stop, if an officer has a reasonable suspicion that the person is armed and dangerous, the officer may search the driver and passenger compartment for weapons. Often, officers make a stop for a minor violation when suspecting more serious crime (known as a pretextual stop; this action has been upheld by the Supreme Court in *Whren v. U.S.*, 1996). If the person is arrested while in or near his or her vehicle, the passenger compartment may be searched as an incident to a lawful arrest. Under the automobile exception, searches of a movable vehicle do not require a search warrant; only probable cause is required (e.g., *Virginia v. Moore*, 2008) (Gardner and

Anderson, 2010; Harr et al., 2011; Samaha, 2012). Vehicles capable of moving fall under what is called the *Carroll* doctrine. If a vehicle is capable of being moved but is stopped and probable cause exists to search, it may be searched absent a warrant. In *Brendin v. California* (2007), the court stated that a passenger who does not consider himself or herself "free to leave" is therefore seized—a violation of a Fourth Amendment right.

Search of Computers/Electronic Devices

Computers are increasingly being used in crime and can be valuable sources of evidence. There are a number of methods by which evidence can be obtained from computers while still complying with the Fourth Amendment. A search warrant and consent are the two most common methods. Government supervisors may, under many circumstances, search employee computers. Finally, anything on a computer in plain view of an officer is covered by the plain view exception if the officer is lawfully in that spot (Gardner and Anderson, 2010; Harr et al., 2011; Samaha, 2012).

Internet crime has greatly increased in the last several years. The most common are crimes against children, threats, abductions followed by identity theft, and computer-hacking crimes. Because of the lack of geographic boundaries of the Internet, the federal government has established task forces to coordinate state and federal laws involving the Internet (Gardner and Anderson, 2010; Harr et al., 2011; Samaha, 2012).

Evidence may also be obtained from other personal electronic services, such as laptops, cell phones, pagers, MP3 players, and PDAs (personal digital assistants). Files indicating evidence of crimes may be saved on these devices. Law enforcement can access these by search warrants for probable cause or by consent searches. The searches must be reasonable under the Fourth Amendment as held by the Supreme Court in *U.S. v. Park* (2007) (Gardner and Anderson, 2010; Harr et al., 2011; Samaha, 2012).

Warrants

The Fourth Amendment and state laws require that magistrates issue warrants only if there is an affidavit by an officer showing probable cause. Further, the warrant must be specific about the place and things to be searched. The issue of anticipatory search warrants is addressed by the Supreme Court in *U.S. v. Grubbs* (2006). The court has stated that all warrants are anticipatory, as cause exists to believe evidence will be found in a search. Additionally, the court has concluded the Fourth Amendment does not require specifying a "triggering" condition in the search warrant, just the persons or things to be searched (Gardner and Anderson, 2010; Harr et al., 2011; Samaha, 2012).

There are a number of different types of warrants. In some jurisdictions, special permission from the magistrate must be obtained to authorize nighttime execution. In some jurisdictions, upon a proper showing, an officer may obtain a warrant that allows the officer to dispense with the usual "knock, announce, and wait" requirements. These are termed no-knock warrants (Gardner and Anderson, 2010; Harr et al., 2011; Samaha, 2012).

Administrative search warrants are used to determine if a person or business is in violation of state laws to protect the public (i.e., health regulation, fire hazards, food services, or structural concerns in public buildings). A lower standard of probable cause is required for these warrants (Gardner and Anderson, 2010; Harr et al., 2011; Samaha, 2012). Sneak-and-peak warrants are issued to allow secret photographing or the placement of listening devices.

Thermal Imaging

Thermal-imaging devices are used to detect temperature or heat differentials in a given area. In *Kyllo v. U.S.*, agents have used such a device to detect a heat differential in a home allegedly growing marijuana indoors using heat lamps. The court has held that the use of such devices is a Fourth Amendment search of a home and will ordinarily require a search warrant (Gardner and Anderson, 2010; Harr et al., 2011; Samaha, 2012).

Wiretaps and Electronic Eavesdropping

In *Katz v. U.S.*, the Supreme Court held that wiretapping and electronic eavesdropping were subject to Fourth Amendment requirements. Congress and most states have passed statutes specifically describing what officers must do to get a court order or warrant to engage in these activities (Gardner and Anderson, 2010; Harr et al., 2011; Samaha, 2012).

Two other frequently used electronic devices are pen registers, or trap-and-trace devices, and telephone wiretapping. Pen registers and trap-and-trace devices identify the phone numbers of ingoing and outgoing calls. Wiretapping is authorized in federal cases and in most states and involves listening to telephone conversations. The law on wiretapping and electronic eavesdropping is lengthy and complex and varies from state to state. In general, such activity is lawful if conducted pursuant to a court order (warrant) or if one party to the conversation consents to the interception. Examples of tape recordings and wiretaps as national news include that of Linda Tripp and the impeachment of a U.S. president. The taping of public statements by public figures does not violate privacy laws (Gardner and Anderson, 2010; Harr et al., 2011; Samaha, 2012).

The USA PATRIOT Act, passed in response to the terrorist attacks of September 11, 2001, has made a number of changes in prior law. In general, the new law expands government authority to wiretap and engage in electronic eavesdropping. Many of these changes deal with the Internet and e-mail (Gardner and Anderson, 2010; Harr et al., 2011; Samaha, 2012).

The Fourth Amendment and the law of most jurisdictions do not require court orders in all situations involving interception of communications. There are no legal problems with police naturally overhearing incriminating conversations in public places. In fact, obtaining evidence by overhearing, monitoring, and/or recording statements or conversations is usually without problems. Undercover officers may testify about incriminating statements made in their presence. Many of the requirements do not apply if one party to the communication consents to the interception or taping (Gardner and Anderson, 2010; Harr et al., 2011; Samaha, 2012).

Surreptitious recording of conversations in police cars, jail cells, and other similar facilities generally does not violate the Fourth Amendment or applicable laws, as there is really no expectation of privacy in these areas. Further, when informants or undercover officers use body wires or transmitters to record or transmit conversations with suspects, there generally are no legal violations. Federal laws and most, if not all, states laws do not have an exception for family members engaging in tape recording, wiretapping, or electronic surveillance. These persons may be subject to civil or criminal sanctions just like other violators (Gardner and Anderson, 2010; Harr et al., 2011; Samaha, 2012).

Use of Search Dogs

Dogs are increasingly being used in law enforcement for tracking and for drug and bomb detection. In general, dog sniffing of vehicles or containers in public places does not implicate the Fourth Amendment. Further, drug dogs may be used during routine traffic stops if the use of the dog does not extend the duration of the stop (Gardner and Anderson, 2010; Harr et al., 2011; Samaha, 2012).

Crime Scene Evidence

Police routinely secure evidence from crime scenes. When such evidence is sought from places covered by the Fourth Amendment, certain legal issues arise. Persons are entitled to Fourth Amendment protection any time the police search a place where the suspect has a reasonable expectation of privacy. If time allows, the most prudent approach is to obtain a search warrant. However, evidence may be lawfully obtained without a warrant if one of the exceptions to the warrant requirement applies. Among these exceptions are searches incident to a lawful arrest, exigent circumstances, and hot pursuit. There are a number of exceptions for exigent (or emergency) circumstances, such as entry to aid injured persons, check on gunshots, rescue persons from fires, etc. In protective sweeps of premises, the courts have not required police to have specific reasons to believe a particular person is necessarily on the premises, e.g., *U.S. v. Mata* (2008). The Fourth Amendment also allows entries based on consent. Further, if the entry is justified, anything seen in plain view may be seized if there is probable cause to seize it (Gardner and Anderson, 2010; Harr et al., 2011; Samaha, 2012).

Upon reaching a crime scene, police may make a quick search for victims, offenders, or dangerous situations. They may control the crime scene until a warrant is obtained. However, there is no exception for extended searches at a crime scene (even the scene of a murder) without obtaining a warrant shortly thereafter. Police must control the crime scene and prevent contamination of evidence, or the investigation will be jeopardized. There is no murder scene exception to the warrant requirement (Gardner and Anderson, 2010; Harr et al., 2011; Samaha, 2012).

There are numerous types of evidence that, if the proper foundation has been laid, can be admissible. Examples are foot or shoe prints, palm and lip prints, hair, bite marks, tire tracks, and of course DNA evidence (Gardner and Anderson, 2010; Harr et al., 2011; Samaha, 2012).

Chain of Custody

Even if there are no Fourth Amendment hurdles, evidence that can be contaminated, altered, etc., generally will be admissible only if the prosecution can prove the chain of custody. How and where the evidence is kept, and by whom (between seizure and trial), must be shown to help assure that the evidence is not tampered with and that it is the evidence from the crime scene. If the item is unique and readily recognizable or not subject to alteration or substitution, the rules on chain of custody are relaxed. Chain of custody evidence is frequently not required in theft or shoplifting cases (Gardner and Anderson, 2010; Harr et al., 2011; Samaha, 2012).

Fingerprints

Because of the uniqueness of each individual's fingerprints, fingerprint evidence is extremely valuable. However, it is only circumstantial evidence that the person who has left the print committed the crime. The chain of custody must be proven, and expert testimony is required. The age of latent prints is impossible to determine, and it is crucial to have other evidence to attempt to show that the print has been left at the time of the crime. Until recently, from a latent print alone, it has been impossible to determine the sex of the person who has left the latent print. However, in 2008, equipment has become available that can analyze prints and not only identify the person but also find if that person has touched drugs, explosives, poisons, or other substances. The FBI and many large police departments have created automated fingerprint identification systems (AFIS). These systems use computers and electronic comparisons (Gardner and Anderson, 2010; Harr et al., 2011; Samaha, 2012).

Tracking Devices

Tracking devices, such as GPS (global positioning system), are helpful in investigations and in locating missing persons. In 2006, the revised Federal Rules of Criminal Procedure provides that federal district court magistrate judges can issue a warrant for the installation of such devices. The warrant must identify the person or property to be tracked. It can be installed in automobiles without a warrant if the vehicle is in a public place; if in a private area, such as a garage, a warrant is needed (Gardner and Anderson, 2010; Harr et al., 2011; Samaha, 2012).

Scent Evidence

One of the more controversial methods of obtaining evidence is scent(s) from a crime scene. This is utilized as a method of identifying a suspect. If clothing or bodily fluids are found, a tracking dog can be used to find the suspect (e.g., *State v. St. John*, Conn. 2007). Scent evidence can be used to enable a trained dog to:

1. follow the trail of a suspect from a crime scene;

2. identify a suspect in a "scent" lineup, e.g., *Risher v. State*, Tex. App. (2006);

3. place a suspect at or near the scene of a crime;

4. establish probable cause to make an arrest or to obtain a search warrant, e.g., *Fitzgerald v. State*, MD (2004);

5. locate a missing person who might be a hostage or dead (e.g., *Trejos v. State*, Tex. App., 2007) (Gardner and Anderson, 2010; Harr et al., 2011; Samaha, 2012).

Documentary Evidence

Photographs and videotapes are demonstrative evidence. Other examples are maps, diagrams, models, and sketches. In addition, surveillance evidence is often utilized and is important in civil personal injury cases, as well as in criminal cases. These all portray or demonstrate things that have occurred outside the courtroom. Demonstrative evidence must be shown to be both relevant and accurate. Gruesome photographs of the victim's body can arouse strong emotions in judges and juries and cause unfairness to the defendant. The judge generally has discretion to determine whether the evidentiary value of the photographs outweighs the possibility of prejudice and can admit such photos (Gardner and Anderson, 2010; Harr et al., 2011; Samaha, 2012).

Videotapes are very powerful evidence and have been used in many famous cases. A person has Fourth Amendment protection against videotaping only if they have a reasonable expectation of privacy in the place where they are taped. Anything that occurs in a public place is not protected. A warrant may not be required in some cases involving government workplaces. The safest practice, however, is to get a warrant should there be any doubts. The chain of custody may also have to be proven (Gardner and Anderson, 2010; Harr et al., 2011; Samaha, 2012).

The privilege against self-incrimination prohibits the government from forcing a person to write or produce a document that is incriminating. However, seizure of documents by the police does not violate the Fifth Amendment. The defendant is not being compelled to produce or create the evidence; the police are seizing it. The party seeking to have writing or documents in evidence must not only show that it is relevant but must also show that it is authentic (or genuine). This means that the party offering the evidence must show that the evidence is, in fact, what the party claims it to be (Gardner and Anderson, 2010; Harr et al., 2011; Samaha, 2012).

Federal Rule of Evidence 901

    (a) General provision.

> The requirement of authentication or identification as a condition precedent to admissibility is satisfied by evidence sufficient to support a finding that the matter in question is what its proponent claims. (Gardner and Anderson, 2010; Harr et al., 2011; Samaha, 2012)

Any type of demonstrative evidence, document, or writing may be authenticated by direct or circumstantial evidence. Some examples of methods of authentication from Federal Rule of Evidence 901b are as follows:

(1) Testimony of witness with knowledge. Testimony that a matter is what it is claimed to be.

(2) Nonexpert opinion on handwriting. Nonexpert opinion as to the genuineness of handwriting, based upon familiarity not acquired for purposes of the litigation.

(3) Comparison by trier or expert witness. Comparison by the trier of fact or by expert witnesses with specimens which have been authenticated.

(4) Distinctive characteristics and the like. Appearance, contents, substance, internal patterns, or other distinctive characteristics, taken in conjunction with circumstances.

(5) Voice identification. Identification of a voice, whether heard firsthand or through mechanical or electronic transmission or recording, by opinion based upon hearing the voice at any time under circumstances connecting it with the alleged speaker.

(6) Telephone conversations. Telephone conversations, by evidence that a call was made to the number assigned at the time by the telephone company to a particular person or business, if (A) in the case of a person, circumstances, including self-identification, show the person answering to be the one called, or (B) in the case of a business, the call was made to a place of business and the conversation

related to business reasonably transacted over the telephone.

(7) Public records or reports. Evidence that a writing authorized by law to be recorded or filed and in fact recorded or filed in a public office, or a purported public record, report, statement, or data compilation, in any form, is from the public office where items of this nature are kept.

(8) Ancient documents or data compilation. Evidence that a document or data compilation, in any form, (A) is in such condition as to create no suspicion concerning its authenticity (B) was in a place where it, if authentic, would likely be, and (C) has been in existence 20 years or more at the time it is offered.

(9) Process or system. Evidence describing a process or system used to produce a result and showing that the process or system produces an accurate result.

(10) Methods provided by statute or rule. (Gardner and Anderson, 2010; Harr et al., 2011; Samaha, 2012)

Best Evidence Rule

The best evidence rule applies when a party wants to admit as evidence the contents of a document at trial, but the original document is not available. In this case, the party must provide an acceptable excuse for its absence. If the document itself is not available and the court finds the excuse provided acceptable, then the party is allowed to use secondary evidence to prove the contents of the document and have it as admissible evidence. The best evidence rule only applies when a party seeks to prove the contents of the document sought to be admitted as evidence (Gardner and Anderson, 2010; Harr et al., 2011; Samaha, 2012).

The Fourth Amendment protects against the search and seizure of these types of evidence if the defendant has a reasonable expectation of privacy in the place searched. If the Fourth Amendment applies, the usual preference for warrants applies as do the usual exceptions. Offices of employees can be places where individuals claim a reasonable expectation of privacy exists. However, in *O'Connor v. Ortega*, 480 U.S. 709 (1987), the Supreme Court has ruled that a public employee's office may generally be searched without a warrant (Gardner and Anderson, 2010; Harr et al., 2011; Samaha, 2012).

Scientific Evidence

Scientific evidence is becoming increasingly important in law enforcement and has resulted in helping to solve many cold cases. DNA and other forms of testing have not only helped locate perpetrators but have also cleared innocent people. The two key issues are (1) the validity of the theory and scientific techniques underlying the evidence and (2) the procedures utilized to gather and test the evidence in the particular case (Gardner and Anderson, 2010; Harr et al., 2011; Samaha, 2012).

Frye Test and *Daubert* Test

For many years, the test in federal and many state courts for admissibility of expert testimony was derived from the federal court of appeals decision in the *Frye* case. This was known as the "general acceptance test." The testimony was admissible if the underlying scientific principles were generally accepted in that field of science. Beginning in the 1980s, additions were made to the *Frye* test. Under the *Frye*-plus test, in addition to general acceptance, the actual procedures and testing used also had to be generally accepted (Gardner and Anderson, 2010; Harr et al., 2011; Samaha, 2012).

In 1993, in *Daubert v. Merrill-Dow Pharmaceuticals Co.*, the Supreme Court rejected the *Frye* (general acceptance) test in federal courts and held that the proper test was found in Rule 702 of the Federal Rules of Evidence. In *Daubert*, interpreting Rule 702, the court set forth a nonexclusive checklist for trial judges to use in assessing the reliability of proposed scientific testimony. The specific factors enunciated were (1) whether the expert witness's theory or technique could be or has been tested—that is, whether the theory can be challenged in some objective fashion or whether it is simply a subjective, conclusory assertion that could not reasonably be assessed for reliability; (2) whether the theory or technique has been subjected to publication and peer review; (3) the potential or known rate of error of the theory or technique when applied; (4) the existence and maintenance of controls and standards; and (5) whether the theory or technique has achieved general acceptance in the scientific community. In the *Kumho Tire* case, the Supreme Court held that this same test applied to technical evidence (engineer's testimony about a tire failure) (Gardner and Anderson, 2010; Harr et al., 2011; Samaha, 2012).

Federal Rule of Evidence 702 ("Testimony by Experts") incorporates the *Daubert* standard: if scientific, technical, or other specialized knowledge will assist the trier of fact to understand the evidence or to determine a fact in issue, a witness qualified as an expert by knowledge, skill, experience, training, or education may testify thereto in the form of an opinion or, otherwise, if (1) the testimony is based upon sufficient facts or data, (2) the testimony is the product of reliable principles and methods, and (3) the witness has applied the principles and methods reliably to the facts of the case.

Although *Daubert* and Rule 702 are applicable only in federal courts, many states use parts of this test but have not adopted the complete test. The general result of *Daubert* has been for courts to become more cautious in many types of cases. Once a scientific theory or technique has been accepted by higher courts, trial courts can take judicial notice of the validity of the underlying theory (Gardner and Anderson, 2010; Harr et al, 2011; Samaha, 2012).

Ballistic Evidence

Ballistic or firearm fingerprinting evidence for identification is crucial, as 40 percent of all criminal homicides are unsolved. Matching bullet fragments to a certain weapon is difficult to do. However, a shell casing with "tool marks" can often be linked to a specific gun (e.g., *U.S. v. Monteiro*, D. Mass., 2006) (Gardner and Anderson, 2010; Harr et al., 2011; Samaha, 2012).

DNA Evidence

Although scientific evidence from a multitude of fields is used in courts, probably no recently discovered scientific technique has had the impact of DNA testing or profiling. All courts have accepted the theory of DNA evidence, and defense attacks usually center on chain of custody, contamination, and faulty procedures in testing. Where DNA evidence is available, it is still subject to the burden of proof requirements. The FBI and many jurisdictions have set up DNA databases. Statutes requiring that convicted felons provide blood samples for DNA databases have been upheld by the courts (Gardner and Anderson, 2010; Harr et al., 2011; Samaha, 2012).

Criminal Procedure

Introduction

In criminal procedure, both formal decision making according to written rules and informal discretionary decision making according to judgments based on official training and experience play a crucial rule. Each step in the criminal process, from investigating crimes to appealing convictions, involves decisions. Each step requires a criminal justice professional to decide whether or not to start, continue, or end the criminal process. Both formal rules and discretionary judgment inform these decisions. The criminal process in practice is a blend of the formal law of criminal procedure and informal influences that enter the process by way of discretion. Discretion and law complement each other in promoting and balancing the interests in criminal procedure (Gardner and Anderson, 2010; Harr et al., 2011; Samaha, 2012).

In the U.S. criminal justice system, government officials must back up with facts every officially triggered restraint on the rights of individuals to come and go as they please (objective basis requirement). The greater the restrictions placed on an individual, the more facts required to back up the official action. For example, probable cause is needed to arrest a person, but proof beyond a reasonable doubt is needed to convict (Gardner and Anderson, 2010; Harr et al., 2011; Samaha, 2012).

Most of the cases involve "guilty" defendants who want to take advantage of the trump card of fair procedures, the exclusionary rule, which requires courts to throw out "good" evidence if the government used "bad" methods to obtain it. "Good" evidence refers to evidence that will prove the defendant's guilt if admitted. "Bad" methods refer to violations of criminal suspects' and defendants' rights guaranteed by the criminal procedure provisions in the U.S. Constitution's Bill of Rights (Gardner and Anderson, 2010; Harr et al., 2011; Samaha, 2012).

You will notice that court opinions refer to past cases to support their reasoning and their decisions. This reliance on prior cases (precedent) is part of how lawyers think. Related to reliance on precedent is the doctrine of stare decisis, which requires courts to follow prior precedent in their decisions (Gardner and Anderson, 2010; Harr et al., 2011; Samaha, 2012).

Criminal Procedure and the Constitution

The law of criminal procedure consists of the rules the government must abide by to detect and investigate crime, prosecute and convict defendants, and punish convicted offenders. The final authority of criminal procedure lies in the U.S. Constitution, especially in the Bill of Rights. Most of the criminal procedure provisions are found in the Fourth, Fifth, Sixth, Eighth, and Fourteenth Amendments. The Constitution and these rights are supreme, making the Constitution the final word in matters involving criminal procedure. According to the principle of judicial review, courts are tasked with the job of interpreting the meaning of the Constitution. The U.S. Supreme Court's decisions bind the lower courts, legislatures, and executives. However, the Supreme Court depends on the lower federal courts, state courts, prosecutors, and law enforcement officials to apply its decisions in the day-to-day operation of the criminal justice system (Gardner and Anderson, 2010; Harr et al., 2011; Samaha, 2012).

Every state constitution guarantees its citizens parallel criminal procedure rights, like the right against self-incrimination and against unreasonable searches and seizures. State courts are a source of criminal procedure law in two types of cases: (1) those involving the U.S. Constitution that the U.S. Supreme Court has not decided yet and (2) those involving their own state constitutions. State courts are the final authority in cases based on their own state constitutions and statutes. State criminal procedure rights might be broader than federal rights, but they cannot fall below the federal minimum standard defined by the U.S. Supreme Court (Gardner and Anderson, 2010; Harr et al., 2011; Samaha, 2012).

From the adoption of the Bill of Rights until the 1960s, the rights afforded to criminal defendants applied only in the federal criminal justice system. The U.S. Supreme Court, in a series of decisions in the 1960s called the "due process revolution," expanded the meaning of these rights within the federal system and ruled that most of these expanded rights also applied in state and local criminal justice matters (Gardner and Anderson, 2010; Harr et al., 2011; Samaha, 2012).

The Supreme Court has relied on two Civil War Amendment guarantees to accomplish its revolution: the due process and equal protection clauses of the Fourteenth Amendment. After a decades-long struggle within the court, a majority have come to agree that "due process" requires the incorporation of the specific criminal procedure provisions in the U.S. Bill of Rights. The court has incorporated all but four of the protections found in the Bill of Rights that are afforded persons accused of crimes: public trial, notice of charges, prohibition of excessive bail, and prosecution by indictment. Since the 1960s, the court has implied in several decisions that the Fourteenth Amendment incorporates all of the Bill of Rights except for indictment by a grand jury (Gardner and Anderson, 2010; Harr et al., 2011; Samaha, 2012).

Defining Search and Seizure

Crime control depends on information, but that information usually comes from reluctant sources. As long as officers can see and hear information that is also available to the general public, they may use it without running afoul of the Fourth Amendment. The Fourth Amendment enters the picture when officials rely on involuntary methods to gather information: searches and seizures, interrogation, and identification procedures (Gardner and Anderson, 2010; Harr et al., 2011; Samaha, 2012).

The Fourth Amendment analysis follows three steps based on answering three questions in the following order:

1. Was the law enforcement action a "search" or a "seizure"? If it was not, the Fourth Amendment is not involved at all, and the analysis ends.

2. If the action was a search or a seizure, was it reasonable? If it was, the inquiry ends because the Fourth Amendment bans only unreasonable searches and seizures.

3. If the action was an unreasonable search, does the Fourth Amendment ban its use as evidence?

The Fourth Amendment is aimed at limiting government authority to infringe on the liberty of people to come and go as they wish and to protect their right to be left alone by the government. The Fourth Amendment balances the government's power to control crime and the right of people to be left alone by banning only unreasonable searches and seizures. Also, it applies only to government actions, not to the actions of private individuals (Gardner and Anderson, 2010; Harr et al., 2011; Samaha, 2012).

If government actions do not invade a reasonable expectation of privacy, the Fourth Amendment does not apply to the actions. They are left to the discretionary judgments of individual officers based on their training and experience in the field (Gardner and Anderson, 2010; Harr et al., 2011; Samaha, 2012).

In its decision, *Katz v. U.S.*, 389 U.S. 347 (1967), the Supreme Court adopted the "privacy doctrine," which held that "the Fourth Amendment protects people, not places," and created a two-pronged test for analyzing the defendant's expectations of privacy: did he or she actually have an expectation of privacy, and was it objectively reasonable? (Gardner and Anderson, 2010; Harr et al., 2011; Samaha, 2012)

Since the *Katz* decision, the court has addressed the reasonable expectation of privacy issue in a number of significant cases involving such things as bank records, electronic surveillance, the use of thermal imagers, numbers dialed from a home telephone, and abandoned trash left on the curb for collection. The court has also ruled that the Fourth Amendment does not apply to discoveries of evidence in plain view, in public places, in open fields, or on abandoned property (Gardner and Anderson, 2010; Harr et al., 2011; Samaha, 2012).

People are not "seized" any time officers approach them and ask questions. According to U.S. Supreme Court's decisions, they are seized when they are either physically detained (actual seizures) or submit to an officer's display of authority. The court has also held that a Fourth Amendment seizure occurs only when, considering all the circumstances, a reasonable person will believe they are not free to leave (Gardner and Anderson, 2010; Harr et al., 2011; Samaha, 2012).

Stop and Frisk

The Fourth Amendment consists of two parts: the reasonableness clause, which applies to all searches and arrests, and the warrant clause, which applies only to searches and arrests based on warrants. Reasonableness is a broad standard and consists of two elements, a balancing element and an objective basis requirement, both of which are determined on a case-by-case evaluation of the totality of circumstances (Gardner and Anderson, 2010; Harr et al., 2011; Samaha, 2012).

Fourth Amendment stops are brief encounters, so law enforcement officials can "freeze" suspicious people and situations to investigate them. In Fourth Amendment frisks, officers protect themselves by conducting pat-down searches of a person's outer clothing, looking for weapons. Stops and frisks generally take place in public places and are less invasive than arrests and searches. They also affect many more people than arrests and searches and raise important policy issues because officers inevitably stop people who have not violated the law and frisk people who are not armed (Gardner and Anderson, 2010; Harr et al., 2011; Samaha, 2012).

Terry v. Ohio, 392 U.S. 1 (1968), has established the framework for stop-and-frisk analysis that continues to the present day. First, in balancing crime control and individual freedom and privacy, the need to control crime must outweigh the invasion of an individual's rights. Second, officers can only stop and frisk suspects based on reasonable suspicion. Hunches, whims, or mere suspicion is insufficient under the Fourth Amendment. Third, officers can protect themselves by frisking people they stop if they have reasonable suspicion that the person presents a danger to them (Gardner and Anderson, 2010; Harr et al., 2011; Samaha, 2012).

Fourth Amendment stops are reasonable if the totality of circumstances, or the whole picture, leads officers to suspect recent or present criminal activity in the case at hand. Officers must be able to articulate the facts that show that criminal activity is happening or about to happen. The whole picture can include direct and/or hearsay information; individualized and/or categorical suspicion, which arises because suspects are a part of a category of people; and actuarial information. People are more likely to be stopped in a high-crime area. Race, ethnicity, unprovoked flight from the police, and drug courier profiles can be part of the totality of circumstances that police can rely on to establish reasonable suspicion but in and of themselves are not sufficient (Gardner and Anderson, 2010; Harr et al., 2011; Samaha, 2012).

Fourth Amendment stops are reasonable in scope if they are brief, on-the-spot detentions, during which time officers question the stopped individuals in order to decide quickly whether to arrest or free the suspects. Fourth Amendment frisks are reasonable if the government interest in protecting law enforcement officers outweighs the individual's privacy right not to be touched by an officer. The elements of a reasonable frisk include the officer lawfully stopping an individual before she frisks him, the officer reasonably suspecting that the person stopped is armed, and the officer limiting her action to a once-over-lightly pat down of the outer clothing to detect weapons only.

Special situation stops and frisks require reasonably balancing special interests. The hundreds of millions of traffic stops every year have to balance officer safety against driver and passenger liberty and privacy. Officers are permitted to demand the driver of a vehicle to get out of a car when the officer lawfully stops a vehicle, even without suspicion that the driver is armed. So also can officers order passengers of a lawfully stopped vehicle out of a car, even without suspicion of wrongdoing, and frisk them if reasonable suspicion develops that a passenger is dangerous (Gardner and Anderson, 2010; Harr et al., 2011; Samaha, 2012).

International border detentions balance the interest in controlling who and what enters and leaves the country against the privacy and liberty interests of U.S. citizens and noncitizens. The expectation of privacy is diminished at the border. The Supreme Court has held that the detention of a traveler at the border, beyond a routine search, is justified if officers, considering all the facts, reasonably suspects the person is smuggling contraband, even if the detention lasts sixteen hours and involves a person smuggling drugs in her alimentary canal (Gardner and Anderson, 2010; Harr et al., 2011; Samaha, 2012).

Roadblocks balance the interest in apprehending specific fleeing suspects against the privacy and liberty interests of innocent people who have been stopped. Checkpoints balance the interest in preventing drunk driving and apprehending drunk drivers. Inspections such as roadblocks can be conducted without individualized suspicion as long as they include all vehicles or all vehicles of a specific type (Gardner and Anderson, 2010; Harr et al., 2011; Samaha, 2012).

Seizure of Persons: Arrest

Arrests are a vital tool that can help law enforcement officers catch the guilty and free the innocent. But arrests have to satisfy the reasonableness requirement of the Fourth Amendment. Arrests are Fourth Amendment seizures but are more invasive than stops. Arrests can last longer, result in being taken to the police station, and are recorded. To satisfy the Fourth Amendment's reasonableness requirement, arrests require both probable cause before and a reasonable execution during and after arrest (Gardner and Anderson, 2010; Harr et al., 2011; Samaha, 2012).

The probable cause requirement balances the societal interest in crime control and the individual right to free movement. Law enforcement officials must have enough facts to believe a crime has been or is about to be committed and that the person arrested has committed, is committing, or is about to commit the crime. Probable cause is more than the reasonable suspicion needed to affect a stop but less than proof beyond a reasonable doubt required to convict. Police apply the probable cause requirement on the streets, having to make quick decisions. Judges have the final say on whether officers had probable cause to arrest (Gardner and Anderson, 2010; Harr et al., 2011; Samaha, 2012).

Officers can use both direct information and hearsay to build probable cause. Direct information includes such things as what officers see, hear, and smell, as well as fingerprints, DNA evidence, resisting an officer, and fleeing the scene. Hearsay is gathered from victims, witnesses, other officers, and informants. Hearsay from an informant can be used to build probable cause if it is corroborated by an officer's direct observations (Gardner and Anderson, 2010; Harr et al., 2011; Samaha, 2012).

Most arrests based on probable cause are reasonable without warrants. Officers, however, often procure warrants in order to have a judge approve the lawfulness of the arrest before it occurs. If officers need a warrant or want one, the Fourth Amendment requires that 1) the warrant be issued by a neutral magistrate, 2) a sworn affidavit accompany the request for a warrant that backs up the facts and circumstances that build probable cause, 3) the warrant identify specifically the person to be arrested. Arrest warrants are required to enter homes to arrest unless exigent circumstances exist. The most common exigent circumstances include hot pursuit, need to protect officers, prevention of the destruction of evidence, and prevention of the escape of suspects (Gardner and Anderson, 2010; Harr et al., 2011; Samaha, 2012).

In *Tennessee v. Garner*, 471 U.S. 1 (1985), the court has ruled that use of deadly force to seize a suspect is subject to the Fourth Amendment's reasonableness requirement, which requires probable cause. The court has also ruled that using deadly force to prevent the escape of a fleeing felon is unreasonable unless the suspect is an immediate threat to the officer or others. In *Graham v. Connor*, the court has ruled that the use of nondeadly force to arrest a suspect is also a Fourth Amendment seizure and that, during and after arrests, officers can use only the amount of force that is objectively reasonable to get and maintain control of suspects they have probable cause to arrest. Under this standard, the Supreme Court has stated that "an officer's evil intentions will not make a Fourth Amendment violation out of an objectively reasonable use of force; nor will an officer's good intentions make an objectively unreasonable use of force constitutional." Furthermore, reasonableness is determined at the moment of the use of force. Not every push or shove, even if it may later seem unnecessary in the peace of a judge's chambers, violates the Fourth Amendment (Gardner and Anderson, 2010; Harr et al., 2011; Samaha, 2012).

After an arrest, felony suspects usually are taken to the police station for booking, photographing, and possible interrogation and identification procedures; misdemeanor suspects usually are issued a citation and not arrested. The Supreme Court has ruled that it is constitutionally reasonable, but not necessarily wise, for officers to make full custodial arrests for fine-only offenses (Gardner and Anderson, 2010; Harr et al., 2011; Samaha, 2012).

Searches for Evidence

Crime control cannot survive without searches, but the power to search comes at a price. The Fourth Amendment does not prohibit all searches, only "unreasonable" searches. To comply with the Fourth Amendment, search warrants have to include a detailed description of the place to be searched and the things to be seized (the particularity requirement) and an affidavit describing the evidence to support the claim that the items named in the warrant will be found in the place to be searched, establishing probable cause (Gardner and Anderson, 2010; Harr et al., 2011; Samaha, 2012).

With important exceptions, when executing warrants to search homes, officers have to "knock and announce" their presence before entering. Exceptions to the "knock and announce" rule include circumstances in which officers need to enter unannounced in order to prevent violence, the destruction of evidence, or the escape of suspects. Officers must wait a reasonable amount of time after announcing their presence to break and enter in the event the occupants refuse to allow them in (Gardner and Anderson, 2010; Harr et al., 2011; Samaha, 2012).

Most searches do not require warrants in order to be reasonable. Some searches require neither warrants nor probable cause. Searches incident to lawful arrests based on probable cause are considered reasonable without warrants because they protect officers, prevent suspects from escaping, and preserve evidence. They include searches of arrested persons and the immediate area within their control—"grabbable area." The "grabbable area" includes the passenger compartment of vehicles that suspects occupied when they have been arrested. The motive of the arresting officer is irrelevant so long as probable cause supports the arrest. Police may also search the containers within the passenger compartment. Searches incident to arrest include the time before, during, and after the arrest (Gardner and Anderson, 2010; Harr et al., 2011; Samaha, 2012).

According to *U.S. v. Robinson*, 414 U.S. 218 (1973), officers can always search anyone they have authority to take into custody, even incident to a misdemeanor arrest. Police, however, do not have the automatic right to search incident to issuing a citation. Pretextual traffic arrests are a powerful, but criticized, investigative tool in the war on drugs; however, the Supreme Court has held that if police officers have probable cause to stop a motorist for a traffic violation and probable cause develops for an arrest, it is not relevant that the initial traffic stop is a pretext (Gardner and Anderson, 2010; Harr et al., 2011; Samaha, 2012).

Consent searches require neither warrants nor probable cause, allowing officers to search where they cannot otherwise do so. The government has to prove that consent is voluntary; consenting persons can withdraw their consent at any time if they can demonstrate their clear intent to stop the search. The scope of the consent depends on whether the officer reasonably believes the person has consented to the scope of the search. Third-party consents are lawful so long as an officer reasonably believes the third person has the authority to consent. Courts look at the totality of circumstances in analyzing whether consent is voluntary (Gardner and Anderson, 2010; Harr et al., 2011; Samaha, 2012).

Searches of vehicles without warrants are reasonable under the Fourth Amendment because vehicles are mobile, and people have a reduced expectation of privacy in their vehicles. Searches of containers in vehicles without warrants are "reasonable" as long as police officers have probable cause to search the vehicle. Officers can also search "containers" attached to people (such as wallets, pockets of clothing, or purses) if they have probable cause to search the vehicle and if the "containers" are capable of concealing the object of the search (Gardner and Anderson, 2010; Harr et al., 2011; Samaha, 2012).

Emergency searches (exigent searches) are based on the idea that it is sometimes impractical to require officers to obtain warrants before they search. Emergency searches can be conducted without a warrant if officers have probable cause to search and a reasonable belief that what they are searching for is about to be destroyed, they are in hot pursuit of a fleeing suspect and must follow him or her into a house without a warrant, or they believe the suspect is violent and dangerous (Gardner and Anderson, 2010; Harr et al., 2011; Samaha, 2012).

Special Needs Searches

Special needs searches are directed at people generally because of a public need, such as public protection. Since they are not the result of individualized suspicion, objective basis like routine procedure are required, while warrants and probable cause are not necessary. Though the procedure is routine, criminal prosecution still results where evidence of a crime is discovered. Frisks are intended to protect officers but also turn up evidence and result in convictions. A special needs search is reasonable when a court finds the government need is more important than the privacy loss that results (Gardner and Anderson, 2010; Harr et al., 2011; Samaha, 2012).

Courts find that inventory searches by law enforcement, when routine, meet a variety of needed public protections, ranging from protecting private property from theft to protection of law enforcement from wrongful blame. When an individual is in custody, the need for security and discipline increases, while the expectation of privacy decreases. Courts maintain that very few privacy rights are retained by prisoners but that they are not lost altogether. DNA databases demonstrate how public need outweighs a prisoner's reduced privacy rights (Gardner and Anderson, 2010; Harr et al., 2011; Samaha, 2012).

Self-Incrimination

Confessions acknowledge guilt, and as such, they are uniquely powerful evidence. Incriminating statements fall short of full confessions. Confessions are made to friends and family, during interrogation, in guilty pleas, and during sentencing in the form of apologies (Gardner and Anderson, 2010; Harr et al., 2011; Samaha, 2012).

Interrogation in the accusatory phase is performed in an intentionally intimidating setting conducive to self-incrimination. Interrogation is an essential tool for crime control. Police will not be able to solve many crimes without confessions. Criminals will not confess if the police cannot interrogate them. As Inbau pointed out, police must use "less than refined" methods when they interrogate suspects. Still, courts warn that the same atmosphere that breaks a criminal's will to lie may break an innocent person's will to adhere to the truth. As Chief Justice Earl Warren has noted, because police interrogations occur in private, our knowledge of what happens in the interrogation room is limited (Gardner and Anderson, 2010; Harr et al., 2011; Samaha, 2012).

The right to remain silent in the face of accusations is an ancient right recognized throughout history. The right is protected by several amendments of the U.S. Constitution. Protections of the Fifth and Fourteenth Amendments apply to all stages of the criminal process, the Sixth Amendment after formal charges are brought, and the Fifth Amendment in custodial interrogation and thereafter (Gardner and Anderson, 2010; Harr et al., 2011; Samaha, 2012).

Courts have adopted different approaches to police interrogation and confessions based on the different constitutional provisions. The influence of these three approaches—due process, right to counsel, and self-incrimination—overlaps in history (Gardner and Anderson, 2010; Harr et al., 2011; Samaha, 2012).

The due process approach requires that confessions be voluntary because involuntary confessions are unreliable. Even if they are truthful, forced confessions violate due process because, in our accusatory system of justice, the government has the burden of proving guilt beyond a reasonable doubt. Finally, courts have reasoned that coerced confessions are not the product of a free will. Under the right-to-counsel approach, involuntary confessions occur during a critical stage, and the suspect's Sixth Amendment right to an attorney is triggered. Finally, in *Miranda v. Arizona*, 348 U.S. 436 (1966), the Supreme Court has applied the Fifth Amendment self-incrimination clause to confessions that occur during custodial interrogation. The Fifth Amendment prevents law enforcement from compelling people to make self-incriminating statements, the Sixth Amendment ensures the right to counsel, and the Fourteenth Amendment guarantees due process (Gardner and Anderson, 2010; Harr et al., 2011; Samaha, 2012).

Compulsion, incrimination, and testimony are all required to prove a violation of Fifth Amendment rights in a criminal case. The Supreme Court has noted in *Miranda* that custodial interrogation is inherently coercive. The "bright line" of *Miranda v. Arizona* defines custodial interrogation. In custodial interrogation, suspects are held against their will. In *Miranda*, the court has rejected the "totality of circumstances" test on a case-by-case basis and instead required that a specific police warning be given in every case at the time suspects are taken into custody. *Custody* is defined as depriving an individual of freedom of action in any significant way. *Miranda* targets interrogation that occurs in coercive atmospheres. The court has ruled that police are not required to give *Miranda* warnings to persons detained in a traffic stop (Gardner and Anderson, 2010; Harr et al., 2011; Samaha, 2012).

The Fifth Amendment protection against being compelled to "witness" against oneself applies to forced testimony but not personal paperwork, weapons, hair samples, blood samples used for alcohol testing, and more. Under the public safety exception, police are not required to give *Miranda* warnings if giving them before questioning a suspect will put the officers or someone else in danger.

The Fifth Amendment's self-incrimination clause prohibits custodial interrogation that is not direct questioning but is subtle coercion that acts as the functional equivalent of a question. The Sixth Amendment's right-to-counsel clause, which is triggered after formal charges have been filed, prohibits officers from "deliberately eliciting a response" (Gardner and Anderson, 2010; Harr et al., 2011; Samaha, 2012).

A waiver of Fifth Amendment and some other rights can be implied, given the totality of circumstances such as age, intelligence, mental condition, education, etc., that indicate the suspect knows his or her rights and wishes to waive them. The Supreme Court has ruled that criminal suspects who want to protect their right to remain silent must speak up and unambiguously invoke it. The court has also ruled that coercive police activity is required for a finding that a confession is not voluntary under the Fourteenth Amendment's due process clause. Voluntary false confessions are not a theoretical risk but a proven fact. Reforms aimed at reducing false confessions focus on police using video records, limiting a suspect's time in custody, and restricting the use of false information intended to elicit confessions (Gardner and Anderson, 2010; Harr et al., 2011; Samaha, 2012).

Identification

For violent crimes committed by strangers, eyewitness identification is the most widely used, and often the only, way to identify a perpetrator and prove his or her guilt. In a lineup, witnesses try to pick the suspect out of a group of individuals who are present. In a show-up, witnesses match the suspect with one person, who is either present or pictured in a "mug shot" (Gardner and Anderson, 2010; Harr et al., 2011; Samaha, 2012).

Courts took a "hands off" approach to identification evidence and its admissibility until 1967. In *U.S. v. Wade*, 388 U.S. 218 (1967), the court held that a lineup after an indictment without counsel violated a defendant's Sixth Amendment rights. In *Stovall v. Denno*, 388 U.S. 293 (1967), the court held that due process was a basis for challenging identification testimony. In *Manson v. Brathwaite*, 432 U.S. 98 (1977), the court made clear that defendants who challenged an identification procedure must prove by a preponderance of the evidence that, under the totality of circumstances, the identification procedure was unnecessarily suggestive and created a substantial likelihood of misidentification. Five factors in the totality of circumstances should be considered: (1) a witness's opportunity to view the suspect, (2) a witness's degree of attention at the time of the crime, (3) a witness's accuracy of description of the suspect prior to identifying them, (4) a witness's certainty about their identification, (5) the length of time between the crime and the identification. Eyewitness identifications are almost never rejected (Gardner and Anderson, 2010; Harr et al., 2011; Samaha, 2012).

Scientists who study memory refute common assumptions about how memory functions and under what circumstances it is likely

DR. JEFFREY C. FOX

to be reliable. When memories are acquired, the brain does not act as a video recorder storing a stream of images. Observational accuracy is affected by how long the witness observed the perpetrator, distractions during the observation, the focus of the observation, stress during the event, and the race of the witness and the perpetrator. Retrieval blends information from the original experience with information added during the retention period. Eyewitness identification is subject to errors of omission (failure to recall) and errors of commission (incorrect recall) (Gardner and Anderson, 2010; Harr et al., 2011; Samaha, 2012).

Suggestion is particularly powerful during the retention and recollection phase. Research finds that witnesses add to a story based on what information researchers give them. People are not good at keeping memories acquired during an incident separate from suggestions that occur thereafter. Identification research uses both new experiments and archival data. Experimental research is subject to concern about whether volunteers are good representatives of average real-world witnesses under stress (Gardner and Anderson, 2010; Harr et al., 2011; Samaha, 2012).

Eyewitness retrospective self-reports are the basis of identification testimony. The social desirability of the response, the need to appear consistent, and reinterpretation of past events due to new events all affect such reports (Gardner and Anderson, 2010; Harr et al., 2011; Samaha, 2012).

The composition of the lineup and the instructions given to witnesses prior to the lineup tend to influence identifications. Instructions that seem reasonable are often more suggestive than we realize. Show-ups are substantially less reliable than lineups. Courts admit show-up identifications even if a witness runs into a suspect in the courthouse, a witness sees police pursuing the suspect, and under other potentially misleading situations (Gardner and Anderson, 2010; Harr et al., 2011; Samaha, 2012). Research shows our reported opportunity to view a culprit varies widely from our actual opportunity to do so. The amount of time spent observing a culprit is less important than what the witness did with the time and where they focused their attention.

Suggestions for reforming identification procedures include using nonsuspect fillers that minimize suggestiveness toward the suspect, using a double-blind procedure, instructing eyewitnesses that the real perpetrator may or may not be present, presenting the suspect and fillers sequentially, assessing eyewitness confidence immediately after the identification, and avoiding multiple identification procedures where the witness views the same suspect more than once. Legal experts suggest that courts implement a per se rule excluding all evidence based on suggestive procedures, loosen the standards for admitting testimony on human perception and memory, require corroboration of eyewitness identification in certain situations, and mandate that police use such reforms as sequential lineups (Gardner and Anderson, 2010; Harr et al., 2011; Samaha, 2012).

DNA is some of the most powerful evidence imaginable, and one of the most important criminal law issues of our day is whether there is a postconviction constitutional right to access DNA evidence for the purpose of exonerating sentenced convicts.

The Exclusionary Rule

The exclusionary rule has been created by the U.S. Supreme Court to enforce constitutional rights. It is not in itself a right. The Bill of Rights does not explain the remedies that judges should use when someone's rights are violated. The term "bad methods" refers to police actions and procedures that violate Fourth, Fifth, Sixth, and Fourteenth Amendment rights. The term "good evidence" is not meant to imply that the evidence has been collected using good methods, only that the evidence is probative of a defendant's guilt. The fruit-of-the-poisonous-tree doctrine excludes evidence indirectly associated with an illegal government action. The premise is that courts should ensure the government is never better off after violating the Constitution than it was before it did so (Gardner and Anderson, 2010; Harr et al., 2011; Samaha, 2012).

Until the twentieth century, the only remedies for constitutional violations were private lawsuits. In 1914, the Supreme Court created the exclusionary rule but applied it only to federal law enforcement. The Supreme Court established that unreasonable searches and seizures performed by state officials violated the due process clause of the Fourteenth Amendment in 1949, and finally applied the exclusionary rule to the actions of state officers in *Mapp v. Ohio* (1961) (Gardner and Anderson, 2010; Harr et al., 2011; Samaha, 2012).

The Supreme Court has articulated several justifications for the exclusionary rule, including arguments that it is based on constitutional rights, it is necessary to preserve judicial integrity, and it is the most effective way to deter officers from breaking the laws. Since the 1980s, the court has relied on the deterrence justification. There are six major exceptions to the exclusionary rule: (1) collateral use (nontrial proceedings such as bail and grand jury hearings), (2) impeachment during cross-examination, (3) the attenuation doctrine, (4) the independent source doctrine, (5) the inevitable discovery doctrine, and (6) the good faith exception (Gardner and Anderson, 2010; Harr et al., 2011; Samaha, 2012).

The exclusionary rule has social costs, and courts seek to mitigate them by defining exceptions. It is difficult to measure what deterrent effect, if any, the exclusionary rule has had on law officers breaking the law to obtain evidence. It is easier to quantify the social impact on successful prosecution. Many professionals agree the exclusionary rule is rarely used and, when it is, does not often involve crimes against persons (Gardner and Anderson, 2010; Harr et al., 2011; Samaha, 2012).

Entrapment

Entrapment occurs when agents get people to commit crimes they won't otherwise commit. The entrapment defense seeks to regulate enforcement tactics by taking criminal disposition into account when assessing guilt. For most of our history, courts have not recognized the entrapment defense. The entrapment defense is not provided by constitutional right. It is an affirmative defense, created and defined by statutes and courts (Gardner and Anderson, 2010; Harr et al., 2011; Samaha, 2012).

Encouragement is likely to result when law enforcement officers pretend they are victims, intentionally entice suspects to commit crime, communicate the enticement to suspects, or influence the decision to commit crimes. Not all encouragement is entrapment. The practice of entrapment arises primarily because it is difficult to detect consensual crimes like drug offenses, gambling, pornography, and prostitution (Gardner and Anderson, 2010; Harr et al., 2011; Samaha, 2012).

The subjective test of entrapment, which is the test in the majority of jurisdictions, prevents conviction in cases where a defendant has had no prior desire to commit the crime and government encouragement has caused the defendant to commit it. The objective test (adopted by a growing minority of courts) does not focus on the predisposition of an individual but on whether the government actions will have caused a hypothetical "reasonable person" to commit the crime in question (Gardner and Anderson, 2010; Harr et al., 2011; Samaha, 2012).

Pretrial Matters

Prosecutor's Decision to Charge

Police officers bring a case to the prosecutor, who then takes over and decides if the case is to be prosecuted. Prosecutors may decide not to prosecute if they think the evidence is weak and they cannot prove the case or if, as "officers of the court," they feel prosecution will not do justice. Prosecutors can also divert cases before a judicial proceeding begins on the condition that the defendant completes certain programs. Selective prosecution is a necessity because resources are limited. The prosecutor's power to charge gives him or her enormous power over peoples' lives and their liberty (Gardner and Anderson, 2010; Harr et al., 2011; Samaha, 2012).

Probable Cause to Detain Suspects

When suspects are arrested without a warrant, magistrates must determine if probable cause exists to detain them. Probable cause to detain a suspect is decided at the suspect's first appearance (probable cause) hearing. In *County of Riverside v. McLaughlin*, the Supreme Court has ruled that a judge's determination that there is probable cause to detain a suspect must happen within forty-eight hours of arrest. If the first appearance does not happen within forty-eight hours, the government must provide evidence of an extraordinary circumstance that caused the delay (Gardner and Anderson, 2010; Harr et al., 2011; Samaha, 2012).

At the first appearance, judges also inform defendants of the charges and their constitutional rights, set bail, and appoint attorneys for those who are indigent. Felony defendants generally do not enter a plea at this time. However, misdemeanor defendants usually enter a plea at first appearance. At an arraignment, felony defendants are required to appear in court to enter a plea (Gardner and Anderson, 2010; Harr et al., 2011; Samaha, 2012).

Bail and Pretrial Detention

Most defendants are released from jail prior to trial. Those who are not released often spend significant amounts of time in jail at considerable public expense. Judges rely on a number of ways to release defendants. Pretrial release and bail take a variety of forms, such as citation release, release on recognizance, and release on money bonds. There is no constitutional right to bail. The Eighth Amendment only prohibits excessive bail. What is excessive is the subject of interpretation. How much bail is excessive is determined by the severity of the offense and the suspect's ability to pay. Constitutional rights that affect bail include due process because being in jail can prevent suspects from preparing a defense and equal protection because being poor can affect whether a suspect is freed (Gardner and Anderson, 2010; Harr et al., 2011; Samaha, 2012).

Right to Counsel

The right to retained (paid) counsel was extended to appointed (free) counsel in state court trials in certain limited circumstances in the 1930s. The right was then extended to all defendants facing federal criminal trials, regardless of their circumstances. Not until 1963, in *Gideon v. Wainwright*, did the Supreme Court rule that all defendants who could not afford to retain counsel, including those in state court proceedings, have a Sixth Amendment right to have counsel appointed. Today most large counties retain public defenders, paid by the public to defend indigent defendants (Gardner and Anderson, 2010; Harr et al., 2011; Samaha, 2012).

The right to counsel attaches to all critical stages of the criminal process, including custodial interrogation, lineups after formal charges, grand jury appearances, and arraignments. The right is not attached to investigative stops, frisks, and first appearances at trial. The right to appointed counsel applies to poor defendants where conviction will result in actual incarceration, even if they face only misdemeanor charges (Gardner and Anderson, 2010; Harr et al., 2011; Samaha, 2012).

Courts uphold the right to effective counsel under the older "mockery of justice" standard or the more modern and common "reasonably competent attorney" standard. This modern standard requires defendants who claim on appeal that they have ineffective representation to prove both that their attorneys' performance is not reasonably competent and that the incompetence is probably responsible for their conviction (Gardner and Anderson, 2010; Harr et al., 2011; Samaha, 2012).

Preliminary Hearing

Preliminary hearings (based on a criminal information drawn up by prosecutors) and grand jury reviews (based on a prosecutor's indictment) test the government's case against the defendant. These hearings have relaxed standards of evidence and testimony. Preliminary hearings are public and adversarial in nature. Judges preside over them and decide if there is sufficient evidence to go to trial. Grand jury proceedings are held in private, and only the prosecution's case is presented to a group of jurors who decide if the matter should be tried. Defense counsel and the defendant are normally not permitted to attend grand jury proceedings (Gardner and Anderson, 2010; Harr et al., 2011; Samaha, 2012).

Arraignment

Arraignments bring defendants to court to hear and answer charges against them, and felony defendants enter a plea of guilty, not guilty, not guilty by reason of insanity, or nolo contendere (Gardner and Anderson, 2010; Harr et al., 2011; Samaha, 2012).

Pretrial Motions

Pretrial motions ask courts to decide important matters that do not require a trial. These matters include double jeopardy, speedy trial, change of venue, and suppression of evidence. The Fifth Amendment protection against double jeopardy ensures the prosecution has "one fair shot" at convicting a defendant. The Sixth Amendment guarantees a speedy trial, so prosecution must begin promptly. The Sixth Amendment also ensures that changes of venue occur only at the defendant's request and only where great prejudice will otherwise exist. Trial judges consider motions to exclude evidence under the exclusionary rule in suppression hearings (Gardner and Anderson, 2010; Harr et al., 2011; Samaha, 2012).

The Trial

Trials promote fact-finding, procedural regularity, and public participation. Negotiating for guilty pleas promotes efficiency and fact-finding (Gardner and Anderson, 2010; Harr et al., 2011; Samaha, 2012).

Trial by Jury

Trial by jury has ancient roots and has been common practice in the American colonies. It promotes several interests (a check and balance on government power), requires citizens to participate in the criminal justice process, and guarantees that accused persons will have other citizens decide their verdict. The Sixth Amendment right to a jury trial extends to all criminal prosecutions except for petty offenses. The Supreme Court uses six months' imprisonment as the dividing line between serious and petty crimes; however, because the right is extended to all crimes of "moral seriousness," under certain circumstances, it can include crimes where the "moral quality" of the offense is serious, even when long prison terms are not at stake (Gardner and Anderson, 2010; Harr et al., 2011; Samaha, 2012).

The twelve-member jury has strong traditional support from legal experts and social scientists but is not an exclusive rule. The Sixth Amendment is satisfied by a jury of fewer members. The court has said that the right demands only enough jurors to find the truth and allow community members to participate in the criminal justice system. The court has held that six-member juries satisfy the Sixth Amendment but that five-person juries do not (Gardner and Anderson, 2010; Harr et al., 2011; Samaha, 2012).

The Fourteenth Amendment ensures that juries are selected from a random cross section of the public using local census reports, tax rolls, city directories, and more. From the jury panel (the list of eligible citizens who have not been excused), the prosecutor and the defense attorney pick the actual jurors during voir dire. The attorneys use peremptory challenges to strike jurors without having to give a reason and challenges for cause to strike jurors who may be biased. Because racial prejudice can sway some jurors, harming a defendant, as well as groups generally, race discrimination in the selection of jurors violates the equal protection clause. In *Batson v. Kentucky*, the court held that if a defendant can make a prima facie case based on the totality of facts that race discrimination has entered into the prosecution's use of peremptory challenges, the burden shifts to the government to provide a race-neutral explanation for striking jurors. The judge will decide if there has been intentional discrimination (Gardner and Anderson, 2010; Harr et al., 2011; Samaha, 2012).

The right to a public trial is based on the Sixth Amendment right to confront witnesses, the Fifth Amendment due process right, and the Fourteenth Amendment due process right. Public trials also protect the right of the public to attend proceedings and the right of defendants to attend their own trials. The right includes every stage of the trial. There are some exceptions to the right. Courtroom size may limit access to the public. Sensitive proceedings may also allow a judge to limit access, as well as the need to protect certain witnesses, such as undercover agents, witnesses who have been threatened, and shy witnesses. Defendants can be excluded defendants if they are disruptive to the proceedings and during the questioning of child witnesses in sexual abuse cases (Gardner and Anderson, 2010; Harr et al., 2011; Samaha, 2012).

The Stages and Rules of a Jury Trial

Stages of a jury trial include opening statements (starting with the prosecution), presenting evidence, closing arguments, instructions to the jury, and jury deliberations. During the presenting evidence stage, the Sixth Amendment confrontation clause allows the defendant the right to cross-examine the prosecution's witnesses. With some exceptions, the clause also limits the prosecution's ability to use hearsay evidence. The amendment also guarantees a defendant's right to compel witnesses to testify in court for them. The Fifth Amendment bars the government from compelling a defendant to testify at his or her trial. The prosecutor is also prohibited from commenting if a defendant refuses to testify (Gardner and Anderson, 2010; Harr et al., 2011; Samaha, 2012).

Defendants do not have to prove their innocence. They do not even have to present any evidence. Instead, due process requires that prosecutors must prove the defendant's guilt "beyond a reasonable doubt" (Gardner and Anderson, 2010; Harr et al., 2011; Samaha, 2012).

Prosecutors have a formal duty not only to convict criminals but also to do justice, prohibiting such behavior as intentionally misstating evidence, misleading juries, or inflaming jurors' passions or prejudices (Gardner and Anderson, 2010; Harr et al., 2011; Samaha, 2012).

Before the jury begins deliberating a defendant's guilt or innocence, the trial judge instructs the jurors about their role to find the facts, explains that defendants are presumed innocent until proven guilty and that the state has the burden of proof, and defines all the elements of the crimes charged. Juries can return "guilty," "not guilty," or "special" verdicts. Special verdicts are generally related to insanity or capital punishment. The requirement for a unanimous verdict instills confidence in the criminal justice process, guarantees careful review of evidence, ensures the hearing of minority viewpoints, and more. Nonetheless, unanimous verdicts are not required by the U.S. Constitution as interpreted by the Supreme Court. The court has upheld a state law that allows a 9–3 guilty verdict but has struck down a nonunanimous verdict of a six-member jury. Juries can engage in jury nullification, meaning they can acquit a defendant even when the facts clearly support a guilty verdict (Gardner and Anderson, 2010; Harr et al., 2011; Samaha, 2012).

Guilty Pleas

Guilty pleas include straight pleas and negotiated pleas (bargaining on the severity of the charges or the severity of the sentence). Defendants who plead guilty waive their Fifth Amendment right to remain silent and the Sixth Amendment rights to trial by jury and to confront witnesses. Guilty pleas are constitutional when defendants waive these rights knowingly and voluntarily. According to the U.S. Supreme Court, the guilty plea must have a factual basis, meaning that defendants' pleas reflect an understanding of the "true nature" of the charges against them. When a judge fails to question a defendant about their plea and establish it as knowing and voluntary, the conviction may be reversed (Gardner and Anderson, 2010; Harr et al., 2011; Samaha, 2012).

Eighth Amendment Considerations

The proportionality principle deems sentences cruel and unusual if they are "grossly disproportionate" to the "gravity of the offense." A minority of judges believe the Eighth Amendment requires no proportionality principle or, if so, that it is up to the legislature to decide what sentences are disproportionate. The Supreme Court has held that the death penalty is proportionate punishment only when a mentally fit adult kills and is convicted of murder. The court is divided on whether the proportionality principle applies to sentences of imprisonment. The court has ruled in *Lockyer v. Andrade* that California's three-strike law does not impose cruel and unusual punishment, even though Andrade has been sentenced to life in prison on two counts of petty theft (Gardner and Anderson, 2010; Harr et al., 2011; Samaha, 2012).

Right of Appeal

Convicted criminals do not base their appeals on any constitutional right but on a statutory right to appeal noncapital convictions in intermediate appellate courts and capital convictions to any court. Under the Constitution, a state does not have to provide any appeal process; however, every jurisdiction has created a statutory right to appeal. Appellate review of criminal cases is affected by principles of mootness (the punishment is complete), raise or waive (the defendant does not object to the error at trial), and plain error (substantial rights are affected, and injustice has resulted). A conviction becomes final when it is affirmed on appeal to the highest court of the land or when the highest court declines to review it (Gardner and Anderson, 2010; Harr et al., 2011; Samaha, 2012).

Habeas Corpus

Habeas corpus is a "collateral attack" where convicted criminals seek to prove they have been unlawfully detained in a civil lawsuit against the government. State courts provide collateral review for defendants convicted in state court. Federal courts review cases brought by defendants convicted in both federal courts and state courts. The broad view of habeas corpus holds that the more judicial review a conviction receives, the more accurate it will be (Gardner and Anderson, 2010; Harr et al., 2011; Samaha, 2012).

Court Procedures

I used to spend a tremendous amount of time in court. I felt like I was really good at testifying but never enjoyed court. It was sad to see how messed up people could be. In addition, you never knew when an attorney was going to viciously attack you on the stand. It was not always about the truth. The best attorneys I ever went up against were true ladies and gentlemen. They were always polite and never made it a personal attack. Yet they represented their clients to a high degree and knew how to win a case. Then there were those who would play games and make personal attacks. And there were those who were lazy and did not do their job, which was to defend their client. I often felt like I cared more about justice for their client than they did. There are many rules to remember in court, but the most important is to never ever compromise one's integrity. I have met officers/troopers/investigators who have said they have never lost a case. Sorry, but they must not have had many go to trial! Mistakes will be made, but they must be honest mistakes. The ends never justify the means.

Steps in the Trial Process

- ✓ Discovery and motions to suppress
- ✓ Direct examinations
- ✓ Cross-examinations
- ✓ Redirect examinations
- ✓ Recross-examination
- ✓ Rebuttal
- ✓ Surrebuttal

- ✓ Closing arguments
- ✓ Might be bifurcated trial

Knowing Rules of Evidence

Officers need a good working knowledge of rules of evidence. They are responsible for collecting and preserving evidence for use by prosecutors. They must be able to distinguish between

- ✓ factual material that is admissible in court and
- ✓ that which is not valid or useful as evidence.

Judicial Notice

The doctrine of judicial notice is an evidentiary shortcut. Judicial notice is designed to speed up the trial and eliminate the necessity of formally proving the truth of a particular matter when the truth is not in dispute.

Types of Evidence

- ✓ Direct Evidence
  - ○ Direct evidence usually is the testimony of witnesses that ties the defendant directly to the commission of the crime.
- ✓ Real Evidence
  - ○ Sometimes referred to as "physical evidence," real evidence is connected with the commission of the crime and can be produced in court.
- ✓ Demonstrative Evidence
  - ○ Demonstrative or illustrative evidence consists of maps, diagrams, sketches, photographs, tape recordings, videotapes, X-rays, and visual tests and demonstrations produced to assist witnesses in explaining their testimony.
- ✓ Circumstantial Evidence
  - ○ The broad definition of circumstantial evidence encompasses all evidence other than direct evidence, provided that it logically relates the defendant to the crime.

✓ Opinion Evidence
  ○ Matters of description in which a nonexpert may give an opinion include color, size, shape, speed, mental condition, identity, race, and language.

Expert Witness

An expert witness is a person who is called to testify in court because of his or her special skills or knowledge and permitted to interpret facts and give opinions about their significance to facilitate jurors' understanding of complex or technical matters.

Hearsay Evidence

The fact that stories tend to be changed when they are repeated makes their reliability and truthfulness questionable. For this reason, the hearsay rule is created. Hearsay is derived from "heard say."

Exceptions to the Hearsay Rule

✓ If the circumstances surrounding the hearsay evidence can ensure a high degree of trustworthiness and reliability, that evidence is admissible as an exception to the rule in order to minimize any injustice.
✓ Confessions
✓ Admissions
✓ Spontaneous and excited utterances
✓ Dying declarations
✓ Former testimony

Evidentiary Privileges

Defendants and other witnesses have a right to have certain matters of communication barred from disclosure in court, such as confidential communications between husband and wife and confidential communications between attorney and client. Grand jury proceedings that are confidential requirements of law are barred.

Testifying and Courtroom Demeanor

General

Duty to Court

- ✓ Be on time.
- ✓ Be quiet and keep the audience quiet.
- ✓ Have protection and security.
- ✓ Be available.

Duty to Prosecution

- ✓ Be prepared.
- ✓ Assist in the preparation for the prosecutor.
- ✓ Have all documents filed.
- ✓ Assure all evidence are available (such as lab reports, recording, records, statements, pictures) and in order.
- ✓ Send copy of report to the prosecutor before court.

Duty of Defendant

- ✓ Testify to the truth.
- ✓ Do not hide things because you think it might hurt the case.

Testifying

- ✓ Avoid constantly using phrases like "I believe," "I do not know," and "I think."
- ✓ Be prepared.
- ✓ Use "Yes, sir/ma'am," and "No, sir/ma'am."
- ✓ Be accurate, do not guess, and use field notes only.
- ✓ Be honest.

Seven Effective Rules for Testifying

- ✓ Have the facts.
- ✓ Know the basic rules (hearsay – venue- ID defendants).
- ✓ Be prepared.

✓ Let the facts speak for themselves.
✓ Speak clearly.
✓ Wear correct uniform or clothing.
✓ Do not lose your temper.

Takeaways

✓ Nothing is ever really off the record.
✓ The Constitution constrains the government, not the people.
✓ Respect the Constitution.
✓ Officers are given an awesome responsibility to uphold and enforce the law.
✓ Recognize the difference between the letter of the law and the spirit of the law.
✓ Know applicable case law. Keep up to date with decisions.
✓ Know and understand the elements of applicable crimes.
✓ Know the rules of evidence.
✓ Understand what direct, real, demonstrative, and circumstantial evidence means and entails.
✓ Know the criminal procedure.
✓ Know the laws of arrest.
✓ Know what reasonable articulable suspicion means.
✓ Know what probable cause means.
✓ Know what proof beyond a reasonable doubt means.
✓ Never compromise your integrity.
✓ The ends never justify the means.
✓ For court, be on time, be quiet, and be available.
✓ For the prosecutor, be prepared, assist as they request, and have all needed documentation. Make sure all filings follow applicable laws.
✓ Testify to the truth, be accurate, and do not hide the truth.
✓ Never argue or criticize the judge.
✓ When testifying, have the facts, be ready, speak clearly, do not lose your temper, and be properly groomed.

This is what the Lord Almighty says: Luke "Administer true justice; show mercy and compassion to one another."
—Zechariah 7:9

Chapter Four
Ethical Behavior

In law a man is guilty when he violates the rights of others.
In ethics he is guilty if he only thinks of doing so.
—Immanuel Kant

Never violate ethical standards.

On patrol one night in the rough part of a city, I stopped a fellow for a couple of traffic violations. He also had a radar detector, which is illegal in my state. I had a trainee with me. As I was writing the fellow a ticket, he asked me if he could give me fifty dollars if I would not give him the ticket. I had been doing police work for about ten years by this point, and no one had ever tried to bribe me in any way. I was caught off guard for a moment. I thought to myself, *How stupid could someone be?* I asked him, "Do you have fifty dollars on you?" He said yes. He then said he would give me and the other trooper fifty dollars each. I again thought to myself, *Is he really saying this to me?* I had never charged anyone with attempting to bribe a police officer. I quickly pulled my codebook out and read the criminal code section. It was pretty straightforward. I said, "Let me see the money." I asked him one more time, "Do you really want to give us fifty dollars each to not give you this ticket?" He said yes. I said, "Okay, step out of the car for a minute." I walked around and put him in the front leaning position and handcuffed him and told him he was under arrest for attempting to bribe the two of us.

We went to the preliminary hearing in district court. It was really an open-and-shut case. The judge certified the case to the grand jury. As the judge was wrapping up, he said jokingly in open court, "I guess the trooper was upset you did not offer more money." I knew this judge well. I think at times he thought he was David Letterman. The people in the courtroom laughed. I ignored it. I thought to myself how unprofessional it was for the judge to say such a thing. Later, the fellow whom I had charged with two counts of attempted bribery pled guilty and received a three-year suspended sentence with time served. The moral to the story is never ever succumb to criminality in any form and do not allow it to occur. Uphold your oath and the law. I am sure bribery does occur, but no person should ever think they can brazenly flaunt the law and that any officer will succumb to such temptation. By the way, it could have been a million dollars, and the thought would have never crossed my mind. The total cost of the ticket would have been about one hundred dollars!

This might be the most important chapter in the entire book. If you do not remember anything else from reading this book, I beg you to remember what you read and learn from this chapter. Over the years, I have seen so many officers destroy their lives by committing unethical acts. The damages have ranged from discipline (such as time off or letters of reprimand) to firings, jail, and suicide. Of course, so far, I am only talking about what happens to the officer. Many times, there are victims involved who must live with the harm done to them. The trust, they have lost, and the community loses in our police because of one bad officer. Then there are all the other officers who end up getting labeled what they are not or getting painted as corrupt.

We have already touched on this subject when we learned about the affective or attitudinal domain. However, this topic is so important that it deserves its own in-depth chapter. We are human and will make mistakes. There are two kinds of mistakes. One is errors of the mind. These are mistakes that are honest in nature. The second is errors of the heart. These are not mistakes and really not even errors. These are choices we knowingly make to do something unethical or criminal.

In our opening quote, Kant says we are guilty ethically if we just think about the act. Kant really sets the bar very high, does he not? The bar must be set high. Consider the following phrase by Samuel Smiles:

Sow a thought, and you reap an act;
Sow an act, and you reap a habit;
Sow a habit, and you reap a character;
Sow a character, and you reap a destiny.

When taking Kant's and Smiles's thoughts together, we clearly see why it is critical to not even have unethical thoughts in the first place. We do, indeed, need to always wear a breastplate of righteousness.

It is important to note that ethics rise above what the law requires. Law is actually the least acceptable level of human behavior a society has decided to tolerate. As we will see, one may well stay within the confines of what is statutorily legal but might still fall outside the bounds of what is ethical.

Defining Terms

In order to better understand what it is meant by the terms *ethics* and *corruption*, it will be instructive to define both. According to Black (1979), ethics relates to moral action, conduct, motive, or character or is ethical emotion. Furthermore, it means professionally right and conforming to professional standards of conduct. Corruption is defined as an act done with the intent to gain advantage that is inconsistent with official duty and the rights of others. Finally, going to the root, corrupt means spoiled, tainted, vitiated, depraved, debased, and morally degenerate and, as a verb, to change one's morals from good to bad. These terms are critical to the issue at hand. The term *corrupt*, especially when used as a verb, goes to the heart of explaining police corruption.

Occupational deviance, as defined, is essentially the concept of employees in positions and deviations from norms binding upon the employee and position (Souryal, 1984). Souryal (1984) defines three basic categories of occupational deviance related to law enforcement—nonfeasance, misfeasance, and malfeasance. These categories of deviance pertain to the conduct necessary to achieve deviance. In this context, they are not defined by statute but as follows: Nonfeasance is failure to perform a prescribed duty. It is failing to do what is required. Misfeasance is the improper performance of an act or duty, which may be properly executed. Malfeasance is conduct that positively violates rules, regulations, or law. Nonfeasance and malfeasance are distinguished by the severity of the act. One is deemed an oversight as opposed to an intentional act. To distinguish between the two, mitigating factors must be used to make the determination.

What difference does it make?

Each year, more officers commit suicide than are murdered by perpetrators. Many of these suicides are a result of an officer's failure to deal with an unethical act in the proper manner. That is, they succumbed to corruption. This is but one of the many reasons why the study of police corruption should be one of criminal justice's greatest concerns (IACP, 1997).

Any democratic society must have faith in a justice system that acts in an ethical manner at all times. If people lose faith and trust in this system of justice, of which policing is a key element and the first and closest to the people, then society will falter, and vigilantism will prevail (Dantzker, 1997). Instilling ethical behavior must be a primary goal of every agency. If we are to expect officers to behave ethically, we must treat them and the citizens they serve ethically (Braunstein, 1992).

On too many occasions, I have seen public figures, including police officers I knew, get caught up in devastating ethical dilemmas or, should I say, get caught having committed a serious ethical violation. My first thought beyond being sad that people do things that will cause harm to themselves and others is that I hope they will not harm themselves physically. This is a tough thing to discuss. One purpose of this book, as it has been with my training, was and is to help prevent officers from committing unethical acts to begin with. This is a difficult topic to discuss, and officers will get offended and upset about it at times. That is perfectly fine if it causes officers to reevaluate things that will cause them or others harm. However low the valley a person may walk through, they need to realize they can survive the situation and hopefully come out on the other side a better person. This transformation will not be easy. Being honest and willing to correct whatever it is that has created the dilemma will not be easy either. As with most things, prevention is the better option. It is a cliché, but it is so true—an ounce of prevention is worth a pound of cure.

In today's society, we are constantly bombarded with negative and unethical behavior. We see it on television and in the movies. We hear it on the news. We also see bad behavior being celebrated and rewarded. We ask ourselves, *What is wrong with today's young people?* All we need to do is look in the mirror. We all have to balance the lines between good and bad, right and wrong, and even more so good and evil. When I was growing up, the good guys wore the white cowboy hats. In almost all cases, good was portrayed as virtuous and right. We wonder why we have kids killing each other, sports teams that cheat yet are defended by their fans no matter what, politicians who are unethical and even go to jail or prison and come back and run for office and win. Do not get me wrong, I believe in redemption. I also believe in consequences. But we have no shame or humility anymore. The media refuses to be neutral and just give us the facts. There are times where I wonder if I have fallen asleep and gone down the rabbit hole with Alice and am now attending the Mad Hatter's party!

Unethical Acts

- ✓ Destroy public trust
- ✓ Ruin careers and destroy lives
- ✓ Can lead to prison
- ✓ Are a major cause of lawsuits
  - ○ Department and individual

Values - beliefs upon which our actions and decisions are made

Integrity - derived from the word *wholeness*

Have character that develops hope, honesty, courage, empathy, etc.

The Current State/Problem

Unethical acts destroy public trust, ruin careers and damage lives, can lead to prison, and are a major cause of lawsuits both for agencies and individuals (Pollock, 1998). Pollock (1998) lists four of the most common motivations of individuals for unethical behavior as anger, lust, greed, and peer pressure.

To add to the conundrum of unethical behavior, loyalty can be misused, thus exacerbating the problem. Pollock (1998) states loyalty is part of the integrity of a social being. Loyalty is a matter of emotional ties and commitments far more basic than cold contractual relationships. Disloyalty is always reviled, but not all failures to act from loyalty are disloyal. Loyalty to principles and loyalty to people can come into conflict. Blind loyalty is an attitude that causes much trouble.

DR. JEFFREY C. FOX

Statistical Data

The National Institute of Ethics (2000) provided the following information. An analysis of 1,080 police officers in the state of Florida who were disciplined by the Criminal Justice Standards and Training Committee between 1990 and 1995 revealed the following data. The average age of the officer was 36. Males made up 94.81 percent, and females were 5.19 percent. The race was as follows: 71.81 percent white, 18.98 percent black, 8.89 percent Hispanic, and 0.19 percent Asian. Level of education was 8.8 percent GED, 68.06 percent high school, 12.13 percent associates, and 11.02 percent bachelor's. By agency, they were 54.06 percent city, 36.97 percent county, and 8.97 percent state. The top six reasons for the discipline were false report or statement, 21.98 percent; battery (simple and aggravated), 13.34 percent; sexual offense or sexual battery, 13.54 percent; larceny, 8.83 percent; fraud or forgery, 7.01 percent; and excessive force, 4.32 percent. Furthermore, from a nationwide survey of unethical acts conducted by the National Institute of Ethics, the following data was collected. The most common motivators of individual acts were anger, lust, greed, and peer pressure. Common causes within an organization were politics, poor background investigations, poor field training office (FTO) programs, and improper role modeling. Most common unethical acts were greed, 26 percent; anger, 23 percent; false reports, 21 percent; lust, 16 percent; and other issues, making up the remaining 14 percent. One key point made by the research finding was one reacted the way one was trained. This is true with all types of training.

The National Institute of Ethics (2000) conducted another nationwide survey on police attitudes toward abuse. The survey found that, in the overwhelming majority of use of force incidents, the police did not use excessive force. On another topic, more than 80 percent of the officers surveyed said they did not accept the "code of silence." However, 24.9 percent agreed that whistle-blowing was not worth trying. Sixty-five percent felt like if they blew the whistle, they would be given the cold shoulder. Fifty-two percent agreed that it was not unusual for police officers to turn a blind eye on other officer's misconduct. Conversely, 85 percent of the officers believed a strong police chief could make a big difference when it came to abuse. Ninety percent agreed that a good first-line supervisor could help prevent abuse.

Ivkovic (2003) offered data from a citizen survey. Gallup polls over the past twenty years have revealed what citizens in general believed, which was that 40 to 50 percent of citizens surveyed felt high or very high that officers were honest and ethical. However, when viewed by race, two-thirds of whites but only one-third of blacks thought police were almost all honest. This finding was consistent with other surveys regarding police actions when viewed by race.

According to the National Institute of Ethics (2000), each year, two to three times as many police officers kill themselves than are killed by assailants. It is preventable and is but one of the sad realities of ethical misconduct in policing. Within the last several years, it has become a recognized fact that ethics training has been and will continue to be the most needed area of improvement in the field of law enforcement. In most cases, there will be a critique of officer-involved shootings; and as a result, training guidelines will be developed. Seldom, if ever, do these critiques offer guidelines on how to prevent police suicides, corruption, and other such unpleasant issues. The trend is to downplay, rationalize, minimize, ignore, or deny that an agency or profession has a problem.

As research conducted by the International Association of Chiefs of Police (IACP) points out, ethics is our greatest training and leadership need. In addition to preventing police suicides, law enforcement must—through ethics training and the ethical administration of their duties—stem the tide of corruption, brutality, discrimination, harassment, and the like. This is not meant as an indictment of the police. To the contrary, a great majority of police officers are fine, admirable people who are willing to give their lives in the call of duty. It is for those who have given their lives, and those willing to, that police officers and leaders must, as a profession, look in the mirror and face ethical issues directly. This commitment is owed to all law enforcement officers and to the communities they serve (1997).

When speaking of unethical acts, the first two things that come to mind are at two ends of the spectrum. The first is gratuities. This is often as far as academy or department training goes. The next is brutality. These issues make the headlines. However, there are a host of unethical deeds that fit into the middle of this continuum. Traditionally, most police administrators and academics alike have placed the blame for unethical conduct on the individual officer. This thought process or explanation is known as the bad apple theory.

When trying to explain, predict, and understand why police officers commit corrupt acts, two basic theories are espoused. Donahue and Felts (1993) state the first and what has often been the most common theory that most call the rotten or bad apple theory. The second theory, which is more controversial and only as of late received the attention it deserves, is organizational or institutional structural theories of corruption. This second theory has many variations and names. The need for ethics goes without saying. What is at issue is the magnitude and variability of police deviance or corruption across departments.

So what might help cause and/or prevent unethical behavior? The values the FTO teaches. The values the sergeant and other officers displays or teaches, the kind of citizens confronted in the first patrol assignment and the level of danger on patrol, whether officers work in a one-officer or two-officer car and whether officers are assigned to undercover work or vice work, whether there are conflicts among officers over ethical issues in the department, the ethical messages sent out by the police executives, the power of the police union to protect officers from being punished, the general climate of civic integrity or lack of it, and the level of public pressure to control police behavior. None of this justifies how officers choose to deal with corruption they face or decide to partake.

The typology of occupational deviance adds further definition to the subject. Typology defines the purpose of deviant conduct. Punch (1985) and Haarr (1997) identify four types of occupational deviance—work avoidance and manipulation, employee deviance against the organization, employee deviance for the organization, and informal rewards. Work avoidance and manipulation include activities such as overlooking a crime that occurs at the end of a shift in order to avoid extra paperwork. Employee deviance against an organization encompasses behavior such as pilfering, stealing, sabotage, or absenteeism. Employee deviance for organizations includes bending the rules and regulations and violating policies, procedures, and the law to get the job done. Finally, on a day-to-day basis, police officers seek a number of informal rewards, such as perks, discounts, services, and presents. Punch's and Haarr's typology of police occupational deviance easily illustrates the intent of the conduct, which is less than honorable. McCafferty's (1998) findings on the subject further validate the typology definitions.

Haberfeld (2006) framed unethical police actions into three categories. First is noble cause corruption. Noble cause corruption involves not making choices for personal gain. The officer acts on behalf of victims by doing what he or she considers the right thing. Violating policy because, in the officer's opinion, it stymies his or her ability to accomplish a task is another example of noble cause corruption. Next is adaptation, which involves considering everyone, including oneself, as an "a——h——." Cynicism, which results from viewing the dark side of humans on a consistent basis, is created. A means-ends conflict occurs. Operating from the premise that the ends justify the means occurs. Finally, economic corruption involves the slippery slope concept. This means starting with relatively small infractions and building up to criminal acts. Corruption is for personal gain. Such corruption involves kickbacks, opportunistic thefts, shakedowns, protection of illegal activities, criminal and traffic charge fixes, direct criminal activities, and internal payoffs.

Ideology

There are two main ways to view or study ethics. One is philosophical or historical. This is done by studying and analyzing such people as Plato, Socrates, Kant, Mills, Jesus Christ, and many others. Notice both religious and secular philosophers are mentioned. This is done to illustrate that ethics can be found in religion and secular humanism. Both can play a significant role in each person's belief system. Each person who enters the field of law enforcement brings with them their own set of values, beliefs, morals, and ideologies. It is here at the personal or micro level that ideologies make the most impact in our discussion. At the macro or group level of policing, we will see how each person's individual ethics can and will be challenged by the subculture itself (Rawls, 1971). The other main way to study or understand ethics is through a practical or real-world application. It is here that we teach and practice everyday ethics. It is here that we often fail.

Ideology can and is

- ✓ societal,
- ✓ subgroup/subcultural,
- ✓ departmental,
- ✓ squad/unit/divisional,
- ✓ individual (public and private).

Sometimes I will see an officer—when I say officer, I mean all types,—who will be beyond the scope of his or her authority and either he or she realizes it but does not take a step back for various reasons (ego, pride, arrogance, anger) or he or she does not realize it at all. We must always know what we can and cannot do. We must also know what we should and should not do. Ethics training is our greatest need.

Common Motivations of Individuals

- ✓ Anger
- ✓ Lust
- ✓ Greed
- ✓ Peer pressure

Most Common Unethical Acts by Officers

- ✓ Greed, 26 percent
- ✓ Anger, 23 percent
- ✓ False Reports, 21 percent
- ✓ Lust, 16 percent
- ✓ Others, 14 percent

The three general reasons for corruption are as follows:

- ✓ Systemic - deviance caused by the relationship between police and the public
- ✓ Institutionalization - general organizational problems
- ✓ Individual - rotten apple

A vast majority of police officers are fine, admirable people who are willing to give their lives in the call of duty. It is for those who have given their lives and those willing to that we must, as a profession, look in the mirror and face our ethical issues head-on. This commitment is owed to all law enforcement officers and to the communities they serve.

Historical Overview

At the end of the nineteenth century and during the twentieth century, police scandals seem to erupt in various large cities about every twenty years. According to Kappeler, Sluder, and Alpert (1998) and Souryal (1998), the scandals often resulted in commissions followed by various reforms. Such commissions included the Lexow Committee in 1894, the Curran Committee in 1913, the Brooklyn grand jury in 1949, the Knapp Commission in 1972, and the Mollen Commission in 1994, all of which were in New York City; the Pennsylvania Crime Commission in 1974; and the Christopher Commission in 1991 and Los Angeles Police Department Rampart Division, both scandals occurring in Los Angeles. All of these commissions came to the same conclusion. Police corruption was widespread and deep. Corruption covered the entire gamut from gambling, narcotics, prostitution, perjury, brutality, drinking, and sex on duty to murder in some cases. One study in 1994 resulted in the following findings from the officers involved. Officers perceived that 39 percent of corruption was from brutality, 22 percent from perjury, 31 percent from sex on duty, 8 percent from drinking on duty, and 39 percent from sleeping on duty (e.g., Delattre, 2002; Ivkovic, 2003; Meese and Ortmeier, 2004).

Oftentimes when police agencies would do mass hiring and lower entrance standards, corruption would follow. According to Delattre (2002), in 1980, Miami hired two hundred recruits immediately, and 80 percent were minority residents of Miami. Recruits were ill-suited as background investigations showed, as well as attempts at training. Field training was poor, supervision was lacking, and internal affairs investigations were poor. By 1988, over one-third of these two hundred recruits had been fired. Twelve of them had been convicted of many crimes ranging from drug trafficking to murder.

According to Delattre (2002), the Los Angeles Police Department's Rampart Division provided for the worst scandal in the history of the agency. Because of the multitude of corrupt acts undertaken by members of the division in one case alone, a plaintiff won a fifteen-million-dollar lawsuit because he had been framed. Approximately one hundred convictions were overturned. Nearly three thousand cases still were being reviewed in 2002.

Kappeler et al. (1998) provided a laundry list of examples where police officers from all levels of government and across the country had committed various illegal acts. In the early 1990s, the DC Metropolitan Police Department did much like Miami did in the 1980s. Mass hiring, lowered standards, and poor backgrounds resulted in 29 police officers being indicted during the first six months of 1992. In 1992, the New York City Police Department underwent another massive investigation where, once again, it was discovered that officers had distributed drugs, accepted bribes, and committed murders. During the 1980s, over 61 percent of the 3,440 citizen complaints against members of the Boston Police Department were levied against 11 percent of the 3,200 officers. The 5 officers receiving the most complaints were still employed. Between the 5 of them, they received 100 complaints and were cleared in 90 of them. These are but a small number of the acts of corruption committed.

Description of the Problem

Grant (2002) states there are eight areas of corruption law enforcement faces. The first issue is acceptance of gratuities. Second is associating with known criminals without department knowledge. Third is disclosing confidential information to unauthorized personnel. Disclosure of ongoing investigations is fourth. Falsifying affidavits and reports is fifth. All forms of harassment are sixth and include but are not limited to sex, creed, religion, and sexual orientation. Seventh is sexual harassment of citizens, coworkers, or subordinates. Eighth and last is failing to protect the rights of citizens and to follow the law or policy when dealing with arrest, evidence, interrogation, and so forth. Grant classifies corruption into three groups. The three groups are individual, organizational, and environmental corruption.

Ethical Frameworks

There are basically two areas where a person will draw or create their ethical framework. They can draw from both, either, or neither actually. One area is based on religion or faith based. The other area is secular in nature. I am not speaking of salvation, so even if one is not particularly religious in nature, there are still many valuable lessons we can learn from faith. Also, if one does base their ethics on religion only, there are still many great lessons one can learn from secular ethics and not violate their faith at all.

Faith plays a major role in so many people's lives. I hope it does in yours. Many officers rely on their faith in many ways. For many of us, we view police work as our calling. It is why God put us here. He has given us skills and the ability to do the hard job an officer faces daily. Faith helps an officer cope with the heartache and despair they see on a daily basis. Many police officers, including me, believe that one of the eight beatitudes of Jesus has direct applicability to their jobs. "Blessed are the peacemakers, for they shall be called children of God" (Matthew 5:3–10). The Ten Commandments and the Bible in its entirety offer great life lessons. A wonderful version of the beatitudes is this version found written on the wall in Mother Teresa's home for the children in Calcutta:

1. *People are often unreasonable, irrational, and self-centered.*
   a. *Forgive them anyway.*
2. *If you are kind, people may accuse you of selfish, ulterior motives.*
   a. *Be kind anyway.*
3. *If you are successful, you will win some unfaithful friends and some genuine enemies.*
   a. *Succeed anyway.*
4. *If you are honest and sincere, people may deceive you.*
   a. *Be honest and sincere anyway.*
5. *What you spend years creating, others could destroy overnight.*
   a. *Create anyway.*
1. *If you find serenity and happiness, some may be jealous.*
   a. *Be happy anyway.*
2. *The good you do today will often be forgotten.*
   a. *Do good anyway.*
3. *Give the best you have, and it will never be enough.*
   a. *Give your best anyway.*
4. *In the final analysis, it is between you and God.*
   a. *It was never between you and them anyway.*

This version is credited to Mother Teresa.

The original version of the Paradoxical Commandments by Dr. Kent M. Keith (2001) is as follows:

1. *People are illogical, unreasonable, and self-centered.*
   a. *Love them anyway.*
2. *If you do good, people will accuse you of selfish ulterior motives.*
   a. *Do good anyway.*
3. *If you are successful, you win false friends and true enemies.*
   a. *Succeed anyway.*
4. *The good you do today will be forgotten tomorrow.*
   a. *Do good anyway.*
5. *Honesty and frankness make you vulnerable.*
   a. *Be honest and frank anyway.*
6. *The biggest men and women with the biggest ideas can be shot down by the smallest men and women with the smallest minds.*
   a. *Think big anyway.*
7. *People favor underdogs but follow only top dogs.*
   a. *Fight for a few underdogs anyway.*
8. *What you spend years building may be destroyed overnight.*
   a. *Build anyway.*
9. *People really need help but may attack you if you do help them.*
   a. *Help people anyway.*
10. *Give the world the best you have and you'll get kicked in the teeth.*
    a. *Give the world the best you have anyway.*

According to Cooper (1998), deontological ethics are duty oriented, whereas teleological ethics are consequence oriented. Kantian ethics are deontological in nature. Mill's and Bentham's utilitarianism are teleological in nature. Ethics can also be classified into two broad groupings, religious and secular. Religious ethics come from many sources on the individual level. Yet when considering U.S. government/citizen relations, ethics, and policy, there is no doubt that those heavily influenced by the Judeo-Christian ethic have founded the nation. The Bible, along with the Ten Commandments, has strongly influenced our founding fathers and the laws that have been passed. As time has passed, secularism has become much more influential in policy development. Yet those same religious ethics or lack thereof drives much of the debate and motivation behind many issues. For our purposes, we shall focus on secular ethics such as Bentham's and Mill's utilitarianism, Aristotle's virtue ethics, and Kantian ethics. These three sets of ethical frameworks have been some of the most influential on government policy development (Pollock, 1998). While this paper addresses secular ethics and decision making, it is not meant to diminish the tremendous role religion plays in many people's lives and in their decision-making process (Pollock, 1998). The Golden Rule of "Do unto others as you would have them do unto you" is key to many people's decision-making process (Pollock, 1998).

Brady (2003) has helped set the stage in our analysis of ethics and public policy. Brady has divided ethics into three categories. Deontology includes duty, principle, will, normative, obligation, law, and rule. These acts are considered morally obligatory regardless of the outcome for human woe. Teleology includes purpose, interest, goal, means-ends, consequences, and hope. These are acts of purpose. The envisioned ends or purpose overrides duty, right conduct, and moral obligation. Finally, axiology includes value, feeling, care, affection, and preference. These are things that are desirable or praiseworthy. Brady has stated that legislators' lives are immersed in the teleological perspective. Two more terms worth analyzing are consequentialism and nonconsequentialism. Beauchamp and Pinkard (1983) have stated that consequentialists view the moral worth of an action by the good or bad produced. Conversely, nonconsequentialists do not view actions based on consequences but more on intrinsic worth.

Utilitarian Ethics

According to Rapaport (1978), Jeremy Bentham was the father of nineteenth-century utilitarianism. James Mill was a protégé of Bentham and carried his works forward, actually forging them into a powerful weapon for enormous social and political change. The foundational point set forth by Mill was that the sole purpose of government, and the test of good government, was promotion of the greatest good for the greatest number. This did not mean less government. It did, however, mean freedom from tyranny and more equality. Thomas Jefferson was profoundly influenced by such thoughts. The U.S. Bill of Rights directly addressed the ideals stressed through such a philosophy. Mill believed that social coercion should only occur when necessary to prevent harm to others. In essence, the government should not interfere except when necessary to prevent harm for the greater good. Although this first principle was to be modified, Mill and Bentham had such a profound and lasting impact on American democracy that more analysis was needed (e.g., Beauchamp and Pinkard, 1983; Pollock, 1998).

Virtue Ethics

Aristotle is the father of virtue ethics. According to Ackrill and Urmson (1998), Aristotle declared that people should seek the mean and avoid the defect or excess in all behaviors. Moral virtues that fall within the defect are cowardice, self-denial, overcautiousness, doing less than what is due, undue humility, laziness, unresponsiveness, being exploitative, understatement, and being stoic/boorish. The mean or those virtues one should strive to achieve include courage, temperance, prudence, justice, pride, ambition, good temper, being a good friend, truthfulness, and ready wit. Finally, those behaviors that go beyond virtuous behavior or excess are rashness, self-indulgence, being carefree, doing more than what is due, vanity, blind ambition, being easily angered, fawning over, boastfulness, and being a vulgar buffoon (e.g., Beauchamp and Pinkard, 1983; Pollock, 1998).

Moral Virtues

Moral Virtues		
Defect	Mean	Excess
Cowardice	Courage	Rashness
Self-Denial	Temperance	Self-Indulgence
Overcautiousness	Prudence	Being Carefree
Doing Less than What Is Due	Justice	Doing More than What Is Due
Undue Humility	Pride	Vanity
Laziness	Ambition	Blind Ambition
Unresponsiveness	Good Temper	Being Easily Angered
Being Exploitative	Being a Good Friend	Fawning Over
Understatement	Truthful	Boastfulness
Being Stoic/Boorish	Ready Wit	Being Vulgar/Buffoon

Kantian Ethics

Pollock (1998) has explained Kant's categorical imperative. Act so that your actions can be a universal rule of behavior for the particular circumstance. Duty requires correct behavior for no other reason than it is the right thing to do. To do the right thing for any other reason will violate Kant's ethical maxim. Ethical formalism is unyielding. For example, lying is wrong all the time and cannot be explained away (e.g., Beauchamp and Pinkard, 1983; Brady, 2003; Pollock, 1998).

Natural Rights

Moral rights such as the right to life, liberty, and the pursuit of happiness are examples of natural rights. Such rights are considered equal and as natural as everything else involving nature such as gravity (Beauchamp and Pinkard, 1983; Brady, 2003; Pollock, 1998).

Other Ethical Thoughts

Covey (1989, 1994) discusses the differences between character-driven and emotion-driven behaviors. A character-driven behavior includes "do right, feel good"; being commitment driven; principle-based decisions; "action controls attitude"; "believe it and then see it"; creating momentum; and asking, "What are my responsibilities?" An emotion-driven behavior includes "feel good, do right"; being convenience driven; popularity-based decisions; "attitude controls action"; "see it and then believe it"; waiting for momentum; and asking, "What are my rights?" Pollock (1998) explains that egoism postulates that what is good for the individual is best. Egoism allows others to be used as an end. The rights and happiness of others are inconsequential.

Pollock (1998) summarizes the major ethical systems as follows. Ethical formalism, or Kantian ethics, decrees that what is good is that which conforms to the categorical imperative otherwise known as the universal rule. Utilitarianism, created by Bentham and Mill, states that what is good is that which results in the greatest utility for the greatest number. Religion, in its many forms, is what is good is what conforms to God's will. Natural law is what is good to that which is natural. Ethics of virtue involves what is good is what conforms to the golden mean. Ethics of care is what is good is that which meets the needs of those concerned. Finally, egoism is what is good is what benefits the individual person.

Utilitarian ethics allows for the most latitude in any decision-making process. The maxim of the greatest good for the greatest number provides the framework for our constitutional democracy. Public policy is steeped in this maxim. Aristotle's virtue ethics allows for some latitude but less than utilitarianism. Finally, Kantian ethics is very rigid and allows little latitude in ethical decision making. Policy and decision making may be better off if those charged with such duties work from Kant to Aristotle and then to utilitarianism. It will appear that little attention is given to or guidance derived from anything but utilitarianism, if even that (Pollock, 1998). Paternalistic principles greatly affect the formation of law, as well as policy. This principle allows the limiting of liberty for one's own good. Such examples of paternalistic laws or policies are seat belt and motorcycle helmet laws (Beauchamp and Pinkard, 1983).

Ethical Maxims

- ✓ Kant's categorical imperative – Act so that your actions could be a universal rule of behavior for the particular circumstance.
- ✓ The Golden Rule – Do unto others as you would have them do unto you.
- ✓ The utilitarian principle – Do things that benefit the greatest good for the greatest number of people.
- ✓ The professional ethic – Only do things that would be considered proper by an objective group of professional associates.
- ✓ Laws usually portray only the lowest level of acceptable conduct. Being ethical means your behavior is usually at a level higher than the law requires.
- ✓ Law is reactive.

Understanding Ethics

Ethics tries to give guidance and support prior to or during difficult ethical dilemmas. The level of ethics within an organization is usually informally established by the chief administrator. The complexity of ethical decision making is created by the organization, professional norms, the individuals involved, and changing society values. Ethical decisions are a necessary part of working within a government or business. There is no single ethical guideline that all managers will agree is the answer to most ethics decision making. Being able to apply a decision-making process composed of practical, effective guidelines can be invaluable.

Loyalty

Loyalty is part of the integrity of a social being. Loyalty is a matter of emotional ties and commitments far more basic than cold contractual relationships. Disloyalty is always reviled, but not all failures to act from loyalty are disloyal. Loyalty to principles and loyalty to people can come into conflict. "My leader (group, friend, department, country), right or wrong" is an attitude that causes a lot of trouble.

Paradigms

We discussed paradigms briefly before, but let us recap this important concept again. Covey (1989, 1994) discusses the role paradigms play in the decision-making process. Paradigms are taken-for-granted commonsense perspectives and unwritten rules. Paradigms are the way our organization and we do things. Paradigms typically can result in damaging perceptions: "Our way or the highway." "We have always done it that way, so it must be right." Personal mastery is one way to overcome paradigms. Personal mastery requires one to understand who he or she is, recognize one's level(s) of competence and commitment, understand one's level of self-esteem, and recognize how fit one is to hold his or her position. Personal mastery can be achieved through the practice of introspection. This is the process of self-analysis and reflection. It can lead to a deeper understanding of ourselves and the beliefs, values, attitudes, and organizational culture that frame our motives. One's paradigm is the source from which attitudes and behaviors flow. A paradigm is like a pair of glasses. It affects the way one sees everything in life.

If you look at things through the paradigm of correct principles, what you see in life is dramatically different from what you see through any other centered paradigm. A "people" paradigm includes such terms as leadership, effectiveness, spontaneity, causes, release/empowerment, programmer, transformation, investment, customer service, principles, synergy, and abundance, whereas a "thing" paradigm includes such terms as management, efficiency, structure, measurement, effects/symptoms, control, program, transaction, administrative efficiency, techniques, compromise, scarcity, and satisficing. Both paradigms are important, but like with all things in life, there must be balance.

Paradigms

The "People" Paradigm	The "Thing" Paradigm
1. Leadership	Management
2. Effectiveness	Efficiency
3. Spontaneity	Structure
4. Causes	Measurement
5. Release/empowerment	Effects/symptoms
6. Programmer	Control
7. Transformation	Program
8. Investment	Transaction
9. Customer service	Administrative efficiency
10. Principles	Techniques
11. Synergy	Compromise
12. Abundance	Scarcity

The influence of illogical factors on our decision-making process causes individuals to engage in a process known as satisficing (Covey, 1989, 1994). Covey (1989, 1994) explains that this process occurs when an individual selects a solution that is just good enough instead of selecting the best course of action. Individuals often engage in satisficing in order to handle a problem with the least uncertainty and risk to themselves. The easiest way out is also caused by the need to appear decisive. This method only addresses the short term and fails to consider the long-term outcomes and impacts. To overcome satisficing, one should practice the art of introspection. Introspection involves assessing one's strengths, weaknesses, understanding, and what and who one is and evaluating personal and organizational expectations. In addition, one should be realistic and not expect perfection from oneself or others. Likewise, one should assess his or her capacity to recognize and deal with problems and understand one's personal biases. Finally, one should change those values and behaviors that need to be changed. Cooper drives this point home when he has stated, "Ethics is concerned about what is right, fair, just, or good; about what we ought to do, not just about what is the case or what is most acceptable or expedient" (1998, p 7).

One way to overcome paradigms is personal mastery.

Personal mastery requires one to

- understand who he or she is,
- recognize one's level(s) of competence and commitment,

- understand one's level of self-esteem,
- recognize how fit one is to hold his or her position.

Personal mastery can be achieved through the practice of introspection. This is the process of self-analysis and reflection. It can lead to a deeper understanding of ourselves and the beliefs, values, attitudes, and organizational culture that frame our motives.

Your paradigm is the source from which your attitudes and behaviors flow. A paradigm is like a pair of glasses. It affects the way you see everything in your life. If you look at things through the paradigm of correct principles, what you see in life is dramatically different from what you see through any other centered paradigm.

Satisficing

The influence of illogical factors on our decision-making process causes individual to engage in a process known as satisficing. This process occurs when an individual selects a solution that is just good enough instead of selecting the best course of action. Individuals often engage in satisficing in order to handle a problem with the least uncertainty and risk to themselves. The easiest way out also caused by the need to appear decisive. This method only addresses the short term and fails to consider the long-term outcomes and impacts.

Introspection

- Assess one's strengths and weaknesses.
- Understand what and who one is.
- Evaluate personal and organization expectations.
- Be realistic, and do not expect perfection from yourself or others.
- Assess one's capacity to recognize and deal with problems.
- Understand one's personal biases.
- Change those values and behaviors that need to be changed.

DR. JEFFREY C. FOX

Kaizen

One way to respond to the results of your self-evaluation is to practice the art of *Kaizen*. Every day, find some small way to improve yourself and the way you perform your function(s).

Why Unethical Acts Occur in Policing

Pollock (1998) explains that police corruption can be described in three general ways. First is systemic. Systemic deviance is caused by the relationship between the police and the public. The second is institutional. These explanations point to general organizational problems such as low managerial visibility, low public visibility, peer group secrecy, poor role modeling by leadership being corrupt, front-line interface with criminals, and the tension between the use of discretion and bureaucracy. The third and final explanation is the individual. This explanation assumes the rotten apple theory. In other words, the individual officer has deviant inclinations before he or she joined the force. Sloppy recruiting and poor backgrounds are a by-product of this. According to Kappeler et al. (1998), there are five neutralizing techniques officers use to rationalize or explain away unethical acts. These neutralization techniques include denial of responsibility, denial of injury, denial of victim, condemning the condemners, and appeal to higher loyalties.

Organizational Structure – Occupational Culture Theory

The organizational theory of police corruption emphasizes the importance of organizational and occupational culture (Klockars, Ivkovich, Harver, and Haberfield, 2000). While the following may seem harsh, it strikes at the heart of one point to be made. Kleinig (1990) says that the essentially nonprofessional lower expectations of police are no doubt partly responsible for the strongly hierarchal, militaristic character of most police organizations. This only reinforces deliberative ignorance and manifests itself in the maxims of police culture "Cover your a— —," "Don't make waves," "Never give up another cop," etc. There are many models or explanations supporting the organizational theory of corruption (Braswell, McCarthy, and McCarthy, 2002). Several of these will be illustrated.

Donahue (1992) says that there are informal codes of ethics in policing just like in any occupational subculture or craft. Donahue goes on to say that understanding the implications bureaucratization plays in causing the failure of an effective code in policing is difficult. Donahue says that bureaucracy precludes bilateral communications, role reciprocity, and the development of binding consensual norms, all of which are needed to create standard normative action. Ironically, the professionalization of policing is meant to eliminate the root causes of corruption. The politics are to be taken out of the selection and retention of officers. The officers are to be military-style crime fighters who are separated from the citizens they are to serve. All of this bureaucratization has the reverse effect regarding corruption (Donahue, 1992; Donahue and Felts, 1993; Pollock, 1998).

The superior-subordinate relationship of military-style policing caused a hierarchical relationship and prohibited two-way communication (Donahue, 1992). Worden (1995) stated, in keeping with authoritarianism or a bureaucratic and military style of management or policing, studies on police pointed out that officers were no greater and maybe even less authoritarian in nature than were any other member of society. Comparison groups such as college students, teachers, and working class people were used in these studies; and little to no difference was found. Again, this lent itself to two points. First, officers may resent such bureaucratic or military-style management, and second, those who did police in such style may be adapting to it as a survival skill or learned mechanism of coping with one's environment (Donahue, 1992; Shernock, 1990).

Muscari went as far as to say, "Indeed, one of the pillars of thought that has been virtually overturned by a structural reassessment of corruption has been the longstanding 'rotten apple' theory—the traditional view which saw corruption as the effect of individual police officers who were simply too weak or dishonest to resist the temptation inherent in police work" (1984, p. 236).

Murphy (1985) paints a clear picture of more elements of organizational corruption. These elements are more pronounced than mere management style. However, they are just as relevant and probably more controversial. Such things as giving choice assignments to friends and allies, hiring and promoting personnel based on reasons other than potential and performance, sowing seeds of corruption through one's own behavior, cronyism, and prejudice all help create fertile soil for the seeds of corruption.

The General Accounting Office (1998) completed a comprehensive report on drug-related police corruption for a member of the U.S. House of Representatives. In this report, it showed that, approximately every twenty years, New York City Police Department has undergone a major corruption scandal. Many other major cities have had cyclical corruption scandals as well. This report, and other research, helps clearly solidify the viewpoint that the causes of corruption are more than just bad apples. It is, at least, partially a result of the given organizational culture.

Discretionary Powers and Authority

Such adages as "Us against them," the thin blue line, the war on crime, and the war on drugs all represent order and disorder. Authority, force, and discretion are all elements inherent in the role of law enforcement. No other criminal justice professional has such power or autonomy. Likewise, no other criminal justice professional receives as much scrutiny from the public or other criminal justice professionals as law enforcement officers (Braswell et al., 2002; Pollock, 1998). Realism allows officers to justify in their minds that the ends truly do justify the means—back to the adage of the war on crime. Viewing the general citizenry or a certain segment of any given population as the enemy in a war model of crime paradigm will only exacerbate the divide or rift between law enforcement and the community they serve. This "take no prisoners" approach will only cause more brutality and corruption (Winright, 1995).

O'Malley (1997) cautions that the idea that community policing will cure corruption has its own potential pitfalls. While community- and/or problem-oriented policing has many benefits, the amount of discretion that both styles allow can lead to corruption by officers who have great latitude to act and make decisions with little oversight. After all, it is the wide-open and political style of policing that lead to reform that ends in a bureaucratic and military style of policing where the police are removed from the public and go into a "patrol and respond" mode.

According to Pollock (1998) and Worden (1995), regarding the use of discretion, there are four general typologies. The first is the old-style crime fighter who is only concerned with crime control. The second is the clean beat officer. This officer seeks to control all behavior in his or her jurisdiction. The third is service style, which emphasizes public order and peace officer tasks. And fourth, there is professional style, which empathizes bureaucratic, by-the-book policing. There is another set of officers described, and they are the professional who balances coercion and compassion and the reciprocating officer who allows citizens to solve their own problems. The other two are the enforcer who operates solely off coercion and the avoider who cannot handle the power and fears it so much that he or she avoids situations where it must be used.

Cultural Indoctrination

Police agencies, like many other organizations, tend to develop their own unique organizational culture. Adcox (2000) and Braswell et al. (2002) state informal values, beliefs, norms, rituals, and expectations come to play as much of, or more of, a role as do the formal expectations. Often, these informal rites are in direct conflict with the formal ones. To some degree, continued employment is affected by how well or how much one adopts or accepts informal rules. There are various stages of development involved in cultural socialization. First, most officers join the force because they believe they identify with many of the goals and values they perceive to be reality. Often, this comes through informal contacts they have developed. Next, the officer enters the academy and is taught the culture. Much of this is subliminal and done through war stories. They are taught what it takes to be a good officer.

Then once they leave the academy, they train with a field training officer (FTO). Here they will learn the unwritten code of conduct. Finally, during the fourth stage, the individual officer learns the realities of police work by using the process of internal adaptation. During this stage, the officer has constant exposure to group norms and often comes to strongly identify with values and beliefs held within the organizational culture while absorbing its standards as his or her own. It is not if the officer will be influenced but rather who will influence him or her (Kleinig, 1990). An informal subculture, which is going to exist regardless, is the most obvious threat to the internalization of ethical standards (Pollock, 1998).

A police officer must act in the role of officer first and person second. The officer must display more self-control and discipline than the average citizen. With this tremendous responsibility comes a heightened sense of duty to the profession. With this and all the duties and responsibilities that are extraordinary to the citizens the officer serves comes a unique work environment. Kappeler (1995) states the environment tends to create a sense of loyalty and trust since officers know that, at any moment, their life may very well depend on a fellow officer. This officer will depend on the skills and courage displayed by his or her fellow officer. In fact, the element of bravery is so strong among officers that to even discuss pain, guilt, or fear can be considered as taboo. This interdependence creates a camaraderie that can either support or undermine the ethical behavior of fellow officers. Officers are trained to cope with actual external dangers. They are not trained to cope with having to confront fellow officers who create internal and external danger by unethical acts. This can be emotionally draining (Dantzker, 1997; Pollock, 1998).

Pollock (1998) illustrates three main themes that are emphasized in a police subculture. The first is cynicism. Their work life leads them to the general conclusion that all people are weak, corrupt, and/or dangerous. Everyone is viewed with suspicion. The second value is the use of force for any situation that is perceived as a threat. The potential for the use of force is a clear symbol of authority and legitimate dominance. And third, there is the general idea by police that they are victims from public scorn and misunderstanding. Pollock goes on to say that some of these values are starting to be chipped away with the inclusion of a more diverse police workforce. Yet one should not think that the police are different from other subcultures. Each has its own set of values and is based on its own unique set of circumstances, be they real, perceived, or both (Graves, 1996). The difference with police and other subcultures is the power the police maintain over other people and society in general.

Misplaced loyalty creates ethical dilemmas for everyone and blurs the distinction between loyalty and as an accessory or accomplice to unethical behavior (Dantzker, 1997; Worden, 1995). Yet loyalty is a common element and, when held in the proper light, is healthy for an agency (Pollock, 1998). Another interesting point, but seldom mentioned, is that police agencies are close reflections of the communities and general morality they serve (Fyfe, Greene, Walsh, Wilson, and McLaren, 1997; Klockars et al., 2000; Pollock, 1998). This stands to reason when considering modeling, socialization, and cognitive dissonance.

Another unique area is how the officer deals with pain. For the most part, officers must develop an emotional barrier between themselves and all victims. This is done as a matter of survival. It will be virtually impossible, on a consistent basis, if one had to deal with everyone else's pain without blocking out his or hers (Pollock, 1998).

Code of Silence

According to the National Institute of Ethics (2000) and Pollock (1998), the code of silence plays a major role in police corruption. Much writing and research has been done on this issue. In some cases, the code only applies to low-level corruption; and in others, it includes the most serious forms of corruption. The majority of studies involving the code of silence reveal that, in general, most police officers will not report other officers for what they perceive to be less serious forms of corruption. The level of reporting goes up as the level of corruption increases. Likewise, the code varies between agencies (Klockars et al., 2000). Two reasons given for the code of silence are (1) that police fear the loss of autonomy and authority as external groups try to limit police discretion and decision-making ability and (2) the potential mistakes officers can make since they are called upon to make split-second decisions (Kappeler, 1995; Pollock, 1998). Pollock (1998) added two more reasons for a fundamental mistrust by officers; they are a mistrust of superiors and bureaucratic administration. Misplaced loyalty is exalted over integrity in many organizational cultures, and the element of camaraderie is at play (Kleinig and Gorman, 1992; O'Malley, 1997). Any formal code of ethics is automatically undermined by a police subculture that requires its members to be loyal and trustworthy at any cost.

Shernock (1990) stated a great many officers tacitly agreed to uphold the code of silence to protect their own from all others. In one study, officers were asked, "What was the most desirable characteristic of a rookie officer?" Forty-seven percent of those surveyed said, "He should keep his mouth shut." Thirteen percent said, "He shouldn't be a stool pigeon." In this study, it was shown that the formal police culture did not accept, ask for, or condone the code of silence. Yet the police subculture did require allegiance to the code in order to be fully accepted. As part of this same study, a sample of the overall group of officers responded when asked if they would report a fellow officer who took money from a drunken citizen. Seventy-seven percent said they would perjure themselves for the officer, and 73 percent said they would not report the incident. Based on research from other studies dealing with the code of silence, it was questionable as to how generalizable these results were, but they may not be too far off.

Another reason for the code of silence is that police operate in an isolated mode. Officers generally take a "we/they" or "us against them" attitude. The attitude the seasoned officer develops teaches other officers that nonpolice cannot understand the true nature of police work (Kappeler, 1995; O'Malley, 1997; Pollock, 1998). Fyfe et al. (1997) indicate that the we/they mentality is increased with a lack of cultural awareness. They go on to say that the code of silence has considerable merit and that without it, widespread corruption cannot exist.

Illustrative Studies

In research conducted by Felkenes (1984), he posed several questions to law enforcement officers in three agencies in California. They were in questionnaire form and asked about officers' attitudes toward police ethics. The results were less than glowing. Fifty-two percent of the officers indicated that they agreed with or were neutral toward the idea that an officer must sometimes use unethical means to accomplish the enforcement of law. More than a third agreed that they would take action if they knew of unethical conduct on the part of a colleague. Most stated they understood ethical principles but that these same principles were not necessarily helpful. Forty-one percent said police professional ethics were too abstract or idealistic to be of much use in actual practice. Over 75 percent said they relied on their personal ethics and not law enforcement ethics to guide them in their job. These research findings were indicative of other findings.

In a national study done by Bryant, Greenspan, Hamilton, Weisburd, and Williams (2000) on police attitudes toward abuse of authority, many significant facts were gleaned from the survey results. This survey involved 925 randomly selected officers representing 121 departments. The survey was done by telephone. The survey consisted of 92 questions. Agencies were municipal and county departments. Some of the findings were as follows. More than 80 percent stated they did not accept the code of silence. Yet approximately 25 percent said whistle-blowing was not worthwhile. Sixty-seven percent of these respondents stated that they would be given the cold shoulder for whistle-blowing. Fifty-two percent agreed or strongly agreed that it was not unusual for an officer to ignore another officer's improper conduct. A staggering 61 percent indicated that police officers did not always report serious criminal violations that involved the abuse of authority by fellow officers. A large majority believed supervisors, mainly the first-line supervisors and chief, could make a difference by the leadership exhibited. There were significant differences between the race and sex of the officer and their views on these issues. The results were but a small sampling of the overall results gleaned from this comprehensive research project.

Dantzker (1997) speaks to the heart of the question in a peripheral manner. Dantzker says that, for a police code of ethics to be effective, it must address the realities that officers are likely to face. Such a code must be reasonable, given the realities of the job. Dantzker goes on to distinguish between what officers think and what they do. We are all tempted at times, but the measure of character is when we resist temptations. Adding more credence to the research at hand, Kleinig (1990) indicates that experienced officers are able to bring moral reflection, wisdom, and realisms of exposure to complexities of situations and pragmatism to their world.

Miller and Braswell (1992) conducted a study wherein they analyzed police perceptions of ethical decision making by looking at the ideal versus the real. They said that police were no different from the rest of society. With that, they said that police learned right from wrong during their employment. Further, most recruits came into the profession with an idealistic attitude. These officers brought their own beliefs and values into the organization but quickly adapted to the new environment. Hence came what the officer perceived as ethical behavior and what they actually did in ethical decision-making situations. Finally, these officers changed over a short period. Sets of hypothetical situations were presented to the officers, and they were asked what they should do and what they would do. The study was longitudinal. The questions were asked again three years later to the same officers. In brief, the data tended to show that officers might not change their moral values or beliefs because of employment. Yet the realistic viewpoint did change. Inferred from this was the assumption that officers came to view unethical acts as more acceptable in the profession.

Continuum of Compromise

Entitlements

Gilmartin and Harris (1998) explain that most police agencies are still reactive to unethical conduct. This method is a stopgap measure and will do little to correct the problems in the end. While it is necessary to be reactive to violations, agencies need to be proactive. Providing officers with a core base of values does this. This begins in the basic academy and with every class afterward. It must continue with one's entire career. A central trait of the deterioration of values is the idea or thought of entitlement. This entitlement mentality allows the officer to rationalize and justify behaviors that are clearly outside the level of acceptance. Entitlements are especially prevalent in police work. By virtue of their position, they should be exempt from what is normally ethically acceptable. Such terms as "professional courtesy," "rank has its privileges," and "half price or free" are all examples of entitlements. Police officers do what most of society will not. Being exposed to the unsavory side of life, coupled with a special authority that few people have, greatly exacerbates this idea of entitlement. Having near-ultimate authority without a firm set of ethics or core values from which to operate places individual officers in a position to act inappropriately. A belief of entitlements can only be offset by a culture of ethical accountability. This accountability must come from within oneself and the organization as a whole.

Gilmartin and Harris (1998) sum up the entire development involving corruption through an organizational process. The transformation from an idealistic officer into a self-serving officer who believes in looking out for number one is subtle and happens without the officer's knowledge. Gilmartin and Harris explain that a series of steps takes place in what they call the continuum of compromise. First is the idea and mind-set of entitlements. Police do what others will not. They are exposed to the bad side of life. They have near-ultimate authority. Coupled with this, they say that most agencies are reactive and employ stopgap measures to corruption. The entitlement mentality allows officers to rationalize and justify unacceptable behavior on their part. Without a firm set of values to operate, officers are placed into a moral vacuum. Likewise, the officer must improvise and become involved in situational ethics. Inciardi (1987) states that police corruption begins with the notion that officers, by some divine right, are entitled to free meals and discounts for everything they buy. What Gilmartin and Harris call the continuum of compromise others call the slippery slope (e.g., Braswell et al., 2002; Delattre, 2002).

Gilmartin and Harris (1998) explain the continuum of comprise as follows:

> The continuum helps to explain how the honest police officer turns into a dishonest officer. It helps explain that not all-dishonest officers are bad apples at first. In many cases, we have the knowledge and foresight to keep many officers from acting dishonestly. In addition to the entitlement versus accountability principle there are several other key factors in the continuum. First, there is the perceived victimization the officer feels. This is especially true when an officer overly invests him or herself into their job. They can have an over identification with their role. What begins with an alienation from the public drifts into an alienation from the agency and the entire criminal justice system. An attitude of the ends justifies the means may develop. No one knows more, and everyone else is stupid. The officer becomes increasingly resentful of anyone who tries to control him or his job. This is not uncommon and many officers travel this path throughout their careers.

A strong loyalty factor plays a role as well. Two key elements in the continuum are loyalty versus integrity and the code of silence.

Another key factor pointed out by Gilmartin and Harris (1998) is the "loyalty versus integrity" issue. Most officers want to be known for being loyal. Likewise, the code of silence is very strong in police agencies. Police work involves many life-and-death situations. Many times, to overcome a threat of bodily harm, an officer will need help. This is a strong factor in loyalty.

The next three areas deal with acts. This is where it all comes together. When an officer has the entitlement mind-set, feels victimized, and believes he has the loyalty of those involved or with potential knowledge, these acts may surface. The first act is the act of omission. This results in decreased work efforts and passive resistance. At this level, little is normally done by the leadership in the agency or the officer's peers. Next come the administrative acts of commission. This is the next logical step. In this stage, violations are administrative in nature. An example of this will be padding arrest numbers. This stage can begin to delve into or near the final act—the criminal act of commission. One such example will be falsifying time slips and receiving money not earned (Gilmartin and Harris, 1998). These criminal acts can run the gamut from forged records to murder. Many officers never make it past the act of omission or the act of administrative commission.

It is when we put together entitlement, victimization, loyalty, and the void—which may exist for a core belief system—that we begin to see more acts of omission and commission. This helps explain why some agencies are more prone to reoccurring incidents of corruption and others are not. This theory of how good officers go bad is not offered as an excuse but as part of the answer. Likewise, it does not mean that bad apples are not hired.

Once these elements are in place, officers become involved in various levels or acts in the continuum of compromise. The first level is acts of omission, which involve such things as reduced work and passive resistance. These involve administrative matters that should be done but are not or not to the degree expected. Administrative acts of commission are next. These include padding arrest numbers and other purposeful things done to violate policy but not the law. Finally come criminal acts of commission. This includes everything criminal, from falsifying time slips for extra money to perjury to murder (Gilmartin and Harris, 1998).

Gilmartin and Harris conclude by saying that, when putting this all together, several patterns emerge. We have entitlements, along with victimization, coupled with strong loyalty and the void of a belief system. This helps explain why some agencies are more corrupt than others. Most officers move in and out of the acts of omission area, some delve into administrative acts of commission, and a few move into criminal acts of commission (Gilmartin and Harris, 1998).

Police do what most people will not. They are exposed to the bad side of life. They have near-ultimate authority. Without a firm set of ethics from which to operate, officers are placed in a moral vacuum. Without an ethical base, they will improvise. They become involved in situational ethics.

This leads us to the continuum of compromise.

- ✓ It helps explain how good officers go bad.
- ✓ It helps explain how and why some agencies have persistent bouts of corruption.

Officer Perceives Victimization Status

This is especially true when officer overinvests in the job. Alienation from the public drifts into alienation of the agency and system. The "ends justify the means" attitude develops. The officer becomes resentful of anyone who tries to tell him or her how to do the job. Strong loyalty factor plays a major role for officers.

The Acts

- ✓ Acts of Omission
  - o Reduced work
  - o Passive resistance, etc.
- ✓ Administrative Acts of Commission
  - o Padding arrest numbers, etc.
  - o Coming close to bordering on criminal in some cases
- ✓ Criminal Acts of Commission
  - o Falsifying time slips
  - o Perjury

- Forgery, assault, sexual acts, extortion, murder, etc.

Putting It Together

When you put together entitlement, victimization, loyalty, and the void—which may exist for a core belief system—we begin to see more acts of omission and commission. This helps explain why some agencies are more prone to corruption than others. Most officers during their career will flow in and out of the acts-of-omission stage. Some will delve into administrative acts of commission. Few will reach the criminal acts of commission.

System-wide corruption demonstrates the existence and power of informal peer group structures and the influence of the code of silence on officer behavior (Rothlein, 2000). My contention is that there is room enough in the many cases of police corruption for both the rotten apple theory and organizational structural theory to stand alone or, in many cases, to merge their synergistic causes and effects together (Muscari, 1984).

As Adcox explains, police agencies each have their own organizational culture. While there are general traits found in most agencies, each one is unique unto itself. Police officers are influenced by the agencies' ethics or lack thereof. The informal rules of any agency can be strong and normally are as strong as or stronger than the formal agency rules (Adcox, 2000). This is where peer pressure comes in. Likewise, Sutherland's theory of differential association plays a major role in the ability of one dishonest officer to bring in other officers under the web or umbrella of corruption.

It is when we put together entitlement, victimization, loyalty, and the void—which may exist for a core belief system—that we begin to see more acts of omission and commission. This helps explain why some agencies are more prone to reoccurring incidents of corruption than others. This theory of how good officers go bad is not offered as an excuse but as part of the answer. Likewise, it does not mean that bad apples are not hired.

Politics

According to Vicchio (1997), one recent survey showed from twelve professions listed that police officers recorded the largest drop in public trust between 1980 and 1995. They dropped five places. Among blacks, police officers went from ninth position in 1980 to eleventh position in 1995. They were one behind politicians and one ahead of lawyers, who were last. The conclusion was that the public, in general, thought that police officers had an integrity problem. Law enforcement did not operate in a vacuum. Corruption and unethical behavior were not limited to the police or to a period in policing (Kappeler et al., 1998).

Kappeler et al. (1998) stated that, from the earliest of times, police corruption and the politics of policing have gone hand in hand. It was this sort of thought that brought about a more militaristic, bureaucratic, and professional style of policing. It was thought that the further the police could be removed from politics and everyday contact with the average citizen, the more incorruptible they would be. There is much argument about this today, especially since most agencies are moving back to the public with community policing. It is the police, after all, who carry out the laws that the legislative and executive branches develop and enact. Often, the police withstand the worst of political ideologies and policies. This does not mean the police can be excused from wrongful actions carried out in the name of the government. It is meant to show the link between the two.

If one chief will not carry out the duties, another one will. If a chief goes against the grain and tries to carry out his or her duties in an ethical manner, he or she may or may not succeed. With a sheriff, it is more hit or miss. It is the will of the people. Commission after commission has studied police corruption. City after city has been plagued with police corruption, often repeatedly. As can be seen, politics play a significant role in ethical policing. We have very briefly touched on politics at the macro level of policing as it involves ethics. All too often, the corrective action taken or needed is half-hearted, is a quick fix, and does not last. By now, it is obvious leadership plays or should play a critical role in police ethics.

This leads us to the political arena. One recent survey showed that that of twelve (12) professions listed police officers recorded the largest drop in public trust between 1980 to 1995. They dropped (5) five places. Among black's police officer's opinions, they went from

9th position in 1980 to 11th position in 1995. They were one behind politicians and one ahead of lawyers who were last. The conclusion was that the public, in general, thinks that police officers have an integrity problem (Vicchio, 1997). Law enforcement does not operate in a vacuum. Corruption and unethical behavior are not limited to the police or to a period in policing.

From the earliest of times police corruption and the politics of policing have gone hand in hand. It was this sort of thought that brought about a more militaristic, bureaucratic, and professional style of policing. It was thought that the further the police could be removed from politics and everyday contact with the average citizen the more incorruptible they would be. There is much argument about this today especially since most agencies are moving back to the public with community policing. It is the police after all who carry out the laws that the legislative and executive branch develop and enact. Often it is the police who bear the brunt of political ideologies and policies. This does not mean the police can be excused from wrongful actions carried out in the name of government. It is meant to merely show the link between the two.

The Leader's Role in the Organization and Unethical Police Behavior

While leadership and management are critical in all organizations, it is especially important for policing because of the authority and impact the police have on all of society. Policing has traditionally been a culture, which is slow to change and very tradition bound. Officers are trained to act independently, and they wield great power and discretion. While certain minimum standards are similar among most agencies, other standards, such as education, vary widely. These issues, among others, create a unique culture.

The first-line supervisor sets the tone for his or her unit (Oldham, 2003). If the first-line supervisor will not do his or her job, then all is lost. Anecdotally speaking, policing—and probably many professions—has more managers than they do leaders. Two mantras are offered to begin this exploration of police leadership. First, one should manage things and lead people. Next, managers do things right, and leaders do the right things (Johnson, 2001).

Community policing requires a different style of management, which is more participative and less bureaucratic. Yet according to Wuestewald and Steinheider (2006), a 2002 national survey has revealed that while 70 percent of police agencies surveyed have decentralized some operations to perform community policing, only 22 percent of the same departments have moved away from a bureaucratic hierarchy. Authority and decision making have not been pushed down. This speaks volumes as to the issue at hand. This data should not be surprising. Alsabrook, Aryani, and Garrett (2001) state that law enforcement has traditionally been very slow to change. This change may take decades. The problem with this is society is changing at a much faster rate. Some agencies are tradition bound, and managers feel they are the guardians of the status quo. Fyfe et al. (1997) and Johnson (2001) state leaders have a zone of influence. This zone is found in the intersection between the goals of the organization and the goals of the individual. Yet every day, the news is filled with examples of poor, unethical, or nonexistent leadership taking place. This void of leadership can be found in all occupations, but nowhere is this void more harmful than in policing. Hansen (1991) states that lack of effective leadership can cause great harm to an agency (Johnson, 2001).

Noble Cause Corruption

Another type, style, or explanation for police corruption is called noble cause corruption. Martinelli (2006) defines this as corruption committed in the name of good ends and happens when police care too much about their work. With noble cause corruption, the ends justify the means. Officers believe there is no accountability and push the limits of what is constitutionally permissible in what they deem in the name of justice. This lack of perceived accountability may be real or imagined. Planting evidence; lying in court, also called "testilying"; and excessive force or street justice are all prime examples of noble cause corruption. Officers do not view bending the rules as misconduct or corruption. They tend to rationalize such action by applying a utilitarian principle of the greatest good for the greatest number. Too much emphasis on enforcement and not enough on the service aspect of the job can help foster such a mentality (Meese and Ortmeier, 2004).

Organizational Structure – Occupational Culture Theory

The organizational theory of police corruption emphasizes the importance of organizational and occupational culture (Klockars, et al., 2000). While the following may seem harsh, it strikes at the heart of one point to be made. Kleinig says that the lower, essentially nonprofessional, expectations of police are no doubt partly responsible for the strongly hierarchal, militaristic character of most police organizations. This only reinforces deliberative ignorance and manifests itself in the maxims of police culture – "Cover your ass;" "Don't make waves;" and "Never give up another cop;" etc. (1990). There are many models or explanations supporting the organizational theory of corruption. Several of these will be illustrated.

Donahue says that there are informal codes of ethics in policing just like in any occupational subculture or craft. He goes on to say that understanding the implications bureaucratization plays in causing the failure of an effective code in policing is difficult. He says that bureaucracy precludes bilateral communications, role reciprocity, and the development of binding consensual norms all of which are needed to create standard normative action (1992). Ironically, the professionalization of policing was meant to eliminate the root causes of corruption. The politics were to be taken out of the selection and retention of officers. The officers were to be military style crime fighters that were separated from the citizens they were to serve. All of this bureaucratization had the reverse affect regarding corruption (Pollock, 1998; Donahue, 1992; Donahue and Felts, 1993).

The superior-subordinate relationship of military style policing caused a hierarchical relationship and prohibited two-way communication (Donahue, 1992). In keeping with authoritarianism or a bureaucratic and military style of management or policing, studies on police point out that officers are no greater and maybe even less authoritarian in nature than are any other member of society. Comparison groups such as college students, teachers and working class people were used in these studies and little to no difference was found (Worden, 1995). Again, this lends itself to two points. First, officers may resent such bureaucratic or military style management, and those who do police in such style may be adapting to it as a survival skill or learned mechanism of coping with one's environment (Donahue, 1992; Shernock, 1990).

Muscari went as far as to say, "Indeed, one of the pillars of thought that has been virtually overturned by a structural reassessment of corruption has been the longstanding 'rotten apple' theory-the traditional view which saw corruption as the effect of individual police officers who were simply to weak or dishonest to resist the temptation inherent in police work (1992, 236)." Murphy paints a clear picture of more elements of organizational corruption. These elements are more pronounced than mere management style. Yet they are just as relevant and probably more controversial. Such things as giving choice assignments to friends and allies, hiring and promoting personnel based on reasons other than potential and performance, sowing seeds of corruption through one's own behavior, cronyism and prejudice all help create fertile soil for the seeds of corruption (1985). The United States General Accounting Office completed a comprehensive report on drug related police corruption for a member of the U. S. House of Representatives. In this report, it showed that approximately every twenty years New York City Police Department has undergone a major corruption scandal. Many other major cities have had cyclical corruption scandals as well (1998). This report, and other research, helps to clearly solidify the viewpoint that the causes of corruption are more than just bad apples. It is, at least, partially a result of the given organizational culture.

The Individual, a.k.a. Rotten Apples

Bad apples do cause some ethical problems within an agency. This may be due to poor hiring, or it may be a deeper internal problem. Usually, it is caused by poor hiring practices. This is but one way people become bad apples. You show me a department that has an ongoing ethical dilemma, and I will show you something more than a bad apple.

Rotten Apple Theory

The theory poses the question are all unethical acts the result of bad apples? Another way to put it is, are police officers who violate the rules predisposed and hired as bad apples? Several years ago, the answer would have been a resounding "yes." There are still those who like to think so. Let us examine why the answer is "no" for the most part.

Until recently, most police administrators have viewed police corruption as a moral character defect within the individual officer who is caught in a corrupt act. Much time, money, and effort has been spent trying to weed out or keep out such bad-apple-type officers. However, in recent years, this theory has come under attack (Dantzker, 1997; Inciardi, 1987; Klockars, Ivkovich, Harver, and Haberfeld, 2000; General Accounting Office, 1998; Muscari, 1984). According to Muscari (1984), the rotten apple theory, which has been the traditional view of police corruption, sees corruption as the result of individual officers who are too weak or dishonest to resist the temptations commonly found in police work. While there can be, and probably are, many complicated answers as to why bad apples are what they are, one simple answer is that they operate off an ethical school of thought called egoism. That is, they are looking out for the number one or their own complete interest (Fair and Pilcher, 1991).

Widespread, reoccurring corruption cannot be explained away by the bad apple theory (Fyfe et al., 1997). Yet trying to explain away corruption with the bad apple theory has been a common mantra by agencies plagued with corruption. By using the bad apple theory, the department can save face and, in a subliminal way, avoid confronting what may very well be at the heart of the problem (Trautman, 1991). Furthermore, how can one explain away the fact that, as time goes by, officers begin to work in groups while performing corrupt activities? Are these bad apples able to just spot one another and know they can trust one another? Not likely.

There is a more plausible explanation to this phenomenon. A slightly expanded version of the rotten apple theory is the rotten pocket theory. This theory brings together several rotten apples to form a pocket of corruption within an organization. What the theory fails to elaborate on is the influence the organization has on such activities. One thing is for sure: failing to investigate and weed out rotten apples, coupled with a code of silence, will eventually spoil many more apples (Felkenes, 1984; General Accounting Office, 1998; Rothlein, 1998). However, credit is given to the code of silence, which helps such pockets of rotten apples survive (Felkenes, 1984; Pollock, 1998; Senna and Siegel, 1984). Striking is the fact that little to no research can be found to prove or disprove the rotten apple theory. While the theory seems to rely on common sense, there is little factual evidence offered to support this theory. One study done by Lersch and Mieczkowski (2000) shows much support for the theory of problem-prone officers. Clearly, this research project shows that a small number of officers seem to generate a large portion of the complaints.

In addition to the bad apple theory, there are two more groups in the corruption network. Fyfe et al. (1997) and Senna and Siegel (1984) state that first is the pervasive unorganized group. This occurs when most department members are corrupt but engage in wrongdoing independent of one another. The second type is pervasive organized corruption. This is the worst type. Two other terms for corrupt officers, used in the Knapp Commission findings, are meat eaters and grass eaters. Grass eaters accept payoffs as part of their everyday job but are not aggressive. They allow corruption to flourish by ignoring unethical behavior. Meat eaters are officers who aggressively solicit bribes and payoffs. This commission has found that the majority of officers are grass eaters (Delattre, 2002). What is troubling about the distinction made and the context it has been reported in is it seems to show grass eaters as less corrupt and more normal than the more aggressive meat eaters (Ivkovic, 2003).

Common Causes for Ethical Problems within an Organization

- ✓ Politics (improper/unwarranted intervention in discipline, hiring, promotion, etc.)
- ✓ Poor background investigations
- ✓ Poor FTO programs
- ✓ Poor role modeling

What to Do

Haberfeld (2006) discusses integrity management. Officers should know the rules, and if they do not, they should be taught and reinforced. Officers should support these rules. If officers do not support the rules, it should be explained to them why they should. Such issues as lawsuits and reduced funding can result. Destroyed lives and tarnished reputations to individuals and entire agencies can result. Citizens can be harmed. Officers should understand what disciplinary actions can be taken. Again, if officers do not understand the discipline process and the levels of discipline, they should be taught. Officers should believe discipline should be fair. If discipline is not fair, it should be made fair. Are officers willing to condone and not report misconduct? If officers are not willing to take action when viewing or having knowledge of misconduct, figure out how to make them willing to act. Several things can be implied from this series of questions. Agency leaders must understand and know their officers. Leaders must train their officers and constantly reinforce ethical behavior.

According to Braunstein and Tyre (1992) and O'Malley (1997), there are a great many things an agency can and must do to increase the level of ethical behavior among its officers and as an agency. The administration must be strong and set a high standard of ethical behavior within the entire agency. The chief and his or her staff must conduct their every action in a manner worthy of emulation. The hiring process must be as thorough as possible and the standards set high. If the hiring process works, along with academy and FTO training, most bad apples will be weeded out. Educational standards must be high. Research has shown and studies have verified that higher education advances ethical behavior among officers. The initial training must be grounded in ethical standards. No class should be taught that does not explain ethics as they pertain to the individual subject. Only positively motivated officers who have the highest of ethical integrity should be FTOs. This is critical. In-service training and all continuing training must include elements of ethics. Ethical simulation training must be taught. Statistical data must be constantly analyzed from such sources as citizens' complaints. Furthermore, needs assessments and surveys should be undertaken at periodic intervals. Discipline must be swift, sure, and fair. We react as we have been trained. If officers have not been trained in how to act in a given ethical dilemma, they will improvise and possibly act in an ethical vacuum.

The National Institute of Ethics (2000), Souryal (1998), and Meese and Ortmeier (2004) provide ethical maxims that help explain how individuals and agencies should act and what drives them to act that way. Kant's categorical imperative states that one should act so that your actions can be a universal rule of behavior for the particular circumstance. The Golden Rule says, "Do unto others as you would have them do unto you." Utilitarian principle says, "Do things that benefit the greatest good for the greatest number of people." The professional ethic advises to only do things that will be considered proper by an objective group of professional associates. In addition, it is important to understand that laws usually portray only the lowest level of acceptable conduct. Just because an officer can do an act legally does not mean he or she should from an ethical viewpoint. Being ethical means your behavior is usually at a level above or higher than the law requires. Law is reactive.

Ethics tries to give guidance and support prior to or during difficult ethical dilemmas. The chief administrator usually informally establishes the level of ethics within an organization. The complexity of ethical decision-making is created by the organization, professional norms, the individuals involved, and changing society values. Ethical decisions are a necessary part of working within a government or business. There is no single ethical guideline, which all managers will agree is the answer to most ethical decision-making. Being able to apply a decision-making process comprised of practical, effective guidelines can be invaluable (Rawls, 1971).

According to the National Institute of Ethics (2000), when deciding any action, a series of questions is worth asking. Am I acting out of anger, lust, greed, or peer pressure? Will my loved ones be proud or ashamed? Is it worth my job or career? Am I following the Golden Rule? If the answer is no to any of these, then the action should not occur.

Media

Law enforcement programs are consistently the most popular shows on television. From the 1960s through the 1990s, themes of crime and criminal justice have constituted the single largest subject matter on television across all types of programming. Most television shows like to portray the police as winning and the bad guy as something less than desirable. This is the good news. The bad news is that television shows seldom portray law enforcement in an accurate light (McNeely, 1995). Having illustrated the public's desire for police-related shows, it is no wonder the media spends such an inordinate amount of time covering police-related issues. As Brooks indicates, the news media has a distinct role to play in our democracy (1999, p. 22). We have a system of checks and balances between the three branches of government. However, who checks them and keeps them honest? It is the press and the First Amendment.

It is through the media that public outcry leads to demands for reforms, ousters, and overall accountability of corrupt agencies and individual officers. It is then up to the various administrations, commissions, and politicians to set change in motion, if done at all. The media and police have an interesting relationship. It is in the best interest of the police to work closely with the media and vice versa. However, both take a guarded approach to their relationship for different reasons. Both entities have or should have a vested interest in each other. After all, crime sells.

The police should not blame the press for airing stories that are unfavorable to them. Likewise, the media should report stories in an impartial and fair manner. The public has a right to know what is going on in their communities. This is especially true when it comes to police corruption or any ethical issue involving the government. In other words, the media plays a key role in keeping the police honest and in keeping the public accurately informed. This role has been forever changed with the augment of video cameras. Now the public can see firsthand the police in action (Braunstein and Tyre, 1992, p. 30).

To help illustrate the important role the media plays in our system of justice, here are a few excerpts from an article written by Witkin (1995) for U.S. News and World Report.

> Mark Fuhrman uttered the "n" word forty-one times as he explained his opposition for putting up a police headquarters in a certain area. He went on to say, "We basically tortured

them. We broke 'em. Their faces were just mush." These were excerpts brought out at the Simpson trial. Witkin went on to explain that New Orleans had more than fifty officers arrested since 1993 for rape, aggravated battery, drug trafficking and murder. New York City had nearly fifty officers arrested since March of 1994 in Harlem and the Bronx for drug trafficking, extortion, brutality and civil rights violations. (p. 20)

While all of these incidents are sickening and beyond comprehension, they are important for the public to know.

The media and police have an interesting relationship. Braunstein and Tyre (1992) argue that it is in the best interest of the police to work closely with the media and vice versa. However, both take a guarded approach to their relationship for different reasons. Both entities have or should have a vested interest in each other. After all, crime sells. The police should not blame the press for airing stories that are unfavorable to them. Likewise, the media should report stories in an impartial and fair manner. The public has a right to know what is going on in their communities. This is especially true when it comes to police corruption or any ethical issue involving government. In other words, the media plays a key role in keeping the police honest and in keeping the public accurately informed. This role has been forever changed with the augment of video cameras. Now the public can see firsthand the police in action.

Resolution of the Problem

The actual or expected outcomes, which can result from implementing the recommendations made, are dependent upon several variables such as the degree and breadth of unethical behavior that exists, agency leadership's willingness to act, and environmental issues such as external or community corruption. Often, agencies will engage in stopgap measures that only temporally fix a problem but do little to cure the issue. Satisficing also occurs wherein only just enough is done to make it appear the leadership has a handle on the matter (National Institute of Ethics, 2000).

There are many areas where improvement may occur if an agency and its employees act ethically. Police suicide because of shame and feelings of hopelessness after being involved in corruption will be reduced. Alcohol abuse, which can also be a cause of corruption, will be reduced. Officers, families, agencies, and the communities they serve will be less negatively affected by unethical actions. Fewer bad apples will be hired with stringent hiring standards that are not lowered. Brutality, rudeness, and lack of civility will be reduced. This can have significant impact on minority communities. Greater faith in the criminal justice system will occur. Lawsuits may be reduced, and awards from judgments will lessen the loss of public monies. Good employees will be less likely to leave. Agency leadership will be more effective, which will result in increased efficiency and effectiveness in all initiatives. Fewer cases will be lost from unethical acts, and better case law will result (National Institute of Ethics, 2000).

Unethical acts are committed by bad apples and those who become bad apples through a process of perceived victimization, perceived entitlements, false loyalties, and finally through a continuum of compromise or slippery slope. This process, coupled with a strong subculture of preexisting unethical behavior and taking into consideration the theory of differential association, is a breeding ground for corrupt departments. Ethics can and must be taught and reinforced. A hiring process must be in place that will employ only those with strong ethical backgrounds and a set of core values that the agency can further build upon and constantly reinforce.

The media plays an important and necessary role in our system of checks and balances. Police agencies should work with the media and not against them in helping gain and maintain the support of the public in their endeavor to provide a professional police service. The politics of policing at the macro and micro levels must be considered, understood, and dealt with always in an ethical manner. Finally, agencies must move beyond soapbox ethics and practice open and honest communications while fostering an environment of inclusiveness and fairness within the entire agency. Every employee, be it the rookie officer or the chief of police, must realize and remember that character is how you act when no one is looking. It is not if any given officer will face an ethical dilemma or choice; it is how he or she will respond when it is time to act. All officers and leaders must be prepared and equipped to reject unethical behavior by anyone at any time.

As Kant argued, policy makers must understand it is not for their own good they act but out of pure duty to others (Bobbio, 1998). Bobbio (1998) speaks within a Machiavellian mind-set when he says it is foolish to demand honesty in political life. This one statement sums up the critical importance of ethical decision making in the public policy process. It is foolish to demand anything less than ethical decision making and honesty in politics. Foster (2001) states society as a whole must demand high standards of human conduct. Such conduct applies to all members, including the policy makers. Lynch and Lynch (2002) state that ethics is not the main goal of the government, just how national defense is, but it is the foundation of everything the government does.

Ethics statements, training, and oversight are all offered as remedies to decrease unethical acts (Mitchell, 1999). Leaders must set the ethical tone, be it in the political arena, corporate world, or public service (Blank, 2003; Sherren, 2005). Ethics training is beneficial as a reinforcement tool. Several legislative initiatives such as the Federal Sentencing Guidelines for Organizations (FSGO) of 1991 and the Sarbanes-Oxley Act of 2002 have created the need for more ethics training in the corporate world (Tyler, 2005). Tyler (2005) states that before ethics training is implemented, standards should be set. Likewise, this training should be for all employees. One ethical decision-making model offers the following questions or statements to ask or abide by: Is the action legal? Does it comply with our values? If you do it, will you feel bad? How will it look in the newspaper? If you know it's wrong, don't do it; and if you are not sure, ask. Keep asking until you get an answer. These are good questions but alone will not provide enough guidance to develop ethical policies.

> *Qui custodiet ipsos custodes?*
> *(Who shall guard the guardians?)*
> (Roman poet Juvenal)

Law is reactive. Ethics are proactive. Ethics tries to give guidance and support prior to or during difficult ethical dilemmas. Ethical decisions are a necessary part of working within a government or business. There is no single ethical guideline, which all managers will agree is the answer to most ethics decision-making. Being able to apply a decision-making process comprised of practical, effective guidelines can be invaluable. Bobbio (1998) speaks within a Machiavellian mind-set when he says it is foolish to demand honesty in political life. This one statement sums up the critical importance of ethical decision making in the public policy process. It is foolish to demand anything less than ethical decision making and honesty in politics. Policy makers and the citizens they serve are all responsible for ensuring that all government actions are ethical (Carlee, 2004; Pollock, 1998).

Training

We react the way we have been trained. How much ethics training have you had?

What can an officer do?

The National Institute of Ethics (2000) and Souryal (1998) proffer that one should understand oneself, his or her religious ethics, secular ethics, the law, and department policy. One should understand the role entitlements play, the role the continuum of compromise plays, and the role loyalty and integrity plays. Likewise, one should understand the role the code of silence plays and the role the organization plays. Last, one should understand the role the community plays and the role all of their experiences play. One must choose to be ethical.

Ask Yourself

- ✓ Am I acting out of anger, lust, greed, or peer pressure?
- ✓ Will my loved ones be proud or ashamed?
- ✓ Is it worth my job or career?
- ✓ Am I following the Golden Rule?

Understand oneself and

- ✓ his or her religious ethics or values,
- ✓ secular ethics or values,
- ✓ law,
- ✓ policy.

Understand

- ✓ the role entitlements play,
- ✓ the role the continuum of compromise plays,
- ✓ the role loyalty and integrity plays,
- ✓ the role the code of silence plays,
- ✓ the role the organization plays,
- ✓ the role the community plays,
- ✓ the role all of their past experiences play.

What can an organization do?

A strong administration sets and lives by a high ethical standard. Hiring process and standards cannot be lowered. Academy and FTO training must teach ethics in every topic. Likewise, they must have the moral courage to weed out the bad apples. High educational standards should be fostered. Conduct periodic needs assessment and act on the same. (Survey employees and the public for real and perceived ethical behavior and the prevalence of the code of silence, anonymous questionnaires should be utilized, make a data analysis involving noncompliance issues, etc.)

Discipline must be swift, sure, and above all fair. Ethics must be taught throughout the employee's entire career. Simulation ethics training and other state-of-the-art training involving ethics must be employed. Move beyond soapbox ethics and practice open and honest communications. Foster an environment of inclusiveness and fairness within the entire agency. Remove the idea of entitlements and replace it with ethical accountability. Remember that character is defined by how you act or what you do when no one is looking!

There are a great many things an agency can and must do to increase the level of ethical behavior among its officers and as an agency. The administration must be strong and set a high standard of ethical behavior within the entire agency. The chief and his or her staff must conduct their every action in a manner worthy of emulation. The hiring process must be as thorough as possible and the standards set extremely high. If the hiring process works along with academy and FTO training most bad apples will be weeded out. Educational standards must be high. Research has shown and studies have verified that higher education advances ethical behavior among officers. The initial training must be grounded in ethical standards. No class should be taught that does not explain ethics as they pertain to the individual subject.

Only positively motivated officers who have the highest of ethical integrity should be FTO's. This is critical. In-service training and all continuing training must include elements of ethics. Ethical simulation training must be taught (Braunstein & Tyre, 1992). Statistical data must be constantly analyzed from such sources as citizens' complaints. Furthermore, needs assessments and surveys should be undertaken at periodic intervals. Discipline must be swift, sure and fair. Remember we react as we have been trained. If officers have not been trained in how to act in a given ethical dilemma they will improvise and possibly act in an ethical vacuum.

Unethical acts are committed by bad apples and those who become bad apples through a process of perceived victimization, perceived entitlements, false loyalties and finally through a continuum of comprise. This process coupled with a strong subculture of preexisting unethical behavior and taking into consideration the Theory of Differential Association is a breeding ground for corrupt departments. Ethics can and must be taught. A hiring process must be in place that will employ only those with a strong ethical background and a set of core values that the agency can further build upon.

Honesty

There are few things more important. Yet in today's society, honesty seems to be a rare commodity. In fact, it seems like dishonesty is rewarded. The more honest one is, the harder the world can be on him or her. A new form of dishonesty can be found with the term "political correctness." I strive very hard to not be politically correct. However, there are times I find myself succumbing to this dogma. When I do falter into political correctness, which is rare, I find I do so out of fear as to what may happen to my family and me as a result. Will I lose my job? Will I be labeled any number of things that will cast doubt and suspicion on my ability to be professional? Do not get me wrong, I seldom shy away from speaking up. I know that, during my career in law enforcement, such truthfulness—while delivered with respect and humility—is not always welcomed and likely hurts me in some circles. There will be those who admire your honesty and those who despise such behavior, especially if it is directed at them.

Final Thoughts!

Fulfillment of Human Needs

- ✓ Live
  - o Life to the fullest. Carpe diem (seize the day).
- ✓ Love
  - o Family, friends, truth, freedom, virtue
- ✓ Learn
  - o Lifelong learning
- ✓ Leave a legacy
  - o Set the benchmark others may emulate; create a positive, lasting impact on all those you meet. When those of you in this room have long since passed into the journals of history, how will you be remembered? Will you be looked at as having been good stewards of your organizations or disciplines? What will be your legacy? Where will your actions (inactions) have carried your organization in the future? (Covey, 1989, 1994)

Takeaways

- ✓ Have character that develops and maintains hope, honesty, courage, and empathy.
- ✓ Create, foster, and maintain these moral virtues: courage, temperance, prudence, justice, pride, ambition, good temper, being a good friend, truthfulness, and ready wit. Avoid the excess and defect of each of these virtues.
- ✓ Act so that your behavior will be a good universal rule.
- ✓ Do unto others as you would have them do unto you.
- ✓ Be mindful of who and what you are loyal to. Ideals and beliefs must trump the individual.
- ✓ Practice introspection daily.
- ✓ Practice *Kaizen* daily.
- ✓ Understand your paradigms and change as needed to be ethical.

- ✓ Avoid satisficing.
- ✓ Do not have a victim mentality.
- ✓ Understand the role entitlements can play.
- ✓ Remember, law is reactive, and ethics are proactive.
- ✓ The law is the least acceptable level of human behavior society allows. Ethics rise above the law.
- ✓ Ask yourself these questions:
  - o Am I acting out of anger, greed, lust, or peer pressure?
  - o Will my loved ones be proud or ashamed?
  - o Is it worth my job?
  - o Am I following the Golden Rule of "Do unto others as I would have done to me"?

Whoever can be trusted with very little can also be trusted with much, and whoever is dishonest with very little will also be dishonest with much.
—Luke 16:10

Chapter Five
Communication Skills

The liberty of speaking and writing guards our other liberties.
—Thomas Jefferson

Hone your communication skills.

I had a fellow officer whom I trained when he got out of the academy who was very bright. He used to like to use what I called fifty-cent words, that is, fancy words, when a more basic word was appropriate or would suffice. One of our sergeants had read an accident report he turned in, and he had used these very flowery fifty-cent words again. The sergeant approached him and half-jokingly said, "Why don't you write in the proper vernacular?" My friend did not know what the word *vernacular* meant, so he had to go look it up. Talk about irony! Do speak and write in the proper vernacular. How you speak and write would be the basis of how you would be judged in many cases. By the way, I had not taught my trainee to do this.

Your communication skills—be they written, verbal, or body language—are critical to the success or failure of your career. This communication takes many forms. This communication is written, verbal, and the body itself. These same communication modes will be important for you to learn how to receive and interpret as well.

On several occasions, I would have a person refuse to sign a traffic summons. On one occasion, I had a female stopped for a speeding violation. She sat next to me while I was in uniform and spoke on the radio in a marked police car. I explained the summons process very clearly to her. When it came time to sign the summons, she said she would not sign. I again explained very clearly and slowly that signing the summons was not an admission of guilt. She was merely saying she would pay the fine or come to court. She said she could not sign it. She wanted me to show her my identification card. That was not our policy, so I told her no. How would that make any difference at this point anyway? I very nicely asked why she would not sign. She said she did not know if I was a police officer or not. I very nicely explained the obvious, such as the police car, the dispatcher I was talking to, and the uniform. I then explained what would happen if she did not sign. I told her I would have to arrest her. I would have to tow her car since her passenger did not have a license and they were on the interstate. Having been through this several times over the years, I then explained what would likely happen once I arrested her. I said, "Once I arrest you, that is it. You cannot then say you will sign the summons. You will likely say you will sign the summons, but it will be too late." I made it very clear. "Will you sign the summons?" She said she could not because she did not know if I was a police officer. I then put her under arrest.

I handcuffed her and went through all the normal steps. She then began to say she would sign the summons. I said that was no longer an option, and I explained to her again what I had said would happen. I called a tow truck and told her friend she would have to go with the tow truck driver. Her friend was furious at her and called her many not-so-nice things. I took her to the magistrate, and she was released from there on her signature. You will be confronted with all sorts of people. Always be calm and patient, be clear with all communications, be professional, do not play games or allow them to play games. Some people will not be rational. They might not be crazy (insane), but they will lack any common sense whatsoever, so take that into account. You must be prepared for these sorts of off-the-wall, weird situations, and do not let them throw you off. Think it through and get advice from a supervisor or a more seasoned officer, but do not violate law or policy. Play it straight always.

Communication is the transfer of information. It is a message sent and a message received. We are communicating all the time. Communication happens through symbols, sounds, and gestures. Put another way, communication might be oral, nonverbal, or written.

The common traits of effective writing are clarity of purpose (why), techniques appropriate to purpose and audience (how), content knowledge (what), and ability and willingness to revise. Academic writings are evidence based, syntheses of literature, scholarly formatted, scholarly citations, developed and defended arguments, constructed new knowledge, and contributing to research.

Writing and Thinking

1. Writing is an expression of your thoughts or telling a story.
2. Writing is an active process.
3. Writing is thinking!
4. Writing is recursive. As we write, we constantly rewrite; we juggle words and then choose, delete, and then choose again.

Benefits of Good Writing Skills

1. Helps you think and learn
2. Improves research skills
3. Improves ability to communicate: inform, persuade, entertain, and speak/write with clarity
4. Teaches tenacity, benefits of hard work, commitment
5. Translates to work and life
6. Bottom line, helps you be smarter and more successful

Communication Processes

Seventy percent of our nonsleeping hours are spent communicating: writing, reading, speaking, and listening. Poor communication is one of the most cited sources of interpersonal conflict. Communication still remains a neglected area.

The Communication Model (Components of Communication)

✓ Source—idea, thought, impression
✓ Encoding—encoded/translated into words or other forms of communication; formulating the message
✓ Transmit Message—oral/written

The Communication Model

✓ Receiving message—through senses: taste, touch, sight, hearing, smell
✓ Decoding—translating the message to a form that can be understood by the receiver

- ✓ Feedback—starting the exchange and clarification process; the check on how successful the message has been received

Barriers to Effective Communication

- ✓ Filtering - The sender consciously or unconsciously manipulates information so it will be seen more favorably.
- ✓ Emotions - How the receiver feels at the time of the receipt of a communication message will influence how she or he interprets it.
- ✓ Selective Perception - The receiver sees and hears things in a selective way, based on his or her needs, motivations, experiences, background, and other personal characteristics, and projects his or her interests and expectations into communications as he or she decodes.
- ✓ Language - Age, education, and cultural background are three obvious variables that influence the language a person uses and definitions he or she gives to words.
- ✓ Nonverbal Cues - If nonverbal cues and communication are in agreement, they complement each other; if they are in disagreement, the receiver becomes confused, and the clarity of the message suffers.

Nonverbal Cues

- ✓ *Facial Expressions* - Probably the most rewarding cue is a smiling face and a nod.
- ✓ *Eye Contact* (a powerful type of nonverbal cue) - When we first encounter another person, we are able to assert dominance over others almost exclusively with eye contact in a matter of seconds.
- ✓ *Hand Gestures* - Next to the face, the hands are probably the most expressive part of the body (clenched fist, open hand, pointed finger).
- ✓ *Body Movement* (an influential type of nonverbal cue) - the degree to which a communicator's shoulders and legs are turned in the direction of, rather than away from, the addressee. Leaning forward is perceived as having a more positive attitude.

- ✓ *Poor Listening Skills* (not listening actively) - listening on the surface (not seriously considering what the person is saying) or giving the impression, through speech or nonverbal cues, of eagerness to end the conversation
- ✓ Showing signs of annoyance or distress of the subject matter being discussed

Tips for Effective Communication

- ✓ Limit you own talking.
  - o God gave us two ears and one mouth so we could listen twice as much as we talk.
- ✓ Concentrate on what the other person is saying.
- ✓ Maintain eye contact (but do not stare).
- ✓ Paraphrase and summarize the other person's remarks.
- ✓ Avoid jumping to conclusions. Be postjudicial, not prejudicial, regarding what the other person is saying.
- ✓ Watch for nonverbal cues.
- ✓ Listen for emotions.
- ✓ Ask for clarification: assume differences, not similarities, if you are unsure of meaning.
- ✓ Do not interrupt.
  - o Unless it is an enforcement issue and enough has been said and it is time to act
  - o You must control the situation and not let the situation control you.
- ✓ Pause for understanding; do not immediately fill the void of silence.

School of Hard Knocks

Everyone wants to be treated with respect. I was teaching an ethics class to a group of troops. I always wanted open and honest communication. That was a two-way street. One student spoke up and said he spoke to people in a language they could understand. Well, one might think that would be a good thing. One might think he was talking about speaking in the proper vernacular. Unfortunately, that was not what he meant at all. He meant he would speak to them in a language he thought they could understand based on what he saw. I would argue that what he meant was he would speak to them in a language he thought they deserved. I pressed him on the statement. I said, "How do you determine what language they would understand? Is it based on their skin color? Is it based on the length of their hair or what they are wearing? Is it based on the area you find them in or their sex? Exactly how do you determine what language they would understand?" The rest of the class was just staring at him in disbelief. No one agreed with his thought process. I urged him to speak with everyone in the same language. That language should be proper English, void of vulgarities, and with respect. It does not matter if the person you are speaking to is speaking in street slang, is using vulgarity, and lacks proper English. You do not act such a way. You should always be a lady or a gentleman. This does not make you a wimp or a lesser person. It does not make you look weak. I am not saying you should kowtow to anyone, especially if they are acting like a miscreant. You can be tough as nails and still be a professional person. Treat everyone with respect and dignity.

When I was a young military policeman, I used a phrase that just came to my mind when dealing with potential problem people, in other words, those who were beginning to show signs of resistance. I would say we could do this the easy way or the hard way. It sounded good at the time. What I found was that some would choose the hard way. I decided to stop using that phrase. Why put such a choice in their head?

"You catch more flies with honey than you do with vinegar" (author unknown).

Thompson and Jenkins (1993), in their book called *Verbal Judo: The Gentle Art of Persuasion*, offer many great communication tips.

Here are some phrases that can be said much better. These are just examples, and some have more merit than others. Think about phrases you have heard used that can be said better. We always want to de-escalate and never escalate any situation.

"Come here."

"Could I chat with you for a minute?"

"You wouldn't understand."

"Let me try to explain this."

"Because those are the rules."

"It is my responsibility to . . ."

"It's none of your business."

"I cannot discuss that with you."

"What do you want me to do about it?"

"I am sorry. I wish I could help, but I cannot provide more information at this time."
(Maybe there are things you could suggest.)

"Calm down."

"It is going to be all right."
"How can I help you?"
"Talk to me."

"What's your problem?"

"What's the matter?"
"How can I try to help?"

"You never . . ." or "You always . . ."

"It seems like . . ."

"I'm not going to say this again."

"It is important that you understand this."
"Please listen carefully."

"I'm doing this for your own good." Thompson and Jenkins offer a few alternatives. I would just not make such a statement.

"Why don't you be reasonable?"

"Let me see if I can understand your position."

One of my favorites deals with arresting people. Do not tell people when you arrest them that you are taking them to jail. Tell them they are under arrest and for what. Every state is different. In Virginia, we rarely, if ever, just take someone directly to jail. After arresting them, we take them to magistrate for a bond hearing and/or to obtain warrants. The magistrate may not put the person in jail. If they cooperate, that helps their cause. If you tell someone they are going to jail, they might just say, "Oh well, let's go for it." I have found that telling them I am arresting them is good enough. If they want to know what is next, then I would explain we are going to the magistrate. It is also to their benefit to cooperate. I do not mean confess; I mean just cooperate and do not fight. Now once at the magistrate, you might have to take them to jail. If that is the case, so be it.

Empathy is a great skill to have and use. This does not mean you do not do your job. This does not mean you need to have sympathy or apathy for the person you are dealing with. Just consider what the person is going through no matter what it is.

Do not take what the person says personally. I know that is easier said than done. Often, the person is drunk. You cannot argue with a drunk. Let them convict themselves. Record them. This is great evidence in court. You cannot stop them from talking.

The five universal truths of human interaction are as follows:

- ✓ People feel the need to be respected.
- ✓ People will rather be asked than be told.
- ✓ People have a desire to know why.
- ✓ People prefer to have options over threats.
- ✓ People want to have a second chance. (Thompson and Jenkins, 1993)

Communication Roundup

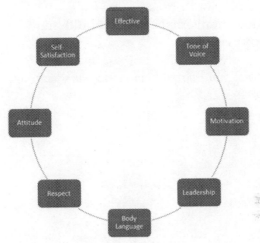

Check your communication as found in the circle. Are you being effective? Is your tone of voice appropriate for the situation? Are you motivated, and are you motivating the person you are speaking to in the way you want them motivated? Are you practicing leadership? Yes, you are the leader as a police officer. Are you holding yourself and the person(s) you are dealing with accountable? Are you being respectful, and is the person respecting you? You must be respectful. Check your attitude. Are you confident but not cocky? Are you pleasant but not flirtatious? Are you firm but fair? Finally, what is your level of self-satisfaction with how you handled that? Will your supervisor be satisfied? Is the subject satisfied, if he or she is reasonable? Remember, communication is a two-way process. So view these same things from the perspective of the person you are in contact with and, I will argue, the public at large. We circle all the way back; are you effective?

Takeaways

- ✓ Make eye contact.
- ✓ Watch for nonverbal cues.
- ✓ Do not jump to conclusions.
- ✓ Ask for clarification.
- ✓ Speak and write in the proper vernacular.
- ✓ Treat everyone with respect.
- ✓ Do not be vulgar or rude.

✓ Use proper English.
✓ Choose your phrasing carefully.
✓ Your nonverbal cues should match your verbal expression.

You shall not bear false witness against your neighbor.
—Exodus 20:16

Chapter Six
Patrol Issues

Morality cannot be legislated, but behavior can be regulated. Judicial decrees may not change the heart, but they can restrain the heartless.
—Martin Luther King Jr.

Expect the unexpected all the time.

You will come across so many things while on patrol. Patrol is the backbone of law enforcement. It was a Tuesday night, and I was heading to the office to drop off some paperwork. I came upon stopped traffic and could see way ahead of me a huge blaze rising up into the night sky. I drove the shoulder and got to the scene of a horrific crash. As I ran up to the scene, there was a full-size tractor trailer that was demolished on the front end. A Mercury Cougar, or what was left of it, was facing the wrong way on the interstate. There was a fellow standing near the crashed car. He was pulling his hair and screaming. The car was fully engulfed in flames. I got up to the car and saw the driver pinned behind the wheel. I used my fire extinguisher, and people started to hand me more fire extinguishers. Each time I would get the fire down, I would try to pull the fellow out, but he was wedged in. The fire continued to lap at his feet and legs. I could hear him gurgling in his own blood. His throat was cut. Once in a while, he would slightly turn his head back and forth. He never spoke, though. I continued to fight the fire and tried to pull him out for at least ten minutes or more. The fire would leap back up each time I would knock it down with extinguishers. The fire department got there and extinguished the fire. A med flight arrived about forty minutes later, and the fellow had been taken from the vehicle. He died before the med flight could lift off. What tremendous pain he went through.

There was a huge pile of spent fire extinguishers next to me and the vehicle when I was done. There were all sizes of fire extinguishers from small ones to large ones that tractor trailers are required to carry. My job now switched from lifesaving efforts to investigation. One fellow walked up to me and asked me why I did not shoot the guy. I explained that I could not do that. He said it so matter-of-factly. Witnesses said the car had pulled onto the shoulder and then made a U-turn into traffic, and that was when the tractor trailer hit him head-on. The driver of the car was legally intoxicated based on blood work.

A twist to the story came when a person said he saw a woman in a blue dress standing on the shoulder with her hands over her face. He described her as if she were a ghost. I put out a "be on the lookout" for a lady in a blue dress. That Friday night, I was contacted by a local agency who found a woman fitting the description wandering around a few miles away. I met them and took her to our office. She was, in fact, the lady in blue I was looking for. She was from Louisiana and was hitchhiking across the state. This fellow had picked her up. He began to put his hand on her leg and come on to her, and she saw he was drinking. She asked to be let out of the car. It was when he had pulled over and let her out that he made the U-turn into traffic. She was suffering from schizophrenia and was off her medication. We contacted her family. She voluntarily allowed herself to be committed to an inpatient treatment center. We first made sure she had something to eat before I interviewed her. I could only imagine what this lady had been through with her already existing condition and then being accosted and then watching this fellow burn to death in a crash. For me, it was just another Tuesday night on patrol. I do not say this callously. I think about this and so many other dramatic events often. I will never forget the carnage that night. It is all so avoidable. We work these events, do our jobs, meet our shift partners for dinner, talk about what happens, and go home happy to be alive.

A law enforcement officer must be many things. One of these things is a warrior. Retired Lt. Col. Dave Grossman—who wrote *On Killing*, *On Combat*, etc.—sums it up best when looking at the role of police. He says there are sheep and wolves. Then there are sheepdogs. The police and our military are sheepdogs. They protect the flock from the wolves. The sheep—many of them, that is—do not care for the sheepdog. He or she is annoying and does not let them do or go wherever they want. Yet the sheepdog protects them and is willing to fight and die for them, even though they do not care for him or her. The sheep do not like the sheepdog, but they are glad he or she is there when the wolves appear. The fundamental question is, are you a sheepdog?

There are sheep and wolves.
Then there are sheepdogs.
The police and our military are sheepdogs.
They protect the flock from the wolves.

A Holistic Approach to Policing

It is very important for you as an officer and for the community you serve to be well-rounded. We all have things we like to do and things we do not like to do. We do not have the ability to pick and choose only those things we like to do. I had a sergeant years ago whose philosophy was to let his officers only do what they liked to do. He and I had discussions about this philosophy being a problem. What if all officers on a shift or in a department did not like to do investigations? What if they did not like traffic enforcement or criminal work or community service? Does not the community suffer by not having a well-rounded police force? Do not the officers suffer as well? Some officers are happy where they are, whether it is in a traffic or patrol unit. What happens when he or she is thrust into a criminal matter and they have not kept up with how to investigate crimes or even make an arrest, including interviews and interrogation, or even how to properly process and handle a criminal arrestee?

What happens if an officer only likes to enforce traffic laws and starts to view people only as numbers to reach the ticket quota he or she created? Such a mind-set is wrong and unhealthy. Sooner or later, an officer will have to deal with all sorts of matters ranging from a minor car crash to a murder. If they are not used to such things, then they will be very much out of their comfort zone. Being out of comfort zones may lead to poor performance or handling of the situation. In other cases, it might lead to avoiding such calls or activities completely.

What happens when the officer has more time on and decides he or she wants to compete for a new position, say, an investigator? He or she will be at a disadvantage in a competitive process since he or she has never dealt with such matters to begin with. Worse yet, what if an officer gets promoted and then cannot help other newer officers become well-rounded or even offer advice or guidance since they have limited or no knowledge of the many situations that will occur?

> *On my honor,*
> *I will never betray my badge,*
> *my integrity, my character,*
> *or the public trust.*
> *I will always have*
> *the courage to hold myself*
> *and others accountable for our actions.*
> *I will always uphold the constitution*
> *my community and the agency I serve.*

Understanding the Oath of Honor

This oath is a solemn pledge individuals make when they honestly intend to do what is said.

Let us examine the oath more closely. Honor means that one's word is given as a guarantee. Betray is defined as breaking faith with the public trust. Badge is the symbol of your office. Integrity is being the same person in both private and public life. Character means the qualities that distinguish an individual. Public trust is a charge of duty imposed in faith toward those you serve. Courage is having the strength to withstand unethical pressure, fear, or danger. Accountability means that you are answerable and responsible to your oath of office. Community is the jurisdiction and citizens served (IACP, n.d.).

The International Association of Chiefs of Police (IACP) adopted the Law Enforcement Code of Ethics in 1957. The code of ethics stands as a preface to the mission and commitment that law enforcement agencies make to the public they serve.

Law Enforcement Code of Ethics
As a law enforcement officer, my fundamental duty is to serve the community; to safeguard lives and property; to protect the innocent against deception, the weak against oppression or intimidation and the peaceful against violence or disorder; and to respect the constitutional rights of all to liberty, equality and justice.
I will keep my private life unsullied as an example to all and will behave in a manner that does not bring discredit to me or to my agency. I will maintain courageous calm in the face of danger, scorn or ridicule; develop self-restraint; and be constantly mindful of the

welfare of others. Honest in thought and deed both in my personal and official life, I will be exemplary in obeying the law and the regulations of my department. Whatever I see or hear of a confidential nature or that is confided to me in my official capacity will be kept ever secret unless revelation is necessary in the performance of my duty.
I will never act officiously or permit personal feelings, prejudices, political beliefs, aspirations, animosities or friendships to influence my decisions. With no compromise for crime and with relentless prosecution of criminals, I will enforce the law courteously and appropriately without fear or favor, malice or ill will, never employing unnecessary force or violence and never accepting gratuities.
I recognize the badge of my office as a symbol of public faith, and I accept it as a public trust to be held so long as I am true to the ethics of police service. I will never engage in acts of corruption or bribery, nor will I condone such acts by other police officers. I will cooperate with all legally authorized agencies and their representatives in the pursuit of justice.
I know that I alone am responsible for my own standard of professional performance and will take every reasonable opportunity to enhance and improve my level of knowledge and competence.
I will constantly strive to achieve these objectives and ideals, dedicating myself before God to my chosen profession . . . law enforcement. (IACP, 1957)

Community Policing and other Policing Options

"Community policing is a philosophy that promotes and supports organizational strategies to address the causes of crime, to reduce the fear of crime and social disorder through problem-solving tactics and community-police partnerships" (National Crime Prevention Council, n.d.).

The oath of honor comes from the International Association of Chiefs of Police (IACP). The oath of honor provides the law enforcement profession with a concise, powerful, and universal process by which officers can affirm and periodically reaffirm their ethical values and beliefs. This concise oath summarizes police values in a simple statement lending itself to continuous and convenient application in both public and professional settings. It is easily institutionalized, understood, and remembered. The law enforcement oath of honor is recommended as by the International Association of Chiefs of Police as symbolic statement of commitment to ethical behavior.

Sir Robert Peel's Principles

1. The basic mission of the police is to prevent crime and disorder.

2. The ability of the police to perform their duties is dependent upon public approval of police actions.

3. Police must secure the willing cooperation of the public.

4. The rest of the principle is "in voluntary observance of the law to be able to secure and maintain the respect of the public."

5. The degree of cooperation of the public that can be secured diminishes proportionally to the necessity of the use of force.

6. Police seek and preserve public favor "not by catering to public opinion but by constantly demonstrating absolute impartial service to the law."

7. Police use physical force to the extent necessary "to secure observance of the law or to restore order only when the expertise of persuasion, advice, and warning is found to be insufficient."

8. Police, at all times, should maintain a relationship with the public "that gives reality to the historic tradition; the police are public and the public are the police. The police being the only full-time individuals charged with the duties that are incumbent on all of the citizens."

9. Police should always direct their actions strictly toward their functions "and never appear to usurp the powers of the judiciary."

10. The test of police efficiency is the absence of crime and disorder, "not the visible evidence of police action in dealing with it."

Community Policing

Police work depends upon public cooperation. Less and less can be controlled by the police officer. The police cannot regard public relations as something separate from the way they do their everyday work. There will never be enough police to police society. Voluntary compliance is the goal. Police community relations is not a public relations program to sell the police image to the people. It is a long-range, full-scale effort to acquaint the police and the community with each other's problems and to stimulate action aimed at solving those problems.

Police are called upon to provide social service functions, such as emergency medical care, and to regulate traffic, enforce law, and bring suspected offenders before the bar of justice. You are supposed to accomplish these and other activities in a professional manner, within the context of the community and its values in which they work, and with as little hostility and antagonism from the public as is possible to obtain. One caveat is offered here: if the community you police has very low values that perpetuate and endorse crime and immoral and unethical action, you cannot lower yourself to such standards.

Police community relations should be viewed not as an aspect of police work but as the outcome of police work. Remember that police have a responsibility to enforce and uphold the law, but society does not give each police officer the right to determine who or what is good or bad. The beliefs and value judgments of police officers are to be held in check as they perform their duties. It is when the police officer fails to hold such beliefs in check that he or she actually discriminates against those with whom he or she interacts and that hostilities and antagonisms are fostered. It is when the interactions between police and the policed are perceived negatively, by either group, that hostile confrontations are most likely to occur. This does not mean an officer must embrace or celebrate values that are not his or her own, but we must be tolerant and not openly judgmental.

Good community relations work is based upon communication and interpretation, and it develops sensitivity to conditions that indicate areas of social unrest. What is public relations? It is the art of achieving goodwill through such techniques as publicity, promotions, and even marketing. Publicity is the technique of telling the story of an organization, person, or cause. It is the advertising of any kind of information with news value designed to advance the interests of a person, place, cause, or institution usually appearing in public print or through some other form of media, such as social media. Publicity is news or information.

We want to foster a positive interaction between members of the police department and members of the community. We need the daily association between you and your fellow person. We need to establish and carry out activities that establish the goodwill of the public and maintain it. The major goal is to establish a better relationship and understanding between police officers and the citizens.

We want to improve awareness of all forces in the community. We need to actively engage in various community relations programs with civic and other organizations to stimulate greater respect for the law. We must develop a positive and true image of the police function in the maintenance of law and order, preservation of peace, and protection of the public. We want to have greater harmony between the police and all people of the community. Our goal is to see a decrease in the rate of crime and delinquency. Our goal is better control of crime and delinquency through the apprehension, punishment, and rehabilitation of law violators.

We want a reestablishment of communication lines within the community so that both community and police problems can be worked on and resolved. We desire an increased working relationship with citizens and official groups. A more professional and influential police department is essential. A much better police image in the community will hopefully be the result of this work. A greater understanding and cooperation between the police department and citizens of the community is needed.

What the Public Deserves of the Police Officer

- ✓ Honesty
- ✓ Good judgment
- ✓ Courtesy
- ✓ Intelligence

- o Further your education when and wherever possible.
- o Know the laws you are required to enforce.
- o Be aware of all recent court rulings; they affect your performance.
- ✓ Self-control
  - o Greatest of all attributes necessary for today's modern police officer
- ✓ Courage
- ✓ Ability to handle all types of people
- ✓ High moral and ethical standards
- ✓ Initiative
- ✓ Knowledge of public affairs
  - o Attend
  - o Participate
  - o Converse
- ✓ Personal appearance
- ✓ Physical ability
- ✓ Uniform and equipment in good repair

Reasons to Foster a Positive Relationship between Law Enforcement and the Community

- ✓ Develop and maintain open communication between law enforcement and the community.
- ✓ Reduce fear and mistrust by some members of the public, especially immigrants whose experience with law enforcement in the other countries have been negative.
  - o Impressions we make on others affect them, ourselves, and our community relations function.
- ✓ Enhance the officer's ability to function as effectively as possible in carrying out daily duties.
  - o The public believes in you.
  - o Proving your service to people is continually in their interest.
  - o Use good judgment.

Consequences that May Result from a Failure of Common Courtesy

- ✓ Lack of respect on the part of the officer toward the public has a ripple effect beyond the immediate situation.

- ○ The public may fail to call for assistance for an officer in trouble.
- ○ They may ignore reporting crime.
- ✓ Negative attitude toward law enforcement, in general, may develop from the actions of one officer.
  - ○ Officer's lack of respect for laws
  - ○ Officer's reluctance to further own knowledge of current community problems
  - ○ Continually finding fault with the public and fellow officers
  - ○ Constant reference to ethnic groups
- ✓ The officer's ability to function effectively in carrying out daily duties will diminish should the officer become known as lacking common courtesy.
  - ○ Do not bring personal problems to work.
  - ○ Be visible.
  - ○ Be compassionate.
  - ○ Be honest.
  - ○ Be truthful.
  - ○ Be patient.
  - ○ Be considerate.
  - ○ Be sensible.
  - ○ Be impartial.
  - ○ Be sincere.

The Basic Concept of Public Service

- ✓ Service orientation
  - ○ Need the support of the citizens to provide better law enforcement
- ✓ Partnerships within a community
  - ○ Positive interaction between police and the community
  - ○ Citizens' support
- ✓ Resource and referral access through law enforcement
  - ○ For the poor and those in trouble, the police department is often the first to be called in times of personal crisis.
  - ○ Compile referral handbook or directory.
    - ▪ Alcohol safety action program for person arrested for DUI

- Alcoholic Anonymous (AA) self-help program for alcohol abuse
- Narcotics Anonymous (NA) self-help program for drug abuse
- Legal services – public defenders
- Health department – free clinics, public health nursing service
- Financial aid
- Mental health – family counseling, family crisis, suicide prevention
- Church organizations
- Aid organizations such as the Salvation Army
- Soup/food kitchens
- Shelters

Ways an Officer Can Individually Contribute to Promoting Success in a Public Service Effort

- ✓ Develop better understanding and improved cooperation with the community to gain public support and confidence
- ✓ Actively engage in various community relations project and develop and present programs that stimulate greater respect for the law
- ✓ Develop a positive image of the police function in maintenance of law and order, preservation of peace, and protection of the public

Crime Prevention

- ✓ Increase the effort – harden targets, control access to facilities, screen exits, deflect offenders, and control tools/weapons
- ✓ Increase the risks – extend guardianship, assist natural surveillance, reduce anonymity, use place managers, strengthen formal surveillance
- ✓ Reduce the rewards – conceal targets, remove targets, identify property, disrupt markets, deny benefits

- ✓ Reduce provocations – reduce frustrations and stress, avoid disputes, reduce temptation and arousal, neutralize peer pressure, discourage imitation
- ✓ Remove excuses – set rules, post instructions, alert conscience, assist compliance, control drugs and alcohol

Patrol Issues, Procedures, and Techniques

Patrol is the backbone of a police agency. Our calm demeanor and decisive action will have a positive psychological effect on our employees, as well as those of other agencies and the victims of an incident. Always consider safety (to officers and others) and the legality of any proposed action. Does the gravity of the crime justify the proposed course of action (for example, forced entry of a house without a warrant)?

Never Compromise – Law, Policy, and Ethics

Patrol Function Categories

- ✓ Crime prevention - proactive deterrence
- ✓ Law enforcement - reactive deterrence
- ✓ Order maintenance - security
- ✓ Social services - community welfare

Patrol as a Function

- ✓ Constant movement
- ✓ Prevent/deter crime
- ✓ Eliminate opportunity for crime

Patrol Activities and Purposes

- ✓ Crime detection and prevention
- ✓ Apprehension of criminals and wanted suspects
- ✓ Data and information collection
- ✓ Report writing and documentation
- ✓ Public assistance
- ✓ Peacekeeping and order maintenance
- ✓ Conflict resolution

- ✓ Traffic control and enforcement
- ✓ Parking enforcement
- ✓ Law enforcement to reduce citizens' fear of crime
- ✓ Detect and enforce code violations
- ✓ Rapid responses to emergencies
- ✓ Public relations
- ✓ Police visibility
- ✓ Property protection
- ✓ Citizen assistance within the scope of duties

Traffic Enforcement

- ✓ Ensure the safety of the public
- ✓ Issue parking citations
- ✓ Reduce accidents and injuries
- ✓ Investigate traffic crashes
- ✓ Collect information
- ✓ Arrest drunk drivers
- ✓ Make criminal arrests
- ✓ Enforce seat belt laws
- ✓ Enforce traffic laws
- ✓ Direct traffic
- ✓ Facilitate traffic flow

Purposes of Criminal Investigation

- ✓ Determine whether or not a crime has been committed
- ✓ Develop and follow up all clues
- ✓ Decide if the crime was committed within the investigator's jurisdiction
- ✓ Locate and apprehend the perpetrator
- ✓ Discover all facts pertaining to the complaint
- ✓ Aid in the prosecution of the offender by providing evidence of guilt that is admissible in court
- ✓ Gather and preserve physical evidence
- ✓ Testify effectively as a witness in court
- ✓ Identify the perpetrator
- ✓ Recover stolen property

Purposes of Patrol

- ✓ Deter crime by being visible
- ✓ Maintain public order (peacekeeping)
- ✓ Respond quickly to emergencies
- ✓ Arrest criminals
- ✓ Aid citizens in distress
- ✓ Facilitate movement of people and traffic
- ✓ Create a sense of safety and security

Proactive Policing

- ✓ Concentrating on hot spots and hot days!
- ✓ Small percentage of offenders, victims, and places involved in most crimes
  - ○ Focus on repeat offenders and career criminals (recidivists).
  - ○ Focus on hot spots for crime.

Policing Models

- ✓ Police-community relations - improving the relationships between the police and public
- ✓ Team policing - decentralized decision making so the police can easily respond to neighborhood problems
- ✓ Problem-oriented policing - identifying and responding to long-term problems

Broken Windows Theory/Model

- ✓ Neighborhood disorder creates fear.
- ✓ Neighborhoods give out crime-promoting signals.
- ✓ Police need citizens' cooperation.

The diagram below functions as a stool. You need an offender, a place, and a target or victim for a crime to occur. Take away the offender, and no crime occurs. If there is a guardian, a crime is less likely in some cases. The police cannot be everywhere at once. Community involvement is essential to crime prevention.

Crime Prevention Stool

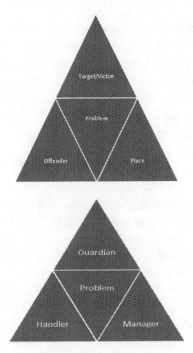

(Tillyer and Kennedy, 2008)

Problem-Solving

We need to ask two questions. One, is there really a problem? Two, is it your problem? If a citizen perceives a problem, then it is a problem to him or her. You might need to try to correct their perception. Further, even if it is a problem, it may be outside the scope of your authority. This does not mean you should just ignore it. You might be able to offer advice or guidance. You might be able to get another agency involved.

In community policing, a four-step process known as SARA is often used:

- ✓ Scanning—identifying problems
- ✓ Analysis—understanding underlying problems
- ✓ Response—developing and implementing solutions
- ✓ Assessment—determining the solutions' effect

Practicing Proactive Policing

The cornerstone of police work is patrol. The cornerstone of patrol is proactive police work. This requires great discretion, abundant common sense, respect for constitutional rights, excellent judgment, maturity, motivation, and a keen understanding of the law. We have covered much of this already, but it is so important that some of it bears repeating. When I was a very young military policeman, just starting out in my career, I had a supervisor who told me that one out of every ten traffic stops would yield more than why I stopped the person. Often, this would be another hidden violation or criminal activity. I never tracked this to determine the exact veracity of the assertion, but I could attest to the general validity of his point. You should always look beyond the initial stop or contact. Not only is it about spotting violations and crimes but it also is about officer safety. Here are a series of critical questions you must ask yourself every time you see a potential violation of law:

- ✓ Do I have a legal right to be where I am?
    - ○ If you do not have a legal right to be there, then you automatically have a problem.
    - ○ Is there another way to approach this now or later?
    - ○ Almost always, if it is not good now, it will not get better.
- ✓ Is what I am seeing illegal?
    - ○ If it is not illegal, then case closed.
    - ○ You might need to explore further by watching, speaking, or using one of your other senses.
- ✓ What should I do about this?
    - ○ You might decide to do nothing or warn, summons, or arrest.
        - Sometimes you will not have time to stop and deal with every violation you see.
        - Some you must deal with if public safety is at stake.
        - Is doing something going to jeopardize everyone's safety and security more than if you did nothing?

- o You might defer action but take action later.
  - Seek advice.
  - Investigate further.
  - Wait until you have a tactical advantage.
- ✓ Why am I doing this?
  - o If it is for any reason other than your sworn duty, then it is wrong.
    - Is it out of anger, revenge, lust, greed, prejudice, ego, etc.?
      - Do not do it ever.

The Constitution is actually a restricting document as much as it is a document about freedom. The Constitution and the Bill of Rights tell the government what it cannot do. The police are probably the most visible form of the government. They are also those who interact with and can affect a citizen's rights and life quicker and more profoundly than anyone else in the government. Never forget this awesome fact and responsibility. Police serve the public. Yes, they do pay all public servants salaries.

It is important to check egos at the door. While I hope it does not happen a lot, sometimes officers' egos get in the way of proper duty. While it would be great if all citizens respect the police, the fact is some do not and will not. Police, however, must respect the public. I have seen situations where a violator will step from a police car and slam the car door. The officer will order the violator to come back and close the door properly. Bad move and idea. Let it go. What right do you have to order someone to open and close a door properly? What if they refuse? There is nothing you can do. Let it go. It is rude and frankly stupid to pass a police car that is doing the speed limit. Unless they are speeding to a level your agency will want you to write them a ticket, let it go. If they are rude, curt, or disrespectful, ignore it. We do not police manners and courtesy. Remember the question you need to ask yourself each time. If you walk up to a vehicle, lean on the vehicle, and put your foot on the car or truck and the violator tells you to take your feet or hands off the vehicle, then do it. The best thing to do is to not do it to begin with. One caveat is needed. If you place your hand on a vehicle for police purposes, such as to leave a fingerprint or to check a door or trunk, that is different.

My practice for citizen or violator contact was always to be as nice as I could be with them. It almost always worked well. If the citizen or violator was rude, curt, or disrespectful, then I went to neutral mode or just bland or matter-of-fact. I never lowered myself to their behavior ever. If their behavior went to confrontational and moving toward threatening or abusive, I would then move to "this is what we are going to do" mode or be stern. Never let the situation get out of control. Never let the violator become in charge of any situation. Remember, no one is happy about being stopped, and people have bad days. A pleasant and professional demeanor will almost always work. Command bearing and clear expectations work as well.

You will have some people who will challenge you and try to get you to act out improperly. Never allow this on your part. Remember what you are allowed to do and not allowed to do. It will not take long, and you will come across an incident or situation that will test you and your judgment. A common occurrence is to have people videotape you on a cell phone or record your actions. You have no right or authority to tell them they cannot do this. As long as they are not interfering with your duties you are trying to carry out, they have every right to record the situation. Ignore it. Let it go. Realize you are being taped, but you should not be doing anything that you will not want recorded anyway. You might be recording it as well. The same holds true for the media. It is not your job to decide what is in good taste.

To avoid civil litigation, evidence suppression, and public criticism, investigative detentions must be accomplished legally. Lawful investigative detentions must adhere to the following constitutional points of law:

1. Officers may approach persons in public places and attempt to engage them in conversation without any suspicion that they may be involved in criminal activity. Such an approach must be voluntary and free of coercion. This action must be voluntary and not a stop of any sort. The person must feel and be free to walk away absent a reasonable and articulable suspicion of crime (Callahan, 2016).

2. The person approached without reasonable suspicion is not required to speak with the officer, produce identification, or otherwise remain in the area. The person may simply walk away, and the officer has no right to detain them (Callahan, 2016). This is what is known as a mere encounter. Do not activate emergency lights or block the person in. It is advisable to even tell the person he or she is free to leave. It is critical to note that any stop and any seizure or search will be challenged as to the voluntariness of the encounter. Your story will likely differ from the defendant once in court.

3. An officer who possesses a reasonable suspicion that a person may be involved in a criminal activity has a legal right to stop and detain the person for a reasonable period to investigate the situation (Callahan, 2016). Notice it does not say "probable cause"; it says "reasonable articulable suspicion."

4. Reasonable suspicion is present when an officer has articulable facts and reasonable inferences drawn from those facts that indicate that a criminal activity may be afoot. You will have to prove this in court (Callahan, 2016).

5. Reasonable suspicion can include a number of factors that, when taken together, combine to support an officer's belief that a criminal activity may be afoot. These factors may include but not be limited to time of day, reputation of the geographical area, reputation of the person to be detained, furtive or evasive behavior, flight, confrontational or abrasive attitude, clothing, etc. (Callahan, 2016). You will have to defend your actions.

6. An officer who detains a person for investigative purposes must be prepared to explain all the reasons as to why he or she detained the person and should make a written record of them as soon as possible (Callahan, 2016). Put another way, the officer must explain the totality of the circumstances.

7. Investigative detentions should take place and continue at the location where the stop has been initiated, absent extraordinary circumstances. Movement of the suspect to the police station or the back seat of a patrol car or other location against his or her will, will likely be construed later as an arrest (Callahan, 2016).

8. Officers must understand that an arrest under the Fourth Amendment must be justified by the higher standard of "probable cause." If an investigative detention becomes an arrest, it will be declared unconstitutional in the absence of "probable cause" (Callahan, 2016). A key point in court will always be that the defendant has felt he or she is not free to leave. There are many cases where judges have ruled both ways on this key issue. How voluntary is the brief detention? What is in the officer's mind matters. Many judges also view what is in the defendant's mind. When it comes to court, the defendant will always say he or she has felt not free to leave.

9. Officers who have reasonable suspicion to stop and detain a suspect have a lawful right to maintain that detention for a reasonable period as long as they are diligently pursuing an investigation to resolve the reason for the stop. The Supreme Court has never set an arbitrary time limit on the investigate detention concept (Callahan, 2016). Rest assured, the time will be questioned. The briefer, the better. You also run the risk of the suspect demanding to leave, and then a decision has to be made.

10. Officers may not detain a person longer than the time required to reasonably investigate the purpose of the stop. Holding a person for a longer time is likely to be interpreted as an arrest, which will be considered illegal in the absence of probable cause (Callahan, 2016). This is why it is important to try to establish probable cause quickly.

11. Officers conducting a *Terry* stop, including a routine traffic stop, are not required to provide the detained individual with *Miranda* warnings prior to asking

questions (Callahan, 2016). Again, this will be challenged in court as to whether the suspect is really free to leave. I have a tendency to read *Miranda* sooner than later to avoid any doubt. Rarely does the person say he or she will not talk. Also, it is better to get your statement or confession before you arrest them. Voluntariness goes down considerably once an arrest is made. You do not want to read *Miranda* too soon, however.

12. Officers who detain a person for investigation based upon reasonable suspicion that a criminal activity may be afoot are not permitted to frisk the person detained unless they possess a reasonable fear for their safety (Callahan, 2016). However, you can ask for consent to pat down.

13. A frisk of a detained person must be limited to a pat down of the person's outer clothing for weapons only. A search for evidence of a criminal activity is not permitted (Callahan, 2016). If during your pat down you feel an item that can be a weapon or illegal material, such as a marijuana pipe, you may retrieve it. Again, it is better to ask to retrieve even if you have probable cause. You want to build a layer of defenses to any objections raised. Consider officer safety in all cases. Ask the person before you pat them down or search them if they have any sharp objects on them that can harm you, such as needles. Do not take their word for it either.

14. Officers making a *Terry* stop of a vehicle may conduct a search of the passenger compartment of the vehicle to look for weapons as long as they possess a reasonable fear that weapons may be hidden in the passenger compartment (Callahan, 2016). You must be able to articulate this. It cannot be a blanket search every time you stop someone. We have discussed furtive movement with *Michigan v. Long* earlier. You can ask for permission to search the vehicle. If you get permission, search the area near the driver first. This is where they will likely have contraband and items they have just hidden. If with consent, remember, they can withdraw consent whenever

they wish. If you have established probable cause during the vehicle search, then even if they withdraw consent, you are good to go with probable cause under the *Carroll* doctrine. It is best to get written permission to search, but verbal is allowed. Follow your agency policy on this.

Now let us review these key terms one more time.

Reasonable Articulable Suspicion

Reasonable suspicion is a standard established by the Supreme Court in a 1968 case, in which it ruled that an officer should be allowed to stop and briefly detain a person if, based upon the officer's training and experience, there is reason to believe that the individual is engaging in a criminal activity. The officer is given the opportunity to "freeze" the action by stepping in to investigate. Probable cause is based upon the standard of a reasonable police officer.

Probable Cause

The court has interpreted the Fourth Amendment use of the word *seizure* to mean both the seizure of evidence and, as in an arrest, the seizure of a person. The court also has applied probable cause to searches, seizures, and arrests conducted without a warrant. According to the court, probable cause to make an arrest exists when an officer has knowledge of such facts as will lead a reasonable person to believe that a particular individual is committing, has committed, or is about to commit a criminal act. The officer must be able to articulate the facts and circumstances forming the basis for probable cause (Garner and Black, 2014).

Probable cause to search for evidence or to seize evidence requires that an officer be in possession of sufficient facts and circumstances as will lead a reasonable person to believe that evidence or contraband relating to a criminal activity will be found in the location to be searched. As with an arrest, if an officer cannot articulate the facts forming the basis for probable cause, the search and seizure will not hold up in court (Garner and Black, 2014).

Beyond a Reasonable Doubt

Beyond a reasonable doubt is the highest standard of evidence that exists in the judicial systems of common-law countries. As the inclusion of the word *reasonable*, however, suggests, proving beyond a reasonable doubt that a person has committed a crime does not mean that there is absolutely no doubt about his or her innocence. Rather, the phrase means that the established facts of the case lead the court to only one logical conclusion: that the defendant is guilty of the charges against him or her. Unreasonable doubt can still exist, but by its very nature, such doubt does not lead a reasonable person to conclude that the accused has not committed the crime in question. This high standard of proof helps reduce the likelihood of wrongful convictions (Garner and Black, 2014).

Totality of the Circumstances

Totality of the circumstances means there is no single deciding factor; one must consider all the facts and the context and conclude from the whole picture whether there is probable cause, whether an alleged detention is really a detention, or whether the officers' actions are reasonable or justified. The primary guide for this kind of substantive rule is the fact patterns from cases in which the courts have found that the criteria have been met (Garner and Black, 2014).

The Bright-Line Rule

A bright-line rule provides specific guidance. For example, any unwanted, nonaccidental touching of the person of another constitutes a battery. Police may not enter a property on which they do not have a right to be without a warrant or other special legal justification. The line is very clear (Garner and Black, 2014).

Adding It All Up

Reasonable articulable suspicion is needed to make a brief stop. Probable cause is needed to make a search or an arrest. Proof beyond a reasonable doubt is needed for a conviction in court. Here is a critical point to memorize and live by. Just because you might have probable cause does not mean you should always make an arrest.

That is what is needed to make an arrest; however, if you know you do not have a case to prove guilt beyond a reasonable doubt in court, then you are wasting your time at this point and really making a poor decision that will not bode well in many ways. Keep working on the case and investigate until you can prove the case beyond a reasonable doubt. Do not make an arrest knowing you cannot prove the case in court with the hope that your case gets better.

Here is another example of when probable cause is good but not good enough. You stop a vehicle for a violation. You smell what you know is the odor of marijuana coming from the vehicle. Based on your probable cause, you search the vehicle. You do not find any drugs. You have probable cause to search the vehicle, but you do not have probable cause to make an arrest. The driver might even say that he has had some marijuana in the car earlier, but it is all gone. Again, you have probable cause, but you will never get a conviction. Your probable cause has gone up in smoke, so to speak! To obtain a conviction, you must be able to prove all the elements of whatever crime it is you are looking to charge the person with. Take good cases to court. Bad arrests create bad case law.

The worst thing you can do as an officer outside of committing a crime is to lose your credibility in court. If the judge does not trust you or believe you, then you cannot be an effective officer. Guard your reputation carefully.

You will come across all sorts of judges. Some will be pro-police and others pro–defense attorney. Some are good and some not so much. Some will follow the law, and others flaunt the law. Some will not convict if they do not like a law. Do your job. Bring good cases. If the judge dismisses your good cases, let it go and do not say a word. I have had to deal with all sorts of judges. In an area I went to as a new sergeant, I noticed my troops were not writing equipment violations. I asked them about this, and they said the judge did not like that type of violation. I told them to write good tickets and let the judge do what he wanted. I went out and wrote a bunch of equipment tickets and went before the judge. He was terrible. He did not follow the law at all. After court, I went up and introduced myself to him. I thanked him for his work. I then told him I was encouraging my troops to enforce all laws, including equipment violations because they were important to traffic safety.

I then smiled and left it at that. My troops started writing equipment tickets again, and that was the end of it. He did what he wanted, but we did our job. I told my troops, "What happens if he tells you he does not like driving under the influence charges? Are you going to stop arresting them as well?" Legislators and the executive branch create law. The executive branch, where the police fall, enforces law. The judiciary tries cases. It is the lower court's job to find guilt or no guilt. They do not get to create statutory law. Higher courts can create case law.

Enforcement Issues

Investigation and Arrest

The process begins with the police discovering something or having it discovered for them. This is known as proactive or reactive policing, respectively. Most policing is reactive, with the police diligently following up, or probing, the truthfulness of any allegations or complaints. Someone becomes a "subject" or "person of interest" of an investigation when he or she is someone the police are looking into, and someone becomes a "target" of an investigation when it is likely he or she will be charged with a crime. Although there are special procedures for when somebody formally becomes a "suspect," all investigative procedures at this level are characterized by suspicion. Police always work up from a state of being naturally suspicious. That is what police do. When they arrest somebody, they have worked up to probable cause. There are many constitutional safeguards at this step of the process, but nobody questions the right of police to investigate and make arrests.

Warn, Summons, or Arrest

There are many things to take into consideration when deciding to warn, summons, or arrest. I will add "take no action" as an alternative. You cannot stop and deal with every violation of law you see. Follow your agency policy regarding when to warn, summons, or arrest and your state law and local ordinances. Often, you will have much discretion as to which you choose. First, you will need to know if it is a traffic or criminal offense. If traffic, you will need to know law and policy dealing with reciprocal agreements between your state and all other states. When it comes to summons or arrest, you will need to know whether what you see is a misdemeanor or felony and what class it is. Some offenses are not jailable, and only a summons is needed or allowed by law. Felonies are not releasable on a summons in most places. You must make sure you have proved all elements of a crime before you make a charge. Remember our discussion about reading the law literally and enforcing it by the spirit of the law. Watch for "may" or "shall." In some offenses, you cannot release the person because they cannot stop committing the act and they are a danger to themselves and everyone else. Drunk driving and drunk in public are two great examples. Some localities have a diversion program for drunk-in-public offenders. They can choose a detoxification center or jail. You do not need to memorize code sections, but it will come with time. What you must know are the elements of all crimes and traffic offenses.

When you arrest someone, you are responsible for their safety and well-being and the property they have in their possession; this includes their vehicle. You must safeguard all such things. Why you choose to warn varies and is up to you. You should follow policy and have some developed criteria to use in a standard manner. Maybe you warn everyone you stop for having a headlight out. Maybe the next time you stop them, you ticket them. Never base your decision on a person's sex or race. It might not have been a good policy, but I had an unwritten policy that, unless it is a serious violation, I would only warn someone I stop who has a Purple Heart or Silver Star license plate. I figured they had shed blood for our freedom and deserved a break. Of course, this is just for minor violations. The funny thing is I have never once, in twenty-seven years, stopped anyone who fits this description. Maybe once you have stopped the person, he or she will offer up a good excuse; or after speaking with them, you have just an ounce of doubt, so no charge is placed. Remember, tie goes to the runner.

Professional courtesy is something officers will ask for. It is up to you if you wish to give another officer a warning. Be fair and consistent. Never ever expect to be given a warning if you are stopped. If you get a warning, be thankful and learn from it. Do not get mad and blame anyone but yourself if you get a ticket. Of course, if you think you are innocent, that is different, and you have the same rights as everyone else. I have never liked the idea of writing traffic tickets just to raise money for a locality. That is a horrible reason to enforce the law. I have known officers and troops who have not written local people tickets but only people passing through. This is wrong as well. People used to joke that I would write my own mother a ticket. I used to write a great many tickets and make a great many arrests every year. The truth is I cannot have done that anyway because my mother died when I was a child as did my father. However, I doubt I would have written them a ticket for a minor violation. Having said that, I would not blame anyone else who have written them a ticket. The way I figure it is there are plenty of other people who can write my family a ticket other than me. Of course, I am speaking of minor traffic violations. I would be the first to fuss at myself or my family for breaking any law.

The diagram below offers an arrest decision flowchart.

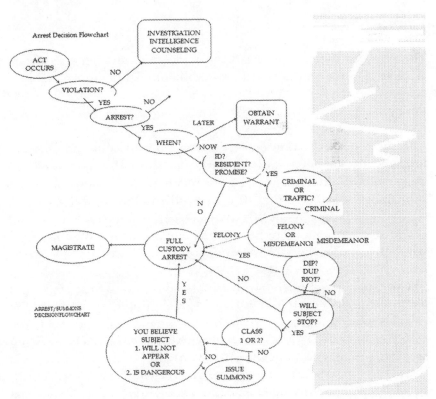

DR. JEFFREY C. FOX

Officer Survival and Use of Force

Officer survival and the use of force go hand in hand. The use of force has been and will always be a major issue for police officers and citizens everywhere.

"This National Consensus Policy on Use of Force is a collaborative effort among 11 of the most significant law enforcement leadership and labor organizations in the United States. The policy reflects the best thinking of all consensus organizations and is solely intended to serve as a template for law enforcement agencies to compare and enhance their existing policies" (National Consensus Policy on Use of Force, 2017). The consensus policy in its entirety follows. My thoughts and comments are added.

Purpose

The purpose of this policy is to provide law enforcement officers with guidelines for the use of less lethal and deadly force.

Policy

"It is the policy of this law enforcement agency to value and preserve human life. Officers shall use only the force that is objectively reasonable to effectively bring an incident under control, while protecting the safety of the officer and others. Officers shall use force only when no reasonably effective alternative appears to exist and shall use only the level of force which a reasonably prudent officer would use under the same or similar circumstances."

The decision to use force "requires careful attention to the facts and circumstances of each particular case, including the severity of the crime at issue, whether the suspect poses an immediate threat to the safety of the officer or others, and whether he is actively resisting arrest or attempting to evade arrest by flight."

In addition, "the 'reasonableness' of a particular use of force must be judged from the perspective of a reasonable officer on the scene, rather than with the 20/20 vision of hindsight . . . The question is whether the officers' actions are 'objectively reasonable' in light of the facts and circumstances confronting them."

Definitions

Deadly Force

Any use of force that creates a substantial risk of causing death or serious bodily injury

Less Lethal Force

Any use of force other than that which is considered deadly force that involves physical effort to control, restrain, or overcome the resistance of another

Objectively Reasonable

The determination that the necessity for using force and the level of force used is based upon the officer's evaluation of the situation in light of the totality of the circumstances known to the officer at the time the force is used and upon what a reasonably prudent officer will use under the same or similar situations

Serious Bodily Injury

Injury that involves a substantial risk of death, protracted and obvious disfigurement, or extended loss or impairment of the function of a body part or organ

De-Escalation

"Taking action or communicating verbally or non-verbally during a potential force encounter in an attempt to stabilize the situation and reduce the immediacy of the threat so that more time, options, and resources can be called upon to resolve the situation without the use of force or with a reduction in the force necessary. De-escalation may include the use of such techniques as command presence, advisements, warnings, verbal persuasion, and tactical repositioning."

Our preference is for the situation to not escalate to begin with. We should do everything legally, ethically, and morally in our power to avoid escalation. It is better to follow the least path of resistance. Having said this, we do not allow the offender to dictate the circumstances or procedures we will follow. We do not cower or shirk our duties to avoid a possible situation. Now having said that, sometimes prudence or discretion is the better part of valor. Do not bite off more than you can chew. Wait for help. Wait until next time. Get a warrant and arrest when the circumstances are to your advantage.

It was the beginning of a midnight shift. I had just gotten a milk shake at McDonald's! I saw a car leave the parking lot sliding sideways and driving recklessly. I went to stop the vehicle, and he took off. We had a short pursuit. The driver drove down a back road and slid to a halt. He jumped out of the car and ran into a huge crowd of hundreds of young black males and females. They were having a party at the end of a dead-end road on someone's property. He was into the middle of the crowd before I could get out of the car. It just so happened the riots were occurring at the same time in California over the Reginald Denny verdict involving the officers' use of force against him. I stepped out of my car and surveyed the crowd. I did not think I could even identify the driver. There was no need to push the issue for so many valid reasons. I got into my car and calmly left. How might this turned out if I had waded into the crowd trying to figure out who the driver was? Use discretion. Now if the driver was wanted for murder, we would have proceeded differently. However, I still would have made a plan, gotten back up, and proceeded cautiously.

Exigent Circumstances

"Those circumstances that would cause a reasonable person to believe that a particular action is necessary to prevent physical harm to an individual, the destruction of relevant evidence, the escape of a suspect, or some other consequence improperly frustrating legitimate law enforcement efforts"

Choke Hold

"A physical maneuver that restricts an individual's ability to breathe for the purposes of incapacitation. This does not include vascular neck restraints."

Most agencies will not allow this action.

Warning Shot

"Discharge of a firearm for the purpose of compelling compliance from an individual, but not intended to cause physical injury"

Note that this is merely offered as a definition. Most agencies do not allow a warning shot. I will never recommend warning shots. There is an old joke that warning shots will just make the offender run faster.

Procedures

A. General Provisions

> "1. Use of physical force should be discontinued when resistance ceases or when the incident is under control."
>
> Street justice is never allowed. When they stop fighting, you stop fighting.
>
> "2. Physical force shall not be used against individuals in restraints, except as objectively reasonable to prevent their escape or prevent imminent bodily injury to the individual, the officer, or another person. In these situations, only the minimal amount of force necessary to control the situation shall be used."
>
> Notice it mentions restraints. Unless circumstances dictate otherwise, you should always handcuff a suspect—hands behind their back, palms out, and thumbs up. Double-lock the handcuffs. Some people are very limber and can slip cuffs in front of them pretty

easily and off as well. Do not leave arrested subjects unattended in a car that does not have a caged back seat. More than one police car has sped away from the stop with the offender driving and the officer standing there!

"3. Once the scene is safe and as soon as practical, an officer shall provide appropriate medical care consistent with his or her training to any individual who has visible injuries, complains of being injured, or requests medical attention. This may include providing first aid, requesting emergency medical services, and/or arranging for transportation to an emergency medical facility."

If the suspect says he or she is injured or hurt, do not ignore this. Do not diagnose them yourself. Render aid you are trained to do. Seek medical care.

"4. An officer has a duty to intervene to prevent or stop the use of excessive force by another officer when it is safe and reasonable to do so."

This is tough, but you must do it. I had a trooper once who had to do just this. The other officer was striking the suspect after he had stopped resisting. The trooper reached up and grabbed the baton and said, "That is enough." This is how you do it. I am very proud of my troop. Later, the agency represented came by to ask what happened. You must act, or you are always guilty of not stopping an offense.

"5. All uses of force shall be documented and investigated pursuant to this agency's policies."

Always report a use of force to your supervisor. Even when you are correct in the use of force, not reporting it makes you look guilty. If you are present, you have a responsibility.

B. De-Escalation

"1. An officer shall use de-escalation techniques and other alternatives to higher levels of force consistent with his or her training whenever possible and appropriate before resorting to force and to reduce the need for force."

"2. Whenever possible and when such delay will not compromise the safety of the officer or another and will not result in the destruction of evidence, escape of a suspect, or commission of a crime, an officer shall allow an individual time and opportunity to submit to verbal commands before force is used."

On more than one occasion, I knew I would have to fight, or use force, to arrest the offender. I called for backup first. Every time, my hunch was right. I had to use force. Some of the hardest people I have ever fought were smaller than me. Do not let size fool you.

C. Use of Less Lethal Force

"When de-escalation techniques are not effective or appropriate, an officer may consider the use of less-lethal force to control a non-compliant or actively resistant individual. An officer is authorized to use agency-approved, less-lethal force techniques and issued equipment."

This will sound bad, but when the use of force is needed, then use it. If you have to strike a person, then strike them. There are some very bad people out there. If you have to shoot, then shoot fast and straight. If you are right in the use of force, then be right with using it. When the threat is over or stops, then you stop using the force. If you hit a person with whatever weapon you are authorized to use and they do not feel it, you have sent a very bad message. An officer may consider using less lethal force

"1. to protect the officer or others from immediate physical harm,

"2. to restrain or subdue an individual who is actively resisting or evading arrest, or

"3. to bring an unlawful situation safely and effectively under control."

D. Use of Deadly Force

"1. An officer is authorized to use deadly force when it is objectively reasonable under the totality of the circumstances. Use of deadly force is justified when one or both of the following apply:

   a. to protect the officer or others from what is reasonably believed to be an immediate threat of death or serious bodily injury

   b. to prevent the escape of a fleeing subject when the officer has probable cause to believe that the person has committed, or intends to commit a felony involving serious bodily injury or death, and the officer reasonably believes that there is an imminent risk of serious bodily injury or death to the officer or another if the subject is not immediately apprehended."

"2. Where feasible, the officer shall identify himself or herself as a law enforcement officer and warn of his or her intent to use deadly force."

"3. Deadly Force Restrictions

   "a. Deadly force should not be used against persons whose actions are a threat only to themselves or property."

   "b. Warning shots are inherently dangerous. Therefore, a warning shot must have a defined target and shall not be fired unless (1) the use of deadly force is justified; (2) the warning shot will not pose a substantial risk of injury or death to the officer or others; and (3) the officer reasonably believes that the warning shot will reduce the possibility that deadly force will have to be used."

Again, most agencies will not allow warning shots. I do not recommend warning shots.

"c. Firearms shall not be discharged at a moving vehicle unless (1) a person in the vehicle is threatening the officer or another person with deadly force by means other than the vehicle; or (2) the vehicle is operated in a manner deliberately intended to strike an officer or another person, and all other reasonable means of defense have been exhausted (or are not present or practical), which includes moving out of the path of the vehicle."

"d. Firearms shall not be discharged from a moving vehicle except in exigent circumstances. In these situations, an officer must have an articulable reason for this use of deadly force."

"e. Choke holds are prohibited unless deadly force is authorized."

E. Training

"1. All officers shall receive training, at least annually, on this agency's use of force policy and related legal updates.

"2. In addition, training shall be provided on a regular and periodic basis and designed to a. provide techniques for the use of and reinforce the importance of de-escalation; b. simulate actual shooting situations and conditions; and c. enhance officers' discretion and judgment in using less-lethal and deadly force in accordance with this policy."

"3. All use-of-force training shall be documented."

This last section is beyond your control within the agency. However, this does not mean you cannot practice on your own. Practice shooting. Stay physically fit. Think through scenarios in your head as to how you will react or what you will do under any given circumstances. Stay up on use-of-force law.

Study this area. Retired Lt. Col. Dave Grossman has written greatly on this topic. I highly recommend you read his material and attend his seminars. Read after-action reports on other officers' use of forces, especially those reports dealing with officers who have been killed in the line of duty. There is much to learn from these.

Use of Force

Many years ago, we had been taught to use force as if climbing a ladder. Move up one step at a time. This seems obvious, but it is not the best practice. It is better to view use of force in a circle. You must look at what force is being used against you or the victim. You do not necessarily match the force with equal force in many cases. You should use only that force necessary to stop the threat. If someone pulls a knife on you, then you will not pull a knife. If someone wants to box you, then you do not have to box them back. There are occasions where you might go from mere presence to having to pull and fire your weapon. In this case, you have skipped many steps. You have jumped over many rungs on the ladder. In a circle approach, you will reach out to the force tool necessary to stop the immediate threat you face. Of course, to pull and fire your weapon means you are facing deadly force.

Be aware of a phenomenon called sympathetic shooting. There have been cases where one officer shot, so other officers fired their weapons as well. I think this comes from one of two things. First, it's from the impulse to fire when one hears a gun going off right near you. Second and very similar, it is reflexive. I will add, in the same realm, that it is an almost innate defense mechanism but not a proper one necessarily. The problem is you should only fire if you think you should fire and never because another officer fires. Remember, you only fire your weapon when the circumstance dictates such use of force and when you are in fear for your life or the life of another person. Keep your finger off the trigger unless you are ready to fire. Do not pull your gun unless you have the probability of having to fire it. You must be aware of the target and your background or backdrop and practice fire control/fire discipline. In the same vein, your orders to the suspect must be in unison or agreement. There have been occasions where some officers are yelling, "Hands up," and others are yelling, "Do not move." It cannot be both. Years ago, we used to say "shoot to kill." Now we say "shoot to stop the threat." You are taught to shoot the center of mass to stop the threat.

Do not put yourself in a position where you have to shoot. In every circumstance, you want to try to de-escalate the situation when possible. This will not always be possible, but do your best. There have been too many occasions where an officer steps in front of a moving car to stop it, only to wind up shooting at the vehicle as it approaches. Then the officer continues to shoot at the vehicle as it has driven by. Neither should occur. Movies are horrible in so many ways. The public gets a terrible view of police in all too many movies. Likewise, the police themselves have drummed into their heads terrible ways to handle any given situation. Do not stand in front of moving cars and order them to stop. Do not stand in front of moving cars and shoot at them. By standing in front of a moving vehicle, you help create a shooting situation that does not have to be. If you do hit the driver, then you might have a totally out-of-control vehicle speeding toward you. Once the vehicle has passed, it is hard to say the threat is still there.

Years ago, I stopped to check on a tractor trailer driver sleeping on the side of the interstate. He was on the edge of the shoulder near the right lane. He was asleep behind the wheel with the engine running. We gave tickets for this. I pounded on the door as I was standing on his rig on the side runner. He finally woke up and put the vehicle in gear and started to drive down the shoulder. I was yelling at him to stop. I could not jump off because of the heavy traffic. He went about a quarter of a mile down the shoulder before he stopped. I arrested him for an aggravated case of reckless driving, and I was going to ask our prosecutor for jail time. Before the trial, the prosecutor and I were preparing the case, and he asked me why I did not shoot the driver. I said, "If I had shot him, then I would have an even worse out-of-control situation with me on the side of this huge rig on the edge of a heavily traveled road." That was the main reason I did not shoot him. The other reason was I felt I had alternatives. I would have broken the window next. The fellow tried to argue he had a sleep disorder. He was found guilty and given thirty days to serve in jail.

Not trying to date the book, but in the last several years, we have seen officers shoot unarmed suspects. The media and some politicians will jump up and down, saying it is improper force by the mere fact the person is not armed with a gun. This is a false narrative, harmful to police psyche, and unfair. Generally speaking, one cannot shoot an armed person. However, if you are truly and reasonably in fear for your life based on the totality of the circumstances, then deadly force might be appropriate. Many years ago, we had a trooper who was arresting a drunk driver. The drunk was able to get the trooper down in a ditch and was strangling the life out of him. If the suspect had strangled the trooper to death, then that was it; he would be dead. Or if the suspect was able to get the trooper's gun, he could shoot him. Or if the suspect merely strangled the trooper to unconsciousness, then he was at the mercy of the suspect. Again, he was as good as dead. The trooper could not get the suspect off him or to stop strangling him. He could not break the choke hold. The trooper shot and killed the suspect at very close range. The suspect was unarmed. It was a proper shooting and use of force.

Use-of-Force Wheel

Here is another way to view the use-of-force continuum.

Use-of-Force Ladder

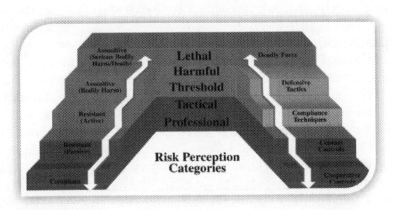

(FLETC, 2003)

Situational Crime Prevention

Situational crime prevention techniques and focused deterrence approaches have been used successfully. Use the techniques of situational crime prevention to understand crime problems, develop interventions, and evaluate the effectiveness of those interventions. Grounded in an opportunity framework that draws on routine activity and rational choice theories, situational crime prevention derives practical implications for prevention from theoretical principles. Initially, situational crime prevention has been designed to address highly specific forms of crime by systematically manipulating or managing the immediate environment in as permanent way as possible, with the purpose of reducing opportunities for crime as perceived by a wide range of offenders. More recently, researchers have recognized that environments and situations not only create opportunities for crimes but also, at times, provide the motivation. More recent techniques have focused on effectively altering opportunity structures and/or motivations of a particular crime by (1) increasing the efforts, (2) increasing the risks, (3) reducing the rewards, (4) reducing provocations, and (5) removing excuses.

DR. JEFFREY C. FOX

Fundamentals of Policing and Patrol Procedures

Below you will see thirty-four categories that cover just about everything you will ever do on patrol or as a result of patrol. The San Jose Police Department has created a field training program in the 1970s, and as part of the program, they have created an evaluation checklist for FTOs to use in training and evaluating new trainees. Under each category are descriptions of what it will take to earn a 1, which is the lowest rating and not acceptable under the standards; a 5, which is the acceptable level; and finally a 7, which will be exemplary performance for a given category. What you will see below is a mix of what will be good to exemplary performance for an officer. Your goal should be to meet exemplary standards at all times. If you focus on each of these categories daily, you will do very well in your future, new, or existing position.

1.   General appearance - physical appearance, dress, and demeanor

Uniform is neat and clean and worn properly. Weapon, leather, and equipment are clean and operative. Hair is within regulations and freshly cut. Shoes are shined and clean. Display command bearing.

2.   Vehicle appearance - appearance and care of assigned or issued vehicle

The vehicle is immaculate inside and outside. Items are put away, no clutter, and one can locate items. The vehicle is kept in an exceptional condition. Items that can be used as weapons are not accessible. There are no excessive items in the vehicle and trunk. The vehicle has no defective equipment. Maintenance schedule is followed and/or documented. Damage is reported immediately.

3.   Acceptance of feedback - accepts constructive criticism, and feedback is used to further the learning process and improve performance from supervisors.

Accept feedback in a positive manner and apply it to improve performance and further learning. Actively solicit constructive criticism/feedback in order to further learning and improve performance. Do not argue or blame others for errors.

4. Attitude toward police work - views career in terms of personal motivation, goals, and acceptance of the responsibilities of the job

   Demonstrate an active interest in career and in police responsibilities. Utilize off-duty time to further professional knowledge and improve skills. Demonstrate concern for the fair and equitable enforcement of the law, maintaining high ideals in terms of professional responsibilities.

5. Department policies and procedures - knowledge of department procedures and ability to apply the knowledge under field conditions

   Have an excellent working knowledge of department policies/regulations, including lesser known and seldom used ones.

6. Criminal statutes - knowledge of the criminal statutes and ability to apply that knowledge in field situations

   Know the difference between criminal and noncriminal activities. Have outstanding knowledge of the criminal codes and apply that knowledge to normal and unusual criminal activities.

7. Traffic codes - knowledge of traffic codes and ability to apply that knowledge to field situations

   Recognize offenses when committed. Know and recognize commonly encountered traffic violations. Apply appropriate sections of the code. Have outstanding knowledge of traffic codes and apply that knowledge to your daily activities.

8. Criminal procedure - knowledge of criminal procedures, including laws of arrest and search/seizure and ability to apply those procedures in field situations

   Follow the required procedure in commonly encountered situations. Conduct proper searches and seizes evidence legally. Arrest within the legal guidelines. Follow the required procedure in all cases, accurately applying law relative to searching, seizing evidence, and effecting arrests.

9. With citizens in general - ability to interact with citizens (including suspects) in an appropriate and efficient manner

   Be very much at ease with citizen contacts. Quickly establish rapport and leave people with a feeling that you are interested in serving them. Be objective in all contacts. Be courteous, friendly, and empathetic. Communicate in a professional and unbiased manner. Be service oriented. Do not be abrupt, belligerent, overbearing, arrogant, or uncommunicative. Do not overlook or avoid the service aspect of the job. Do not be introverted, insensitive, and uncaring.

10. With ethnic groups other than own - ability to interact with members of ethnic or racial groups other than own in an appropriate efficient manner

    Do not be hostile, overly sympathetic, prejudicial, subjective, and/or biased. Be at ease with members of other ethnic/racial groups. Serve their needs objectively and with concern. Do not feel threatened when in the presence of other ethnic/racial groups. Understand the various cultural differences and use this understanding to competently resolve situations and problems. Be totally objective and communicate in a manner that furthers mutual understanding. It is very important that you always remain mindful of special-needs populations you will deal with. They are vast and varied. You might not even know you are dealing with a member of these groups at first. You will receive or should receive training in this area. Having knowledge of these groups and the various issues each group (members) has can mean the difference between a peaceful and a hostile encounter.

11. With other department employees - ability to effectively interact with other department employees of various ranks and in various capacities

Do not gossip. Be a "team player." Adhere to the chain of command and accept your role within the organization. Have good peer relationships and be accepted as a group member. Be at ease in contact with superiors. Understand superiors' responsibilities; respect and support their positions. Be a peer group leader. Actively assist others.

12. With persons of the opposite sex - ability to effectively interact with persons of the opposite sex both in a written capacity and outside the department

Be at ease with members of the opposite sex. Work objectively and without prejudice with members in this grouping. Do not feel threatened when in their presence. Create a positive work environment through a nonjudgmental attitude and do not partake in sexual harassment. Understand the various sexual differences and simultaneously use this understanding to competently resolve situations and problems. Be totally objective and communicate in a manner that furthers mutual understanding. Do not tolerate sexual harassment.

13. Driving skill in normal conditions - skill in the operation of the police vehicle under normal driving conditions

Obey traffic laws when appropriate. Maintain control of the vehicle. Perform vehicle operations while maintaining alertness to surrounding activities. Drive defensively. Set an example for lawful and courteous driving. Maintain complete control of the vehicle while operating the radio and observing traffic.

14. Driving skills in moderate- and high-stress conditions - skill in vehicle operation under emergency situations and in situations calling for other than the usual driving skills

Use lights and siren properly. Maintain control of the vehicle and evaluate driving situations properly. Display a high degree of reflex ability and driving competence. Anticipate driving situations in advance and act accordingly. Practice defensive driving techniques. Respond very well relative to the degree of stress present.

When traveling at high rates of speed, you are most likely outrunning your siren. Do not drive at 100 percent capacity. To do so leaves no room for error or adjustment as needed. It is more important to get there safely than fast. Pick your traffic stop location carefully. If not a good spot, move the vehicles. Practice light discipline when stopped. Do not blind oncoming vehicles. Wear your seat belt. Some states allow the officer to use his or her discretion regarding wearing seat belts while on a call. Wear your seat belt until you get where you are going. It is not worth getting killed or injured over.

15. Orientation/response time to calls - awareness of surroundings and ability to find locations and arrive at destinations within an acceptable period

Be aware of the location while on patrol. Properly use a map. Relate the location to the destination. Arrive at the destination within a reasonable period. Remember locations from previous visits to not need a map or GPS to get there. Be aware of shortcuts and utilize these to save time. Have a high level of orientation to the area.

16. Routine forms – Accuracy/completeness - ability to properly utilize departmental forms necessary for job accomplishment

    Make sure forms are complete, accurate, and properly used. Know the commonly used forms and understand their use. Complete these forms with reasonable accuracy and thoroughness. Consistently make accurate form selection and rapidly complete a detailed form without assistance. Display a high degree of accuracy.

17. Report writing – Organization/details - ability to prepare reports that accurately reflect the situation and do so in an organized and detailed manner

    Complete reports, organizing information in a logical manner. Make reports that contain the required information and details. Make reports that are complete and contain a detailed accounting of events from beginning to end. Ensure they are written and organized so that any reader understands what has occurred.

18. Report writing – Grammar/spelling/neatness - ability to use proper English, to follow spelling rules, and to write neatly

    Ensure reports are legible and grammar is at an acceptable level. Make sure spelling is acceptable and errors are rare. Make certain that errors, if present, do not impair an understanding of the report. Create reports that are very neat. They should contain no spelling or grammatical errors.

19. Field performance – Nonstress conditions - ability to perform routine, nonstress police activities

    Properly assess routine situations, determine the appropriate action, and take the same. Properly assess situations, including unusual or complex ones.

20. Field performance – Stress conditions - ability to perform in moderate- to high-stress conditions

Do not be timid. Do not lose temper or display cowardice. Do not overreact. Maintain calmness and self-control; determine the proper course of action and take it. Do not allow the situation to further deteriorate. Maintain calmness and self-control in even the most extreme situations. Quickly take command and gain control of the situation. Determine the best course of action and take it. Make sure the course of action is always correct.

21. Investigative skills – Crime scenes - ability to conduct a proper investigation with an emphasis upon crime scene investigatory procedures

Discern readily available evidence. Protect scenes. Collect, tag, log, and protect evidence in a proper manner. Always follow proper investigatory procedures and be always accurate in diagnosis of what offense has occurred. Connect evidence with the suspect even when not apparent. Have "evidence technician" collection and identification skills. Collect "readable" fingerprints from any possible surface when available.

22. Investigative skills – Accident investigation - ability to conduct a proper investigation of accidents

Promptly call for wrecker/rescue squad. Subpoena needed witnesses. Collect all necessary information and ensure that information has been exchanged. Respond, position the vehicle, and check for injuries. Draw diagram(s), photograph the scene when needed, open the roadway quickly, always collect needed information, and make correct charge(s). Interview and match physical evidence to the statements of the driver(s). Know how to handle a fatal crash investigation with minimal assistance.

23. Interview/interrogation skills - ability to use proper questioning techniques, to vary techniques to "fit" the

person being interviewed/interrogated, and to follow proper procedures

Elicit the most available information and record the same. Execute the "advice of rights" form as needed. Always use proper questioning techniques. Establish rapport with all victims/witnesses. Control the interrogation of even the most difficult suspects and conduct successful interrogations of the same.

24. Self-initiated field activity - interest and ability to initiate a police-related activity, to view the same, and to act on even low-priority situations

    Do not avoid activity. Follow up on situations. Do not rationalize suspicious circumstances. Recognize/identify suspicious/illegal activity. Have a broad orientation of the job, including low-priority activity. Develop cases from observed activities. Show inquisitiveness. Seldom misses observable activities. Make good quality arrests and/or proper dispositions from observed activities. Think well "on your feet."

25. Officer safety in general - ability to perform police tasks without injuring self/others or exposing self/others to unnecessary dangers/risks.

    Follow accepted safety procedures, for example, (a) do not expose weapons (baton, handgun, etc.) to the suspect; (b) keep your gun hand free during enforcement situations; (c) do not stand to the front of the violator's car door; (d) control the suspect's movements; (e) keep the violator/ suspect in sight; (f) use illumination when necessary and properly; (g) (maintain a good physical condition; (h) utilize or maintain personal safety equipment; (i) anticipate potentially dangerous situations; (j) do not stand too close to passing vehicular traffic; (k) do not be careless with a gun and other weapons; (l) do not stand in front of doors when knocking upon the same; (m) make the appropriate choice of which weapon to use and when to use it; (n) provide cover to other officers; (o) do not stand between the police car and the violator's vehicle during stops; (p) wear a reflective safety vest when exposed to traffic other than traffic stops; (q) always wear a bulletproof vest; (r) do not reach into a vehicle with the driver behind the wheel to turn the car off or remove the keys; (s) foresee dangerous situations and prepare; (t) keep your partner informed and determine the best position for yourself and your partner; (u) do not be overconfident; (v) use light or other illumination appropriately.

Always be mindful of your stance. Put the weapon away from suspects. Never ever surrender your weapon. Three strikes and you are not out. Never give up if you are in a struggle with a suspect. Being shot or injured does not mean you will die. Fight and survive. Sometimes this might be the case: "There is nothing wrong except there is nothing wrong." Be aware of your surroundings at all times on and off duty. Wear your bulletproof vest. If you have an in-car camera or a body camera, use it. Wear your traffic vest when exposed to traffic longer than a normal traffic stop. Wear the traffic safety vest while investigating crashes, directing traffic, or conducting a checking detail or DUI sobriety checkpoint. Consider approaching stopped vehicle from the passenger side. This gives you the element of surprise since they usually expect you to approach from the driver side, and they hide items from that view. I have found many illegal items that way, and many are guns. Approaching from the passenger side also gives you protection from traffic and a place to run. Check the trunk as you approach. Lift up on the trunk lid. Also, leave your latent prints on the trunk and rear window.

26. Officer safety with suspects/suspicious persons/ prisoners - ability to perform police tasks in a safe manner while dealing with suspects, suspicious persons, or prisoners

Follow accepted safety procedures with suspects, suspicious persons, and prisoners. Foresee potential danger and eliminate or control the same. Maintain a position of advantage in even the most demanding situations. Be alert to changing situations and prevent opportunities for danger from developing.

27. Control of conflict – Voice command - ability to gain and maintain control of situations through verbal command and instruction

   Speak with authority in a calm, clear voice. Properly select words and have knowledge of when and how to use them. Completely control with voice tone, word selection, inflection, and the bearing that accompanies what is said. Restore order in even the most trying situations through the use of voice.

   We had a great saying at our state police academy. "You can be as tough as nails and still be a gentleman" or a lady.

28. Control of conflict – Physical skill - ability to use the proper level of force for given situations

   Be physically able to perform task. Obtain and maintain control through the use of the proper amounts of techniques of force application. Have an excellent knowledge and ability in the use of restraints. Select the right amount of force for the given situation. Be in superior physical condition.

29. Problem-solving/decision making - performance in terms of ability to perceive, form valid conclusions, arrive at sound judgments, and make proper decisions

   Be able to reason through even the most complex situations and to make appropriate conclusions. Have an excellent perception. Anticipate problems and prepare resolutions in advance. Relate past solutions to present solutions.

Discretion is the better part of valor.

30. Radio – Appropriate use of plain language/procedures - ability to use the police radio in accordance with department policies and procedures

Follow policy and accepted procedures. Have a good working knowledge of the most often used sections of the code. Always use plain language and comply with policies and procedures.

31. Radio – Listening and comprehension - ability to pay attention to radio traffic and to understand the information transmitted

Be aware of own radio transmissions and traffic in the area. Be aware of traffic elsewhere in the department/ division/precinct. Use previously transmitted information to your advantage.

32. Radio – Articulation of transmission - ability to communicate with others via the police radio

Use proper procedures with clear, concise, and complete transmissions. Transmit clearly, calmly, concisely, and completely in even the most stressful situations. Make sure transmissions are well-thought-out and do not have to be repeated.

33. Court testifying - skill reference his/her testifying in court

Prepare cases prior to presentations. Do not be hostile to the defense attorney, prosecuting attorney, and/or judge. Present the facts of the case in a clear, concise, and relevant manner. Make sure to be seldom requested to explain your testimony. Be polite and professional to the court officials. Have a full understanding of proper courtroom demeanor. Prepare your cases in an exceptional manner and be totally familiar with the facts.

34. Criminal interdiction

Look beyond issuing a summons. Obtain backup before searching. Attempt to obtain consent to search a vehicle; get it voluntarily through conversation. Notice the "indicators" that are consistent with a possible criminal activity. Utilize assistance (other police officers). Check criminal history; run wanted checks on persons and weapons (property). Understand when probable cause exists. Completely search vehicles. Understand that racial profiling is not permitted. Before trying to obtain consent, observe actions or items that are consistent with a criminal activity. Obtain consent and understand when a search can be conducted only using probable cause. Be aware of uncommon hiding places. Recognize cues given by suspects. Be current in interdiction case law.

Traffic Management

Traffic management in the context of an incident may include managing the queue (those in line to pass by the incident), managing those trapped between the incident and detour route, managing traffic backups and secondary crashes, and driving and monitoring alternate routes and placing patrols on them to assist disabled or lost motorists.

Traffic Incident Management

Goals of Incident Management

- ✓ Reduce detection time
- ✓ Reduce response time
- ✓ Reduce clearance time
- ✓ Provide effective scene management
- ✓ Provide timely and accurate motorist information

Who is in charge? Who is the incident scene commander?

- ✓ In many cases, it will be you or maybe the fire chief or both, and a unified command should be used.
- ✓ If the police are in charge, then you are in charge until a supervisor gets there. That might be thirty minutes to a

couple of hours in some cases. Even if the police are not the lead, you are still in charge for the police functions, so act appropriately.

✓ What you do or do not do until the supervisor's arrival can be critical to the success or failure of the incident.

✓ The bigger question is, who is in charge of what? Put another way, who has the duty and responsibility for what? We need to work in a unified fashion. Use the incident command system as needed and appropriate for the level of the event.

Think broadly and act locally.

✓ What is going on behind you?
✓ How far is the backup?
✓ Is the backup affecting other routes?

Control the situation.

Murphy's Law says what can go wrong will go wrong. Hope for the best but plan for the worst. Incident management is more of an attitude than an activity. Work with others and know each role. In a general sense, this is what each stakeholder wants.

✓ Transportation wants the road open as quickly and safely as possible.

✓ Fire departments want to put out and prevent fire. Deal with hazardous material.

✓ Emergency medical services want to treat and transport the injured.

✓ The media want the story as quickly as possible.

✓ Wrecker drivers want to tow and recover.

✓ Citizens and motorists want the road open and to be able to get where they want and need to be.

✓ Those involved want help.

✓ Local agencies (police and other officials) want to be kept informed and local roads open.

✓ Police want what everyone else wants. We also want to investigate the crash.

✓ All of us want it done with safety in mind.

Whether it is a crime or crash scene, remember the order of priority.

1. Life safety
2. Scene stabilization
3. Property preservation

When you get there, do the following:

- ✓ Begin your accident investigation.
- ✓ Create a safe scene.
    - o Park properly.
    - o Create a safety zone for all to work in.
    - o Wear the proper traffic/safety vest for visibility purposes.
    - o Create and maintain proper emergency vehicle light discipline.
        - ▪ Moth effect can occur.
        - ▪ Do not want to blind oncoming traffic of disorient oncoming drivers.
- ✓ Begin with the end in mind.
- ✓ Assess the scene.
- ✓ Get the roadway open.
- ✓ Get help that is needed.
    - o Render aid as trained.
- ✓ Help may be needed other than at the scene.
    - o Detours
    - o Others patrol congested areas
    - o The queue
        - ▪ Manage the funnel where traffic merges to get by.
        - ▪ Be sure oncoming traffic has ample warning.
- ✓ Get the necessary wreckers en route.
    - o Find out what wreckers are needed and call right away so the closure time is minimized.
- ✓ Do an initial assessment of the crash.
- ✓ Conduct a thorough and accurate investigation.
    - o Many of the principles and techniques discussed in the criminal investigation chapter apply here equally.
- ✓ Photograph as needed.

- ✓ Sketch the scene as the vehicles are found at rest.
  - ○ Get the vehicles off the road once the photos are taken and the scene sketched. Record skid marks and debris location as well.
  - ○ Some crashes will require a reconstruction team to respond before moving vehicles.
- ✓ Collect driver and witness information.
- ✓ Conduct interviews.
  - ○ It is good practice to have all witnesses write their statements down. You can then ask additional questions at the end of their statement and have them sign at the bottom. It is hard to say they have not said that when it is in writing. It is hard to say that is not what they meant when it is written.
- ✓ Complete the investigation.
- ✓ Make the appropriate charge.
- ✓ Complete other investigative and administrative matters.
- ✓ Transportation agencies and public works have a lot to offer.
  - ○ Heavy equipment
  - ○ Personnel
  - ○ Road signs/barricades/cones
  - ○ Funds
  - ○ Expertise
- ✓ Keep the media in the know so people can detour.
- ✓ When a wrecker tells you a specific time for clearance, you can almost without any doubt plan for more time than that.
  - ○ It is better for you to under promise and over deliver when setting time estimates.
- ✓ Do not make promises you cannot keep.
- ✓ Fire and rescue may need a lane for safety; put yourself in their shoes.
- ✓ Be ready to get the lanes open.
- ✓ Keep everyone involved apprised and moving.
- ✓ Let the other agencies know immediately that they may be dealing with detour routes, coordinate, and communicate.
- ✓ Remember that once the debris is off the road, cleanup can take place later.

- o Less traffic
- o Barricades and detour signs up
- o Better equipment can respond
- ✓ Each stakeholder has a role to play. Input should be received from each and given to each. Practice unified command.
- ✓ Keep supervision apprised until their arrival.
  - o The bigger the incident, the more help you will need. Get the help needed.
- ✓ Keep the dispatcher informed of lane closures, etc.

Scene Management Follow-Up

- ✓ Check congested area for disabled motorists.
- ✓ Plan the opening.
  - o People back in vehicles.
  - o Let everyone know it is open.
    - ▪ The media
    - ▪ Truckers CB-19
- ✓ Make sure no one is going the wrong way.
- ✓ Make sure you tell the dispatcher when it is clear or when things change.

Until a supervisor gets there, you are in charge for the police. Your actions or inaction will have laid a great deal of groundwork for what the supervisor has to work with. Life safety must come before all other incident priorities.

Incident Command

In emergency management, there are four traditional phases.

1. Mitigation
2. Preparedness
3. Response
4. Recovery

As a police officer, you will be involved in response all the time. However, you might well find yourself in the other three phases as well.

Structure and Principles of Incident Command

The incident command system (ICS) is based on an organizational structure that includes the incident commander(s) (as well as information, safety, and liaison officers) and four supporting sections (planning, operations, logistics, and finance/administration) as needed. This is all scalable depending on the situation and need (Bullock, Cappola, Haddow, and Yeletaysi, 2009; Lindell, Prater, and Perry, 2007).

Incident command is composed of the on-scene leadership for the incident, emergency, or disaster. This may initially be the first person to respond to the incident. Later on, command may be taken over by the highest-ranking official in a single organization or shared among the leadership of several responding agencies to facilitate coordination. Incident command may also be given to the person(s) with the most expertise in certain disasters or response functions (Bullock et al., 2009; Lindell et al., 2007).

The incident commanders have ultimate responsibility to oversee and coordinate response operations. If needed, three officers work with and report directly to the incident commander(s) (Bullock et al., 2009; Lindell et al., 2007).

1. The information officer works with the media to answer their questions about the event and release information to the public.

2. The safety officer monitors the hazardous conditions of the emergency or disaster to ensure protection of responding personnel.

3. The liaison officer is the point of contact between incident command and other organizations responding to the incident.

If needed, the incident commander establishes and works with four sections that facilitate effective on-scene emergency and disaster management (Bullock et al., 2009; Lindell et al., 2007).

The planning section

- ✓ collects and evaluates information about the emergency or disaster,
- ✓ defines operational priorities in collaboration with the incident commander, and
- ✓ disseminates information about the incident and the use of resources during response operations (Bullock et al., 2009; Lindell et al., 2007).

The operations section

- ✓ is responsible for implementing the strategy to respond to the incident as determined by the incident commander and the planning section (Bullock et al., 2009; Lindell et al., 2007).

The logistics section

- ✓ acquires and provides materials, services, and facilities to support the needs of responders as directed by the incident commander and the operations section (Bullock et al., 2009; Lindell et al., 2007).

The finance/administration section has the goal of

- ✓ tracking costs,
- ✓ completing and filing paperwork, and
- ✓ recording expenses of operations and logistics (Bullock et al., 2009; Lindell et al., 2007).

There is one more often vital position to be filled, and that is the intelligence or information officer. This position/section can be placed wherever the incident commander wishes to put it. It can be the general or command staff.

The incident command system is based on a number of vitally important principles.

- ✓ Common terminology. Because there are so many response organizations involved in the response, common vocabulary (plain English) must be used instead of "ten" codes (i.e., 10-4).
- ✓ Modular organization. Depending on the nature and scope of the emergency/disaster, the incident command system may consist of the incident commander and one responding unit, or it may be composed of the incident commander(s), support sections, and additional layers as needed (i.e., division, branch, strike teams, etc.). The system is flexible.
- ✓ Integrated communications. In order to accommodate each of the participating agencies, a common communications plan is utilized, and assigned frequencies are clearly identified.
- ✓ Unity of command. As a way to limit organizational confusion, each person reports to one commanding officer only.
- ✓ A unified command structure. When there is more than one responding organization, the command structure expands to include all major agencies to facilitate joint decision making.
- ✓ Consolidated incident action plans (IAPs). The incident commander(s) and the planning section identify operational goals and produce written incident action plans to guide operations (typically over recurring twelve-hour periods).
- ✓ A manageable span of control. Each supervisor should manage between three and seven individuals (with five being the optimal number).
- ✓ Designated incident facilities. All of those responding to disaster should be made aware of the location of the incident command post (ICP), staging areas, camps, helispots, casualty collection points, etc.
- ✓ Comprehensive resource management. Human, material, and equipment resources are always checked in and given assigned, available, or out-of-service status

to consolidate control and maximize the use of resources (Bullock et al., 2009; Lindell et al., 2007).

What is incident command?

- ✓ A set of personnel, policies, procedures, facilities, and equipment integrated into a common organizational structure designed to improve emergency response operations of all types and complexities.
- ✓ ICS is the model tool for command, control, and coordination of a response and provides a means to coordinate the efforts of individual agencies as they work toward the common goal of stabilizing the incident and protecting life, property, and the environment.
- ✓ The purpose of incident command is to allow its user(s) to adopt an integrated organizational structure equal to the complexity and demands of single or multiple incidents without being hindered by jurisdictional boundaries (Bullock et al., 2009; Lindell et al., 2007).

Response and Recovery

Response is defined as an immediate reaction or relief effort focused on saving lives, and *recovery* is the process of repair and restoration. The key elements of this definition are "saving lives." *Evacuation*, a related term is usually discussed under mitigation, but it can be mentioned here that comprehensive evacuation planning should have already calculated behavioral estimates of the percentage of the population that will evacuate when directed, the levels of transportation assistance and special needs required, and the number of people who may seek refuge at public shelters (Bullock et al., 2009; Lindell, et al, 2007).

Interagency Cooperation

Unified command works best when there is a multiagency response, and such a response is characterized by backup communications systems, shared intelligence architectures, shared public information services, and multijurisdictional accountability. An ICS must be robust enough to provide for the adaptability needed when large numbers of personnel from multiple government agencies need to work together. Flexibility is built in by allowing breakdown positions (branches, groups, task or strike forces) to be staffed only if the event dictates the need. To some extent, incident command is already capable of this flexibility because an ICS blends agency autonomy, management by objectives, unity integrity, and functional clarity and practices good span of control (Bullock et al., 2009; Lindell et al., 2007). Play nice in the sandbox!

The Five Cs of Incident Command

- ✓ Command
  - ○ Control
- ✓ Communication
  - ○ Human
  - ○ Technological
- ✓ Cooperation
- ✓ Coordination
- ✓ Collaboration

The below diagram illustrates a very basic ICS structure.

Incident Command Structure

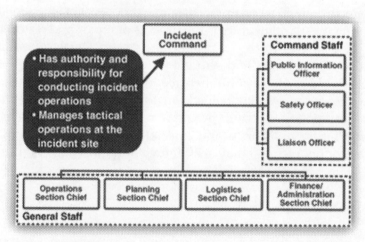

(Bullock et al., 2009; Lindell et al., 2007)

Remember, we always want to de-escalate situations, not make them worse. There will be many times where you are on the scene of a potentially volatile situation with members of other law enforcement agencies. Do not let them drag you into a bad situation and then make it worse. Try to practice a unified command. This may or may not work. There are certain situations that we do not get to formally plan for but that we do know how to handle in a general nature. Hostage situations are different than barricade situations. With hostage situations, we may be pressed to act. In barricade situations, we do not have as much pressure. He or she is not going anywhere if we have them properly contained. If he or she fires on us, then we might need to return fire. Other than that, we have plenty of time. No need to rush. No need to get you, another officer, or even the offender killed.

Many years ago, I and several of my troops responded to a barricade situation. We were in an isolated parking lot at the top of a mountain with no civilians around. Another agency was there already. The subject was alone in his vehicle with a gun he was pointing at himself. I deployed my troops and vehicles so he had nowhere to go. I had a canine in the woods. We had time. It was controlled. Without a word, an officer from the other agency began to move forward past the cover of the vehicles and approached the subject. I was very unhappy at this moment. This was totally not needed. The subject was pushed into a situation where he had to surrender right then, turn the gun on us, and create a suicide-by-cop situation or shoot himself. As the officer got near the door of the car, the subject shot himself in the chest. We all stood there and listened to him softly say "ouch" several times until he died. He was dead in less than a minute. This fellow may have shot himself anyway, but there was no need at all to push the issue. Remember, stay calm, do not do stupid things, de-escalate, and maintain discipline in all ways. The officer did not kill this man. The man chose to kill himself. It was a very poor tactical decision to make. I could not have ordered this officer to not do that, but if I had known, I could have at least said it was a bad idea.

Serving and Educating the Public

We have spent a great deal of time learning about enforcement activities. However, there are other parts to being an officer. Public service involves helping people as well. Your agency will set parameters on what you can and cannot do. Your agency may or may not want you unlocking car doors when the keys are locked in a car. There are many things that will be civil in nature, and you cannot intercede. You have no authority here other than to ensure no violation of criminal law occurs. Your agency might do funeral escorts. Some do, and some do not do this. You might do money escorts for businesses. You might do security checks and health and welfare checks.

A very important area of service is educating the public. We do this through speaking engagements, public service announcements, helping at events such as Toys for Tots, fingerprinting children, bicycle rodeos, and the list goes on. Early on, I have said you should be a well-rounded officer. This includes speaking with the public. Your agency should be heavily involved in community outreach and education. I hope you are involved as well. If you are not a great speaker, you can learn. When you see a child, never miss the opportunity to say hello and smile at him or her.

Takeaways

- ✓ Wear your bulletproof vest all the time.
- ✓ Wear your reflective traffic safety vest when exposed to traffic longer than a normal traffic stop.
- ✓ Never give up.
- ✓ Never surrender your weapon.
- ✓ Do not outdrive your lights and siren.
- ✓ Three strikes and you are not out in officer survival.
- ✓ Getting there safely is more important than getting there quickly.
- ✓ There is no such thing as routine in police work.
- ✓ Be a well-rounded officer.
- ✓ Expect the unexpected.
- ✓ Have courage in all things.
- ✓ Never compromise your integrity, policy, or law.
- ✓ Have a strong work ethic.
- ✓ You can hear and smell more with your window rolled down and AM/FM radio off or very low while on patrol at low speeds.
- ✓ You can find things on foot patrol that you cannot in a vehicle.
- ✓ Never lose radio contact.

- ✓ It is hard to focus on good police work when riding around and talking on the cell phone or sitting around texting.
- ✓ Do not snub officers from other agencies. Be friendly. We are all in this together. Every agency has good and not-so-good officers. The same holds true for other first responders.
- ✓ Do a vehicle inspection every time you start your tour of duty. Pull up in front of a plate glass window and check all your lights.
- ✓ Do not let people just walk up to you in the patrol car. When you see someone approaching, get out and speak with them in a safe stance and a good distance.
- ✓ Do not reach into a vehicle to remove the keys or turn the car off if the driver is behind the wheel.
- ✓ Always operate within what the law allows.
- ✓ Always be aware of special-needs populations you will encounter.
- ✓ Know and understand the law and procedural issues.
- ✓ Always work toward de-escalation.
- ✓ Never use excessive force or allow others to use it.
- ✓ Strive for excellence.
- ✓ Take charge and be a leader.

Lying lips are an abomination to the Lord, but those who act faithfully are his delight.
—Proverbs 12:22

Chapter Seven
Investigations

I am not bound to win, but I am bound to be true. I am not bound to succeed, but I am bound to live by the light that I have. I must stand with anybody that stands right, and stand with him while he is right, and part with him when he goes wrong.
—Abraham Lincoln

Sweat the little things.

On one occasion, I had a citizen stop by our office to complain about a theft from his home. He had been told by another agency there was nothing they could do. I was not sure why that was the answer they gave him. Our policy was we did not interfere with other agencies' investigations unless they asked us. However, in this case, they had done no investigation at all. It was a theft from his savings account for fifty dollars. My first question was who had access to his home. The list was small. The maid service was at the top of the list. I obtained a list of employees who had cleaned the gentleman's house from the maid company. I ran a check on each, and one had a criminal history for theft. She was my first stop.

I went to her home without notice. The funny thing was, when I went to her house to question her, she had a rather large giant of a husband who was not a nice guy. He was standing in the driveway with an ax, cutting wood when I drove up. I had arrested him several years earlier for drunk driving and being a habitual offender. He gave me a false name, and I figured out who he really was by speaking with his wife on the phone. Oh my! He was not happy to see me. He just stood there and stared at me the entire time.

At this point, I was starting from a strong hunch. She sat in my car, and as soon as I confronted her, she started to cry and admit to everything and started pulling all the stolen rings off her fingers. She went inside and got more rings she had stolen. She had already used all the savings withdrawal slips she had stolen from various people.

I contacted the maid company and asked them to contact the people's homes she serviced so they could check their records and belongings, or I could call them. At first, they said they did not want to do that. It was bad for them, they said. I explained that if they did not want to do that, I would go to the local newspapers and get it out that way. They agreed to call each client she had served.

Most of the victims did not even know they were victims. She stole rings, and she always took the last check or withdrawal slip from the savings or checkbooks. She would always write the check for fifty dollars each time. Most people did not even realize what she had done. Fortunately, one person did, and that led to dozens and dozens of charges in four jurisdictions. This lady was not a rocket scientist either. Most criminals are not that smart. Many people had lost family jewelry that had not just monetary value but also sentimental value. It was all recovered.

There are many morals to this story. One is to not ignore citizens when they make complaints. Do your preliminary work and develop leads and suspects. Do not announce yourself if you can help it. Had I called her first, she would have prepared and likely destroyed evidence and maybe even gotten a lawyer first. Who knows? Her husband may have been better prepared for me. Follow up on other potential crimes. Most criminals do not just commit one crime. I have heard many say that when I have arrested them for whatever, that has been the first time they have ever done such a thing. It is possible but not likely.

When it comes to criminal investigation, every agency will be different. In many agencies, minor offenses and misdemeanors are responded to and investigated by the patrol officer. Even if the case is turned over to investigators, it is likely the preliminary investigation will be handled by the patrol officer. When it comes to felonies, often, an investigator, detective, or agent will handle the case from start to finish or take it from the patrol officer. In some cases, the patrol officer will just get help from an investigator. In serious cases, a crime scene unit with forensically trained personnel may come out. Caution: forget everything you see on television. It rarely, if ever, works the way it is shown on television. There is such a thing, though, as the CSI effect. The phenomenon has affected many trials. Juries expect to see the same thing they see in the popular *CSI* shows when you present your cases.

Many students or potential officers want to jump right into investigations without working the road or patrol first. This might happen in some cases, but you are better off to do your time on the road or patrol and work your way into investigations full time. Depending on the size of the agency, investigations might be generalist or specialist in what they investigate. While some crimes are obviously more important than others, we must treat them all with the time, attention, and effort we would give the most serious of crimes. To the victim, it is important. Another important point is that criminals often commit multiple crimes, and your simple investigation might lead to bigger things. How would you want your loved one treated?

Why We Investigate

Why do we investigate crime? One reason is to determine if a crime has been committed. Another reason is to determine who did and did not commit the crime. We look for inculpatory and exculpatory evidence. We eliminate potential suspects from the list until, hopefully, we determine who the real offender is. Then we build the best case possible for an effective prosecution. Our goal is to provide enough evidence to move beyond probable cause to reach beyond a reasonable doubt.

What makes for a great investigator?

Many students want to be forensic investigators. This is a good goal. However, most of the time, it takes time, effort, and patience to earn such a position. Experience is important, as well as training and education. Investigators collect evidence. Evidence comes in many forms. A lot of evidence is physical in nature. Much evidence is verbal. Interviewing is an art. I have always found that almost everyone wants to rationalize his or her behavior. I would let them. It is critical to know the elements of the crime being investigated. Each element must be proven. Hard work, knowledge, common sense, excellent people skills, excellent written and verbal skills, and a very inquisitive mind are some of the many traits that make for a good investigator.

Do the ends justify the means?

No! Sometimes in policing, and criminal investigation specifically, one may be tempted to make the evidence fit even if it does not. *After all*, thinks the investigator, *this person must be guilty. He or she deserves justice, so I will do a good thing and exaggerate, modify, or manipulate to obtain a conviction.* Unfortunately, this happens, and justice is perverted. For those not in policing, please do not get the impression that everyone does it. They do not, but it does happen. Discover the facts and let them speak for themselves.

> *The end doesn't justify the means.*
> —Ovid (c. 43 BC–AD 18)

Great investigations take hard work.

There are report takers, and then there are investigators. We need to be both. Writing a report is only one part of a good investigation. Good report writing is critical. All too often, reports are filed away and never see the light of day again. Evidence goes stale, leads fade, and justice goes unserved.

Great investigators seek the truth.

It is indeed the truth that will set a person free or get them arrested! Case law allows police officers to be deceptive during investigations. Sometimes officers pretend to be something they are not. I argue that such deception should only be used when absolutely necessary. Lying can be a tool for a lazy investigator and sometimes a necessary tool when used only as a last resort and only in a thought-out, measured way. It should also be remembered that while case law permits some deception during an investigation, it does not to one's supervisor, the public in general, and never to the courts or a jury. Deception does not look good to a jury.

The Investigator's Role in Justice

Every step an investigator takes must stay within the pathway of legality. All evidence must be obtained legally. All evidence must be handled in a legal manner so as not to invalidate its usefulness because of contamination or lacking a proper chain of custody. It is not the investigator's job to mete out justice. This is the job of the judge or jury. It is the investigator's job to gather evidence, present the evidence, and let justice be done.

It is better to let one hundred guilty go free instead of convicting one innocent person. Of course, this does not have to be the case. Do your best to charge the correct person. When the wrong person is charged, a great injustice is done. First, the real criminal remains at large. Second and most important, an innocent person has been arrested. That person can be you or your loved one. Imagine going to prison for a crime you have not committed. This leads us to two critical terms: inculpatory and exculpatory evidence (Garner and Black, 2014). Both terms are of equal importance. Exculpatory evidence tends to indicate the innocence of the defendant or suspect. Inculpatory evidence tends to show a person's involvement in an act or evidence that can establish guilt. Part of the investigative process is to eliminate suspects as much as it is to find the guilty party.

Crime Scenes

Police routinely secure evidence from crime scenes. When such evidence is sought from places covered by the Fourth Amendment, certain legal issues arise. Persons are entitled to Fourth Amendment protection any time police search a place where the suspect has a reasonable expectation of privacy. If time allows, the most prudent approach is to obtain a search warrant. However, evidence may be lawfully obtained without a warrant if one of the exceptions to the warrant requirement applies. Among these exceptions are searches incident to a lawful arrest, exigent circumstances, and hot pursuit. There are several exceptions for exigent (or emergency) circumstances, such as entry to aid injured persons, check on gunshots, rescue persons from fires, etc. In protective sweeps of premises, the courts have not required police to have specific reasons to believe a particular person is necessarily on the premises (e.g., *U.S. v. Mata*, 2008).

The Fourth Amendment also allows entries based on consent. Further, if the entry is justified, anything seen in plain view may be seized if there is probable cause to seize it.

Upon reaching a crime scene, police may make a quick search for victims, offenders, or dangerous situations. They may control the crime scene until a warrant is obtained. However, there is no exception for extended searches at a crime scene, even the scene of a murder, without obtaining a warrant shortly thereafter. Police must control the crime scene and prevent contamination of evidence, or the investigation will be jeopardized. Again, there is no murder scene exception to the warrant requirement.

There are numerous types of evidence that, if the proper foundation has been laid, can be admissible. Examples are foot or shoe prints, palm and lip prints, hair, bite marks, tire tracks, DNA evidence, and many more types of trace evidence.

The Investigator and Physical Evidence

The investigator gathers, documents, and evaluates evidence. He or she needs strong professional training and experience and a strong degree of self-discipline. You must only use legally approved and ethical methods. Strong people skills are key. You include and seek all evidence of innocence, as well as guilt. You will use a systematic method of inquiry. Use both inductive and deductive reasoning. You want to be compassionate, not calloused and cynical. It is good to have a wide range of contacts across many occupations. It is critical to remain objective always. Leave nothing to chance during an investigation. Be sure to secure the crime scene(s). Properly document, collect, store, and transfer all evidence.

The Investigative Process

The objectives of an investigation are to

- ✓ establish if a crime has been committed;
- ✓ collect, document, and preserve evidence;
- ✓ identify and apprehend the suspect(s);
- ✓ recover stolen property;
- ✓ assist in the prosecution of the person(s) charged with the crime(s).

The Preliminary Investigation

The actions taken at the scene of a crime immediately following its detection and report to the police are

- ✓ receipt of information and initial response,
- ✓ emergency care,
- ✓ crime scene control,
- ✓ "be on the lookout" (BOLO) alerts,
- ✓ crime scene determination,
- ✓ evidence,
- ✓ the report.

Crime Scene

- ✓ Location(s) where the offense(s) was committed
  - ○ may include surrounding areas where evidence may be located or
  - ○ may involve a dump site
    - property,
    - incriminating evidence,
    - body.
- ✓ Always start big. It is much easier to make it smaller than to expand it at a later time.
- ✓ There may be more than one crime scene.
- ✓ Consider macroscopic versus microscopic scenes.

Categories of Evidence

- ✓ Corpus delicti evidence
  - ○ Evidence that helps prove the elements of the crime(s)
  - ○ The body of the crime (not literally necessarily, though)
- ✓ Associative evidence
  - ○ Evidence that connects the suspect to the scene and/or victim or connects the scene/victim to the suspect
  - ○ Bidirectional
- ✓ Trace evidence

- ○ Small or microscopic evidence or evidence in limited amounts
- ○ The Locard principle states that any time two objects come into contact, there is a transfer of material (Osterburg and Ward, 2014).

Crime Scene Control

Crime scene control is the actions that the first arriving officer at the crime scene takes to make sure that the integrity of the scene is maintained. This is critical to the case. Control also includes preventing people at the scene from becoming combatants and separating witnesses. Caution should be used to safeguard people, property, and evidence. Be mindful of contaminants, such as blood-borne pathogens. Do not destroy evidence or allow evidence to be destroyed. Make the crime scene bigger than expected and shrink as necessary. There can be more than one crime scene. You might find a body at a dump site, not the original crime scene, for instance. Do not overlook fruitful areas for exploration. Do more than a cursory examination (Osterburg and Ward, 2014).

Documentation

Constant activity starts with

- ✓ rough shorthand field notes,
- ✓ sketches,
- ✓ diagrams to scale.

Ways to document a crime scene visually include the following:

- ✓ Videotaping
  - ○ Consider the use of drones for aerial views.
- ✓ Photographing
- ✓ Sketching
- ✓ 3-D laser scanning
- ✓ Computerized diagramming
- ✓ Using an infrared wave signal for total stations to read slopes and measure distances, capturing one point at a time. If you are documenting small crime scenes and

routine crashes, this is a practical tool for vehicle crashes and crime scenes.
✓ Computerized diagramming

Major Considerations of the Crime Scene Search

✓ Boundary determination
✓ Choice of search patterns
✓ Instruction of personnel
✓ Coordination
✓ Documentation

Primary Investigative Questions

Primary questions meet most investigative information needs. There are six recognized categories of primary questions:

✓ Who
✓ What
✓ When
✓ Where
✓ Why
✓ How

Crime Scene Evidence

Class and Individual Characteristic Evidence

✓ Class is a group of objects or persons with characteristic physical evidence common to it.
  ○ Examples include soil and hair.
✓ Individual characteristics can be identified as having originated with a particular person or source.
  ○ It establishes individuality.
  ○ Examples include fingerprints and footprints.

Locating and Handling Soil Evidence

Soil evidence is important when the suspect drives/walks on unpaved areas. It is picked up by

- ✓ tire treads,
- ✓ shoe bottoms,
- ✓ pant cuffs.

It may also be located in

- ✓ subject's vehicle,
- ✓ articles in a suspect's trunk.

Collecting Glass and Paint Evidence

- ✓ Paint may be collected from the suspect's tools or clothing.
- ✓ Paint can often be collected in dried chips.
- ✓ Glass is a common form of evidence at burglary scenes.
- ✓ Before any glass fragments are removed from a glass window, it should be photographed (Osterburg and Ward, 2014).

Collecting and Storing Fibers, Cloth Fragments, and Impressions

Fibers are of greater value as evidence than rootless hairs. Fibers may be located on the body of the victim and/or the suspect. Cloth fragments may be found at the scene of a violent crime. Cloth fragments may also be found at the suspect's point of approach or exit.

Categories of Latent Fingerprints

- ✓ Plastic prints
  - ○ Created when the fingers touch against some material such as putty
- ✓ Contaminated/visible prints
  - ○ Formed when the fingers are contaminated with such things as ink or blood and touch a clean surface
- ✓ Latent/invisible prints
  - ○ Left on a surface from the small amounts of body oil and perspiration that are normally found on friction ridges

DR. JEFFREY C. FOX

Forensic Dentistry

Forensic dentistry is a specialty that relates dental evidence to investigation. Analyses of bit marks have played a major role in many cases. Teeth marks may be left in food, pencils, or other items left at crime scenes. Bite marks can help eliminate or identify suspects (Osterburg and Ward, 2014).

Identifying and Analyzing Bloodstains

If blood at the crime scene is fresh and relatively uncontaminated, identification is not difficult. If the conditions at a crime scene are otherwise, it is more difficult to identify. One preliminary field test involves the use of Hemident. Blood analysis is important because of the value of DNA typing (Osterburg and Ward, 2014).

Sources of DNA Evidence

These are common sources of blood and DNA evidence that investigators need to be aware of when conducting crime scene searches.

Determination from firearms evidence lab examinations of firearms evidence may answer the following questions:

- ✓ Was this bullet fired from this weapon?
- ✓ What else can be learned from the bullet?
- ✓ What determinations can be made from cartridge cases?
- ✓ What miscellaneous determinations can be made by examination of firearms evidence? (Osterburg and Ward, 2014)

You may use a gunshot residue (GSR) test or paraffin. Caution: if a subject comes back positive for GSR, that does not mean he or she fired a weapon. It does mean he or she was near or close to a weapon when it was fired.

Ways to Locate People

- ✓ Law enforcement records

- ✓ National Crime Information Center (NCIC)
- ✓ DMV – driver's license, vehicle registration
- ✓ Integrated Automated Fingerprint Identification System (IAFIS)
- ✓ Specialized sources – EPIC, LEO, etc.
- ✓ Violent Criminal Apprehension Program (VICAP)
- ✓ Government (public record)
- ✓ Land deeds and titles
- ✓ Birth/death certificates
- ✓ Securities and Exchange Commission (SEC)
- ✓ FAA
- ✓ Business records
- ✓ Insurance
- ✓ Utilities
- ✓ Credit
- ✓ Cell phone data
- ✓ Social media sites
- ✓ Automobile GPS tracking – OnStar, etc.
- ✓ Unions
- ✓ Telemarketing databases
- ✓ Fraternal organizations
- ✓ Combined DNA Index System (CODIS)
- ✓ With the marrying of DNA and computer technology, a counterpart of Automated Fingerprint Identification System (AFIS) can be created.
- ✓ States enacted laws requiring the collection of DNA samples from certain categories of offenders.
- ✓ NCIC databases

Thus law enforcement will have more information available in a timely fashion (Osterburg and Ward, 2014).

Criminal Profiling

The process of inferring distinctive personality characteristics of individuals responsible for committing crimes has commonly been referred to as criminal profiling. Despite its successes, profiling as a field is not without criticisms. Included in these criticisms are

- ✓ untrained or inadequately trained profilers,
- ✓ promising too much and delivering too little,

✓ relying on inadequate or dated databases,
✓ overstating the meaning of physical evidence.

Role of Profiling: Investigative Phase

✓ Reduces the pool of suspects
✓ Links similar crimes through unique indicators and behavior patterns
✓ Assess potential for escalation in crime seriousness and frequency
✓ Provides investigators with potential leads and approaches
✓ Assists in evaluation of evidence
✓ Assists in developing interview strategies
✓ Helps gain insight on offender motivation
✓ Helps suggest a crime scene linkage by modus operandi and signature behavior (Osterburg & Ward, 2014)

Do not conduct racial profiling.

Common Internal Sources of Case Information

✓ Incident and supplemental reports
✓ Physical evidence seized
✓ Jail booking reports
✓ Field interview/information reports
✓ Inventories of impounded vehicles
✓ Traffic citations
✓ Crime lab reports
✓ Vehicle canvass
✓ Neighborhood canvass
  ○ A fundamental aspect of most investigations is the neighborhood canvass.
  ○ The investigator contacts residents, merchants, and others in the immediate vicinity of the crime.
  ○ It includes information of any video footage taken and/or stored.
    ▪ Fixed recorded video footage
    ▪ Cell phone footage/imagery
  ○ A systematic neighborhood canvass soon after the crime may be useful in 20 percent of the cases.

- o The extent of the canvass depends on
  - the type of offense,
  - the time of day,
  - the characteristics of the crime scene (Osterburg and Ward, 2014).

Information Needed Before Conducting a Neighborhood Canvass

- ✓ Information relating to the offense
- ✓ A description of the suspect
- ✓ Any injury sustained by the suspect
- ✓ The type of property taken

Possession of these facts is essential for
- ✓ officer's safety and
- ✓ the intelligent questioning of possible witnesses (Osterburg and Ward, 2014).

Informants

Information provided by informants often plays a vital role in a successful investigation. Such information may provide evidence of an unreported crime. Such information may provide the basis for a search warrant. Such information may constitute the basis for an arrest (Osterburg and Ward, 2014). Corroborating evidence is very useful in such situations.

Major Categories of Information

- ✓ Mercenary - information provided for financial reward
- ✓ Rival - information provided to establish monopolistic control over the activity in question by eliminating a competitor
- ✓ Plea bargaining - information provided to obtain reduced charges or a lenient sentence
- ✓ Self-aggrandizing - information provided to obtain an enhanced sense of self-importance
- ✓ Fearful - information provided because they are worried they will be endangered by the criminal activities of an associate

✓ False - information provided that is misleading to direct the investigation away from herself or himself, friends, and relatives
✓ Anonymous - information provided by an unknown person
✓ Legitimate - information provided by a law-abiding citizen out of a sense of civic duty (Osterburg and Ward, 2014)

Effective Uses of Surveillance

✓ Establishing the existence of a violation
✓ Obtaining probable cause for a search warrant
✓ Apprehending violators in the commission of illegal acts
✓ Identifying the violators' associates
✓ Verifying informant reliability
✓ Providing protection for undercover investigators or informants
✓ Locating persons, places, or things
✓ Preventing crime
✓ Gathering intelligence on individuals and premises prior to the execution of a search warrant
✓ Gathering intelligence on illegal groups' activities (Osterburg and Ward, 2014)

Area under Video Monitoring

The use of video surveillance camera in public places is becoming common. Such systems may deter crime. Video systems may also store evidence of a crime.

Procedures for Photo Lineups

Include only one suspect in each identification procedure. Select "fillers" (nonsuspects) who generally match the witness's description of the perpetrator. If multiple photos of the suspect are available, use the one made closest to the time when the crime has been committed. Lineups should include a minimum of five fillers. If there are multiple witnesses, consider placing the suspect in different positions each time a lineup is shown to a witness. If a new suspect is developed, avoid using fillers who have been used in a previous lineup for the same witness. Make sure that no writing or information about the suspect's previous criminal history can be seen by the witness. Before the witness views the lineup, check again to make sure the suspect does not unduly stand out. Record the presentation order or the lineup and handle the original photographs as evidence. Write a supplemental report that chronologically describes what has happened (Osterburg and Ward, 2014). Never coach or suggest to a witness.

Objectives of the Interrogation Process

Successful interrogation accomplishes four objectives:

1. Obtaining facts
2. Eliminating the innocent
3. Identifying the guilty
4. Obtaining a confession

Similarities between Interviews and Interrogations

Interviews

- ✓ Planning important
- ✓ Controlling surroundings important
- ✓ Privacy or semiprivacy desirable
- ✓ Establishing rapport important
- ✓ Careful listening
- ✓ Proper documentation

Interrogations

- ✓ Planning critical
- ✓ Controlling surroundings critical
- ✓ Absolute privacy essential
- ✓ Establishing rapport important
- ✓ Careful listening
- ✓ Proper documentation

Difference between Interviews and Interrogations

Interviews

- ✓ Aims to obtain information
- ✓ Minimal or no preinterview legal requirements; no rights warning
- ✓ Cooperative relationship between interviewer and subject likely
- ✓ No guilt or guilt uncertain
- ✓ Moderate planning or preparation
- ✓ Private or semiprivate environment desirable

Interrogations

- ✓ Aims to test information already obtained
- ✓ Extensive preinterrogation legal requirements; rights warning required
- ✓ Adversarial or hostile relationship between interviewer and subject likely
- ✓ Guilt suggested or likely
- ✓ Extensive planning preparation
- ✓ Absolute privacy essential

Preparation for Interviews or Interrogations

Know as much as possible about the witness. Know what crime or crimes have been committed. Learn as much as possible about the victim. Evaluate what is known about the suspect.

Steps in Interview Process

An interview consists of beginning, middle, and end.
- ✓ Beginning should be a time
  - ○ when the investigator can identify himself or herself,
  - ○ when the investigator can discuss the purpose for the interview,
  - ○ when the investigator establishes rapport.
- ✓ Middle

  o   The investigator gathers information.
✓   End
  o   Thank the witness for his/her cooperation.

Interview to Confession: The Art of the Gentle Interrogation

Behavior: Evaluate only the behavior that is in response to and has resulted from the asking of the question. Do not consider movement that occurs between questions and can be considered movement that is the norm for that person during the questioning (Bowden and Lane, 2012).

Eye Contact: Look for breaks in eye contact when the subject is answering the question. A truthful subject will maintain good eye contact. When the deceptive person answers the question, they may break eye contact, however briefly. They may resume eye contact after the question, sometimes as if they are looking to see whether you are accepting the answer (Bowden and Lane, 2012).

Answer: Evaluate the actual answer itself. Look for the following characteristics: Does the person use harsh or soft terms? Does the answer spread or focus suspicion? Does the person include or omit themselves from suspicion? Does the person give you a direct answer, or is the answer evasive or irrelevant to the question? (Bowden and Lane, 2012)

Timing: Check the answer for timing and consistency. Is the answer on time, or are they thinking before answering? The bottom line is to evaluate the timing of the answer with the type of question. As Paul Ekman states, "Is the person thinking when they shouldn't have to?" (Bowden and Lane, 2012)

Voice Characteristics: Does the person's voice tone go up, go down, or remain in the middle? Is the speech clear or mumbled? Does the voice volume increase in anger when accused or remain neutral? (Bowden and Lane, 2012)

One word of caution—this model is just a tool to observe and quickly analyze behavior. It is not full proof, and there is a significant amount of learning required to become proficient at reading and interpreting behavior (Bowden and Lane, 2012).

The Impact of *Miranda v. Arizona* and Other Supreme Court Cases

The Supreme Court in the 1960s established many legal requirements regarding interrogation of suspects. Issues involved included

✓ Fifth Amendment protection against self-incrimination,
✓ Sixth Amendment guarantee of right to counsel.

Miranda v. Arizona was the critical decision underscoring rights for suspects being interrogated.

Requirements Imposed on Police by *Miranda v. Arizona*

The police are required to advise in-custody suspects of the following:

✓ The right to remain silent
✓ The right to be told that anything said can and will be used against him or her in court
✓ The right to consult with an attorney prior to answering any questions and the right to have an attorney present during the interrogation
✓ If the suspect cannot afford to pay for an attorney, the court will appoint one.
   ○ Do not do what you have seen on television—do not repeat *Miranda* rights from memory. Always read it from a card or a *Miranda* rights acknowledgment sheet.

Eyewitness Identification

Research indicates this form of identification is often unreliable. Human perception and memory are selective and do not make exact copies.

Managing Cases and Case Reconstruction

Follow-Up Investigation

Subsequent investigation includes the following:

- ✓ Contacting witnesses who left the scene
- ✓ Checking out suspect(s) alibi
- ✓ Gathering additional evidence from other locations
- ✓ Talking with informants
- ✓ Attempting to locate additional witnesses
- ✓ Evaluating evidence collected and laboratory results of tests
- ✓ Obtaining search and/or arrest warrants
- ✓ Recovering stolen property
- ✓ Conferring with the prosecutor (Osterburg and Ward, 2014)

Requirements for a Valid Search Warrant

An application for a warrant must be supported by a sworn, detailed statement made by an officer appearing before a judge or magistrate. The Supreme Court has said that probable cause exists when the facts and circumstances within the officer's knowledge provide a reasonably trustworthy basis for a person of reasonable caution to believe that a criminal offense has been committed or is about to take place (Osterburg and Ward, 2014).

Details in a Warrant Application

The Fourth Amendment requires not only that warrants be supported by probable cause offered by an officer but also that the warrant "particularly" describe the person or place to be searched or seized. Warrants must provide enough detail so that an officer with the warrant can ascertain with reasonable effort the persons and places identified in the warrant. For most residences, a street address usually satisfies the particularity requirement, unless the warrant designates an apartment complex, hotel, or other multiple-unit building, in which case the warrant must describe the specific subunit to be searched. Warrants must describe individuals with sufficient particularity so that a person of average intelligence can distinguish them from others in the general population (Osterburg and Ward, 2014).

Ensure all search warrants—and for that matter all warrants, including arrest warrants—are valid on their face. In other words, they are complete, they are correct, and they are served timely. When searching, you must be reasonable in the scope of your search. If you are searching for a seventy-two-inch color flat-screen television, you cannot look in kitchen drawers. If you are in a home and you move anything, then you are searching. When applying for your search warrant, be mindful of this: almost all crimes can now involve cyber technology. When I started out in policing, there was no cyberspace or computers. As the years went by and I was handling evidence as a supervisor, I began to see large computers being placed into evidence storage. Now you will see thumb drives, PDAs, cell phones, and the list goes on. You must be reasonable but remember to include evidence that might be stored on any such electronic device. This will allow the search for any such device based on your search warrant scope. Again, it must be logical and reasonable.

Investigative Solvability Factors

Can the identity of the suspect/s be established through?

- ✓ Usable fingerprints being discovered
- ✓ Significant physical evidence being located
- ✓ Victim/witness/informant information
- ✓ A license number or a significant description of the vehicle known to have been used in the offense

Is there serious physical harm or threat of serious physical harm to the victim?

Did the suspect(s) utilize a deadly weapon or dangerous device? Is there a significant method of operation (MO) that will aid in the solution of the offense(s)? Is it a sex offense in which the victim and suspect(s) had physical contact? Can a suspect be named? Can a suspect be identified? Can a suspect be described? Is there another reason that leads you to believe that the offense should be assigned for a follow-up investigation? It is often useful to return to the scene of the crime during the same period the crime has occurred.

Legal Issues and Evidence

Evaluating the Case

Investigators must consider risk factors in deciding when to arrest, whether the suspect will flee if allowed to remain free, the potential danger to others if the suspect is free, and the hardships imposed on the suspect by early incarceration. Once an arrest is made, cooperation with the suspect is likely to go down. The speedy trial rule kicks in.

Takeaways

- ✓ Do not dismiss citizens' complaints out of hand.
- ✓ Do your preliminary work and develop leads and suspects.
- ✓ Do not forewarn suspects that you are coming when possible.
- ✓ Gather as many facts as you can before interviewing or interrogating suspects.
- ✓ Never show the suspect your hand or let them know what you know or do not know.
- ✓ Work to always corroborate all your facts and evidence.
- ✓ Follow up on other potential crimes within your jurisdiction and in other jurisdictions.
- ✓ Criminals do not respect jurisdictional boundaries.
- ✓ Most criminals commit more than one crime.
- ✓ Exculpatory evidence is as important as inculpatory evidence.
- ✓ Your goal is to provide facts and evidence that shows a crime has or has not been committed and to prove all the elements of the crime and who has done it.
- ✓ It is all about the who, what, when, where, why, and how.
- ✓ The ends do not justify the means.
- ✓ Great investigations take hard work.
- ✓ Time is not on your side.
- ✓ Great investigators seek the truth.
- ✓ Always maintain crime scene integrity.

✓ There can be more than one crime scene.
✓ Be mindful of the frailty of eyewitness identification.
✓ Written statements are better than verbal.
✓ Document interviews with video.
✓ Maintain the chain of evidence.
✓ Separate suspects as soon as possible. Never let them see each other when interviewing them to avoid not only hearing each other's statements but seeing their body language as well.
✓ Trace evidence is everywhere. Remember the Locard principle of two objects exchanging material.
✓ Treat suspects with respect.
✓ Empathy works well with suspects even when you cannot empathize with them at all, such as child molesters, etc.
✓ Never coerce a confession.

When justice is done, it is joy to the righteous but terror to the evildoers.
—Proverbs 21:15

Chapter Eight
Dealing with Juveniles

Silence in the face of evil is itself evil: God will not hold us guiltless.
Not to speak is to speak. Not to act is to act.
—Dietrich Bonhoeffer

We were all children once.

Throughout my career, I have often dealt with juveniles. I have never avoided dealing with them out of fear of having to deal with juvenile court. Juveniles enjoy almost the exact same rights adults do, but they are very different indeed. Several things make them uniquely different. Obviously, it is their age that creates the legal difference. When you come across a juvenile in need of services or supervision, you will very likely have a legal responsibility to care for him or her. The Latin term is *in loco parentis*. Each state will handle this differently, but be aware of this concept and the possible legal duty. The same laws that apply to adults apply to juveniles except juveniles will have extra laws that apply to them. These are known as status offenses. Status offenses are things such as underage drinking, smoking, curfews, etc. Do not take your duties and responsibilities lightly. We were all young once, and we did stupid things. Often, you might be tempted to exercise much discretion with warnings. This is up to you, your agency, and of course what the laws allow. However, you cannot give away your duty to care for the child. Yes, if under eighteen, they are a child.

One late night—or early morning, if you will—I was traveling along a residential road on patrol. I came along a little tyke who was probably between six and nine years old. I stopped and asked him what he was doing. He said he had been to the local store. I put him in my car and drove him home. I knocked on the door and woke his parents. I said, "Do you know where little Johnny is?" They said he was asleep upstairs. I said, "No, he is in my police car." I explained what had happened and turned him over to his parents. Sometimes it could be as simple as that. However, it could also be painfully hard. Dealing with teenagers who ran away and parents who did not want them back could be gruelingly hard. The parents had an obligation but were at their wits' end. What to do? In cases like this, an intake officer may be needed. Social services or juvenile authorities would likely be needed.

One very cold winter day, I was patrolling the interstate and came across three older teenagers—two girls and one boy. I think they were sixteen and seventeen years old. They did not come back as wanted, but their story did not make sense. They were from several states away and were hitchhiking to Florida. I took them to the local police station and contacted their parents by phone. One mother was distraught. She had tried to have her daughter listed as a runaway, but they would not do it for the first twenty-four hours. The other two parents said to let them go. They were tired of fighting them, so they wanted to let them go. I told the one mother to go to the police station in her state and tell them to enter her as a runaway and that we would hold her until she came and got her daughter. They finally entered her, and we held her. Meanwhile, it was time to use psychology. I kept the one girl in the police station and had the other two wait outside. I told her what her parents had said. The one girl decided she did not want to go further without her friend. I explained that she wanted to be on her own and that her parents said okay. By the time we were done talking, all three of them wanted to go home. I spoke to the one grieving mother again, and she said she would be happy to take all three of them back home. Whatever you do, never ignore issues involving juveniles. They need us badly. Also, I hope there are no police agencies that make citizens wait twenty-four hours to report their child as a runaway or missing. The first twenty-four hours are the most important in finding a child.

Juvenile Justice Overview

Major court decisions have laid down the constitutional requirements for juvenile court proceedings.

The juvenile justice process consists of a series of steps:

- ✓ Police investigation
- ✓ Intake procedure in the juvenile court
- ✓ Pretrial procedures used for juvenile offenders
- ✓ Adjudication, disposition, and postdispositional procedures
- ✓ Possible diversion from court

There are conflicting values in contemporary juvenile justice. Some experts want to get tough with young criminals, while others want to focus on rehabilitation. Crime control advocates want to reduce the court's jurisdiction over juveniles charged with serious crimes and liberalize the prosecutor's ability to try them in adult courts. Child advocates suggest that the court scale back its judicial role and transfer its functions to community groups and social service agencies.

Note the difference between prevention and intervention efforts to reduce juvenile delinquency:

- ✓ Prevention efforts target children and teens to prevent the onset of delinquency.
- ✓ Intervention efforts target children and teens considered at higher risk for delinquency and are designed to ward off involvement in more serious delinquent behavior.

Police Work with Juveniles

Officers must have a thorough knowledge of the law, especially the constitutional protections available to juveniles.

Major court cases have influenced juvenile police practices:

- ✓ Through the *Terry v. Ohio* decision, along with others, the U.S. Supreme Court has established that police may stop a suspect and pat down for weapons without a warrant under certain circumstances.
- ✓ Through the *Miranda v. Arizona* decision, the U.S. Supreme Court has established clearly defined procedures for custodial interrogation.
- ✓ Most courts have held that the Fourth Amendment ban against unreasonable search and seizure applies to juveniles and that illegally seized evidence is inadmissible in a juvenile trial.
- ✓ Most courts have concluded that parents or attorneys need not be present for children to effectively waive their right to remain silent.

✓   Juvenile judges vary in dealing with juveniles in such areas as interviewing juveniles without their parents present. Seek legal advice from your prosecutor.

Policing allows for use of discretion, a low-visibility decision made in the administration of adult and juvenile justice. Discretionary decisions are often made without guidelines from the police administrator. Numerous factors influence the decisions police make about juvenile offenders, including

✓   the seriousness of the offense,
✓   the harm inflicted on the victim,
✓   the likelihood that the juvenile will break the law again.

Discretion is essential in providing individualized justice. Problems with discretion include

✓   discrimination,
✓   unfairness,
✓   bias toward particular groups of juveniles.

The major policing strategies to prevent delinquency include the following:

✓   Aggressive law enforcement
✓   Police in schools
✓   Community-based and community policing
✓   Problem-oriented policing

There are pros and cons of police's use of different delinquency prevention strategies. Innovation in policing strategies can address the ever- changing nature of juvenile delinquency, and tailoring policing activities to local conditions and engaging the community and other stakeholders show promise in reducing delinquency. Saturation patrols that include targeting gang areas and arresting members for any law violations have not proven to be effective against gangs. Maintaining the level of intensity and cooperation of the many agencies involved in problem-oriented policing strategies, which are essential to their success, is not easy and requires sustainable funding.

Juvenile Court Process

The main players in the juvenile court are the prosecutors, judges, juvenile intake officers, and defense attorneys.

- ✓ The juvenile prosecutor is the attorney responsible for bringing the state's case against the accused juvenile.
- ✓ The juvenile judge must ensure that the children and their families who come before the court receive the proper help.
- ✓ Defense attorneys representing children in the juvenile court play an active and important part in virtually all stages of the proceedings.

Key issues of the preadjudication stage of juvenile justice include

- ✓ detention,
- ✓ intake,
- ✓ diversion,
- ✓ pretrial release,
- ✓ plea bargaining,
- ✓ waiver.

Many decisions about what happens to a child may occur prior to adjudication. Because of personnel limitations, the juvenile justice system is not able to try every child accused of a crime or status offense. Therefore diversion programs seem to hold greater hope for the control of delinquency. Thus such subsystems as statutory intake proceedings, plea bargaining, and other informal adjustments are essential ingredients in the administration of the juvenile justice system.

The Juvenile Adjudication Process

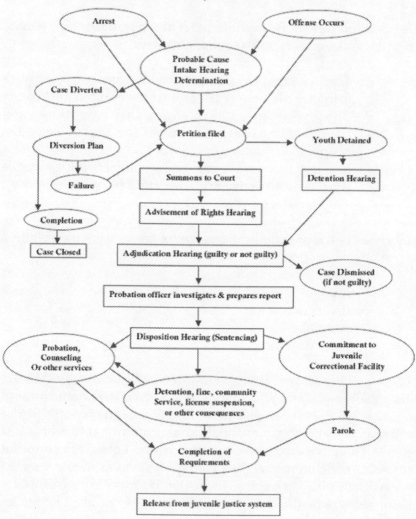

Most jurisdictions have a bifurcated juvenile court system that separates the adjudication hearing from the dispositional hearing. Juveniles alleged to be delinquent have virtually all the constitutional rights given a criminal defendant at trial—except possibly the right to a trial by jury. Juvenile proceedings are generally closed to the public.

Court Cases regarding Juvenile Due Process

- ✓ *In re Gault* is the key legal case that has set out the basic requirements of due process that must be satisfied in juvenile court proceedings.
- ✓ *Roper v. Simmons* is where the U.S. Supreme Court has ruled that the death penalty for juveniles is prohibited because it constitutes cruel and unusual punishment.
- ✓ *Graham v. Florida* is where the U.S. Supreme Court has put an end to the practice of life sentences without the possibility of parole for juveniles convicted of nonhomicide crimes.

Many state statutes require that juvenile hearings be closed and that the privacy of juvenile records be maintained. This is done to protect the child from public scrutiny and to provide a greater opportunity for rehabilitation. This approach may be inconsistent with the public's interest in taking a closer look at the juvenile justice system.

In addition to dealing with juveniles who commit crimes, you will encounter children in need or supervision or services. You will work closely with juvenile authorities and/or social workers in placing children in foster facilities on emergency custody matters. Families can often help here. Most states will have statutes that allow and require officers and others to take a child into their care if the child is in danger. The child does not have to have committed a crime but may be a victim of severe neglect or immediate abuse or have no parental authority available. When this happens, you can make a big difference in a child's life.

Takeaways

- ✓ You are responsible for people under eighteen, that is, children.
- ✓ Juveniles have the same rights as adults.
- ✓ Do not avoid dealing with juveniles.

- ✓ Juveniles are subject to status offenses.
- ✓ Be a positive influence with children.

Let no man despise thy youth; but be thou an example of the believers, in word, in conversation, in charity, in spirit, in faith, in purity.
                                        —1 Timothy 4:12

Chapter Nine
Understanding the Intelligence Process

The only thing worse than no intelligence is corrupt intelligence.
—Paul Sperry

Never underestimate the role intelligence plays in policing.

While on patrol, I stopped a vehicle and obtained consent to search. There was a male, a female, and a baby. The male was holding the baby. I immediately saw pieces of crack cocaine on the driver's side floorboard. All of a sudden, the male literally threw the small baby at me. I caught the baby. He took off. I had to make a split-second decision. What to do? First, I would have had to hand the baby to the woman. What would she then do? I could not leave the car because, again, what would she do? I let him go. I recovered all the evidence. I got all the information from her. I knew who the runner was.

I went to track him down so I could arrest him for possession of cocaine and other charges. A few days later, a drug investigator from a rather large metropolitan agency to the north of my area called me and asked me to let him go because he was a good informant for them. He had contacted them and asked them to speak on his behalf! Now let me say informants are a necessary evil. However, I have never bought into the idea of letting informants break laws to catch other criminals. I told the investigator I would not let him go. He did not wish to help me track him down. We ended our phone call not agreeing, to say the least. I relied on information I gathered from some of this fellow's family. I knew if he saw me coming, he would run every time. I got the call from a family member that he was there. I had two detectives from a local agency, whom I worked closely with, intercept him in their vehicles. Their cars were undercover cars. We cornered him with the three cars, and he gave up without a fight.

Information versus Intelligence

The terms "information" and "intelligence" are frequently used interchangeably. Consequently, the use of the term "intelligence" is often a misnomer. For example, in 2003, researchers have conducted a survey of officers from three different police departments. The study has shown that 83 percent of the officers surveyed have indicated they complete and submit intelligence reports at least once a month. In reality, those reports are not intelligence reports but rather informational reports (Brown, 2007, p. 339). There is an important difference between information and intelligence.

Information is the raw data that is collected. Information is like a jigsaw puzzle, each puzzle piece representing a piece of information. It is not until all the pieces of the puzzle are completely put together that the whole picture is revealed. Therefore information must undergo a process to derive meaning. Intelligence is the result of processed information that answers questions and allows decision makers to make informed decision (Brown, 2007, p. 338).

Intelligence Defined

Defining intelligence is difficult. The definition of intelligence is largely dependent upon the individual or organization defining it and is usually tailored to the individual's or organization's function.

From a law enforcement perspective, Ratcliffe (2003) defines *intelligence* as "a value-added product, derived from the collection and processing of all relevant information relating to client needs, which is immediately or potentially significant to client decision-making" (p. 3). In simplest terms, intelligence is the product resulting from the collection, processing, integration, analysis, evaluation, and interpretation of available information.

In broader terms, intelligence is three things: structure, process, and product. Federal, state, and local agencies have intelligence functions (agencies, sections, or units) that serve as the structure. The intelligence analysts working in the intelligence functions utilize the intelligence cycle as the process to create intelligence products. Intelligence products are the result of processed information that facilitates decision making as to what actions and resources are required in effectively addressing problems in the environment (Ratcliffe, 2003).

Levels of Intelligence

Another important aspect is to understand the three different levels of intelligence that decision makers use depending on specific situations. These levels of intelligence are strategic, operational, and tactical (Lowenthal, 2015).

Strategic intelligence is intelligence that is required for the formulation of strategy, policy, plans, and operations that are designed to further the advancement toward goals. This level of intelligence considers the "big picture," assists in assessing future problems, and supports planning and decision making (Lowenthal, 2015).

Operational intelligence is intelligence that is required for supporting operations in the field. It focuses on the monitoring of activities to identify and detect strengths, weaknesses, opportunities, and threats. This level of intelligence is used in military, business, and law enforcement operations (Lowenthal, 2015).

Tactical intelligence is intelligence that is required immediately for supporting current operations or addressing existing problems. Tactical intelligence depends on short-term, timely collection and analysis of critical changes in the environment and is usually required every twelve to twenty-four hours. This level of intelligence is used by military and law enforcement officers who are in the field and actively engaged in operations (Lowenthal, 2015).

The Intelligence Cycle

The intelligence cycle is a concept that describes the fundamental cycle of intelligence processing in a civilian or military intelligence agency or in law enforcement as a closed path consisting of repeating stages. The stages of the intelligence cycle include planning and direction, collection, processing, analysis, and dissemination of intelligence. The cycle is not complete until decision makers provide feedback and issue revised requirements (Lowenthal, 2015).

Planning and direction. In the planning and direction phase, decision makers determine and then issue intelligence requirements.

In law enforcement agencies, the chief of police or his or her staff will determine intelligence requirements for the intelligence staff to satisfy (Lowenthal, 2015).

Collection. To satisfy decision maker requirements, the intelligence staff will develop an intelligence collection plan. The intelligence collection plan is used to keep track of available sources and methods of collecting required information. Depending on the organization and its access, sources may include HUMINT (human intelligence), IMINT (imagery intelligence), ELINT (electronic intelligence), SIGINT (signals intelligence), OSINT (publicly available or open-source intelligence), etc. (Lowenthal, 2015).

Processing and collation. Once the collection plan is executed and information is obtained, it is processed for exploitation. This entails the translation of raw intelligence data, evaluation for relevance and reliability, and collation of the raw intelligence in preparation for exploitation or use of it (Lowenthal, 2015).

Analysis. The analysis phase establishes the significance and implications of processed intelligence. Analysis integrates it by combining disparate pieces of information to identify collateral information and patterns and then interprets the significance of any newly developed information (Lowenthal, 2015).

Dissemination. Finished intelligence products take many forms such as intelligence estimates, briefs, indications and warning (I&W) bulletins, and other publications. The type of product is dependent upon the needs of the decision maker and reporting requirements. Typically, an intelligence organization or community establishes the level of urgency of various types of intelligence (Lowenthal, 2015).

Reevaluation. The intelligence cycle is a closed loop, meaning that feedback is a crucial part of the intelligence cycle. In the reevaluation phase, feedback is received from the decision makers, and revised requirements may be issued (Lowenthal, 2015).

Collection Disciplines

During the collection phase, the intelligence function may employ the following collection disciplines:

Human Intelligence (HUMINT). HUMINT involves the collection of information from people on the ground. In policing, this might involve witnesses or informants of all types. The oldest of the collection disciplines, HUMINT is derived from human sources. Until the mid- to late twentieth century, HUMINT has been the primary source of intelligence collection for all governments. However, with the advent of sophisticated technologies, HUMINT has taken a back seat to other collection disciplines. Nevertheless, HUMINT still remains the mainstay of intelligence collection activities for many nations that cannot afford or does not have access to technologies (Lowenthal, 2015).

HUMINT involves overt, sensitive, and clandestine collection activities. Overt HUMINT collectors conduct their activities openly and include military attaches, diplomatic personnel, and members of official delegations. During overt collection, collectors exploit unclassified publications and conference materials or debrief travelers who have recently visited a country of interest. Most HUMINT collection is performed by overt means (Lowenthal, 2015).

Signals Intelligence (SIGINT). SIGINT involves the collection of information by intercepting signals from communications and electronic emissions. In policing, this might take the form of a wiretap. I have made some very good cases just from listening to radio traffic of the citizens band (CB) radio. Signals intelligence is derived from the interception of signals. These signals include communications intelligence (COMINT), electronic intelligence (ELINT), and foreign instrumentation signals intelligence (FISINT). COMINT is one of the primary signal disciplines and involves the interception of communications transmissions. Things such as voice traffic, Morse code traffic, facsimile messages, and video are COMINT targets. It is also possible to collect COMINT from other transmission medium such as airwaves (cellular telephones), fiber optics, and cable (Lowenthal, 2015).

Open-Source Intelligence (OSINT). OSINT involves the collection of information gathered from nonclassified, nonsecret sources. Sources include television, newspapers, magazines, the Internet, and commercial databases to name a few. Social media, such as Facebook, is a great tool for gathering intelligence and evidence. With an abundance of electronic databases available, it has become easier to collect and organize large quantities of information and to structure that information to meet the needs of the collector. Extremely valuable information can be derived from open-source information (Lowenthal, 2015).

Quite often, open-source information can provide data on the activities, capabilities, dynamics, technical processes, and research activities of organizations that cannot be found elsewhere. As in the fairly recent case of WikiLeaks, classified material can sometimes be found by individuals surfing the web. With the advent of the Internet and the media broadcasting breaking news as it happens twenty-four hours a day, seven days a week, open-source information is generally timelier. During a crisis or emergency situation, open-source information may be the only information available during the early stages (Lowenthal, 2015).

Measurement and Signature Intelligence (MASINT). MASINT involves a highly technical, multidisciplinary approach to intelligence collection to provide detailed characteristics of targets, including radar signatures of aircraft and telemetry of missiles. This source is not usually available to law enforcement. Of the six collection disciplines, MASINT is the least understood. MASINT involves scientific and technical intelligence information obtained by quantitative and qualitative analysis of data derived from specific technical sensors (Lowenthal, 2015).

Geospatial Intelligence (GEOINT).

GEOINT involves the collection of information related to the earth from imagery, imagery intelligence, and geospatial information. Google Earth and other such sources are a great place to gather information for planning special events, raids, surveillance, etc. Information that identifies a natural or constructed feature on the earth by its geographic location and other characteristics is known as geospatial information. When geospatial information is superimposed with imagery and IMINT and analyzed, the result is GEOINT (Lowenthal, 2015).

Imagery Intelligence (IMINT). IMINT involves the representation of objects reproduced optically or by electronic means from a variety of sources, including radar, infrared sources, and electro-optics. IMINT involves the use of satellites and aerial photography to gather information and is a product of imagery analysis. IMINT includes the exploitation of imagery data to detect, classify, and identify objects or organizations (Lowenthal, 2015). Police use such devices often, but they must be commercially available and not military grade, where the public cannot use them as well. Drones and commercial aircraft are often used by police. Aviation administration standards must be maintained.

Imagery provides significant benefits for the intelligence community (IC). Imagery sensors can cover large areas to facilitate the mapping of areas of interest (Lowenthal, 2015).

All-source intelligence integrates information derived through all disciplines. All source intelligence enables the IC to develop reinforcing information and to use multiple sources to corroborate key data. The advantage of an all-source approach is that each of the collection disciplines is suited to collecting a particular type of data, which allows the intelligence organization to examine all aspects of an intelligence target and gain a better understanding of its operation (Lowenthal, 2015).

The second phase of the intelligence cycle is collection. The collection process involves the management of various activities, including developing collection plans that ensure the best use of available intelligence resources. Intelligence collection requirements are developed to meet the needs of consumers. Once intelligence requirements are identified, collection managers task specific disciplines to collect information (Lowenthal, 2015).

Analysis is the third phase and an integral part of the intelligence cycle. There is a difference between information and intelligence. Information is like pieces of a jigsaw puzzle. It is not until all the pieces of the puzzle are carefully put together that the picture or significance of the puzzle is revealed. Likewise, intelligence cannot be produced until all disparate pieces of information are collected and properly analyzed. Through the process of analysis, information is transformed into intelligence, which gives meaning and relevance to issues or events. A properly analyzed information paints a picture or tells a story that enables consumers to make decisions based on the knowledge gained from the intelligence (Lowenthal, 2015).

The analysis that is required to transform information into intelligence products is not achieved haphazardly. Intelligence analysis is an art, and the individuals that conduct analysis must possess the necessary traits, knowledge, skills, and qualities to achieve it. To produce useful intelligence products, the IC depends on intelligence analysts, sometimes referred to as intelligence officers, who possess these qualities and are trained in the intelligence craft. Intelligence analysts play a significant role within the IC. Intelligence analysts are tasked with making sense of issues and events, identifying potential threats, and creating appropriate intelligence products for policy and decision makers (Lowenthal, 2015).

Intelligence Analyst

Most police agencies do not have actual intelligence analysts. More are hiring them, and they are a great asset. I will argue that every police officer is an intelligence analyst, though. It is important that you become familiar with the attributes of analysts and their role in the agency. As you can see, a police officer has or should have all of these attributes.

Role and responsibilities. Intelligence analysts are more than just another source, collector, or provider of information. The intelligence analyst plays a vital role in the IC. Intelligence analysts participate in supporting IC programs where the overall mission is to advance the gathering, analysis, sharing, and use of both open-source and sensitive material. Intelligence analysts provide support through several key functions:

- ✓ Conducting research and gathering information
- ✓ Identifying intelligence gaps
- ✓ Interpreting and evaluating information from multiple sources

✓ Monitoring trends and events related to a particular country or issue

✓ Preparing written and oral assessments based on historical and current events (Lowenthal, 2015)

Desired attributes of an intelligence analyst. Not just anyone can be an intelligence analyst. Individuals aspiring to enter into the intelligence tradecraft as an intelligence analyst must possess certain personal traits, knowledge, skills, and qualities to excel. Desirable traits include judgment, professionalism, flexibility and adaptability, initiative and motivation, the capacity to learn, curiosity, and tenacity (Lowenthal, 2015).

Judgment. An intelligence analyst, or officer, must be able to make sound decisions related to the gathering and use of information. They must be able to develop and then evaluate alternative solutions and select and commit to a course of action (Lowenthal, 2015).

Analysis Techniques

Law enforcement entities all require skilled analysts to interpret growing amounts of information. During the course of their duties, intelligence analysts use many analytical techniques. These techniques include clustering, link analysis, time series, visualization, data mining, and social network analysis (Lowenthal, 2015).

Cluster analysis. Cluster analysis is an exploratory data analysis tool used for grouping similar objects into categories, which allows analyst to exploit the most useful data first (Lowenthal, 2015).

Link analysis. Link analysis is a technique used to evaluate the connections between a known problem and individuals. Through link analysis, relationships may be identified among various type of objects, such as organizations, people, and transactions (Lowenthal, 2015).

Time series analysis. Time series analysis is a technique used to identify time trends. By charting meaningful statistics and other characteristics of data, analysts can predict future values based on previously recorded values (Lowenthal, 2015).

Visualization analysis. Visualization analysis is a technique that allows intelligence analysts to view large amounts of complex information in new forms, such as graphs, charts, or diagrams (Lowenthal, 2015).

Data mining. Data mining is a repetitive process of selecting, exploring, and developing large amounts of information to identify meaningful, logical patterns and relationships among key variables. Data mining is used to reveal trends, predict future events, and assess the advantages of various courses of action (Lowenthal, 2015).

Social network analysis. Social network analysis is used to identify, connect, or link individuals and their relationships within a network (Lowenthal, 2015). Hopefully, you have already realized how useful these techniques are with serial offenders, gangs, terror cell, organized crime, etc.

In response to the terror attacks of September 11, 2001, The National Strategy for Homeland Security was enacted in July 2002. The strategy recognized the importance of state and local law enforcement agencies in preventing, deterring, and responding to terrorism. Additionally, the strategy set forth an additional responsibility for state and local law enforcement agencies. While law enforcement agencies would continue to investigate and prosecute criminal activity, they would now assign priority to preventing and interdicting terrorist activity within the United States. The federal government recognized that the nation's state and local law enforcement officers would be a critical component in the effort to keep another 9/11 from occurring (Lowenthal, 2015).

Implementation of Intelligence-Led Policing

For more than twenty years prior to 9/11, law enforcement agencies across the nation conducted their operations utilizing the community-oriented policing or problem-oriented policing philosophies. However, following 9/11, the Department of Homeland Security (DHS) called upon state and local law enforcement agencies to adopt a homeland security model of policing, which included an emphasis on intelligence gathering, covert operations, greater information sharing, and enforcement of immigration laws. To persuade law enforcement agencies to adopt a homeland security model of policing, the federal government significantly reduced grant funding for community policing and problem-oriented policing projects. DHS offered hundreds of millions of dollars in grant funding to law enforcement agencies for training, equipment, and program funding (Ratcliffe, 2005).

The intelligence community and law enforcement in the United States realized that a process was required to enhance coordination, cooperation, and information sharing to prevent another terrorist attack. In 2002, the International Association of Chiefs of Police (IACP) and the United States Justice Department identified and adopted the intelligence-led policing philosophy and encouraged federal, state, and local law enforcement to do the same. The National Criminal Intelligence Sharing Plan was created and echoed the IACP and United States Justice Department's recommendation (Ratcliffe, 2005).

However, the guidelines, tenets, and components of intelligence-led policing that are necessary to successfully develop and implement a framework are still foreign to most law enforcement agencies today. The idea behind intelligence-led policing is that the effective use of intelligence to drive decision making and deploy resources can enable law enforcement to prevent, deter, and respond to crime issues and terrorism in a more efficient and cost-effective manner (Ratcliffe, 2005).

The environment is where the criminal activity takes place and where law enforcement collects information. Police officers document criminal violations, arrests, and other information on crime incident reports, field interview reports, and traffic summons and by other reporting mechanisms. Law enforcement agencies warehouse the collected information in record management systems. Intelligence units within law enforcement agencies then access the information. Crime analysts and intelligence investigators analyze and evaluate the information to interpret what is going on in the environment. The interpretation of information results in the identification of crime trends and patterns and the identification of criminal suspects (Ratcliffe, 2005).

The Intelligence Cycle

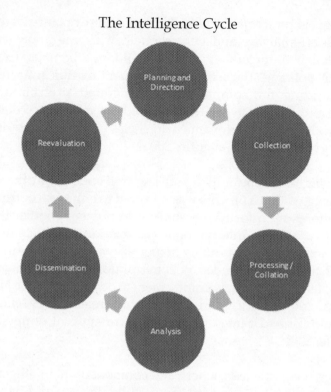

Once all information is analyzed and evaluated, the intelligence unit creates intelligence products in the form of alerts, bulletins, and hot spot maps. The intelligence unit disseminates intelligence products to decision makers to influence them in deciding what courses of action and resources are required to affect or address problems in the environment (Ratcliffe, 2005).

The Intelligence Cycle

Police must master the ability to prompt the various assets available to their agencies in order to pull information from the environment, analyze that information to gain understanding, and use that understanding to reduce public safety threats. The intelligence cycle is at the heart of the intelligence-led policing philosophy. Successful implementation of intelligence-led policing depends upon law enforcement leaders' ensuring that all officers under their command receive training on the intelligence cycle. Through the proper application of the intelligence cycle, law enforcement agencies can achieve more effective and efficient policing and crime control. The

National Criminal Intelligence Sharing Plan provides guidelines for the application of the intelligence cycle (Ratcliffe, 2005).

Planning and direction. The planning and direction phase is an important part of the intelligence process. Successful outcomes are dependent upon planning that is well coordinated and focused. When law enforcement agencies identify problems in the environment, information requirements must be determined. During the planning and direction phase, analysts work closely with intelligence investigators to determine what information is available and what information needs to be collected to close information gaps. The agency closes information gaps by identifying assets in the organization best suited to collect specific information and then directing them to collect it. A well-planned and focused collection effort will achieve desired outcomes (Ratcliffe, 2005).

Collection. The collection phase involves the proactive gathering of large amounts of information required to produce intelligence products. Since the collection phase "is the most labor intensive aspect of the intelligence cycle" (Peterson, 2005, p. 6), collection of all relevant information requires a systematic approach. A collection plan is extremely useful to keep track of what information is available, what information is required, who is tasked to collect specific information, and a time frame specifying when the information is required. All available sources should be used to collection information. Sources include the Internet, criminal databases, record management systems, undercover and patrol officers, businesses, and the community. Law enforcement agencies should take every precaution to ensure that collection of information complies with federal guidelines so as not to violate citizen privacy and civil liberties (Carter, 2008, p. 29–30).

Processing and collation. As information is collected, it must be processed and organized so that analysts can more easily work with the volume of information received. It is during this process that analysts sort and categorize information and the validity and reliability of information is established (Ratcliffe, 2005).

Analysis and production. The analysis and production phase is where the rubber meets the road. In this phase, analysts synthesize information to derive meaning. As Peterson (2005) notes, "Without the explicit performance of this function [analysis], the intelligence unit is nothing but a file unit" (p. 7). The systematic analysis of all relevant information allows analysts to identify the current and emerging threats in the environment. Thorough analysis of information enables analysts to identify crime trends and patterns and potential suspects, which assist investigators in furthering an investigation. From the analyzed information, analysts create actionable intelligence products that should provide situational awareness and allow officers to do something with it. Furthermore, the finished intelligence products assist commanders in strategic and tactical planning to address crime issues (Carter, 2008, p. 30).

Dissemination. The dissemination phase is also a critical step in the intelligence process. Failure to disseminate intelligence products to the right people at the right time negates any good collection and analysis process (Peterson, 2005, p. 7). When possible, intelligence products should be disseminated as widely as possible on a "right-to-know" and a "need-to-know" basis. The *right to know* means that the person receiving the intelligence product has a legal standing to access it. The *need to know* means that the person requesting the intelligence product requires it by virtue of their position and responsibility to act on it (USDOJ, 2005, p. 7).

Reevaluation. The final step of the intelligence process is the reevaluation of the intelligence products and process. The reevaluation of intelligence products involves end users—such as managers, investigators, and officers—providing constructive feedback on intelligence products (Peterson, 2005, p. 7). If the products fail to provide users with actionable intelligence, then feedback allows the intelligence function to determine what improvements are required. Conversely, analysts can provide valuable feedback used to improve the collection process. Every member of a law enforcement agency plays an important role in the intelligence cycle, and each has a responsibility to provide his or her unique perspective toward improving it (USDOJ, 2009, p.10).

Enhancements to the Criminal Intelligence Enterprise after 9/11

In an effort to provide greater sharing of information and intelligence, many states and large cities have established fusion centers. The state fusion or regional intelligence centers are designed to collect information from the jurisdictions in the state and to provide intelligence information to law enforcement agencies so as to enable them to identify, assess, and manage potential threats to public safety. Another primary role is to ensure that valuable intelligence information is coordinated between federal, state, and local law enforcement via the Homeland Security Information Network (HSIN).

Privacy and Civil Liberty Concerns

Many individuals and organizations are highly skeptical about the intelligence activities carried out by law enforcement (Carter, 2008, p. 6). When implementing an intelligence-led policing framework, a primary goal of law enforcement agencies should be the protection of citizen privacy and civil liberties. Accomplishing this goal involves establishing policies and procedures for the appropriate collection and retention of intelligence information in criminal databases. A rule of thumb is the requirement of the articulation of a criminal predicate before permanently warehousing information in criminal databases. Law enforcement agencies that comply with 28 C.F.R. Part 23 demonstrate good faith, and it contributes to protecting the agency from liability (Ratcliffe, 2005).

The Threat Environment in the Twenty-First Century

Cyber Threats

Computer networks are critical components for infrastructure such as communications, energy, transportation, banking and finance, government, and defense.

Drug Trafficking

The illicit trafficking and abuse of drugs present a significant threat to the United States.

Organized Crime

Organized crime is both a national and transnational problem. The dynamics of organized crime have changed significantly compared to years past, and the threat is broader and more complex than ever. In addition to prostitution, human trafficking, and drug trafficking, organized crime rings now excel at stealing millions of dollars each year through stock frauds and financial scams, often from afar by utilizing technology. These organizations utilize extortion, intimidation, and even murder to further their enterprises.

Challenges for the Intelligence Community

Since 9/11, the IC has done a good job overall in supporting policy makers, the military, and law enforcement in securing the nation and keeping Americans safe. Police face a multitude of challenges in dealing with crime in general. Intelligence can and should be used to deal with all sorts of crimes and criminals, such as gangs, drug offenders/dealers/cartels, terrorists, repeat/career offenders, serial offenders such as rapists and murderers, hot spots for crimes, anarchists, organized crime, etc.

Informants

Informants have a special role in the intelligence process in policing. Most informants are not exactly pillars of the community. Often, they know what they know because of their own ills or affiliations with others ills. The use of informants is a necessary evil. Whenever one uses an informant, they must proceed with caution. Some parts of certain investigations will be difficult without them. They should make every effort to corroborate the information. Never become attached personally to an informant. Always measure what is gained with what can be lost.

Several issues arise when information supplied by informants is used. One concerns Fourth Amendment protection against unreasonable searches and seizures. This depends on if the information provided by the informant allows for probable cause or not. The other concern involves the Sixth Amendment and whether the identity of the informant needs to be revealed. As for the first question, the biggest problem for probable cause depends on the credibility of the informant. Did the informant actually use his or her own senses in witnessing the crime, or was it hearsay? In *Draper v. United States*, the court has approved the use of an informant's hearsay information in allowing for a warrantless arrest. In *Spinelli v. United States*, a two-pronged test has been devised to determine if an informant's information can be used to show probable cause. First, the informant must be reliable. Second, the information the informant supplies is credible (Osterburg and Ward, 2014).

Informants often work off time by working with police. They should never be allowed to commit more crimes because they are informants. I have rarely seen or heard of informants who have informed out of the goodness of their heart. I call that type "witnesses." Some informants are working against their competition. Judges and juries will weigh the evidence as to its veracity and relevance—"weight of the evidence." Cross-examination is a crucial step in any trial. This is an issue in and of itself when it comes to informants being confidential. The exclusionary rule is important. Corroboration is very important.

The police agency should have strict rules and policies in place for dealing with informants. I have seen more than one officer get in trouble usually because they have gotten too close to an informant. Paid and unpaid informants also make a difference. The motives and truthfulness or reliability of informants will always be a point of attack in any trial. Outside the fact that many informants are not upstanding citizens to begin with, for me, the weakest part of informant use is the lack of ability to cross-examine. This makes it critical for the police to be always 100 percent above board in the use of informants.

Legally, the use of informants is permissible. Ethically, it can sometimes be questionable. Remember, the codified law is the least acceptable level of human behavior. Ethics rise above the law. What may be legal may not be ethical, and the reverse is true as well.

Takeaways

- ✓ Do not underestimate the role intelligence plays in policing.
- ✓ The only thing worse than no intelligence is corrupt intelligence.
- ✓ Information is raw data that is collected.
- ✓ Intelligence is the result of processed information.

- ✓ Regarding the collection and use of intelligence, an officer must be professional, use good judgment, be flexible and adaptable, be motivated and have curiosity and tenacity, and be willing to learn.
- ✓ Understand the various types of intelligence collection available.
- ✓ Respect the Constitution and laws regarding all collection and use of intelligence.
- ✓ When implementing and using intelligence-led policing, respect the rights of citizens.
- ✓ Police must have strict rules when dealing with human intelligence, a.k.a. informants.

Truthful lips endure forever, but a lying tongue is for a moment.
—Proverbs 12:19

Chapter Ten
Report Preparation and Case Management

We are what we repeatedly do. Excellence, then, is not an act but a habit.
—Aristotle

The job is not done until the paperwork is complete.

When I was a first sergeant, I was reading a sergeant's report on a use of force he had investigated involving one of our troops. We were new with working together. I read the report and found it straightforward and uneventful. After I was done, he said he had left one detail out because he did not want to muddy the water. I asked about the detail. He said the arrestee told him the trooper had handcuffed him and then pounded his head against the floor. The trooper had chased the guy into a bar and had to get him down and handcuff him. I told my sergeant he could not leave such information out of a report. If that was what the arrestee said, then he should write it down as he said. I told him he now needed to go back and try to prove if that happened. "If it did not happen, then great, we have cleared the trooper. If it did happen, then we are going to have an issue that will be addressed. It is up to us to find out the facts and prove or disprove the allegation made, if possible." He went back and found witnesses who confirmed that what the arrestee said never happened. It was a lie. I was happy it was not true and that we cleared the trooper. Never leave out facts ever. It might not be the truth, and that is our job to find out as well.

Incident Report

While the exact layout for incident reports typically varies from one jurisdiction to another, they all have a "face" with blanks into which the officer conducting the preliminary investigation enters basic case information.

- ✓ Suspects: It provides additional information about suspects.
- ✓ Witnesses: This is information from witnesses, including their descriptions of events and things as they experienced them through their four senses.

✓ Evidence: The evidence seized, how it was marked, the chain of custody, and the numbers assigned by the property or evidence control room are recorded.
✓ Interviews: All persons with whom the investigator talked during the course of the inquiry should be identified, even if they could not provide information at the initial contact.
✓ Investigation: A description of the crime scene may be given to permit a basic conceptualization of it by persons to whom it is unfamiliar.
✓ Reconstruction: The reconstruction is a narration of the probable way the crime was committed.

NIBRS

The National Incident-Based Reporting System (NIBRS) is administered by the FBI (Uniform Crime Reporting [UCR] phasing out). Its format allows for much more data about an offense to be gathered. Data gathered allows police to look for relationships between victims and offenders and drugs/alcohol and crime. The NIBRS incident report collects a significant amount of information for later analysis by investigators.

Report Approval Process

Police reports are subject to supervisory review for corrections and guidance before their final disposition. Well-written reports are very helpful to investigators who may be conducting follow-up investigations at a later date and to prosecutors who have to handle the case.

The Report Disposition Process

Supervisory options for report disposition following approval include as follows:

✓ The case may be retained for further investigation by uniformed officers.
✓ It may be unfounded (i.e., the complaint is false).
✓ The case may be inactivated because of the lack of leads.

✓ It may be referred to plainclothes investigators.
✓ It might be closed arrest.
   ○ This means the suspect was arrested.
   ○ The case should not be closed until there is a final disposition of any evidence in police custody.
✓ It might be closed exceptional means.
   ○ An example will be the suspect is known but cannot be arrested because he or she has been killed.
   ○ Sometimes the suspect is known, and a case can be made, but the prosecutor declines to prosecute.

Writing Effective Reports

If incident reports are going to serve the many uses to which they can be put, they must meet certain standards. Fill in all the blanks on the incident report. Write the report in the first person. Avoid unnecessary technical or legalistic jargon. Write short but complete sentences. Use shorter paragraphs for the same reason. Support any conclusions you express with details. Do not repeat facts more than once. Check your spelling. Edit what you write. Write in chronological order of the events as you know them. Include attachments such as evidence logs, crime scene sketches, written statements, etc.

Supplemental Reports

Supplemental reports are written to:

✓ document new or corrected information;
✓ document specific acts or accomplishments, such as the issuance of a warrant, arrest of a suspect, or the recovery of property;
✓ unfound an offense;
✓ exceptionally clear an offense;
✓ inactivate a case.

It should be written as leads are developed and work is completed. Every ten days is a good goal.

DR. JEFFREY C. FOX

Writing Effective Investigative Reports

Criminal Investigative Reports

The criminal justice system partially functions through investigative reports. These are used by police officers to document crimes reported to them. These tend to document the preliminary investigative actions of the police. Many times, these reports are written before the police have a suspect in the case. These reports detail all the information that links the suspect to the crime and the investigation that led to the suspect's arrest. This report should include identification of the crime, the parties involved, witness statements, crime scene specifics, officer's observations, etc.

Writing an Effective Police Report

Avoid jargon and wordiness. (Remember your audience.) Write facts, not opinions, although impressions might be important to document. Select an appropriate word to describe the incident and other important factors. Organize by using paragraphs and headings.

Write in the first person. Use chronological order from the officer's perspective (I arrived, I spoke to witness 1, I discovered A, B, and then C). Use proper tense, normally past tense. Use active voice. Use proper grammar, spelling, and punctuation; have subject/ verb agreement ("I have," not "I has"). Verb and noun agreement is needed as well. Use correct pronoun reference (I, he, she, it, etc.).

Quality Investigative Reports

It is very important that your police report be of high quality. The report will document the effort you have put into the investigation. If the report is not clear, the investigation may seem ambiguous. An effective police report is clear, concise, complete, and accurate.

A police report should start with the date and time you received the call, when you arrived, and exactly what you found (saw and heard) when you arrived. Of course, you secure the scene. You will collect evidence in accordance with the law and interview everyone. Follow-up interviews will be needed in many cases. You must conduct thorough interviews of every witness. The entire trial process hangs on the police officer's ability to find and remember details; thus you must take notes. You are telling a fact-based story.

You need to make sure that you give sufficient details about the incident that you create a mental picture for the prosecuting attorney and later for the judge or jury. It should read neutrally. There is no such thing as too much information in a police report so long as it is relevant.

To make reports easy to read and understand, you should write in the first person. You, as the writer of the report, will refer to yourself as *I* and use the first-person pronouns *me, my,* and *mine*. Some departments may want you to use the more formal third person, such as *this officer* or *this writer*. Leave no holes in your report unless you do not know.

You must make sure that all relevant information is included in the report. Any holes in your report can be exploited by the attorneys defending the case. Remember, the attorneys were not at the scene, so you need to add sufficient details to paint the picture of the scene. Gaps in your report can also cause a jury to think you are incompetent.

Chronological order is order by time. Your report should tell what happened in the order that the events took place from your perspective. Get the facts and list them in the order in which they happened. Witnesses might not give you information chronologically, so probe to get all the important information.

Everything you write in your report has already happened, so use the past tense.

If you do not know the answer, then you will need to give that reply. You want to avoid having to say that you do not know something in front of a jury too often; it makes you look sloppy or incompetent. If it is written in the past tense, you can easily say that the victim did work there when the report has been written.

Reports should be written in active voice whenever possible. Active voice is when the subject performs the action described by the verb. Use correct spelling and punctuation. Make sure that you compose your sentences so that the reader knows who or what the pronoun refers to. Avoid police jargon. Attorneys who need to read your report will not be familiar with radio codes or other jargon. Use simple words. Avoid wordy phrases. Report facts, not your opinions. Make sure you tell where you got the information. Be specific with your words. Accuracy involves detail; detail is important to be able to show that what someone did violated a law and is not just your opinion. Be sure your sentences are specific enough to provide a clear picture.

An arrest is only as good as the report that supports it. It is the building block that the entire criminal justice system uses to build a case. People are convicted based on good report writing. People are not charged or cases are lost because of poor report writing.

Who uses police reports, and for what purpose?

There are often limits on who is allowed access to open and closed criminal investigative reports.

Police and Administration

- ✓ Keep statistics
- ✓ Make a record of an incident
- ✓ Release information to the media
- ✓ Aid detectives in their investigation
- ✓ Examine by supervisors all that took place
- ✓ Analyze and compare crimes
- ✓ Judge the quality of your work and efforts
- ✓ Help manage your case

Prosecutors

- ✓ Decide who to charge
- ✓ Decide who not to charge
- ✓ Decide what to charge

✓ Help to map out prosecution course of action and questions

Defense Attorneys

✓ Help in defense of client
✓ Information will be garnered on serious cases during motion for discovery

Judges

✓ Weigh evidence
✓ Determine admissibility of evidence

Insurance Companies

✓ Insurance claims

Probation Officers

✓ Used in sentencing recommendation

Elements of information gathering

✓ Observe
✓ Listen
✓ Smell
✓ Touch
✓ Record
✓ Question
  ○ Open ended
  ○ Do not assume; ask.

Basic Report Structure

✓ Block information
✓ Narrative
✓ Conclusion
✓ Attachments
✓ Basic report structure

✓ Block information

Conclusion

✓ Disposition of case (What did you do to finish the case?)
✓ Follow-up needed

Attachments

✓ Probable cause affidavit (search or arrest warrant)
✓ Search-warrant-related documents
✓ Evidence collection information
✓ Witness's and/or suspect/accused's written statement(s)
✓ Suspect advised of rights, etc.

Field notes should/are

✓ the basis of a good report,
✓ contain information obtained through inquiry and investigation,
✓ help recall for report writing,
✓ help organize the investigation,
✓ help recall for testifying in court,
✓ serve as a reference for police activities performed during a particular shift.

Characteristics of Good Field Notes

✓ Clear
✓ Complete
✓ Concise
✓ Accurate
✓ Objective

Purpose of Field Notes

✓ Aid in remembering the incident
✓ Aid in the investigation of a crime or incident
✓ Aid in writing the report
✓ Serve as a valuable aid when testifying in court

Field notes are what you can testify from in court. Technically you cannot testify from a finished report that has been created/made after the fact. It is a common practice for attorneys to ask to see your notes while on the stand, so do not write anything on them that you do not want others to see. Another practice by some attorneys is to ask for your notes while on the stand and then ask you questions based on your notes or ask other questions without the aid of your notes. Judges will handle this, and hopefully you have a good prosecutor who will contest this type of action.

Another common mantra is if it is not written in your notes or in your report, then it did not happen. Of course, this may not be true, but you will often be challenged with this concept by attorneys.

Your field notes might be written in a spiral pad, a legal pad, or other type of paper. It is best to write in black ink only.

Often, with minor offenses and traffic offenses, your notes will be written on your copy of the ticket/summons. You should always complete your field notes before you leave the scene. These are your original notes. It is also when you will recall the events most clearly. Also, you will be handling other calls and making other charges, so do one thing right before you move on to the next. Your field notes should be complete, copious, and extremely detailed.

If you have made a charge against someone, make sure you have written down all elements of the crime or offense they have committed. Leaving one element off will ensure a "not guilty" verdict. The summons may capture much of the needed data, but you will need to write down everything else.

Basic Report Structure

- ✓ Synopsis
- ✓ Body
- ✓ Conclusion

DR. JEFFREY C. FOX

Synopsis

It tells the reader what the report is all about. You are telling the entire story from beginning to end as you know it.

You want to try to answer these questions:

- ✓ Who
- ✓ What
- ✓ Why
- ✓ When
- ✓ Where
- ✓ How

Body of the Investigative Report

It is the comprehensive narrative of what the officer saw, heard, and did. Quote people when appropriate. Answers the questions who, what, why, when, where, and how. How and why = motive and mental state. If how and why are not answered, it tells the reader follow-up is needed. Not all crimes require that a motive be proved. It should be written in first person, active voice, and past tense.

Conclusion of the Report

It indicates if any follow-up is needed. It states whether or not the case is closed. It ties up loose ends and comes to a brief ending. It is not an opinion. Conclusions are logical reasoning based on facts observed.

Completing a Summons or Traffic Ticket

On a summons, there will be mainly "fill in the blanks." You want to ensure you use the correct code section and standard acceptable verbiage for the violation. Most information will come from the driver's license of the person. You may have to ask certain questions that might be sensitive, but you are better off to ask than to guess. You might have to ask weight, sex, eye color, or even race. Explain why you are asking. Just say, "I need to ask this so I can complete the summons accurately." If you guess and guess wrong, two things can happen. The person can become very upset. The case can be lost in court when it is discovered that you have charged a male when she is a female or that you have said the person is black when he or she is white. I have seen all of this happen more than once. Be sure to explain why you are asking. I have seen people think you are flirting when you ask about eye color or weight. I have also seen people get upset when you ask about weight. Better off to ask than guess.

Another important issue when completing a summons is to make sure the person is telling you the truth. If they do not have a license or other form of official identification, they might well be lying to you as to who they are. This will happen. If they are lying, it is usually one of four things: they are wanted, they are committing an illegal act right now, they are not supposed to drive, or they just want to get out of a summons by using another person's name. Look and listen for clues. Do not let them see the summons so they can just repeat what they have said before. Go back and subtly ask them the same questions again. Look for inconsistencies. Check further through the various means available such as a license, registration, criminal history check, etc. Another great trick is to go ask anyone with them who the person is, but do not let on that you have suspicions. Ask each person separately as well.

Takeaways

- ✓ Never leave out pertinent information for any reason.
- ✓ Avoid technical jargon.
- ✓ Write in the first person.
- ✓ Write in the past tense.
- ✓ Write short but complete sentences.
- ✓ Check your grammar.
- ✓ Check spelling.
- ✓ Write in chronological order.
- ✓ Use paragraphs and headings.
- ✓ You are telling a fact-based story.
- ✓ Make sure you have proper subject-verb agreement.
- ✓ Do not try to create brevity. Write as much as is needed to tell the entire story.
- ✓ Ultimately, if an arrest is made, you will need to show that a crime has been committed, the person charged did it, and you have all the elements of the crime.

- ✓ You cannot testify from the final report in court.
- ✓ You can testify from your field notes in court.
- ✓ Complete your field notes while still at the scene or move to another safer spot and complete before you go on to the next call or patrol.
- ✓ The attorneys or judge can ask to see your field notes on the stand.
- ✓ Keep your case effort up to date, with supplemental reports filed often.

The tongue has the power of life and death, and
those who love it will eat its fruit.
—Proverbs 18:21

Chapter Eleven
Liability and Complaints

Power tends to corrupt, and absolute power corrupts absolutely.
—Lord Acton

If you are doing your job, you will get complaints sometimes.

I was assigned a case that involved a possible impersonation of a trooper. A letter of commendation had been written to our agency head. The letter was from two teachers who wanted to commend a trooper who had stopped and helped them on the side of the interstate in my assigned county. The problem was we had no trooper by that name in the department. My first thought was to check and see if we had anyone by that name who had worked with the agency before or who had applied to the agency. From time to time, there would be what we called wannabes. These were people who wanted to be police officers who carried it too far and pretended to be officers. My first act was to call our personnel department. Lo and behold, on the same day as the incident, they had tested for new troopers, and this fellow had been at our headquarters and tested to be a trooper. Now I had a name and could tie him to a place. I contacted his last place of residence, and he had moved, but they were familiar with him. He was an odd fellow who liked to pretend to be an officer in subtle ways. He had moved to an adjoining state, though. I got his information and called him. I told him I needed to talk with him about employment. He agreed to come back to Virginia and meet me at our office.

When he came into the office, I presented him with the letter of commendation and asked him to explain. He opened up and told the truth. I had already spoken to the teachers he had helped. They were husband and wife. They told me they had a flat tire on the side of the interstate. This trooper pulled up in an unmarked Mercury Cougar. He helped them. He flashed a badge at them. He had a red light on the dash. He had a beard and told them he was the only trooper allowed to have one. He took the tire off, had the fellow's wife go with him, drove up the on-ramp the wrong way, and got the tire changed. When she got in the car, she saw handcuffs, and she thought the CB radio was a police radio! He then brought the wife and tire back, thank God. The fellow admitted to everything. These were past misdemeanors, so I asked him if he would go with me to obtain warrants, and he did. I was hoping to find more evidence in the car, such as the red light, handcuffs, badge, gun, etc. He had a red light and CB he used for a police radio. He was charged with impersonating a police officer, reckless driving, and a few other things. I subpoenaed the two teachers to court. They were furious at me for bothering them and this nice young man. He was found guilty and appealed. I had to again subpoena the teachers. Now they were incredulous with me. They could not understand the problem. They had to be treated as hostile witnesses on the stand by the prosecutor! The fellow was again convicted of all charges.

I actually felt sorry for the young man. Luckily for the couple, he was not a dangerous person. He could have taken the wife off and done great harm to her, but they did not seem to grasp the danger. There have been cases where people have impersonated police officers and abducted victims who never lived to tell their stories.

The thought of being sued is scary and a reality unfortunately. There is an old saying in policing: "Better to be tried by twelve than carried by six." The most important thing is that you, as an officer, go home safe and unharmed at the end of your shift. Of course, we must be legal and ethical in everything we do. We must always act in good faith. Try as we might, we cannot completely safeguard ourselves from lawsuits. We can do a great deal to avoid them and to ensure we win if we are sued.

While I do not like lawsuits, they are a necessary process in order to seek redress. The same holds true for complaints. I only had a few complaints during my career, and none of them were ever found to have any merit. That did not take away the angst it caused me. Most were very trivial. There is an old saying that you do not have to worry about the dog that is barking at you as far as being bitten. It is the quiet one that will bite. I cannot say if this old saying has any merit, but it does seem to be that way with complaints. Some people will give it to an officer verbally and make all sorts of threats. Then you never hear from them again. It always seems to be the one who has not said a word who will complain later. Then there are officers who always get the same type of complaint over and over. Complaints such as being rude and crude often cannot be proven.

Usually the complaint cannot be proven one way or another since there are no witnesses, but the old saying is "Where there is smoke, there is fire."

Government Liability

Suing the government is very popular in America, and police are often the targets of lawsuits, with over thirty thousand civil actions filed against them every year, between 4 and 8 percent of them resulting in an unfavorable verdict. With lawsuits against large police departments, the average jury award is two million dollars. This is not counting the hundreds of cases settled through out-of-court settlements, which—if added up—will probably run in the neighborhood of hundreds of millions of dollars. Further, it may take five years or more to settle a police liability case.

Because police work involves risky split-second decisions, officers become subject to a wide range of investigations, complaints, and legal actions against them. Investigations and prosecutions may take place on multiple overlapping jurisdictions (i.e., both state and federal).

When police fail to perform their duties, perform them negligently, or abuse their authority, the possibility of civil liability exists. Unlike criminal cases, liability cases are tried in civil court. It is common to name everyone associated with the injury or damage as the defendant (officers, supervisors, agencies, even the government entity) in order to reach the "deep pockets." Chances are the higher-ups will have the ability to pay larger awards either personally or by raising taxes. At other times, it is common for an individual officer to be the target of a single accusation; and in such civil action, the officer's personal assets may be at risk.

There are two ways to sue the police. One, the lawsuit may be filed in state court as a tort law claim. This is the preferred method since torts can only be settled by money awards, and the standard of proof is preponderance of the evidence—a standard much lower to convict than in a criminal case. Two, the lawsuit may be filed in federal court as a violation of Title 42 of the United States Code section 1983. This is referred to as a civil rights claim and is essentially a charge that someone has had their constitutional rights violated. States cannot be sued in a civil rights claim, but municipalities and sheriffs can be sued if they are (a) acting under color of state law and (b) violating a specific amendment right in the Constitution. The standards under federal law are custom or policy and deliberate indifference—a rather poorly defined concept that is similar to totality of circumstances. Although federal lawsuits can result in money awards, the amount is usually less since the purpose is theoretically at least to win and get the agency to change the way it operates (i.e., obtain injunctive relief) (Gardner and Anderson, 2010; Harr et al., 2011; Samaha, 2012).

State (Tort) Liability Law

There are three types of torts under state law, each with different levels of proof and focusing upon different elements of the injury or damage. Evidence rules, precedent, and judicial discretion play a role in determining what type of tort law will be applied.

Strict Liability—In this case, the injury or damage is so severe and it is reasonably certain that the harm could have been foreseen that the law dispenses with the need to prove intent or mental state. The only issue is whether the officer or department should pay the money award, and since officers do not usually have ample money, the department almost always pays (for example, reckless operation of vehicle).

Intentional Tort—In this case, the officer's intent must be proven, using a foreseeability test involving whether or not the officer knowingly engaged in behavior that was substantially certain to bring about injury (for examples, wrongful death, assault, false arrest, false imprisonment).

Negligence—In this case, intent or mental state does not matter. What matters is whether some inadvertent act or failure to act created an unreasonable risk to another member of society (for example, speeding resulting in traffic accident, not responding to 911 call). Most states have three levels of negligence: (1) slight or mere (absence of foresight), (2) gross (reckless disregard), and (3) criminal. To be prosecuted under tort law for negligence usually requires at least level 2 since to be prosecuted for mere negligence requires considering foreseeability that will support charging the person with an intentional tort or not (Gardner and Anderson, 2010; Harr et al., 2011; Samaha, 2012).

There are additional details of state tort liability associated with specific types of lawsuits, such as the following:

Wrongful death—These are typically cases when the officer thinks a suspect is reaching for a weapon and shoots the suspect, and then no weapon is found on the suspect. Courts have ruled that the totality of circumstances must be looked at, especially the reason why the suspect came into contact with the officer in the first place. Merely alleging that a suspect appeared to be reaching for a weapon is no defense.

Assault and battery—A police assault will be if an interrogator threatens to throw a suspect out a second-floor window; a police battery is (paradoxically) defined more loosely as any offensive contact without consent.

False arrest—The unlawful restraint of a person's liberty without their consent (e.g., using the caged area of a patrol car as a holding area, several officers surrounding somebody, or ordering someone to remain at the station) could be interpreted as false arrest.

False imprisonment—This is different from false arrest in that an officer may have had probable cause to arrest but later violates certain pretrial rights, such as access to a judge or bondsman.

Hot pursuits—This high-liability area typically involves reckless or negligent operation of a motor vehicle. It is also typically a strict liability area, and here are some of the acts used by the courts to infer intent or state of mind: not using emergency lights and sirens, not considering alternatives to chase, excessive or reckless disregard of traffic control devices, not securing the chase path, not warning the public, using cutoff maneuvers and roadblocks that create the possibility for overreaction, not stopping to assist any innocent injured bystanders. The duties are threefold:

- ✓ To warn and protect
- ✓ To secure the scene

✓   To render assistance

Federal Liability Law

Two elements have to be present simultaneously under federal liability law. If a person loses in federal court, they still have recourse under state law.

Acting under Color of Law—This means that the behavior of officers not related to employment is not actionable. It does not mean that off-duty officers cannot be sued. Officers moonlighting in a security job can be held liable since they are acting under color of law in performing a police function. And it sounds like a contradiction, but police behavior that is clearly illegal and violates departmental procedure, like beating up a citizen, is regarded by the court as acting under color of law. By strict definition, employees are acting "under color of law" when they are either actually carrying out their official duties or acting in a manner that makes it seem as if they are. Clearly, any behavior while on duty counts; and in addition, an off-duty police officer showing his or her badge is most likely acting under color of law (Gardner and Anderson, 2010; Harr et al., 2011; Samaha, 2012). These federal codes are 42 U.S.C. 1983, which is civil, and 42 U.S.C. 1982, which is criminal.

Violation of a Constitutional Right—These involve whatever the court believes to be specifically prohibited conduct regarding freedom of religion, speech, press, or assembly (First Amendment); freedom from unreasonable search and seizure (Fourth Amendment); freedom from double jeopardy and self-incrimination (Fifth Amendment); rights to a speedy, public, impartial jury trial and to be informed of the charges, confront and compel witnesses, and have assistance of counsel (Sixth Amendment); freedom from excessive bail, fines, and cruel and unusual punishments (Eighth Amendment); and freedom from deprivations of life, liberty, or property without due process (Fourteenth Amendment) (Gardner and Anderson, 2010; Harr et al., 2011; Samaha, 2012).

The leading case in police department liability under federal law is *Monell v. Dept. of Social Services*, 436 U.S. 658 (1978). Under this ruling, it must be shown that the department has adopted or promulgated (however informal) a "custom" or policy that has been the driving force behind the officer's violation of constitutional rights. In essence, this is the doctrine of respondeat superior since a policy maker (or "custom maker") has to be found to declare the department liable. A "pattern" of constitutional violations and an awareness of them by high-ranking officials must be demonstrated. However, there is precedent holding departments accountable for one single act as fulfilling the "pattern" requirement (Gardner and Anderson, 2010; Harr et al., 2011; Samaha, 2012).

Examples of gross negligence or accumulations of mere negligence constitute deliberate indifference. This standard is usually satisfied by looking at whether or not the agency administration has engaged in supervisory negligence. Virtually every decision a police administrator makes subjects them to possible liability. The following are examples of supervisory negligence:

- ✓ Negligent hiring—hiring persons unfit for police work, not conducting psychological exams, not conducting full background checks
- ✓ Negligent supervision—inadequate monitoring of employee performance, failure to reprimand when appropriate, tolerating sloppy police work, hearing rumors and not acting
- ✓ Negligent retention—keeping employees on the job or promoting them on the basis of favoritism or friendship when they clearly should have been severely disciplined, demoted, or dismissed
- ✓ Failure to train—inadequately preparing employees to perform their duties, minimal or too easy academy training, little or no in-service training
- ✓ Negligent entrustment—inadequately preparing employees prior to entrusting them with responsibilities, a synergistic combination of failure to train and negligent supervision
- ✓ Negligent assignment—assigning known problem employees to critical or inappropriate duties, reckless drivers to patrol, racist officers to minority areas, sexist officers with an opposite sex partner
- ✓ Failure to direct—not giving officers clear, articulated guidance in how to perform their duties; not having

policies and procedures; having officers "sign off" on the same without understanding them

✓ Failure to discipline—not having an effective discipline process, not following progressive discipline principles

✓ Failure to investigate—also a liability of officers; with supervisors, not having an effective internal affairs unit or inspections or integrity checks, a difficult (for citizens) complaint process, or a difficult (for employees) grievance process

✓ Failure to protect—also a liability of officers and jail managers; not inspecting safety conditions, allowing victims or witnesses to come in contact with suspects (protection of public is an individual liability addressed with failure to direct for supervisors or writ of mandamus)

✓ Failure to treat—also a liability of officers and jail manager; not providing first aid, ambulance service, or counseling (given the foreseeability of suicide)

✓ Negligent classification—a jail manager liability; throwing adults in with children or dangerous inmates in with nondangerous ones (Gardner and Anderson, 2010; Harr et al., 2011; Samaha, 2012)

Defenses to Liability

Contributory negligence—This is where the government shows that the plaintiff has also been negligent and has contributed to their own injury or damage. No money award is granted if this defense is successful.

Comparative negligence—This is when the court decides on a percentage split (say 60–40) in terms of who is negligent. This defense tends to mitigate or reduce the size of the money award. Not all states use comparative negligence.

Assumption of risk—This is when the court decides that the suspect engaged in behaviors (e.g., fleeing from police) that assumed the risk of damages or injuries and cannot expect to sue the police to recover.

Absolute immunity—This is a section 1983 lawsuit defense that is limited to participation in the judicial process (i.e., testifying in court). If a police officer commits perjury on the stand, he or she cannot be threatened with civil liability, only the criminal offense of perjury. The courts reason that it is difficult enough to get people to testify without the threat of civil liability.

Qualified immunity—This is a section 1983 lawsuit defense covering duties of a discretionary nature, such as when a police administrator decides to increase or decrease the number of patrols for drunk drivers. A motorist hit by a drunk driver charging that the department has not had enough patrol cars out protecting her will not win her lawsuit.

Probable cause—This is the standard defense to false arrest charges.

Good faith—This covers a wide range of behaviors, even unconstitutional ones, if the officer is executing a warrant believing in good faith that the warrant is valid, but it later turns out the warrant is defective or invalid (Gardner and Anderson, 2010; Harr et al., 2011; Samaha, 2012).

Individual Rights under Liability Law

The watershed case that has given law enforcement officers a constitutional right to immunity is *Garrity v. New Jersey*, 385 U.S. 493, 500 (1967), and it applies to internal affairs investigations where the officer is ordered (i.e., upon being served with a *Garrity* order) to answer questions relevant to the investigation or else face immediate discharge. The Supreme Court has held that "the choice imposed on [officers] was one between self-incrimination or job forfeiture"—a choice the court has termed "coercion." In a particularly strong language, the court has held that "policemen, like teachers and lawyers, are not relegated to a watered-down version of constitutional rights" and ruled that statements that a law enforcement officer is compelled to make under threat of possible forfeiture of his or her job cannot subsequently be used against the officer in a criminal prosecution. Further, the fruits of their answers cannot be used for criminal prosecutions. Despite this ruling, police departments continue to utilize *Garrity* orders, and a subsequent case the following year—*Gardner v. Broderick*, 392 U.S. 273 (1968)—has held it unconstitutional for departments to get around *Garrity* by making officers sign immunity waivers. Since then, police departments "get around" both *Garrity* and *Gardner* by (a) ensuring that internal affairs investigations are "specifically, narrowly, and directly" tailored to the employee's job; (b) making sure that any refusal to answer questions will only result in charges of insubordination, not criminal charges; and/or (c) making it ambiguous over whether an internal affairs or "administrative investigation" is going on and asking the employee to simply write a report. (Note: the law is unsettled over exactly how formally a *Garrity* order must be given and whether asking for a routine report is covered.) Some employers also utilize polygraph testing as part of their "administrative investigations." Nonetheless, the *Garrity* rule applies whenever an officer or any public employee is required by a supervisor to answer questions as a condition of employment, and the level of discipline imposed for not answering the question must constitute a "substantial economic penalty" (Gardner and Anderson, 2010; Harr et al., 2011; Samaha, 2012).

Many agencies will conduct a parallel investigation. What this means is the criminal investigation will take the lead with the administrative investigation one step behind and somewhat paralleling it. A decision may have been made to not go the criminal route. In some cases, the criminal route will be pursued, and an administrative investigation will follow. An officer cannot be compelled to offer a verbal testimony against his or her interests in a criminal investigation. They can be compelled in an administrative investigation, but such statements and any fruits resulting from such statement will not be admissible in a criminal trial.

The area where officers are most likely to face charges involves serious traffic crashes when it is found they are operating well outside the bounds of policy and law. If they are not operating under the law, that is, they are horse-playing and not on a call or in pursuit, then the case becomes worse. Under either scenario, they might face a traffic or criminal charge and/or civil litigation. An officer is also subject to internal discipline. Remember, it is more important to get there safely than fast. No call or stop is worth your or someone else's life. Unfortunately, there are other times officers are charged with crimes whether they are on or off duty when such crimes are committed.

Criminal Charges against Police

Police officers can be charged with crimes for instances of misconduct. For example, an officer who illegally shoots and kills a person may have committed homicide. Illegal arrests may be false imprisonment. Illegal searches may be criminal trespass and perhaps breaking and entering. However, it is not often that police officers will be charged with crimes. For police officers to be charged with crimes, the prosecution must prove criminal intent beyond a reasonable doubt—a very tough thing to prove. Officers who honestly believe they are enforcing the law are generally protected.

Civil Actions

Civil lawsuits that seek damages based on police misconduct can be filed against the individual officers involved in the incident, their supervising officers, the law enforcement agency where they are employed, and the government units in charge of the officers and departments (towns, cities, counties, states, and the federal government). Civil actions against the federal government and its officers; local, county, and state officers; law enforcement agencies and government units; and other government employees are controlled by different statutes, court decisions, and government units (Gardner and Anderson, 2010; Harr et al., 2011; Samaha, 2012). Civil lawsuits against federal officers have been first accepted by the court in 1971 and are called constitutional tort (*Bivens*) actions. Civil lawsuits against the federal government for their officers' constitutional torts are called federal tort claims actions. Civil Rights Act actions are lawsuits against individuals in state and local law enforcement for violating someone's constitutional rights. Law enforcement officials are protected by qualified immunity from many lawsuits. They cannot be held personally liable if their actions are objectively reasonable as measured by the clearly established law at the time of the incident (Gardner and Anderson, 2010; Harr et al., 2011; Samaha, 2012).

The right to recover damages for injuries caused by official torts must be balanced against law enforcement's job of protecting the public, and official immunity limits liability to malicious wrongdoing. Not all states allow citizens to bring suits against them for the constitutional violations of their officers. These states give vicarious immunity to officers and other law enforcement officials (Gardner and Anderson, 2010; Harr et al., 2011; Samaha, 2012).

Courts have not imposed a constitutional duty to protect, and plaintiffs cannot sue officers when they fail to prevent other individuals from committing crimes or violating their rights. There is an exception to the no-affirmative-duty-to-protect rule. A special relationship exists between the government and persons in their custody, and the state has a duty to protect them and prevent other prisoners from injuring them or violating their rights. A special circumstance exists whereby the government is held responsible for protecting people from state-created dangers (Gardner and Anderson, 2010; Harr et al., 2011; Samaha, 2012). A general duty to protect does not exist; however, an officer might create one if certain promises are made.

Judges cannot be sued for misconduct because of their special status of absolute immunity, and prosecutors can hardly ever be sued because of functional immunity, which applies whenever they act as advocates.

Other barriers to successfully suing officers and governments include expense, court limitation on injunctions against police techniques, and the preference of juries for police testimony.

Administrative Remedies

Administrative remedies discipline public officials to remedy misconduct. There are two types of administrative reviews: (1) internal affairs units (IAU) review, which is a review by special officers inside police departments, and (2) external civilian review, which involves participation by individuals who are not police officers. Though there has traditionally been a fair amount of controversy over civilian reviews, the rates of sustainment of complaints in civilian review are about the same as the rates in internal affairs units.

"The government of the United States has been emphatically termed a government of laws, and not of men. It will certainly cease to deserve this high appellation, if the laws furnish no remedy for the violation of a vested legal right" (John Marshal, *Marbury v. Madison*).

Chronology of Training and Selected Municipal Liability

1956—*Meistinsky v. City of New York* (State)
State tort claim for negligent training—firearms and deadly force

1961—*Monroe v. Pape*
The court has ruled a municipality is not a person. Yet a state officer acting under color of law (even if unlawful under state law) can be sued.

1978—*Monell v. Department of Social Services*
Local government officials are persons under 42 U.S.C. 1983 and must implement or execute a policy, ordinance, regulation, or official decision.

1979—*Popow v. City of Margate* (State, New Jersey)
An officer accidentally shot a person. Initial training was ten years earlier, and the only other training shooting was every six months at the range. The court said, yes, it was minimum training yet not lifelike or realistic. It needed moving targets, night shooting, and residential topic covered.

1989—*Will v. Michigan Department of State Police*
The state is not a person under 42 U.S.C. 1983. However, the federal government and most, if not all, states allow for some level of compensable liability by statute.

1989—*City of Canton v. Harris*
A municipality can be held liable for inadequate training of its employees. Liability occurs when failure to train amounts to deliberate indifference.

1989—*Bordanaro v. McLeod* (U.S. First Circular)
The department was found to be operating off rules from the 1960s. There was no training beyond basic academy. Leaders actively discouraged officers from seeking training. Discipline was haphazard. It all amounted to deliberate indifference.

1991—*Hafer v. Melo*
The municipality, in reality, is a defendant when the suit was filed against an individual officer in official capacity.

1993—*Zuchel v. City and County of Denver* (U.S. Tenth Circular)
Failure to have "shoot/don't shoot" and no street conditions amounted to deliberate indifference.

As you can see, over the years, sovereign immunity has lost much of its strength. Section 42 USC 1983 has increased in usage with the watering down of immunity and the wider interpretation of who a person is. Training has become more of a focus for several reasons— one is deeper pockets, and it can attach this way. Two, more and better training is examined. And three, contextual-based, lifelike, and realistic training is sought after.

In *Canton v. Harris*, the Supreme Court laid out four elements for liability to attach:

1. Focus must be on adequacy of the training in relation to the task the person—in this case, the officer—must perform.

2. The individual shortcomings of the person—in this case, the officer—may be from something other than the training.

3. It must show more than the need for more or better training.

4. The identified training deficiency must be closely related to the injury or proximate cause. In other words, failure to train must be linked to some specific policy related to training.

In essence, *Canton* does not just require more training; it requires better training. It requires employees to know the things they can be expected to do on the job. To not meet the training standards set forth in *Canton* invites liability.

Three links are required for successful litigation for failure to train:

1. There must be a constitutional violation.

2. It must establish that the training is deficient and that the deficiency is due to department policy or custom. The design and administration of the program must be so lacking that they demonstrate deliberate indifference on the agency's part.

3. The third link requires a causal connection. The plaintiff must prove that the identified deficiency in the training program is closely related to the ultimate injury.

Certain professions are high liability, and that will never change. The police and medical professions are and will always be in this high-liability category. To say we live in a litigious society will be an understatement.

Frequency of Police Liability

- ✓ Between 1978 and 1990, there were 191,359 cases involving police liability decided by U.S. courts alone.
- ✓ Between 1967 and 1976, the number increased over 500 percent.
- ✓ Between 1967 and 1976, 1 in 34 officers was sued, or 3 percent.
- ✓ Between 1978 and 1990, 11 percent of all 42 U.S.C. 1983 suits were for inadequate training.
- ✓ Plaintiffs were successful in a range of 53.5 to 77 percent of training cases.

The above statistics are meant to merely offer a glimpse into but one profession. No profession or occupation is immune from litigation. It is unfortunate, but the ability to sue is needed for proper redress, and it also causes some public agencies and some professions to change outdated or inadequate training, along with other issues. The settlements, in many of these cases, are astronomical. Will it not be better just to provide more and better training? A caveat must be offered here. Even the best training and policies will not prevent a suit from occurring, but it can protect the employee and the agency from losing. We often hear politicians provide knee-jerk reactions calling for more training before they even know what happened in many situations. These sorts of actions are often misinformed and harmful. Of course, none of the aforementioned case laws cover private companies, and their liability is quite different. Negligent retention, hiring, training, supervision, and assignment can all be reduced with great training.

Every twenty years or so, law enforcement commissions have been established to determine why police are doing such and such, which is usually unethical behavior. Overall, the various commissions have consistently found the following:

- ✓ More and better training is needed.
- ✓ Training should change behavior.
- ✓ Training must incorporate the agency's values.
- ✓ Training must be lifelike and realistic.
- ✓ Training must sensitize officers to others.
- ✓ Training must continue past recruit level.

I mention this not as an indictment on police or policing. Police agencies have improved greatly over the last twenty to thirty years and continue to show great advancements in all areas. The same arguments can be made for most professions. These findings apply to any agency, company, or profession.

What role do ethics have in training liability?

Firearms are high risk and low frequency, and we train for it. Dealing with the public day in and day out is one of the highest frequency functions officers do. Do we train for it? One study showed 40 percent of liability cases have been brought about by officers' misconduct, not just technical errors or minor rights violations. A legally defensible program must have, as its cornerstone, training that encompasses, in a comprehensive manner, ethics and values. Whatever profession or occupation it is, what we see is that, while accuracy and skill are critical, knowing when to act or not to act and to what degree to act is also critical. I used to tell my new trainers that giving a new officer a test only tells me if the officer knows the knowledge or has retained the elements needed to pass a test.

Scoring 100 percent does not tell me if the officer knows how and when to use discretion. Common sense and good judgment are often the wildcards in the equation, but we can help this as well through good and better training.

Takeaways

- ✓ By its very nature, officers will get complaints.
- ✓ Complaints need to be investigated to protect all parties, including the officer and the citizenry.
- ✓ Police are subject to criminal charges when they act outside the scope of their authority.
- ✓ Police are subject to civil liability when they act outside the standards and scope of their authority.
- ✓ Police enjoy the same rights as every other citizen when it comes to defending themselves against criminal or civil actions.
- ✓ Police must answer questions when posed in an administrative, noncriminal manner.
- ✓ The best way to protect yourself from criminal or civil action is to be professional, stay within policy and law, and follow your training.
- ✓ Do not compound matters by lying about anything.
- ✓ Do not ever let others drag you into the muck.
- ✓ Police are not above the law.
- ✓ Power corrupts, and absolute power corrupts absolutely.
- ✓ Make good notes and record everything you can for your own defense.
- ✓ You are never really off duty.
- ✓ People are watching and listening to you all the time, so act appropriately all the time.

I strive always to keep my conscience clear before God and man.
—Acts 24:16

Chapter Twelve
Managing Your Career and Life

The qualities of a great man are vision, integrity, courage, understanding, the power of articulation, and profundity of character.
—Dwight D. Eisenhower

Life is funny like that—not!

It was a quite weekday when, all of a sudden, our dispatcher began to call for help at the police department. I got there quickly. As I started down the steps to the police department, I saw a male in an army coat holding a fish filet knife. His hands were soaked in blood. I had him drop the weapon. I handcuffed him. He was yelling he had killed someone. I checked on the dispatcher, who was fine. I asked where the fellow he killed was. He told me, and off we went. I and a fellow officer went into the dark, dank local bar where we found the victim lying dead in a pool of blood. The other officer began to render life support, but it was very obvious the fellow was dead. I had the suspect secured in my back seat in a caged car. So off we went to interrogate him, while others processed the crime scene. It was an open-and-shut case. The fellow I had under arrest was a bad local guy. The fellow lying dead on the floor was a good local guy. They had a running feud. The bad guy came up behind the victim and stabbed him repeatedly with a fish fillet knife. The fellow said the victim had a bat. He did, but the rumor was it was for his protection. The offender really did not get that long of a sentence for this brutal murder, but that is all too often par for the course. The story ends here, kind of.

Later that year, right before Christmas, we were experiencing a light snow. I had court that morning but was patrolling until then. I came across a car in a shopping center parking lot that had come to rest against a steel light pole. The car came back to the father of the fellow I had arrested for murder earlier that year. It was a few minutes later when we received a disturbance call at the residence of the owner of the car and father to the fellow I had arrested for murder, who was now serving time. Several of us were working that morning, and when we arrived at this two-story older home, it was apparent we had a big problem.

The father, a.k.a. problem, was running around the house naked and had broken all the windows out of the house. It was snowing outside! He kept placing a piece of broken glass to his throat and was holding a broken cast-iron skillet in his other hand. I had recommended to my sergeant a proper course of action, but before we could act, a few relatives had gotten into the house and were trying to get the man down. My sergeant then told all of us to go get him. Not exactly the best tactical decision process I have ever seen but oh well. So off three or four of us went. We were wrestling with this man, who was very large, very angry, very naked, and sweaty. We were able to subdue him, but he had to be tied to a stretcher and then have another stretcher put on top of him and in handcuffs. We took him to the hospital for treatment. I was late for court that morning. He was upset his son was in prison. I doubt he was happy to see me!

Professionalism

The Five *Is* of Police Professionalism

1. Integrity
   a. Moral leadership - personal values such as trustworthiness, courage, honesty, self-discipline, and tolerance
   b. Yes, as an officer, you are leader.

2. Intellect
   a. Procedural and technical duties
      i. Report writing, legal codes, department policies, and law
   b. Discretionary authority/enforcement issues
      ii. Issues of force, search and seizure, emergency driving, arrest, and detention
   c. Conceptual attitudes relevant to police education (CARPE)
      iii. Professionalism, ethics, diversity, and harassment issues

3. Industry
   a. A well-developed sense of industry is one of the most important examples a police officer can set.

      b. Industrious officers are those who possess work habits that are results oriented as opposed to activity driven.

      c. Officers with a sense of industry are heavy on follow-through and always have the end result in mind.

      d. Industrious officers possess work history that reflects an ability to manage and supervise complex tasks through effective delegation and influence.

4. Initiative
   a. Three types of people
      i. Those who make it happen
      ii. Those who watch it happen
      iii. Those who wonder what happened

5. Impact
   a. Presence of
      i. confidence,
      ii. competence,
      iii. positive attitude.
   b. Characterized by a continual effort to set the highest standard of excellence in all professional endeavors through the axiom of leadership/ service by example
   c. Well-developed communication skills
      i. Verbal
      ii. Nonverbal
      iii. Active listening

Do not overinvest, and have balance in all things.

Promotions, Career Progression, and Advancement

It is not only how hard you work; it is also how smart you work. I want you to be as marketable and competitive as possible. That is one reason I have written this book. I want you to be incredibly successful. I want this for many reasons—first, for you and then for your agency and the community you serve. When you are the best officer you can be, that helps your agency achieve its goals.

When that happens, then you and your agency have made a positive difference in the community. That is what it is all about.

Right now, you might be trying just to get hired, make it through the academy, or get through your probationary period. You might be a seasoned officer or a supervisor. You might be content with where you are now, and that is great. Many people do not want to get promoted. However, many do and often those who do not want to change their minds as years go by. Prepare yourself now. First, be a great officer. Then look at the position(s) that interest you and plan for them. Look at the position description and ask yourself, "Do I have these traits or skills?" If you do, hone them. If you do not, get them. Study, practice, go back to college. Take advantage of training opportunities. Let your supervisors know you are interested. Pick the brains of those who have those positions now. Competition for jobs and promotions are fierce. Never step on anyone on the way up the career ladder. Watch out for those who will try and step on you.

If you do not define yourself, others will be happy to do it for you. I have always been kind of hardheaded. That can be good or bad. I always thought hard work will be enough. It ought to be, but it is not. There is nothing wrong with networking. I have never been a "suck up" and do not care for it. However, I have always been pro supervisor. I have never viewed them as bad guys or gals. I always got along with them. Not everyone feels that way. Some think it is an "us against them" way of doing things. You will have some great leaders, some okay ones, and unfortunately some who are terrible. You usually do not get to pick and choose. The same is true for them. I have seen supervisors who have been poor employees before becoming a supervisor, and now they truly live in a glasshouse, and everyone knows it. Do not live in a glasshouse.

Priority Principle

- ✓ Efficiency is the foundation for survival!
- ✓ Effectiveness is the foundation of success!

Specializing

I have mixed feelings about being specialized versus being a generalist. In some agencies, one does not have the choice. I think both are okay, and often, general is necessary because of personnel resource allocation and the number of crimes committed of a certain type. Generally speaking, we see vice and drug investigations in one section and then general investigations in another. If I was a victim of a crime, I would like to have a specialist investigate it versus someone who was not as well versed. When deciding on a field or profession, I believe we need to search ourselves to see what our calling is. There can be a burnout factor, so keep that in mind. It is good to be well-rounded. Also, some positions will help you with your next career when you retire more so than others.

Some specialty positions are part time and in addition to your main duties. These might be instructor, honor guard, canine unit member, tactical team member, critical incident stress management team member, etc. My theory on this has always been that if you are not doing your main job properly, then you should not have extra jobs. Remember to maintain a balanced work life.

I have had so many criminal justice students say they do not want to do police work, but they want to be investigators, more specifically forensic investigators. This is understandable because of all the cool crime dramas that flood the airways. There are only a handful of police agencies in any given state that hire civilian forensic technicians. Usually, you have to have an advanced degree in the field. You are much better off to join a police agency and work your way up and into such a position. You will be better prepared and much more respected by other officers and agents. The Crime Scene Investigation effect (CSI effect) is a phenomenon in modern society. It affects courts in jury trials because so many on juries have watched these forty-two-minute crime dramas, and they expect the same results in real life in all cases.

Stress Management and Balance

Do not overinvest in the job. That is hard for me to say because I did. It was a choice I made freely and fully. I loved my job. I loved police work. I was and am a workaholic. I never really viewed it as work. It was what I loved to do. Being an officer is who you are or will be. That is how people will see you except those who know you personally, like your family. You are an individual. However, you will be judged based on what all officers do. You will be judged on the reputation of your agency or even the type of agency.

Resiliency is all about the ability to bounce back. Often, elderly people have a harder time with resiliency when they get sick because of their overall health condition. It is critical that you are in the best physical, mental, and spiritual shape you can be. You will be hit with illness like everyone else. But you will also be hit with things many people are not. You will see the worst in people. You will see death, injury, evil, depravity, and just bad behavior in general on a daily basis. You will be tempted in many ways. You must be prepared for all of us. Yes, you will receive complaints. You will make mistakes. Make sure they are honest mistakes of the mind and not the heart. Try your best to not make mistakes, though. You will be assaulted in many ways. You will be attacked in court. You will be disappointed at times in your agency, shift partners, and even yourself. We have discussed all of this and ways to prevent and deal with it. Be ready for the storms because they are going to come. Do your best to prevent and mitigate these storms. Respond to them appropriately. Be prepared for them. Finally, recover. Pick yourself up. Be resilient. Remember, you are never alone. Do not take on a "helpless victim" mentality.

Manage Stress

- ✓ Work out at least thirty minutes three to five days a week. Five is better. Get your cardio up—sweat. Build muscle. Build stamina.
- ✓ Learn relaxation techniques. Drinking is not one of them.
- ✓ Reduce use of caffeine. Maintain a proper diet—eat right.
- ✓ Pray—put it in God's hands. Meditate.
- ✓ Use good time management skills.
- ✓ Have fun, laugh, enjoy life. Have a sense of humor. Practice smiling.
- ✓ Get plenty of sleep.
- ✓ Be thankful.
- ✓ Be nice to everyone even when they are not nice to you.
- ✓ Do not try to keep up with the Joneses. Simplify things.

- ✓ Set reasonable goals. Have a sense of purpose in life.
- ✓ Forgive others even if they do not want it or deserve it.
- ✓ Be optimistic but also realistic.
- ✓ Do not operate off rumors or spread them (Sewell, 2002).
- ✓ Stay positive.
- ✓ Have a positive future outcome mind-set.
- ✓ Do not neglect your family.

Life is 10 percent what happens to us, and 90 percent how we react to it!

> *What lies behind us and what lies before us are tiny matters compared to what lies within us.*
>
> —Walt Emerson

Our attitudes cannot stop our feelings, but they can keep our feeling from stopping us.

> *Attitudes are nothing more than habits of thought, and habits can be acquired. An action repeated becomes an attitude realized.*
>
> —Paul Meier

Reframe your attitudes by keeping paramount that, while you may not be able to change the world you see around you, you can change the way you see the world within you.

Do not participate or listen to rumors. Stay away from negative officers. They will be more than happy to drag you down because misery truly does love company. You will never know the entire story when it comes to personnel matters. You will hear one side but should never hear the side from management because it is improper for them to discuss it with you unless it is about you. Believe half of what you see and none of what you hear when it comes to rumors, complaints about others, and general gossip. Base your decisions about how you feel about your agency only on what you know firsthand. Be a leader, not a follower.

Takeaways

- ✓ Never compromise your integrity.

- ✓ Always keep developing your intellect.
- ✓ Work hard and smart.
- ✓ Have a positive impact on everyone you can.
- ✓ Do not overinvest in the career but do invest appropriately.
- ✓ Maintain a balanced life.
- ✓ If you are not moving forward, you are moving backward.
- ✓ If you do not define yourself, other will be happy to do it for you, and it may not be want you want or like.
- ✓ Do not live in a glasshouse.
- ✓ Make sure you are always able to be resilient. You will get knocked down. Get back up.
- ✓ Recognize you will have stress. Manage it appropriately.
- ✓ Do not participate or listen to rumors.
- ✓ Stay away from negative officers.
- ✓ Be a leader, not a follower.

The man of integrity walks securely, but he who
takes crooked paths will be found out.

-Proverbs 10:9

Chapter Thirteen
Wrapping It Up

We must reject the idea that every time a law's broken, society is guilty rather than the lawbreaker. It is time to restore the American precept that each individual is accountable for his actions.
— Ronald Reagan

No Other Job like It

Many of you have heard of the DC sniper back in 2002. It is safe to say the country, especially places like Virginia and even more so the northern part, is still trying to get used to the new norm created by 9/11. I was a field lieutenant with the state police in the metro Richmond area of Virginia. The sniper was active and seemed to be expanding his target area. We worked with several of the metro Richmond police agencies to develop a plan in case the sniper struck in our area. I worked with a committee of police leaders for an entire week every day, putting together a major plan of action. Friday night came, and we had a plan in place, but it had not been reviewed by the agency heads. Little did we know there would be no more time for planning. The next night, Saturday, a man and his wife stepped out of their car to go eat dinner right off Interstate 95 when the shot rang out. The fellow was struck in the abdomen by a high-powered bullet. Within minutes, hundreds of police officers within a fifty-mile radius went into action.

We were looking for a white van based on intelligence from most of the other shootings. This night, the two snipers lay in the woods behind the restaurant. One shot rang out. This completely innocent man and his wife were traveling and had stopped to eat. The restaurant was not too far from a major trauma center that happened to have a fantastic surgeon working. This sniper victim lived. On this attack, the sniper left a note saying he was God. We learned later, after they were caught in Maryland along the interstate, that on this attack they had calmly walked back to their dark-colored sedan and put the rifle away. They then walked into their hotel room very near the scene of the shooting and watched from their window. They left the next day, I think. For two solid weeks after this shooting, the area was on pins and needles. Schools shut down. There was real fear in many people's hearts. It seemed like 9/11 had just happened, and now we were dealing with this. I was responsible for our troops during the twelve-hour day shift, and another lieutenant had the night shift. When they decided to open schools back up several days later and it was time for me to go to work, I went early and drove to my daughter's school. I wanted to check out the wood line just for my own peace of mind. The sniper had shot a child at a school in Maryland before he struck our area. Looking back, we had a good plan. I think we might have stood a chance of catching them except our intelligence was bad as is often the case. We were looking for a white van, not a dark sedan. I prayed many times each day during this ordeal to not let anyone get hurt, especially our children.

Later this same year, I would go to our academy as the assistant training officer. This was my last year working the road, so to speak. I will be lying if I say I do not think about all my years of law enforcement. I miss it every day. I miss my friends, my shift partners, my brothers and sisters in blue, gray, and brown. The camaraderie one gets from those you serve with in uniform, be it a military uniform or police uniform, is a bond truly of brothers and sisters. They are people who will risk their lives for you and you will for them in a heartbeat. I often think about those who have died either too young by illness or in the line of duty. I think of all those who have been injured some to the point of having to retire. I think of their families. I am honored to have known them. Whenever I hear taps or bagpipes, I think of those who have given their all. These sounds are hauntingly beautiful and stir my soul. I thank God for those who serve in uniform, for those sheepdogs who watch over the flock and protect them from the wolves.

Think Ahead

Many years before you retire, you need to think about it and plan for it. Financially, you need to plan. Plan for the worse case as well. What happens to your spouse if, heaven forbid, you are killed or injured in the line of duty? Make plans financially. Invest wisely. Do not live beyond your means. Make sure your insurance policies name the correct beneficiaries. I have seen too many times where someone is listed as a beneficiary who should no longer be.

Have a contingency plan. What happens if you are injured and cannot do the job any longer? In many jobs, you can still work if disabled. In police work, it is hard to do. There can be some adjustment made but only within reason. Have backup plans. Having other skills or a trade and a college degree will help a lot.

In many cases, when you retire, you will be young enough where you want to and need to keep working. Some call this double-dipping. You have earned it! Some want to do jobs similar to what they did before and maybe even the same job in another state or locality. Being older now, I can greatly appreciate how hard it was for my troops who were still working the road in their fifties. Police work is a young person's job. Know when the time is right to retire or go.

Prepare yourself mentally. I will be brutally honest; when I left my police career behind after twenty-seven years of giving it my very all, it was extremely hard. I felt like part of me had died. It took me years to get to the point where the pain subsided. For many officers, retiring or ending their career is welcomed and very easy. For others, it is extremely difficult. I think many officers will also say the best part of their career is working the road on patrol with their shift partners. There is no way to describe the camaraderie and feeling that doing such work creates.

Go out on a high note. Stay positive. Leave a positive, lasting legacy for your fellow officers, your family, and the community you serve. Do an honest day's work for an honest day's pay.

The Adjustment

Several years ago, I had been forwarded the below message. The author is unknown. I have found the words quite moving and true. Wherever you are in your life's journey, whether you are contemplating becoming an officer, you are a new or seasoned officer, or you are at the twilight of your career, I wish you the very best. Be safe, and may God bless you and yours.

For those of you who are Cops, you will find this very true. For those of you who aren't . . . this gives you a little insight as to why we are, the way we are.

Always a Cop

Once the badge goes on, it never comes off, whether they can see it, or not. It fuses to the soul through adversity, fear and adrenaline and no one who has ever worn it with pride, integrity and guts can ever sleep through the "call of the wild" that wafts through bedroom windows in the deep of the night.

When Cops Retire

When a good cop leaves the "job" and retires to a better life, many are jealous, some are pleased and yet others, who may have already retired, wonder. We wonder if he knows what he is leaving behind, because we already know. We know, for example, that after a lifetime of camaraderie that few experience, it will remain as a longing for those past times. We know in the law enforcement life there is a fellowship which lasts long after the uniforms are hung up in the back of the closet. We know even if he throws them away, they will be on him with every step and breath that remains in his life. We also know how the very bearing of the man speaks of what he was and in his heart still is.

These are the burdens of the job. You will still look at people suspiciously, still see what others do not see or choose to ignore and always will look at the rest of the law enforcement world with a respect for what they do; only grown in a lifetime of knowing. Never think for one moment you are escaping from that life. You are only escaping the "job" and merely being allowed to leave "active" duty.

So what I wish for you is that whenever you ease into retirement, in your heart you never forget for one moment that, "Blessed are the Peacemakers for they shall be called children of God," and you are still a member of the greatest fraternity the world has ever known.

Civilian Friends vs. Police Friends

Civilian Friends: Get upset if you're too busy to talk to them for a week.

Police Friends: Are glad to see you after years, and will happily carry on the same conversation you were having the last time you met.

Civilian Friends: Have never seen you cry.

Police Friends: Have cried with you.

Civilian Friends: Borrow your stuff for a few days then give it back.

Police Friends: Keep your stuff so long they forget it's yours.

Civilian Friends: Know a few things about you.

Police Friends: Could write a book with direct quotes from you.

Civilian Friends: Are for a while.

Police Friends: Are for life.

Civilian Friends: Have shared a few experiences.

Police Friends: Have shared a lifetime of experiences no citizen could ever dream of . . .

There are those that think they understand. And then . . . there are cops.

I do not think it is wrong or unwise to want to make a difference in this world. To the contrary, I think that is why we are here. You may never know the big and little differences you make in someone's life. These differences might be good or bad. Hopefully, they will be good differences. Honestly, it might seem bad for the person at times, though. I arrested a fellow once on a cocaine charge, along with many other charges involving contributing to the delinquency of minors, etc. He had been in a car crash where he was smoking marijuana in a cul-de-sac with two underage girls. They were drinking and making out with him. They got sick, and one girl was driving down an icy road. The thirtysomething man was helping her drive from the passenger seat by holding the steering wheel with her. The vehicle ran off the road and flipped, and he was partially ejected. His head was caught under the car. It mangled him up pretty good. Everyone was charged, but he went to prison for a couple of years. When he got out, he came to see me and thanked me for helping change his life. I believe he was sincere. I hope he was. We cannot single-handedly change everything that is bad with the world, but we can do our part. I think it is very important to remember the serenity prayer.

The Serenity Prayer

God, grant me the serenity
to accept the things I cannot change,
courage to change the things I can,
and wisdom to know the difference.
Living one day at a time;
Enjoying one moment at a time;
Accepting hardships as the pathway to peace;
Taking, as He did, this sinful world
as it is, not as I would have it;
Trusting that He will make all things right
if I surrender to His will;
That I may be reasonably happy in this life
and supremely happy with Him
Forever in the next.
Amen. (Reinhold Niebuhr)

Takeaways

- ✓ Plan your retirement early on.
- ✓ Do not retire while on duty. In other words, work or retire.
- ✓ Have an exit plan.
- ✓ Have contingency plans during your career.
- ✓ Prepare yourself mentally.
- ✓ Go out on a high note.
- ✓ Leave a positive legacy.
- ✓ Do an honest day's work for an honest day's pay.
- ✓ You have one of the most important jobs in the world. Treat it that way.
- ✓ Remember the serenity prayer.
- ✓ Remember, during those darkest hours of your career, you are never alone.

And let us not grow weary of doing good, for in due
season we will reap, if we do not give up.
—Galatians 6:9

Chapter Fourteen
A Few More War Stories for the Road

Let's have faith that right makes might; and in that faith let us, to the end, dare to do our duty as we understand it.

—Abraham Lincoln

The Jewelry Store Alarm

You should take every alarm call seriously. Many will be false because the store is opening or closing, the weather is bad, etc. However, once in a while, it will be a real alarm call. It was a midnight shift, and all was very quiet when the alarm sounded for a jewelry store in one of our strip malls. My shift partner and I were at the office. We jumped in our cars and headed to the store. I came in from one entrance to the shopping center, and my partner came in from another. I was approached by a car speeding toward me. I stopped, angled my vehicle, and hit my lights. The driver jumped from the car and ran to the rear. Then the driver crawled under the car. I was ordering the driver out. Meanwhile, my partner gave pursuit in his vehicle to several suspects who were running from the scene on foot. He was a very good officer and observant. Before he gave chase, he noticed another car in front of the jewelry store and got the tag number. Little did he know more suspects were lying down in the car. As I was occupied with my person and he gave chase, they drove off with no lights on in another direction.

I got my suspect out from under the car and under arrest. His suspects got away. The jewelry store had all the windows broken out of the front, and a massive amount of jewelry had been stolen. In the trunk of my suspect car was a huge pile of jewelry. We put out a lookout for the vehicle. By daybreak, the other car had been stopped, four more people were arrested, and a trunk load of jewelry had been recovered. They were part of a huge burglary ring in Northern Virginia. Our arrest on a quiet midnight shift solved many crimes. I realized that night how much of a markup was on jewelry as we counted the massive amount of jewelry and recorded the retail and wholesale prices. The suspects who had gotten away all had glass particles in their clothes that were matched pretty closely to the glass from the shattered windows. Never take an alarm as anything but real and serious. All the suspects were convicted.

Not Smoky and the Bandit: Tractor Trailer Pursuit

While all pursuits are very dangerous, there is probably no type of pursuit that is more dangerous than one involving a tractor trailer. I was at the office, and my troops and I heard over the speaker that a tractor trailer pursuit was coming into our area on the interstate. The vehicle had already knocked several passenger cars off the road. The vehicle was stolen from two counties away. We did not know how much gas he had or what he was hauling at the time. We were trying to ascertain this. My area was fifty miles south of Washington, DC. The interstate was always busy, but it was midday and not as bad as normal. I took charge of the pursuit and told all available units in every jurisdiction to block the on- and off-ramps going northbound. We set up a row of police cars to follow the vehicle so as to keep all other traffic way behind us. We started deploying stinger spike strips. The spike strips were catching under some of the wheels of the tractor trailer, but they are designed for passenger cars. We deployed a good number of spike strips. After a while, the driver realized what we were doing and moved from the left to the center lane, making it hard to deploy the strips. As time went by, some of his tires started to break apart from the damage from the strips. Two of my guys were getting right up beside him, and I had to tell them several times to back away. There was nothing they could do with their cars. He could have hit them and sent them spinning. My and several other police cars stayed close behind him. We were soon to leave my area of responsibility, but there was no higher-ranking officer on scene, so I kept the situation as mine to handle. I had radioed our headquarters and told them we might need to shoot the vehicle soon. I did not hear back. We entered another county after having traveled through my two counties and city. We were moving closer to DC. A sergeant had set up a roadblock with tractor trailers across the interstate, but the driver wove around them. Once in another division, I heard on the radio that taking a shot was authorized. I was getting ready to do that anyway. I told my units to get someone in position to shoot the radiator of the tractor trailer. Doing this would shut down the engine after a little time has passed.

The first trooper shot, but the round went through the passenger side's front windshield. I had another trooper get in position, and he shot. This time, the round hit the radiator. It probably took about five more miles before the tractor trailer came to a stop. The wheels on the tractor were fully engulfed in flames by this point. My troops dragged the driver from the vehicle and arrested him. We had gone through six jurisdictions and were about twenty miles from DC. The driver faced a multitude of charges in every jurisdiction from attempted murder for striking the vehicles with the tractor trailer and grand larceny to multiple counts of reckless driving. No one was hurt. We ended up paying for a lot of passenger cars to get tires fixed since our stinger spikes were in shambles as the tractor trailer hit them and left the spikes all over the road. Maintaining calm in a situation like this is of paramount importance. Stay low key, keep control, and make good decisions. I was very proud of my troops and all the officers that day, which probably numbered well over a hundred.

Jeff, Stop Running!

I had just marked on duty when I was given a "be on the lookout" for a person who had escaped custody. It was a young male who had stolen a vehicle and was under arrest when he escaped. Several of us were converging on a shopping center parking lot. As I headed in that direction, I went past a deputy whom I knew well. He and I had gone to the local academy together several years back. He had a white German shepherd as a patrol tracking dog. I drove on by. A few minutes later, I spotted the suspect. I drove up near him, jumped out, and began a foot chase. I was gaining on him and about to pounce on his back. I heard my deputy friend now yelling, "Jeff, stop! Jeff, stop!" I looked down, and running right beside my leg was the white canine. I stopped and froze. The canine stopped and looked at me. The suspect stopped for a second. He then took off running, and in a millisecond, the canine was all over him. Ugh, that was too close. Somehow the canine handler whom I had passed a few minutes ago had caught up to everyone else. All I saw was a ball of white fur and the suspect. I had never been bit by a canine and was glad it did not happen that day. My first thought was *Why does the deputy want me to stop running? I got this guy!*

The Heroin Addict Christmas Story

I was called to investigate a possible forge-and-utter case at a local video store. The evidence led me to a home where the lady I was looking for lived. When I got there, I found her son and daughter-in-law living there. They were very cooperative. His mother had a drug problem. She was a recovering heroin addict. They were nice people who seemed to be doing the right thing. They had allowed her to stay there, but she had left a few weeks ago. She had not paid any rent and had no expectation of privacy to anything that was left, considering she had abandoned things and cut off contact. I found more evidence that she was involved in many attempts to forge and utter checks and other documents. Once the family got a lead on where I could find her, I went to her new place of abode. I took two other troopers with me and placed one outside the first-floor town house window, and the other came in with me.

It was a very nice, well-maintained town home. She had moved in with her boyfriend, who seemed like a pretty reputable fellow. I explained why I was there. I already had enough to arrest her by this point. She confessed and cooperated. The house was decorated for Christmas and had a warm feeling to it. Knowing what I knew about the lady and her method of operation, I spoke to her boyfriend and suggested he check his checkbook, etc., to make sure everything was okay. Sure enough, she was stealing from him and attempting to forge and utter his name. It was all very sad actually. She was arrested on numerous felony charges. I did not find any drugs, such as heroin. I did not check back on their relationship status. She had thrown away a chance to have a relationship with her son. Now she had betrayed her boyfriend. I have always thought of this case as my heroin addict Christmas story. What a sad world this can be. Remember, criminals rarely commit one crime. It is very unlikely the one crime you are investigating or arresting them on is the only one he or she has committed. Dig deeper.

Riot Duty

If you have not been involved in a riot, you have not lived. That sounds bad, does it not? I have seen a great many riots on television, but when I was a young trooper, I got to experience one firsthand. I had been assigned to many potential events where civil unrest was possible. Based on the history of a particular event in one of our beach communities during the Labor Day weekend, we were assigning extra troops to the beach area. I was not originally assigned. It was Sunday morning, and I was home asleep. My wife and daughter were at church. I, like many other troops around the state, received a phone call to be at the beach area within five hours. I left a note, packed, and headed out. The closer I got to the beach area, the more trooper cars that fell in line, forming a very large caravan. When we arrived, we checked in at an old military base and got our assignments. The night before had seen heavy rioting. This night, there would be hundreds of more officers. We formed up at a pavilion near the beachfront. At about sunset, squads started to be called out. Before long, my group was the last squad not on the street. We could hear sirens blaring from every direction. Then we were called out. We had practiced riot control training almost every day in the academy. Now we would put our training to use.

We were not on the street but a few minutes before the action started. We had about twenty in our squad, and at the time, we used V formations. The order had been given to everyone to clear the streets. We were met by hundreds of rioters who were several hundred feet in front of us, throwing anything and everything. Troopers on each side of me were getting hit with bottles and other items. We kept marching forward. We cleared the way and made a turn to come down another street. As we marched by, I saw several platoons of local officers on the side street, waiting in formation to fall in behind us and seal off the roads we were clearing. From time to time, we were confronted with rioters. At one point, we were stopped in front of a restaurant that was pretty much all glass front. Rioters were swarming into the restaurant where vacationers were trying to eat. The rioters were running in and out of the restaurant. Each time, we would pursue them but stopped at the door. Finally, we were ordered to go get them. The next time, we did not stop at the door. Tables were going everywhere, and the rioters were going out any door they could find. Then the police horses appeared. They were a beautiful sight and could really move a crowd, but they must be protected.

With our wedge, we had an arrest squad behind us and an armored vehicle to place prisoners and to house our tactical team in case we took fire. We would spot the agitators and so-called leaders in the crowd. Our line would open, and the arrest squad would go out and retrieve the individual rioters. They would then bring them back, and we would close the line again. The system worked pretty well, but the arrest squad should not go too far out if they did not get the offender quickly. I recall one of our salty old veterans would come up beside the person the squad had just arrested and laugh at him, saying, "This is going to look good on your résumé, sport!" That is funny, but do not do that.

We continued. We were met by a large crowd of rioters at a hotel parking lot. They were ripping the hotels apart and throwing toilets over the balcony of the high-rise hotels. We were ordered to drive them back. We drove them all the way to the hotel doors. I stopped and looked, and there was nowhere else to go but in the hotel. So we reformed and moved on. This went on all night. At daybreak, we made it back to the pavilion. Some of the troops had minor injuries but nothing major. The next night, things were quieter. For each of the many years after that, we had to send hundreds of troops to this beachfront area in anticipation of more riots, but they did not occur. This riot literally started over nothing—nothing, that is, but a bunch of people who wanted to steal and destroy property because they could. Years later, I was involved in more potential civil unrest issues with hate groups, but enough for now.

Hot Summer Nights and Guys on a Hot Roof

Often, the police officer's job extends way past making arrests and investigating crimes. There is and should be a significant service component. It was a quiet midnight shift when the local fire department alarm sounded. I asked the dispatcher what the fire department had. It was a volunteer department, and I knew it would take a few minutes to get out and to the scene of the fire. The dispatcher said it was a house fire on the other side of town. I drove over there and saw the smoke billowing up from down the hill where an old home sat. I told the dispatcher I was going down to the fire. Another officer told the dispatcher he would be joining me. Our sergeant told the other officer not to go down there and stay at the road. My fellow officer ignored him and came with me. The house was old and built out of wood with asbestos-style siding. The other half was cinder block. Vehicles had caught fire in the yard, and the house was burning heavily. We saw three older gentlemen sitting on the roof over the wooden part. They were stuck and would not jump. My partner and I pulled an old reclining chair to the side of the house and gingerly stood on the side and top of the chair. We grabbed each of the men and dragged them off the roof. The last fellow really resisted, and he tore his pants on the gutter. He might have ripped the skin; I could not recall for sure. They were yelling about another person being in the house. My partner and I entered the dwelling on our knees and went as far as we could. The smoke was thick, and the fire was out of control. I think we made it about halfway through on the floor but could go no further. We made our way out. The fire department had arrived and started to work on the fire. We went around to the rear of the house, and we could hear someone pounding on a wall, but the room was engulfed in flames. Within a few minutes, the pounding stopped. We could not get to him. That morning, the last person in the house was found in the fetal position in a bed at the wall where we heard the pounding. We could never have reached him, but we tried our best. Our sergeant never said a word to my shift partner about him disobeying his order. Smoking in bed and heavy drinking were apparently the cause of the fire. Never forget the service part of the job.

Blind or Bad Luck and Squeaky Floors Make for a Bad Ending

We were dispatched to a "shots fired" call at a home in town. When we got there, the lady who lived in the house met us outside. She had been shot in the leg. Multiple officers from three agencies were there. The lady told us her husband had been in the basement. There was an old green army blanket acting as a curtain at the top of the basement steps. When he heard the floor squeak as she walked in front of the blanket, he shot and hit her in the leg. They had been arguing, and he was drunk. My sergeant decided we would go into the house and get him. This was a very bad tactical decision to make. We should have set up a perimeter and negotiated. It was a barricade situation with no hostages. We had plenty of time. We could have deployed tear gas if needed. Following orders, we did as the sergeant told us. I and another officer from one agency came in through the front door. Two other officers, one from our agency and the other from another agency, went in through the basement door. The suspect had already killed himself before we got there. He was lying on a cot in the basement with a bottle of liquor and a police scanner next to him. He had shot himself in the head. We were very lucky that night. If he had been alive, one of us could have easily been shot, or we may have had to shoot him. Looking back, we all should have told the sergeant his plan was very poor and that we would create a better plan of action. If you work for one agency, you do not have to listen to the orders of someone from another agency. Even in your own agency, if the orders are illegal or unethical, you can and should disobey, but be ready to defend yourself. In this case, the order is not illegal, just very stupid. If the orders are given from a supervisor in another agency, make sure your agency is okay with said order first.

Leave My Daddy Alone! He Has a Bad Heart!

I was conducting a checking detail on a hot Saturday evening. An off-duty supervisory agent from my agency drove up and told me of an accident down the road a little ways. I headed that way, and he followed me. When I got there, I began to investigate a run-of-the-mill crash. The female driver had been drinking but was not legally drunk. She was at fault. The area was near a railroad underpass and in a rural part of the county. If one went straight down that road, he or she would end up on the Potomac River. Down there was a small beach. The area, at that time, was a hot spot for problems. As I was working the crash, a person came up to me and said a drunk driver was heading my way. I saw the vehicle heading our way. The driver pulled over and got out. Just my luck, it was the husband of the lady of the crash I was working. I wanted to finish dealing with her before I dealt with him. I had seen him drive up, so there was a potential drunk driver charge. He kept coming around and opening the car door on her side and telling her to get out. I instructed him to stay back and let me finish what I was doing. More people were leaving the beach, and a lot of drinking had been done. A crowd was gathering. I called for some help to head my way if something went wrong. A rather large deputy showed up. When I finished with the lady, I then went to address her husband.

He was very drunk and a huge man. His grown kids were there as well. Many people were drunk. It was a mixed crowd of people. The fellow was not going to cooperate with testing for drunk driving, so we went straight to "You are under arrest." He did not want to be under arrest. He refused to turn around and be handcuffed. He was ready to rumble, so to speak. The deputy tried to get him to cooperate, and he decided to use force on him to effect the arrest. He struck this fellow across the arms and chest area with his PR-24—a nightstick. We did not have OC spray or Tasers back then. I am not sure if they would have worked with this fellow. I went ahead and called for more help. "Just go ahead and send everyone you have. Send the paddy wagon." The fellow just stood there as if to say, "Is that all you have?" He was combative and resisting still. I took my hat off and took a running start and hit him full speed ahead. We hit the hood of a car, and it was on. We went to the ground, and the deputy and off-duty supervisory special agent all landed on top of him. It was everything we could do to keep him down. We were trying to get his hands behind his back to handcuff, but he was huge, very strong, and real drunk. His family, except for his wife, was trying to come up on us. I distinctly remember hearing his daughter yelling, "Leave my daddy alone! He has a bad heart!" I could not help but think, *I would hate to see if he had a good heart.* She came up behind me grabbing hold, and I gave her a stiff arm, and off through the air she went flying. I ordered everyone to leave the scene. That has been a law in Virginia. An officer could order people to leave the scene of a crash. Help began to pour in, and many were arrested. One of the best sounds to a police officer was when you could hear the sirens coming to help and that they were getting closer. We finally got the fellow in handcuffs and arrested. My hat had been crushed in the melee. So off we all went to the magistrate and to jail. It was just another hot summer Saturday night.

If You Think I Look Bad, You Ought to See the Other Guy!

It was a quiet Sunday night at shift change. I had gone out to my police car and was speaking to my friend who had just gotten off. I saw a car pull up in police parking and leave. A little later, I saw the same car again driving down the road. I followed the car, and it was weaving very badly. I stopped the car at the edge of town. A stout female wearing a softball uniform was driving alone. She had her hands concealed. She was obviously very drunk. I said, "Let me see your hands." She pulled her hands out of her sleeves. She had blood all over both hands. I asked about what happened to her. She said she had been playing softball in the next county over, and she and another person had gotten into a fight. She said, "You think I look bad? You should see the other person!"

After running her through some sobriety tests, which she failed badly, I went to arrest her for driving under the influence of alcohol. Another officer had pulled up by this time. She resisted arrest and started to run away. We tackled her, and she went face first into the gravel shoulder. She came up spitting gravel and blood out of her mouth. She fought like crazy, but we got her to the magistrate and to jail. Once at the jail, we had to fight her to get her into a cell. As we pushed her into the cell, the officer who had been helping me ended up going in with her. He had to keep fighting her off and pushing her back to get out of the cell so we could close the door. It was serious but funny at the same time.

When it came time for the court date, I got a note saying she could not be there since she was in a hospital in another area because she had been bitten by a police canine during another unrelated event. She had apparently resisted arrest and ran from the police again. Several years later, I was a trooper, and I heard over the scanner that she had been involved in cutting a bunch of police car tires. I often wondered what the other person she had fought with did look like! Never think because of a person's size or sex that he or she was any less dangerous. Later, there was talk that she may have been involved with an unsolved murder. I would not be at all surprised.

You Are Never Really Off Duty

I had been in police work for about six years when I went to the state police. I was sworn in and had powers of arrest, but we had very strict orders to not get involved when away from the academy. We had a live-in academy and only went home on weekends. It was a Friday night, and I had gotten to my hometown. I saw an officer I used to work with on Main Street as I was driving to my home. I stopped, and we were chatting. We were talking about him joining the department, which he did later. It was close to seven, and the street was empty. He got a call of a disturbance at a home, so he had to go. I got back in my car and began to drive off. Suddenly, this car came by slowly with three men in it. They were yelling and screaming at me, making threats. I had just stepped into my car. I pulled off and made a turn to go toward my home, and they were in front of me. They stopped, so I figured I better stop and not try to go by them. I was not sure what they might do. Before I could do anything, they had gotten out of the car and were back at my door. I quickly exited my vehicle. This all happened in a matter of seconds. One very large man was completely out of control. He appeared drunk and, I think, very high on cocaine. That was the main drug of choice then and around there. The other two were smaller and not as engaged but with him all the way. The main guy grabbed me, and the fight was on. He knew I had been a police officer. He had been a troublemaker and in the middle of many bad things. He was the reason for the call the other officer had gone to. The reality was he had left the scene, and now he was coming after me for no reason other than I was an officer.

We were not allowed to carry a weapon and were told very firmly not to get involved. Well, now I was involved but not by choice. This guy attacked me harder and more ferociously than I had ever been attacked before. We hit the ground, and he ended up on my back. He yelled, "I killed people in Vietnam, and I am going to kill you!" He bit into my back so hard and pulled that I thought for sure he had taken a chunk of meat out of my back. I already had some scars from being bitten in each armpit from other assaults. We must have fought on the ground and up and down for five minutes. Every time I would try to throw a punch, his buddies were blocking my moves. Finally, he stood up and walked toward his car. I went to the trunk of my car and got my tire iron out. I told the other two to stay out of the way. They stepped back. I had to end this assault one way or another. He was going to be arrested one way or another. About this time, an officer pulled up. He said, "What do you want to do?" I said, "We are going to arrest him." I wish I had arrested the other two, but this guy was enough to deal with between the two of us. A citizen had finally driven by and called the police. I wish we had cell phones then. The guy gave up without a fight.

He was charged with a felony and misdemeanor. I had to go to the hospital for the bite and lacerations. I was bleeding on my forehead, face, back, and left wrist. I had a scar on my left wrist where my watch had dug into my skin and took out a piece of skin. My shirt was about ripped off. It literally was a fight for my life. From what I could gather, I did not have a scar on my back. A local state police first sergeant had to come out and investigate the matter. He did not know me at all. When he went to interview the guy in jail, he made one statement. He told the first sergeant, while screaming from his cell, "F—— y——." Then he spelled it out for him. That was all he would say. I got to know the first sergeant as years went by, and we became friends. From time to time, he would remind me of this incident on this hot summer night so many years ago.

I went back to the academy that Sunday night worried to death I would be fired for having gotten involved. They treated me great. The staff was very curious as to what happened. I had to tell the story over and over. I was completely cleared. I was asked why I did not shoot the guy. I told them I did not have a gun because I was told I could not have one. I was then told I could carry one for the rest of the school. As I was fighting for my life, I was more worried about getting in trouble than I was fighting this guy trying to kill me, which he was. When it went to court, we had a very weak prosecutor and judge, and this fellow's mother was a big wheel in town; so between these factors, he was given a slap on the wrist. He only served a few days in jail and had to pay for all the damage, such as clothes and hospital bills. He received a suspended sentence. I was not surprised. I had been doing police work for a long time and was used to some judges and prosecutors being very weak on criminals. I have seen other judges who would put this guy under the jail for assaulting an officer. I do not know whatever happened to this fellow.

But, Honey, It Is Not What You Think

One of my first experiences with how people could be as a police officer came when I was a very young military policeman in West Germany. My partner and I got a call of a man running down the street bleeding and was all cut up. We came upon the man and stopped him. He was a soldier. He was hysterical, and he had small cuts all over him. It was a very hot summer night, and he was sweating and had no shirt on. We took him to the army hospital on post. He was telling us what had happened. He and a woman were lying out behind a housing area on the ground. They were being affectionate with each other. Apparently, this woman's husband looked out his apartment window from several floors up and saw this affection taking place. He grabbed a butcher knife and decided to put an end to the affection. The next thing he knew, the husband was there, and the woman was between him and her husband. She was putting her hands in the air as if to say stop to her husband, who was also a soldier. Her husband swung the butcher knife and cut down between the joints of two of her fingers.

When we got to the hospital, we were walking the fellow to a room for treatment. We were passing several doors in the emergency room. We passed one door, and there the lady was getting her hand stitched up as her husband stood beside her. Our guy about freaked out. We took him to his room. We then went back and asked the husband to step outside with us. He did with no problem. The next thing I knew, here came his wife running out of the emergency room into the parking lot with her hand half-stitched up. She began to hit me and my partner, trying to stop us from apprehending her husband. We defused the matter, and her husband came with us. The Uniform Code of Military Justice frowns on this sort of thing! Love can be funny sometimes.

Sometimes You Just Have to Call It like It Is

It was a very hot summer night. I met a trooper from the next county over who was investigating a bad hit-and-run felony. She had an address of the suspect vehicle. I told her I would go to the residence and check it out. This home was out in the middle of nowhere. Sitting right there in the driveway was a smashed-up car. I knocked on the door, and a woman with two kids came to the door. My dispatcher knew where I was and what I was doing. She invited me in. We were standing in the kitchen. It was a small home. I asked if someone had been driving the car outside tonight. She said yes, her husband. I asked if he was there. She said yes and called for him. All of a sudden, the door leading to the kitchen opened, and her husband came out, moving toward me quickly. He had no shirt on, was very drunk, and was extremely muscular. He was not huge, but it was obvious he was strong. I quickly opened the kitchen door and motioned for him to step outside with me. I moved to the side as he stepped outside. I asked a series of questions quickly to establish that, in fact, he was driving the car and was involved in the hit-and-run. It took a minute to get the statements I needed to charge him with a hit-and-run felony. I had him up against the police car. I had already told the dispatcher to send some help my way but figured help might take ten minutes or longer to get there. I saw his wife and children looking out the window at us. As I began to cuff him, I felt him tighten up. I had been through this exact action many times over the years. He was getting ready to resist, and it would be on. I leaned into him and softly told him, "Your wife and kids are watching us from the window. I know what you are getting ready to do. I am going to arrest you and handcuff you. I am going to do what I have to if you decide you want to fight me. Do you want your family to see that? I am going to win this fight one way or another. Now loosen up." He loosened up immediately, and I handcuffed him with no further incident. I said this in a very matter-of-fact tone while maintaining a very firm grip of him. Nonpolice types might be aghast that I explained it to him that way. It really was not a threat at all. I would have had to use force on him if he resisted, and I was just telling him that. I was giving him an option. We did not have Taser or OC spray back then. I am not recommending that this is how each situation is handled. Each situation will be different. You must use the proper amount of force to overcome the resistance being offered. You must win the fight. Sometimes you have got to just tell it like it is. Some of you will work with partners. Some will have backup within a few minutes on any given call. Many of us work in areas where backup might be thirty minutes away at times. When possible, have backup before you start. Never use excessive force. Never abuse anyone. Never give up or lose the fight. People must know you are serious.

Kids Say the Darndest Things!

I worked a very bad hit-and-run felony. The rear end of the struck vehicle was torn up pretty badly, and the other vehicle left the scene. It was an easy case, though. The other car left its bumper with the license plate. The vehicle was registered to someone who lived just down the road. I worked the scene and drove to the suspect's home. There was the vehicle with damage and no bumper. I knocked on the door. An older woman came to the door in her pajamas. She allowed me in. Her young grandson was there. He was probably five or six years old. I sat at her kitchen table with her. I could barely breathe; the cigarette smoke was so thick that you could see it in the air. All around me were generic empty beer cans piled up all over the house. It was very nasty. I asked her a series of questions about the crash. First, she lied about driving and then admitted to it but did say she had not hit anyone. When I asked her how much she had drunk tonight, she said she had nothing to drink. Her grandson spoke up and said, "Grandma, you were drinking tonight. Grandma, you drink every night." I was laughing inside, but it was all very sad. She finally admitted she drank that night. I asked if it was before or after the crash. She said before. I said, "How much did you drink last night?" She said ten beers. Tonight it was ten beers, and every night for as long as she could remember, she always drank ten beers. This lady was a chronic alcoholic. I arrested her on the felony hit-and-run. By the time I got her to the magistrate for warrants, two hours had passed since the crash or offense. I also charged her with driving under the influence and reckless driving. I asked if she would take a blood test, but she said no. Two hours had passed since the offense, and I could not force her to take a test. At trial, she fought hard. The judge found her not guilty of driving under the influence, but she was found guilty of everything else. Later, the judge told me I was so close on the DUI and that he used his fingers to show just a little bit of space but not quite enough. That was fine with me. I think back to incidents like this and wonder whatever happened to that honest little boy.

What We Have Here Is a Failure to Communicate

I was starting another night on midnight shift when I was called to a traffic fatality. Each year, as a trooper, I worked at least a couple of fatalities, and not one was a straight up run-of-the-mill fatality, if there was such a thing. This one was no exception. I got to the scene, which was a residential front yard on a busy two-lane road. The passenger vehicle had run off the road right, hit a mailbox, traveled on and hit a huge brick pillar on the corner of the yard, and then hit a large cedar tree. The vehicle overturned, and the lone driver was partially ejected, and his head landed under the vehicle as it came to a rest. We got the vehicle off him and removed his body. A rescue squad worker handed me a sealed envelope and said it had been taped to the dash of the car. The envelope contained a suicide note. In the note, he spoke badly about one of his ex-wives. He asked that his body be removed from the vehicle before it started to stink because he wanted to give the vehicle to someone. His body had a very strong odor of alcohol about it.

After working the scene, it was time to go to his home and try to make a notification to his next of kin. I and another trooper went there. No one was home. The house smelled absolutely horrible. I wondered if there was a dead body inside; it was so bad. It took several hours, but we finally got one of his ex-wives to come to the house. She was also his first cousin, and they had a child together. I was told the child and mother had gone to the scene and that the child was playing in the yard where her dad had just lay crushed under a car. The child appeared to not be fully aware of things. Once we were let in, we found nobody and no more notes. I did find a few addresses on mail I would have to follow up on. I needed to tell this fellow's wife he was dead. In the suicide note, he had given or sold for one dollar his tractor—from a tractor trailer rig to his friend. That was not up to me to determine the legality of that deal, thank goodness.

So what I had was fatality that might have been drunk driving or suicide or both. One has to be very careful when ruling something a suicide for many reasons. My interpretation was that he had planned on shooting himself in the vehicle and wanted to be removed because he had plans to give the vehicle to a friend. In the trunk of the vehicle was a VCR. Several days later, his ex-wife was caught climbing over the fence at the wrecker facility to pry the trunk open to get the VCR she said was hers!

I was able to figure out he had two ex-wives and a current wife. We finally tracked down his current wife, who had left him over a month before and moved out West. I was not sure he ever figured out she had left him, though. By the time we found her, his other family had already buried him. The autopsy showed he had brain aneurism. So between being drunk, the brain aneurism, and the way the suicide note was written, we ruled it was an accidental death. In this and similar cases, I had to take shoes, cut out dashboards, take brake and gas pedals, and send them to the lab to try to determine if he was braking or accelerating.

It Is Not the Fall that Kills You; It Is the Landing, Maybe

For many years, I never had a bridge jumper; then in a couple of years, it seemed like everyone came to my area to jump off interstate bridges. I was involved with at least three. Each time, the person jumped. One time, the person lived. It was a regular two-lane bridge over the interstate. We were assisting the city since the bridge was in the city over the interstate. I was in charge for the troopers. We had the guy locked in on one side so we could keep the northbound lanes of the intestate open. People could be heard yelling and screaming as they drove by for him to jump. It is indeed a cruel world. I had placed two of my troops below the bridge if, by some miracle, he was able to survive and try to run away.

The city officers did a great job talking with him, but finally, he leaned back and did a dive onto the pavement. His back and head hit the pavement below. You could hear the pop and bang noise as his head hit the ground. His head then came off the pavement and hit again. We had EMS there immediately, and they flew him out. He actually lived. It was the second time he had jumped off a bridge!

Oh, That Is Just Nasty!

To say police work is a nasty job is an understatement. Likewise, to say it is a dangerous job is an understatement. During my career, I was very lucky. I never considered myself to have been seriously hurt. I had my finger double dislocated. The doctor said he wanted to look at it as he braced himself against me. Before I knew it, he had pulled my finger extremely hard. I heard and felt a pop. I had a chip in the bone, and it took many years for my finger not to hurt when it rained! I went to the hospital several other times for being bitten by a crazed drunk and for chemical inhalation of some sort. I had many friends become disabled on the job. I had some of my troops shot at, and some were struck. I carried the casket of several troopers and witnessed my troops die in the line of duty. I think about all of them often.

I have had so many drunks vomit and urinate in my car that I lost count. The key is to turn their head toward the window so it does not get on you. I have solved crashes as to who was driving based on tuna vomit and hair in the driver's side window! I have been transporting drunks who have fallen asleep, and their false teeth have fallen on the floorboard, only to put the teeth in their pocket later. The number of mangled and burned bodies from car crashes is too many to remember, but I do remember them all. Watching people cut or shoot themselves and take their last breath in front of you is a thing you do not forget. Knocking on a door to give a death notification and seeing a parent break down and hit your chest out of anguish are things that stay with you. Sometimes you do not have to even say a word; they just know when they open the door and see you there. I was helping one of my troops with a fatal crash. I went to the family farm with him to give the death notification. Their husband and father had been driving a farm tractor down the road when he was hit and killed. My trooper told his wife. The three children were playing in the yard. She asked if we could tell them. I told the trooper I would do it. There is no easy way to tell and explain to three little kids that their dad is not coming home.

I was called out to help a trooper one night with a fatal crash. When I got there, it was a very dark backcountry road. I had to walk down one side of the scene to the other end, where everyone was. I was walking down the pavement with my wonderful flashlight! I heard this squeaking noise coming from my shoes. I looked down, and the entire road was covered with blood. It was as if someone had rolled the blood onto the road. I stepped onto the grass. As I kept walking, I saw a perfect piece of a face lying on the pavement. This was the eye area and nose. Then I came upon a large body torn up with cut marks. The face was completely gone, and the entire contents of his head were gone. Nothing was in the head cavity at all. No brain. Nothing! This fellow had been hit and dragged up and down the road over and over. A few people stopped once they realized what they were hitting.

What a Shame; Children Do Not Get to Pick Their Parents

When I was a sergeant, I had a trooper who had just begun a potential child abuse investigation. He transferred to another area, so I took over the case. The trooper had recognized dry vomit in this little girl's hair when her mother dropped the child off at a babysitter. Apparently, the vomit had been there for a good while. I decided to go to the trailer where the mother lived and to visit her early one Saturday morning. She was not expecting me. I knocked on the door, and she answered. I asked if I could speak with her. She said yes and invited me in. I told her why I was there. She had a small baby who I think was about a year old. She also had a little girl around five or six years old. The trailer was filthy. The crib was on the floor with no bottom to it. Right outside the crib was a cigarette butt can with butts, and a nail was sticking out on the outside edge. I asked her about this. "Yes, that was where the baby often stayed," she said. She saw no problem that the baby could reach out into the butt can or catch her hand on the nail. She said the baby could not stand yet, even with aid or support. I asked her where the baby food was. There was little to nothing. I asked how she handled the children on her own. She said she let the little girl watch the baby. Other than the crib on the floor, there was no place to put the baby. In the little girl's room on the other end of the trailer was a bathroom with a commode that did not work and had dried feces in it, and it had been there for some time. Everything about the situation was terribly wrong. I took notes and pictures. There were questions about bruising on the little girl, but she said the child bruised easily and fell on the playground.

I obtained two felony warrants for child abuse by acts of omission. It was what the mother was not doing that was so wrong. One can be very poor but still be clean. One could get aid for the children. In court, she pled guilty and was given a suspended sentence and ordered to undergo parenting training and be under the supervision of a child support social worker. The problem was that social services already knew of her. I had asked her if the social worker had ever stepped foot in the trailer, and she said no. I asked this social worker to come into the hallway with me after court. I very clearly told him what I thought of his work ethic. I also explained that he had failed to do his duty, I would be watching this case, and if those children ever had to go through this again, I would be making an official complaint on him and work hard for him to be fired. He was sweating pretty good as I spoke to him. There was really nothing he could say. He had failed these vulnerable children immensely.

My goal was not to see this lady lose her children or go to prison. My goal was to make sure these innocent and helpless children had what they needed to survive and hopefully thrive in life. It was clear both children were not developing in the manner they should be from their age, and this was most likely based on nutrition, health, and other physiological reasons. The dried vomit had been there for a good number of hours, but she was too rushed to take care of it before dropping her child off. I did not take charging a parent lightly, especially when it was based on omission from what a parent should do and what a child needs. However, the totality of the circumstances in this case warranted the intervention and charges. In such cases, it is important to understand child developmental issues.

What Is Good for the Goose Is Not Good for the Gander

I was called to a hit-and-run in a person's private driveway. The driveway was very long and led up to a grand home. When I got there, I met the complainant. He said a fellow had backed into his car as he left his home and then fled. Something just did not seem right at first glance. He knew who the person was. I asked what had happened. He said this fellow and another guy came to his home, they argued, and the guy jumped back in his car and backed up quickly, striking his car, and left. I left and contacted the other fellow. He confirmed everything that was said. I said, "Why did you leave without exchanging information?" He said he had gone to the fellow's house to confront him about sleeping with his wife. He and his friend were standing in the driveway. "The guy came out, and my friend said, 'Watch out, he has a gun.'" They argued quickly, and out of fear, they jumped in the car and fled. The gun was not brandished. The other fellow kept the gun behind his back, but it was visible.

I went back and saw the complainant. I explained what I had found out. I asked him if he was sleeping with this man's wife. He said he was. I said, "Well, I tell you what I will do. I will charge that fellow with hit-and-run and reckless driving, but if I charge him, I will need to charge you with adultery. Now do you not think that is fair?" He said, "Never mind, just forget it." I said okay. The matter was dropped. The odd thing was this man who had a gun and who was sleeping with this fellow's wife had a wife who had been killed by an unknown assailant in her own bedroom several years before while he had taken his kids to the bus stop. I passed along what had happened in my case to the investigating agency and prosecutor's office, but there was not enough there for them to proceed. Just odd circumstances I guess! On a side note, I did not have enough to charge the fellow with adultery really.

You Made It!

Congratulations, you made it to the end of the book. Thank you for taking the time to read this. I truly hope you have found it useful. You are special in God's eyes. Working in the criminal justice system is not easy. For those of us who are or who have been in it, we can attest that the world can be a harsh place. You will face many challenges throughout your career. I am not sure many officers will admit it, but if one spends a career in this field, I do not know how they do not live with some degree of post-traumatic stress, whether they know it or not. There are other occupations that see these horrible things, but I do not know of any other one, except for the military, where you have people who want to hurt and/or kill you. You will often see unfairness in the courts. Some judges will let criminals go or slap them on the hand after you have risked your life to arrest them. It might seem like the world is your enemy, but it is not actually. There are way more people who support you and care for you than who do not. There are way more good people than there are bad ones, and they need you.

You will never be alone. Never succumb to temptations. Never succumb to corruption. The more honorable you are, the harder it will be. Along with honor must come humility. This can be a tough tightrope to walk because if you are a road officer or someone who comes into contact with the bad guys and gals, you must be humble but confident and brave and never give up. A badge can be a heavy weight if worn by one who lacks integrity and moral turpitude. I do not mean it to be doom and gloom, but I wanted to share this with you. You can make a positive difference. One day, each of us will lose our earthly bodies. I hope to see you in hand hear the Lord say to you and me, "Well done, good and faithful servant."

To borrow a phrase from Stephen Covey, "Live, love, learn, and leave a lasting legacy."

May God bless you, your families, and your community. I leave you with the police officer's prayer.

A POLICE OFFICER'S PRAYER

Lord I ask for courage

Courage to face and
Conquer my own fears . . .

Courage to take me
Where others will not go . . .

I ask for strength
Strength of body to protect others
And strength of spirit to lead others . . .

I ask for dedication

Dedication to my job, to do it well
Dedication to my community
To keep it safe . . .

Give me, Lord, concern
For others who trust me
And compassion for those who need me . . .

And please, Lord,

Through it all
Be at my side.

(Author unknown)

Takeaways

- ✓ Take every alarm seriously.
- ✓ Stay calm.
- ✓ Maintain control.
- ✓ Make good decisions.
- ✓ Rely on your training.
- ✓ Never forget the service aspect of your job.
- ✓ Visualize your plan of action.
- ✓ Never let a person's size or sex fool you.
- ✓ Never let their current demeanor fool you.
- ✓ Be careful on all calls but even more so on domestics.
- ✓ Follow up leads quickly.
- ✓ You must win the fight.
- ✓ Never use excessive force.
- ✓ Never abuse anyone.
- ✓ People must know you are serious.
- ✓ Carefully and fully examine all crimes and crashes. Keep an open mind. Do not jump to conclusions.

- ✓ Expect the unexpected.
- ✓ Treat people fairly and equally.
- ✓ Things will never be fair. Understand it and get used to it. Do your job anyway.
- ✓ Ask for help if you need help. Do not travel this journey alone.
- ✓ Look for the positive things and moments in life. They are there and all around you.

Greater love hath no man than this, that a man
lay down his life for his friends.

—John 15:13

References

Ackrill, J. L., and J. O. Urmson. 1998. *Aristotle the Nicomachean Ethics.* Oxford, UK: Oxford University Press.

Adcox, K. 2000. "Doing Bad Things for Good Reasons." *The Police Chief* 67 (1): 16–27.

Ahn, M. J., S. A. Adamson, and D. Dornbusch. 2004. "From Leaders to Leadership: Managing Change." *Journal of Leadership and Organizational Studies* 10 (4): 112–124.

Alsabrook, C. L., G. A. Aryani, and T. D. Garrett. 2001. "Five Principles of Leadership." *Law and Order* 49 (5): 112–116.

Atkins v. Virginia, 536 U.S. 304 (2002).

Ballew v. Georgia, 435 U.S. 223 (1978).

Beauchamp, T. L., and T. P. Pinkard. 1983. *Ethics and Public Policy*, 2nd ed. Upper Saddle River, NJ: Prentice-Hall.

Bee, H. L. 1994. *Lifespan Development.* New York, NY: Harper Collins College Publishers.

Best, R.A. 2011. "Intelligence Issues for Congress." CRS Report for Congress. Washington, DC: Congressional Research Service. Retrieved from http://www.fas.org/sgp/crs/intel/RL33539.pdf.

Best, R.A. 2011. "Intelligence, Surveillance, and Reconnaissance (ISR) Acquisition: Issues for

Congress." CRS Report for Congress. Washington, DC: Congressional Research Service. Retrieved from http://www.fas.org/sgp/crs/intel/R41284.pdf.

Black, H. C. 1979. *Black's Law Dictionary*, 5th ed. St. Paul, MN: West.

Blank, D. 2003. "A Matter of Ethics: In Organizations Where Honesty and Integrity Rule, It Is Easy for Employees to Resist the Many Temptation Today's Business World Offers." *Internal Auditor* (February).

Blum, L. N., and J. M. Polisar, J. M. 2004. "Why Things Go Wrong in Police Work." *The Police Chief* 71 (7): 49–52.

Bobbio, N. 1998. "Ethics and Politics." *International Council for Philosophy and Humanistic Studies* 182: 13–42.

Bordanaro v. McLeod, 871 F.2d 1151 (1st Cir. 1989), *cert. denied*, 493 U.S. 820 (1989).

Bordua, D. J., and A. J. Reiss. 1966. "Command, Control, and Charisma: Reflections on Police Bureaucracy." *The American Journal of Sociology* 72 (1): 68–76.

Borsuk, A. J. 2006. "Government Ethics Worse Than in Past, Residents Say in Poll." *Milwaukee Journal Sentinel* (June 30).

Bowden, J. C., and M. E. Lane. 2012. *Interview to Confession, The Art of the Gentle Interrogation.* Duncan, OK: APTAC Publishing.

Brady, F. N. 2003. "'Publics' Administration and the Ethic of Particularity." *Public Administration Review* 63 (5): 525–536.

Braga, A. A. 2012. "Pulling Levers Focused Deterrence Strategies and the Prevention of Gun Homicide." *Journal of Criminal Justice* 36 (4): 332–343.

Braswell, M. C., B. R. McCarthy, and B. J. McCarthy. 2002. *Justice, Crime, and Ethics,* 4th ed. Cincinnati, OH: Anderson Publishing.

Braunstein, S., and M. Tyre. 1992. "Building a More Ethical Police Department." *The Police Chief* 58 (1): 30–35.

Brendlin v. California, 551 U.S. 249 (2007).

Brigham City v. Stuart, 547 U.S. 398 (2006).

Brown v. Texas, 443 U.S. 47 (1979).

Brown, S. 2007. "The Meaning of Criminal Intelligence." *International Journal of Police Science and Management* 9 (4): 336–340, doi:10.1350/ijps.2007.9.4.336.

Brooks, M. E. 1999. "The Ethics of Intentionally Deceiving the Media." *The FBI Law Enforcement Bulletin* 68 (5): 22–25.

Brown, S. 2007. "The Meaning of Criminal Intelligence." *International Journal of Police Science and Management* 9 (4): 336–340, doi:10.1350/ijps.2007.9.4.336.

Bryan v. McPherson, 630 F.3d 805 (9th Cir. 2009).

Bryant, K. A., R. Greenspan, E. E. Hamilton, D. Weisburd, and H. Williams. 2000. *Police Attitudes toward Abuse of Authority: Findings from a National Survey.* National Institute of Justice. Research in Brief (5).

Buck v. Bell, 274 U.S. 200 (1927).

Bullock, J., D. Cappola, G. Haddow, and S. Yeletaysi. 2009. *Introduction to Homeland Security: Principles of All-Hazards Response,* 3rd ed. Boston, MA: Butterworth-Heinmann.

Bullock, K., R. Erol, and N. Tilley. 2006. *Problem-Oriented Policing and Partnerships.* Portland, OR: Willan.

Callahan, M. 2016. "The Objectively Reasonable Officer: Fourteen Things Cops Need to Know to Successfully Use 'Stop and Frisk.'" PoliceOne.Com. Retrieved from https://www.policeone.com/Officer-Safety/articles/185192006-14-things-cops-need-to-know-to-successfully-use-stop-and-frisk/.

Carroll v. United States, 267 U.S. 132 (1925).

Carlee, R. 2004. "Ethics in Local Government: It's More Than Not Doing Bad Things." *Public Management* 86 (6): 3–5.

Carter, D. L. 2004. "Law Enforcement Intelligence: A Guide for State, Local and Tribal Law Enforcement Agencies." United States Department of Justice. Retrieved from http://www.cops. usdoj.gov/files/RIC/Publications/leintelguide.pdf.

———. 2008. "The Concept and Development of Intelligence-Led Policing (ILP)." Intelligence Program/School of Criminal Justice, Michigan State University. Retrieved from http:// intellprogram.msu.edu.

Chimel v. California, 395 U.S. 752 (1969) [1].

City of Canton v. Harris, 489 U.S. 378, 109 S. Ct. 1197, 1989 LEXIS 1200; 103 L. Ed. 2d 412 (1989).

Coker v. Georgia, 433 U.S. 584 (1977).

Cooper, T. L. 1998. *The Responsible Administrator: An Approach to Ethics for the Administrative Role*, 4th ed. San Francisco, CA: Jossey-Bass.

Colby, A., L. Kohlberg, J. Gibbs, and M. Lieberman. 1983. "A Longitudinal Study of Moral Judgment." *Monographs of the Society for Research in Child Development* 48 (1–2, serial no. 200). Chicago: University of Chicago Press.

County of Riverside v. McLaughlin, 500 U.S. 44 (1991).

Covey, S. R. 1989. *The Seven Habits of Highly Effective People*. New York, NY: Simon & Schuster.

———. 1994. *First Things First*. New York, NY: Simon & Schuster.

Crawford v. Washington, 541 U.S. 36 (2004).

Dantzker, M. L. 1997. *Contemporary Policing—Personnel Issues and Trends*. Boston, MA: Butterworth-Heinemann.

Daubert v. Merrell Dow Pharmaceuticals, 509 U.S. 579 (1993).

Davis v. Washington, 547 U.S. 813 (2006).

Dawson v. State, 20 So. 3d 1016 (2009).

Delattre, E. J. 2002. *Character and Cops Ethics in Policing*, 4th ed. Washington, DC: American Interprise Institute.

Densten, I. L. 2003. Senior Police Leadership: Does Rank Matter? *Policing* 26 (3): 400–419.

Dickerson v. United States, 530 U.S. 428 (2000).

Dinse, C. F., and K. Sheehan. 1998. "Competence and Character: Developing Leaders in the LAPD." *FBI Law Enforcement Bulletin* 67 (1).

Donahue, M. E. 1992. "Crisis in Police Ethics: Is Professionalization an Answer?" *American Journal of Police* 11 (4): 47–70.

Donahue, M. E., and A. A. Felts. 1993. "Police Ethics: A Critical Perspective." *Journal of Criminal Justice* 21: 339–352.

Draper v. United States, 358 U.S. 307, 79 S. Ct. 329, 3 L. Ed. 2d 327 (1959).

Dubrin, A. J. 1986. *Managerial Deviance*. New York, NY: Mason/Charter.

Duncan v. Louisiana, 391 U.S. 145 (1968).

Eberheart v. State, 239 Ga. 407 (Ga. 1977).

Ermann, D. M., and R. J. Lundman. 1987. *Corporate and Governmental Deviance*. New York, NY: Oxford.

Fair, F. K., and W. D. Pilcher. 1991. "Morality on the Line: The Role of Ethics in Police Decision-Making." *American Journal of Police* 10 (2): 23–38.

Farrow, J., and T. Pham. 2003. "Citizen Oversight of Law Enforcement: Challenge and Opportunity." *The Police Chief* 71 (10): 22–29.

Felkenes, G. T. 1984. "Attitudes of Police Officers toward Their Professional Ethics." *Journal of Criminal Justice* 12: 211–220.

Federal Law Enforcement Training Center (FLETC). 2003. "Use of Force Diagram." Retrieved from https://www.bing.com/images/search?view=detailV2&ccid=%2bQXCEl4x&id=615E0C0B3EDD9AA815EF5EAC926495E99822E889&q=fletc+use+of+force+continuum&simid=608049873082057381&selectedIndex=2&ajaxhist=0.

Fitzgerald v. State, 384 Md. 484, 508, 864 A.2d 1006, 1020 (2004).

Foster, G. D. 2001. "Ethics, Government and Security: The Democratic Imperative." *Humanist* (May).

Fraser, B. W. 2003. "Regaining the Public Trust: Two Top Business Leaders Discuss the Deteriorating Regard for Corporate America and What Can Be Done to Win Back the Public's Confidence – Peter G. Peterson – Henry A. McKinnell, Jr." *Internal Auditor* (February).

Fry v. Pliler, 551 U.S. 112 (2007).

Furman v. Georgia, 408 U.S. 238 (1972).

Fyfe, J. J., J. R. Greene, W. F. Walsh, O. W. Wilson, and R. C. McLaren. 1997. *Police Administration,* 5th ed. New York, NY: McGraw-Hill.

Gardner, T.J., and T. M. Anderson. 2010. *Criminal Evidence, Principles and Cases,* 7th ed. Florence, KY: Wadsworth Cengage Learning.

Garrity v. New Jersey, 385 U.S. 493, 500 (1967).

Garner v. Broderick, 392 U.S. 273 (1968).

Garner, B. A., and H. C. Black. 2014. *Black's Law Dictionary,* 10th ed. St. Paul, MN: Thomson Reuters.

Garland, N. 2009. *Criminal Law for the Criminal Justice Professional,* 2nd ed. Boston, MA: McGraw-Hill.

General Accounting Office. 1998. *Report to the Honorable Charles B. Rangel, House of Representatives: Law Enforcement—Information on Drug-Related Police Corruption* (GAO publication no. ADM GAO/GGD-98-111). Washington, DC: U.S. General Accounting Office.

Georgia v. Randolph, 547 U.S. 103 (2006).

Gideon v. Wainwright, 372 U.S. 335 (1963).

Giles v. California, 554 U.S. 353 (2008).

Gilligan, C. 1977. "In a Different Voice: Women's Conceptions of Self and of Morality." *Harvard Educational Review* 47 (4): 481–517.

Gilmartin, K. M., and J. J. Harris. 1998. "The Continuum of Compromise." *The Police Chief* 65 (1): 25–28.

Graham v. Connor, 490 U.S. 386 (1989).

Graham v. Florida, 560 U.S. 48 (2010).

Grant, J. K. 2002. "Ethics and Law Enforcement." FBI Law Enforcement Bulletin, 71 (12): 4–8.

Graves, W. 1996. "Police Cynicism: Causes and Cures." *The FBI Law Enforcement Bulletin* 65 (6): 16–20.

Gregory v. Missouri Pacific R. Co., 32 F.3d 160 (1994).

Gregg v. Georgia, 428 U.S. 153, 227, 231 (1976).

Grossman, D., and L. W. Christensen. 2008. *On Combat: The Psychology and Physiology of Deadly Conflict in War and Peace,* 3rd ed. China: Warrior Science Publications.

Hafer v. Melo, 502 U. S. 21, 112 S. Ct. 358, 116 L.Ed. 2d 301 (1991).

Haarr, R. N. 1997. "They're Making a Bad name for the Department. Exploring the Link between Organizational Commitment and Police Occupational Deviance in a Police Patrol Bureau." *Policing: An International Journal of Police Strategy and Management* 20 (4): 786–812.

Harr, J. S., K. M. Hess, and C. H. Orthmann. 2011. *Constitutional Law and the Criminal Justice System,* 5th ed. Florence, KY: Wadsworth Cengage Learning.

Haberfeld, M. R. 2002. *Critical Issues in Police Training.* Upper Saddle River, NJ: Prentice Hall.

–––. 2006. *Police Leadership.* Upper Saddle River, NJ: Prentice Hall.

Hammon v. Indiana, (05-5705) Appealed from: Supreme Court of Indiana Oral Argument: March 20, 2006 (2006).

Hansen, P. 1991. "Developing Police Leadership." *FBI Law Enforcement Bulletin* 60 (10): 4–8.

Harrington, L. K. 1996. "Ethics and Public Policy Analysis: Stakeholder's Interests and Regulatory Policy." *Journal of Business Ethics* 15 (4): 373–383.

Herrmann, F. M. 2004. "Empowering Governmental Ethics Agencies." *Spectrum* 77 (3): 33–34.

Hiibel v. Sixth Judicial District Court of Nevada, Humboldt County, et al. Citations: 542 U.S. 177 (2004).

Hilgenfeldt, K. 2001. "Where Have All the Leaders Gone?" *Law and Order* 49 (11): 117.

Holmes v. South Carolina, 547 U.S. 319 (2006).

Hope v. Pelzer, 536 U.S. 730 (2002).

Hudson v. McMillian, 503 U.S. 1 (1992).

Hudson v. Michigan, 547 U.S. 586 (2006).

Hughbank, R.J. and D. Githens. 2010. "Intelligence and Its Role in Protecting against Terrorism." *Journal of Strategic Security* 1 (3): 30–37.

Humphrey v. State, 995 So.2d 510 (2008).

Iannone, N. F. 1987. *Supervision of Police Personnel*, 4th ed. Englewood Cliffs, NJ: Prentice Hall.

Idaho v. Wright, 497 U.S. 805 (1990).

Illinois v. Allen, 397 U.S. 337 (1970).

Inciardi, J. A: 1987. *Criminal Justice*. New York, NY: Harcourt Brace Jovanovich Publishers.

In re Gault, 387 U.S. 1 (1967).

In re Kemmler, 136 U.S. 436 (1890).

International Association of Chiefs of Police. 1997. *A Report by the Ethics Training Subcommittee of the IACP Ad Hoc Committee on Police Image and Ethics* [Online]. http://www.theiacp.org/pubinfo/pubs/ethictrain.htm [2007, January 15].

International Association of Chiefs of Police (IACP) Code of Ethics. n.d. Retrieved from http://www.iacp.org/codeofethics.

Ivkovic, S. K. 2003. "To Serve and Collect: Measuring Police Corruption." *Journal of Criminal Law and Criminology* 93 (2/3): 593–624.

Jacocks, A. M., and M. D. Bowman. 2006. "Developing and Sustaining a Culture of Integrity." *The Police Chief* 73 (4): 16–22.

Johnson, C. E. 2001. *Meeting the Ethical Challenges of Leadership.* Thousand Oaks, CA: SAGE Publications.

Kappeler, V. E. 1995. *The Police and Society: Touchstone Readings.* Prospect Heights, IL: Waveland Press.

Kappeler, A. M., R. D. Sluder, and G. P. Alpert. 1998. *Forces of Deviance Understanding the Dark Side of Policing,* 2nd ed. Prospect Heights, IL: Waveland Press.

Katz v. U.S., 389 U.S. 347 (1967).

Kelly, S. F. 2003. "Internal Affairs: Issues for Small Police Departments." *FBI Law Enforcement Bulletin* 72 (7): 1–6.

King, V. R. 1991. "Redirecting Ourselves to Leadership and Ethics in Law Enforcement." *FBI Law Enforcement Bulletin* 60 (1): 24.

Kleinig, J. 1990. "Teaching and Learning Police Ethics: Competing and Complementary Approaches." *Journal of Criminal Justice* 18: 1–18.

Kleinig, J., and A. J. Gorman. 1992. "Professional Courtesies: To Ticket or Not to Ticket." *American Journal of Police* 11 (4): 97–113.

Klockars, C. B., S. K. Ivkovich, W. E. Harver, and M. R. Haberfeld. 2000. *The Measurement of Police Integrity.* National Institute of Justice: Research in Brief. Washington, DC: U.S. Department of Justice, Office of Justice Programs.

Knight, D., and D. Gilgoff. 2006. "House of Horrors." *U.S. News and World Report* 141 (9): 52–6.

Kohlberg, L. 1958. "The Development of Modes of Thinking and Choices in Years 10 to 16." PhD Dissertation, University of Chicago.

– – –. 1984. *The Psychology of Moral Development: The Nature and Validity of Moral Stages* (Essays on Moral Development, 2). New York, NY: Harper & Row.

Kyllo v. United States, 533 U.S. 27 (2001).

Lersch, K. M., and T. Mieczkowski. 2000. "An Examination of the Convergence and Divergence of Internal and External Allegations of Misconduct Filed against Police Officers." *Policing: An International Journal of Policing Strategies and Management* 23 (1): 54–68.

Lincoln Jr. v. State of Maryland, No. 742 Sept. Term, 2004 (2004).

Lindell, M. K., C. Prater, and R. W. Perry. 2007. *Introduction to Emergency Management*. Danvers, MA: Wiley.

Lockyer v. Andrade, 538 U.S. 63 (2003).

Lowenthal, M. M. 2015. *Intelligence: From Secrets to Policy*, 6th ed. Los Angeles, CA: Sage.

Lynch v. Commonwealth, Ky., 74 S.W.3d 711 (2002).

Lynch, T. L., and C. E. Lynch. 2001/2002. "Virtue Ethics: A Policy Recommendation." *Public Administration Quarterly* 25 (3/4): 462–498.

Maccoby, M. 2000. "Understanding the Difference between Management and Leadership." *Research Technology Management* 43 (1): 57–59.

Manson v. Braithwaite, 432 U.S. 98 (1977).

Mapp v. Ohio, 367 U.S. 643 (1961).

Marbury v. Madison, 1 Cranch 137; 2 L.Ed. 60 (1803); 5 U.S. 137; 1803 U.S. Lexis 352.

Martinelli, T. J. 2006. "Unconstitutional Policing: The Ethical Challenges in Dealing with Noble Cause Corruption." *The Police Chief* 73 (10).

Massey, M. E. 1980. *The People Puzzle*. Upper Saddle River, NJ: Prentice Hall.

Mattox v. United States, 156 U.S. 237 (1895).

McCafferty, F. L., and M. A. McCafferty. 1998. "Corruption in Law Enforcement: A

Paradigm of Occupational Stress and Deviancy." *The Journal of the American Academy of Psychiatry and Law* 26 (1): 57–65.

McLean, J. 2005. "Management and Leadership Dispelling the

Myths." *The British Journal of Administrative Management* 16 (October/November).

McLeod, S. A. 2013. "Kohlberg." Retrieved from www.simplypsychology.org/kohlberg.html.

McMullan, J. L. 1998. "Policing Reform and Moral Discourse: The Genesis of a Modern Institution." *Policing* 21 (1): 137–161.

McNeely, C. L. 1995. "Perceptions of the Criminal Justice System: Television Imagery and Public Knowledge in the United States." *Journal of Criminal Justice and Popular Culture* 3 (1): 1–20.

Meese, E. III, and P. J. Ortmeier. 2004. *Leadership, Ethics, and Policing*. Upper Saddle River, NJ: Prentice Hall.

Meistinsky v. City of New York, 309 N.Y. 998 (1956).

Michigan v. Long, 463 U.S. 1032 (1983).

Miller, L. S., and M. C. Braswell. 1992. "Police Perceptions of Ethical Decision-Making: The Ideal vs. the Real." *American Journal of Police* 11 (4): 27–45.

Mills, A. 2003. "Ethical Decision-Making and Policing—The Challenge for Police Leadership." *Journal of Financial Crime* 10 (4): 331–335.

Minneapolis & St. Louis R. Co. v. Bombolis, 241 U.S. 211 (1916).

Miranda v. Arizona, 348 U.S. 436 (1966).

Mitchell, C. E. 1999. "Violating the Public Trust: The Ethical and Moral Obligations of Government Officials." *Public Personnel Management* 28 (1): 27–38.

Monell v. Department of Social Services, 436 U.S. 658, 98 S. Ct. 2018, 56 L. Ed. 2d 611 (1978).

Monroe v. Pape, 365 U.S. 167; 81 S. Ct. 473; 1961 U.S. Lexis 1687; 5 L. Ed. 2d 492.

Morreale, S. A., and P. J. Ortmeier. 2004. "Preparing Leaders for Law Enforcement." *The Police Chief* 71 (10): 89–97.

Murphy, P. V. 1985. "Ethical Issues in Policing." *Criminal Justice Ethics* 4 (2): 2–96.

Muscari, P. G. 1984. "Police Corruption and Organizational Structures: An Ethicist's View." *Journal of Criminal Justice* 12: 235–245.

Napue v. Illinois, 360 U.S. 264 (1959).

National Consensus Policy on Use of Force (NCPUF). 2017. Retrieved from file:///C:/Angel/Documents/National_Consensus_Policy_On_Use_Of_Force.pdf.

National Institute of Ethics. 2000. *The Ethics Instructor Certification Course.*

O'Conner v. Ortega, 480 U.S. 709 (1987).

Ohio v. Roberts, 448 U.S. 56 (1980).

Oldham, S. 2003. "Are You Leading?" *Law and Order* 51 (6): 136.

O'Malley, T. J. 1997. "Managing for Ethics: A Mandate for Administrators." *The FBI Law Enforcement Bulletin* 66 (7): 20–27.

Osterburg, J. W., and R. H. Ward. 2014. *Criminal Investigation: A Method for Reconstructing the Past,* 7th ed. Boston, MA: Anderson Publishing.

Paul, R. W., and L. Elder. 2002. *Critical Thinking: Tools for Taking Charge of Your Professional and Personal Life.* Upper Saddle River, NJ: Prentice Hall.

Penry v. Lynaugh, 492 U.S. 302 (1989).

People v. Harris, 60 Cal. App. 4th 727, 70 Cal. Rptr. 2d 689 (1998).

People v. Pope, 811 N.E.2d 801 (2002).

People v. Wilkinson, 2008 NY Slip Op 28192 [20 Misc 3d 414] (2008).

Peterson, M. 2005. "Intelligence-Led Policing: The New Intelligence Architecture." Bureau of Justice Assistance, NCJ 210681. Retrieved from https://www.ncjrs.gov/pdffiles/bja/210681.pdf.

Piaget, J. 1932. *The Moral Judgment of the Child.* London: Kegan Paul, Trench, Trubner & Co.

Plummer, L. C. 1995. "In Pursuit of Honest Leadership." *FBI Law Enforcement Bulletin* 64 (4): 16–18.

Pollock, J. M. 1998. *Ethics in Crime and Justice,* 3rd ed. Belmont, CA: West/Wadsworth.

Popow v. City of Margate, 476 F. Supp. 1237 (D. NJ. 1979).

Powell v. Alabama, 287 U.S. 45 (1932).

Punch, M. 1985. *Conduct Unbecoming.* New York, NY: Tavistock.

Rapaport, E. 1978. *J. S. Mill on Liberty.* Indianapolis, IN: Hackett Publishing.

Ratcliffe, J. H. 2003. "Intelligence-Led Policing." *Trends and Issues in Crime and Criminal Justice* 248. Retrieved from https://www.iadlest.org/Portals/0/Files/Documents/DDACTS/Docs/Integrated%20Intelligence%20and%20Crime%20Analysis.pdf.

Ratcliffe, J. 2005. "The Effectiveness of Police Intelligence Management: A New Zealand Case Study." *Police Practice and Research* 6 (5): 435–451, doi:10.1080/15614260500433038.

Rawls, J. 1971. *A Theory of Justice,* 1st ed. Cambridge, MA: Harvard University Press.

Rest, J. R. 1979. *Development in Judging Moral Issues.* Minneapolis, MN: University of Minnesota Press.

Richelson, J. T. 2012. *The U.S. Intelligence Community.* Boulder, CO: Westview Press.

Riley, K. J., G. F. Treverton, J. M. Wilson, and L. M. Davis. 2005. "State and Local Intelligence in the War on Terrorism." RAND Corporation. Retrieved from http://rand.org/pubs/Monographs/2005/RAND_MG394.pdf

Risher v. State, 227 S.W.3d 133 (Tex. App. 2007).

Robbins, S. P. 1996. *Management,* 4th ed. Englewood Cliffs, NJ: Prentice Hall.

Robinson, P. A. 2004. "Shared Responsibility: The Next Step in Professional Ethics." *The Police Chief* 71 (8).

Rosen, B. 1980. "Moral Dilemmas and Their Treatment." In *Moral Development, Moral Education, and Kohlberg*, edited by B. Munsey, pp. 232–263. Birmingham, AL: Religious Education Press.

Rothgery v. Gillespie County, 554 U.S. 191 (2008).

Roof, J., and K. Presswood. 2004. "Is It Leadership or Management?" *College and University Journal* 79 (4): 3–7.

Roper v. Simmons, 543 U.S. 551 (2005).

Rothlein, S. 1998. "Fostering Integrity in Policing: A Corruption Prevention Strategy." *The Police Chief* 67 (10): 68–76.

Samaha, J. 2012. *Criminal Procedure*, 8th ed. Florence, KY: Wadsworth Cengage Learning.

Samson v. California, 547 U.S. 843 (2006), [1].

Scott v. Illinois, 440 U.S. 367 (1979).

Senna, J. J., and L. J. Siegel. 1984. *Introduction to Criminal Justice*, 3rd ed. St. Paul, MN: West Publishing Co.

Sewell, J. D. 2002. "Managing the Stress of Organizational Change." *FBI Law Enforcement Bulletin* 71 (3): 14–20.

Sherren, J. 2005. "Ethics in the Workplace." *Summit*.

Shernock, S. T. 1990. "The Effects of Patrol Officers' Defensiveness toward the Outside World on Their Ethical Orientations." *Criminal Justice Ethics* 9 (2): 24–42.

Siegel, Larry J., and Brandon C. Welsh. 2012 *Juvenile Delinquency: Theory, Practice, and Law*. Belmont, CA: Wadsworth Cengage Learning.

Skinner v. State of Oklahoma, ex. rel. Williamson, 316 U.S. 535 (1942).

Slahor, S. 1999. "Ethical Leadership." *Law and Order* 47 (7): 123–124.

Sokolow v. U.S., 490 1 (1989).

Souryal, S. S. 1984. *Police Administration and Management*. St. Paul, MN: West.

– – –. 1998. *Ethics in Criminal Justice in Search of the Truth*, 2nd ed. Cincinnati, OH: Anderson Publishing.

Spinelli v. United States, 393 U.S. 410 (1969).

Stanford v. Kentucky, 492 U.S. 361 (1989).

State v. Gagnon, 2009-Ohio-5185 (2009).

State v. Hayes, 2006-Ohio-1467 (2006).

State v. Hughes, 142 Wash. App. 213, 173 P.3d 983 (2007).

State v. Mainaaupo, No ... 386, 98 P.3d 250, 257 (App. 2004).

State v. Poetschke, 750 N.W.2d 301 (Minn. Ct. App. 2008).

State v. St. John, No. 17189 Conn. (2007).

Staveley, S. 2002. "Taking a Closer Look at Leadership." *Journal of California Law Enforcement* 36 (1): 18–26.

Stovall v. Denno, 388 U.S. 293 (1967).

Taylor v. Curry, 17 F. 3d 1434 (1994).

Tennessee v. Garner, 471 U.S. 1 (1985).

Terry v. Ohio, 392 U.S. 1 (1968).

Thompson, G. J., and J. B. Jenkins. 1993. *Verbal Judo: The Gentle Art of Persuasion*. New York, NY: Quill.

Tillyer, M. S., and D. M. Kennedy. 2008. "Locating Focused Deterrence Approaches within a Situational Crime Prevention Framework." *Crime Prevention and Community Safety* 10 (2): 75–84.

Trautman, N. E. 1991. *How to Be a Great Cop.* Dallas, TX: Standards and Training, Inc.

Trejos v. State, 243 S.W.3d 30 (Tex. App. 2007).

Trop v. Dulles, 356 U.S. 86 (1958).

Tyler, K. 2005. "Do the Right Thing: Ethics Training Programs Help Employees Deal with Ethical Dilemmas." *HR Magazine* (February).

United States Department of Justice. 2005. "National Criminal Intelligence Sharing Plan." Retrieved from http://it.ojp.gov/ documents/National_Criminal_Intelligence_Sharing_Plan. pdf.

United States Department of Justice. 2009. "Navigating Your Agency's Path to Intelligence-Led Policing." Retrieved from http://it.ojp.gov/docdownloader.aspx?ddid=1082.

United States Commission on National Security/Twenty-First Century. 2001. "New World Coming: American Security in the Twenty-First Century." Retrieved from Federation Association of Scientist: http://www.fas.org/man/docs/ nwc/index.htm.

United States v. Alfonso D. Lopez, Jr., 514 U.S. 549 (1995).

United States v. Arnold, 523 F.3d 941 (9th Cir. 2008).

United States v. Arvizu, 534 U.S. 266 (2002).

United States v. Ary, 518 F.3d 775 (2008).

United States v. Caruto, No. 07-50041 (9th Cir. 2008).

United States v. Cronic, 466 U.S. 648 (1984).

United States v. Cruikshank, 92 U.S. 542 (1875).

United States v. Drayton, 536 U.S. 194 (2002).

United States v. Gonzales-Lauzan, 01/30/2006, 04-12536 - U.S. 11th Circuit (2006).

United States v. Grubbs, 547 U.S. 90 (2006).

United States v. Hsu, 155 F.3d 189 (3rd Cir. 1998), 97-1965 (1998).

United States v. Leon, 468 U.S. 897 (1984) [1].

United States v. Mata, 02/11/2008, 06-40957 - U.S. 5th Circuit (2008).

United States v. McClain, 444 F.3d 556, 559 (6th Cir. 2005).

United States v. McConney, 728 F.2d 1195, 1199 (9th Cir.), *cert. denied*, 469 U.S. 824 (1984).

United States v. Monteiro, 407 F.Supp.2d 351 (2006).

United States v. Park, U.S. Court of Appeals, Second Circuit. 218 Fed. Appx. 74 (2d Cir. 2007).

United States v. Robinson, 414 U.S. 218 (1973).

United States v. Sprague, 282 U.S. 716 (1931).

United States v. Wade, 388 U.S. 218 (1967).

Vernon, R. 2003. "Inspirational Leadership and Ethics." *Law and Order* 51 (10): 218.

Vicchio, S. J. 1997. "Ethics and Police Integrity." *The FBI Law Enforcement Bulletin* 66 (7).

Virginia v. Moore, 553 U.S. 164 (2008).

Weeks v. United States, 232 U.S. 383 (1914).

Whitten v. Georgia, 47 Ga. 297, 297–301 (1872).

Whren v. United States, 517 U.S. 806 (1996).

Will v. Michigan Department of State Police, 491 U.S. 58, 109 S. Ct. 2304, 105 L. Ed.2d 45 (1989).

Williams v. Florida, 399 U.S. 78 (1970).

Wilson, J. Q. 1997. *The Moral Sense*. New York, NY: Simon & Schuster.

Winright, T. L. 1995. "The Perpetrator as Person: Theological Reflections on the Just

War Tradition and the Use of Force by Police." *Criminal Justice Ethics* 14 (2): 37–56.

Witkin, G. 1995. "When the Bad Guys Are Cops: While Professionalism Is Increasing, a Vicious New Breed of Rogue Officer Has Experts Worried." *U.S. News and World Report* 119 (10): 20–23.

Worden, R. E. 1995. "Police Officers' Belief Systems: A Framework for Analysis." *American Journal of Police* 14 (1): 49–81.

Wolf, P. 2002. "COINTELPRO." Retrieved from http://www.icdc. com/~paulwolf/cointelpro/cointel.htm.

Wright, K. N. 1999. "Leadership Is the Key to Ethical Practice in Criminal Justice Agencies." *Criminal Justice Ethics* 18 (2): 2–5.

Wright, L. 2006. *The Looming Tower: Al-Qaeda and the Road to 9/11*. New York, NY: Vintage

Wuestewald, T., and B. Steinheider. 2006. "Shared Leadership: Can Empowerment Work in Police Organizations?" *The Police Chief* 73 (1): 48–55.

Yukl, G. 1989. "Managerial Leadership: A Review of Theory and Research." *Journal of Management* 15 (2): 251–289.

Zuchel v. City and County of Denver, 997 F.2d 730 (10th Cir. 1993).

Other Books by Dr. Fox

Fox, J. 2009. *Analyzing Leadership Styles of Incident Commanders* (Doctoral Dissertation). Retrieved from ProQuest LLC (3383115). http://search.proquest.com/docview/305173788.

———. 2015. *The Ultimate Guide to Excellent Teaching and Training: Face-to-Face and Online.* Thorofare, NJ: Xlibris (ISBN 9781503577701).

About the Author

Dr. Jeff Fox served for twenty-seven years in the field of criminal justice, twenty-one of which were with the Virginia State Police (VSP). He began his law enforcement career as a military policeman in the U.S. Army and served as a town police officer, trooper, sergeant, first sergeant, and lieutenant. He served as a field lieutenant with the state police and served as the assistant training officer, where he managed the daily operations of the training academy. He also served as the statewide incident management program manager for the Virginia Department of Transportation in the operations and security division.

Jeff earned an AAS degree in police science from Germanna Community College, a BLS degree in criminal psychology and sociology from Mary Washington College, and an MS degree in criminal justice administration from Virginia Commonwealth University. He earned an MBA degree with specialization in criminal justice, and he earned a PhD in business administration with specialization in homeland security from Northcentral University. He was a graduate of the Southern Police Institute Administrative Officers Course and the Virginia Commonwealth Management Institute. Jeff completed the Virginia State Police Basic Academy, Rappahannock Regional Criminal Justice Academy, and Military Police School.

Jeff has been teaching at various colleges and universities since 2001. He retired from state service as the program coordinator and assistant professor for the Homeland Security and Emergency Preparedness and Criminal Justice Cohort Programs for Virginia Commonwealth University in Martinsville, Virginia. Jeff served as an assistant professor and chair of the Public Safety Adult Degree Completion Programs (bachelors) (Criminal Justice and Homeland Security and Emergency Management) for a private college in Virginia. While the assistant training officer for the VSP, he collaborated with the University of Virginia; and together, they created the National Criminal Justice Command College (NCJCC). Jeff's full-time job now is as public safety trainer/educator/consultant for his company called Fox - Public Safety Training, Educating, and Consulting, LLC.

He has been an associate dean, program chair, program coordinator, associate and assistant professor, lecturer, and adjunct.

Jeff spent 20 years instructing over 4,000 hours at various criminal justice academies in a variety of criminal justice, leadership, ethics, and instructor development courses as a certified instructor. Jeff has taught hundreds of academically based criminal justice and homeland security/emergency preparedness classes, which included over 18,000 classroom hours. Jeff has spent over 22,000 hours instructing. He has taught over 85 criminal justice topics in police academies. Jeff has received over 140 commendations during his career in public service. These commendations range from criminal and traffic enforcement, major drug seizures, educational efforts, community service, crime prevention, and traffic safety to lifesaving attempts.

For more information about Jeff's training, education, and consulting services through Fox Public Safety, LLC, contact him at
https://www.fox-publicsafety.com/home.html
or
info@fox-publicsafety.com.

Index

Printed in the United States
By Bookmasters